AF531611

The book has a sweeping account of how West came onto dominate Asia around Indian ocean. How the West used its superior maritime forces to take control over Asia is quite enthralling. The book starts with Portuguese sailor Vasco Da Gama whose journey from Lisbon to Calicut in 1498 opened gates for Europeans. The book has an interesting account of wars between Portuguese and King of Travancore which latter won keeping Portuguese limited to the Western coast. After Portuguese, came the Dutch and then the British. The author has divided the book in certain phases and focuses on three main countries in these phases—India, China and Japan. After all these countries mattered most in the Indian Ocean setting. Towards later years, the discussion also moves to Russia as it became a stakeholder in China and Japan wars.

Born in 1895, **Sardar K.M. Panikkar** was educated in Madras and Oxford. He was a scholar of Christ Church and was later called to the Bar (Middle Temple). After a period as a professor at Aligarh Muslim University, he became editor of *The Hindustan Times*. Later he went to Patiala State as Foreign Minister, during which period he was also Secretary to the Chancellor of the Chamber of Princes. He then went to Bikaner as Foreign Minister, later becoming Prime Minister of that State.

In 1948 he was appointed India's Ambassador to China. Continuing as Envoy after the establishment of the People's Republic of China, it was his proper assessment of the situation there that led India to advise the United Nations to recognise the new regime and to desist from carrying the Korean War beyond the Yalu river. After a successful tenure in China, he went as Envoy to Egypt in 1952. When the State Reorganisation Commission was set up at the end of 1953, Sardar Panikkar was appointed a memeber and he returned from Cairo early in 1954. In 1956 Sardar Panikkar was appointed Indian Ambassador to France.

Asia and Western Dominance

Asia and Western Dominance

A Survey of the Vasco Da Gama Epoch of Asian History 1498–1945

K.M. Panikkar

First Published 1953
First LG Edition 2020
Reprinted 2024
ISBN 978–93–83723–63–8

Published by
LG PUBLISHERS DISTRIBUTORS
49, Street No. 14, Pratap Nagar
Mayur Vihar Phase I, Delhi 110091
lgpdist@gmail.com

Printed at
D.K. Fine Art Press, Delhi

CONTENTS

Part VI

THE RECOVERY OF ASIA

Part VII

CHRISTIAN MISSIONS

Part VIII

ORIENTAL INFLUENCES IN EUROPE

ILLUSTRATIONS

MAPS

ACKNOWLEDGMENTS

I AM indebted to many friends and colleagues for their kind and willing assistance in my work. More especially I wish to express my deep gratitude to Mr C. S. Venkatachar, I.C.S., who read through the book in manuscript and helped me with many valuable suggestions; to Mr Guy Wint, who saw the work through the press, undertook the necessary but tedious task of reading the proofs and generally helping with the publication. During a period of over fifteen years I have had many occasions to discuss with Mr Wint the problems which have been treated in the present work and I gratefully acknowledge how much I have profited by his profound knowledge of European history in Asia. To Mr Geoffrey Hudson, Fellow of All Souls, my obligations are twofold. It is his invaluable and masterly essay on China and the West which has been a guide-book to me as to all other students of Chinese relations with Europe before the nineteenth century. He also laid me under great personal obligation by reading through the manuscript and checking, among other more important things, the spelling of unfamiliar foreign names.

I also wish to express my thanks to—

The fathers in charge of Peitang—the Catholic Cathedral—Peking, for making available to me the pictures of St Francis Xavier and Ricci;

the Portuguese Government for supplying the sketches of the ships in which Vasco da Gama's first voyage of discovery was made;

the Kunsthistorische Museum of Vienna for a photograph of the tapestry depicting John de Castro's landing in India; and

Mr J. V. Ford of the British Embassy, Peking, for making available to me his unpublished translations of important Chinese historical material.

INTRODUCTION

THE 450 years which began with the arrival of Vasco da Gama in Calicut (in 1498), and ended with the withdrawal of British forces from India in 1947 and of the European navies from China in 1949, constitute a clearly marked epoch of history. It may have passed through many stages, undergone different developments, appeared in different periods under different leadership, but as a whole it had certain well-marked characteristics which differentiated it as a separate epoch in history. Its motivations underwent changes; one major strand in the original idea, that of a crusade against Islam and a strategic outflanking of Muslim power, disappeared after the menace to Western Europe from the growth of Islamic imperialism ended with the Battle of Lepanto. The original desire for the monopoly of the spice trade changed in a hundred years to the import into Europe of textiles, tea and other goods, which again changed after the Industrial Revolution in Britain into an urge to find markets for European manufactured goods and finally for investment of capital. Originally confined to trade, European interests became in the nineteenth century predominantly political over many years. The leadership of European peoples in this period also underwent change. From Portugal the supremacy in trade was wrested by the Dutch. In the middle of the eighteenth century Britain and France contested for it for a short time. Since then, the authority of Britain was never seriously challenged till the beginning of the Second World War.

In spite of these changes and developments, it is none the less true that the da Gama epoch presents a singular unity in its fundamental aspects. These may be briefly stated as the dominance of maritime power over the land masses of Asia; the imposition of a commercial economy over communities whose economic life in the past had been based not on international trade, but mainly on agricultural production and internal trade; and thirdly the domination of the peoples of Europe, who held the mastery of the seas, over the affairs of Asia. It was an age of maritime power, of authority based on the control of the seas. Till the beginning of the present century, for a period of 400 years from the time of Vasco da Gama, sea power, capable of deciding Oceanic policies, did not exist outside the Atlantic. The control of the Atlantic thus meant the mastery of the Indian Ocean and ultimately of the Pacific. During the first hundred years the Iberian powers had the mastery of the Atlantic, but from the time of dispersal of Philip of Spain's Armada, that supremacy began gradually to diminish and was inherited by other European Powers. The essential feature, that of the control of the Asian seas, remained.

The imposition of a commercial economy on the peoples of Asia and the gradual revolution in almost every aspect of life that it brought about are among the principal themes of this study and they do not require any discussion here. All that need be said is that from the beginning of the period to its end they constituted the dominant features of Europe's relations with Asia. Even when the motive of weakening Islam was proclaimed as a major objective, it is significant to note, as Albuquerque said in his speech to his soldiers at Malacca, that it was by excluding the Moors from the spice trade that the Portuguese hoped to sap the strength of Islam. Trade, enforced by a naval supremacy, was the simple policy of the Portuguese. The creation of a world market in spices as a result of the immense quantities which began to be shipped to Europe led to a change in the economy of the coastal and island regions which produced these commodities, but it did not seriously affect the bigger land Powers, at least in the time of the Portuguese. However, with the arrival of the Dutch and the British the position began slowly to change. The British trade with India was not to any large extent in spices, but in cotton textiles, luxury goods, indigo and saltpetre, necessary for the manufacture of gunpowder. The demand for these goods was so great that during the course of the eighteenth century India's economy became to a large extent dependent on her seaborne trade. The shift of economic and political power from the inland areas to the coast, and the growth and rise to power of a commercial class in alliance with the foreign mercantile interests, are major developments both in Indian and Chinese history after European trade became nationally important. Through all the changes, from the first monopoly in spice trade to the large-scale export of capital in the three decades preceding the First World War, the dominance of a commercial economy on the life of Asian people is what gives the epoch its distinctive colouration.

The third feature, the political domination of European peoples over almost the entire territory of Asia, which was a spectacular development and naturally attracted the most attention, was but the result of the first two factors. The control of the sea made it possible for the European nations to bring their strengths to bear on any point in Asia, especially after the economic and political strength of the great empires had been undermined by the European monopoly of maritime trade. Political domination brought in its train a doctrine of racialism and a feeling of European solidarity as against the Asians; and in the consideration of the relations between Asia and the West these two factors gain a significance which they did not possess in the earlier periods.

There is a further feature which gives unity to this period and that is the attempt made during the time by European nations to Christianize Asia. It would, however, be a mistake to think that this was an essential characteristic of Europe's relations with the East. The Portuguese during the age of discovery were undoubtedly animated by the spirit of the great Crusades: but that was essentially an anti-Islamic spirit and did not seriously include the problem of evangelization. It was only during the great upsurge in the Catholic world known in history as the counter-reformation that the spirit of evangelization began to take Asia into its sphere. St Francis Xavier was the embodiment of that spirit and for a short period, following his example, there was a great movement to convert the heathen in Asia. It was not the Jesuits in Peking who represented that spirit but the evangelists in Japan. But this was a temporary phase. After the arrival of the Dutch and the English and the decline of Portuguese power in the East there was but little missionary activity anywhere in Asia for over a century. Actually the Protestant sects began to feel interest in evangelization only by the end of the eighteenth century and their missionary activities in India and China, which became so prominent a feature of European relations with Asia, were connected with Western political supremacy in Asia and synchronized with it.

These features give to the epoch its special character and stamp it as the reflection in history of a great movement. It may be objected that though the European political authority over Asian countries has ceased the chapter of their relations is not closed: that Europe continues to have even closer connections than before in many spheres of Asian activity: that trade between Asia and Europe is much larger today than it was before. Undoubtedly all that and much more is true. But the essential difference is that the basis of relationship has undergone a complete change. If economic relations are closer they are on the basis of reciprocity and as determined by the national interests of both parties and not imposed by Europe. The political relations between the Asian and European nations are as between independent countries. Asia and Europe confront each other and many vitally important historical results may flow from this new confrontation. But it is no longer the relationship of the da Gama epoch, for a revolutionary and qualitative change intervenes between the new era which has now opened and the epoch that preceded it.

Another major fact which marks the change in the character of the epoch lies in the increased influence of the Soviet Union and Ameria in the affairs of Asia. The USA reached the Pacific coast in 1844. By the first two decades of the twentieth century American influence in the Pacific had already become very great. After the First World War it became dominant, leading to the slow eclipse of European authority in the Far East. The development of Russian influence was in a sense parallel to the American movement. While American expansion was from the East across the sea, the Russian approach was along the land frontier of Continental areas. Both had the result of shifting the balance of power from the colonizing nations of Europe, whose influence was finally to be overshadowed by these two new Powers whose traditions of relationship with Asia were altogether different from those of Western nations.

It is outside the scope of the present treatise to deal with the Russian and American policies in the East and they are discussed in this book only to the extent necessary for a proper appreciation of European policies. One point may, however, be emphasized here. Russia is permanently in Asia, a geographical fact, the influence of which will become increasingly apparent as time goes on. The three major States in the East, India, China and Japan, border on Soviet territories. Also the Soviet influence is Continental and not maritime and in this respect it differs fundamentally from the influence that Europe exercised on Asia for 400 years. Contact with America also is inherent in the facts of geography, for though the Pacific is a wide oceanic space and was unexplored in the ages before European arrival in Asia, today the Far Eastern countries and America are neighbours and will continue to be so in an increasing degree with the improvement of air communications. For all these reasons it would be obvious that the disappearance of European political authority from Asia marks the end of a definite epoch.

The final failure of the European effort to conquer and hold Asia is an example of the limitation of sea power and has lessons which no one can overlook. Hilaire Belloc, discussing the failure of the Crusades in Palestine, claimed that it 'is an illustration of something which you find running through all military history, to wit, that dependence on sea power in military affairs is a lure leading to ultimate disappointment. In the final and decisive main duels of history the party which begins with high sea power is defeated by the land power; whether that sea power be called Carthage or Athens or the Phoenician fleet of the Great King, it loses in the long run and the land power wins'. Ultimately in Asia also, the land masses asserted themselves against the power based on the sea, and the withdrawal of European power from Asia is in effect a reassertion of the power of land empires shaking themselves free from the shackles of maritime mercantilism.

Some European writers have been inclined to view the European expansion as the effect of a civilization on the march. Sir George Sansom, for example, observes: 'It (the invasion of the Asian world) was the expression, the inevitable expression of a civilization on the march. It marked a new phase in the development of human society.'[1] Professor Tawney, on the other hand, sees in the early European invasions of Asia only the hand of the grasping merchants of Antwerp.

Actually the early European expansion in Asian waters was neither 'a civilization on the march' as Sansom would have us believe, nor a puppet show managed by clever merchants from behind the scenes. It was, as we shall try to establish, an attempt to get round the overwhelming land power of Islam in the Middle East, supplemented by an urge to break through the 'prison of the Mediterranean' to which European energies were confined. By the nineteenth century, Europe, with its social, economic and political structure reorganized by the tremendous industrial and revolutionary upheavals of the end of the eighteenth century, represented indeed a civilization on the march. It challenged the basis of Asian societies; it imposed its will on them and brought about social and political changes in Asia which are of fundamental importance. But to see in the commercial adventurism of the first three centuries of European contact the grand conception of an epic conflict between the East and the West is perhaps reading into past events the meaning of what happened much later.

Though this epoch, because of its importance, has been the subject of many valuable studies, so far they have been concerned mainly with special areas. No study of the relations of Europe with non-Islamic Asia as a whole has yet been attempted. On the purely historical side there are many works of great value dealing with each country separately and ignoring the basic unity of the problem, which was to a large extent obscured by the position of the British Empire in India which a distinguished Foreign Secretary of that Government once described as neither the Far East, nor the Middle East, but INDIA. The British position in India was thus isolated from the rest of the problem, rendering a correct perspective of Asia difficult if not impossible.

The present attempt, therefore, is to restore that perspective, which was well understood and fully realized in the seventeenth and eighteenth centuries. Also it may be added as a final word that this is perhaps the first attempt by an Asian student to see and understand European activities in Asia for 450 years.

[1] Sansom: *The Western World and Japan*, London, 1950.

Part I

THE AGE OF EXPANSION

1498–1750

CHAPTER I

INDIA AND THE INDIAN OCEAN

(i)

VASCO DA GAMA arrived at the port of Calicut on the south-west coast of India on May 27, 1498. Without doubt his arrival marks a turning-point in the history of India and Europe.

India had been known to Europe from the earliest days of history Indian soldiers had fought under the Persian banner on Greek soil in 480 BC and, long before Alexander reached the Indian frontiers, friendly relations had existed between Hellas and India. Roman ships based on Egypt regularly visited Indian ports and the Arikkamedu excavations have now established that a flourishing trade had developed in the first century AD between the Roman Empire and the States of South India. Greek and Roman geographers had known the Indian coast and had described even the Indonesian Archipelago. In the dark ages of Europe, though the contact was neither so regular nor so intimate, India continued to excite the imagination of the West, and we have some evidence of the knowledge of Asian countries in Europe. After the early Crusades Europe's interest in Asia increased greatly and both Venice and Genoa possessed detailed knowledge of Indian conditions and trade. Even in distant Antwerp, India was known and Indian products esteemed. In the thirteenth century India was visited by many European travellers, among whom Marco Polo, Friar Odoric and Monte Corvino deserve special mention. In fact, as Hegel noted later: 'India as a land of Desire formed an essential element in general history. From the most ancient times downwards, all nations have directed their wishes and longings to gaining access to the treasures of this land of marvels, the most costly which the earth presents, treasures of nature – pearls, diamonds, perfumes, rose essences, lions, elephants, etc. – as also treasures of wisdom. The way by which these treasures have passed to the West has at all times been a matter of world historical importance bound up with the fate of nations.'

The full significance of da Gama's arrival at Calicut can be recognized only if we appreciate that it was the realization of a 200-year-old dream and of seventy-five years of sustained effort. The dream was shared by all the mercantile peoples of the Mediterranean, with the exception of the Venetians; the effort was mainly that of Portugal. To understand the religious, political and economic urge behind this dream and this effort, it is necessary to survey briefly certain trends of European history during the previous two centuries.

From the time of Saladin, who recaptured Jerusalem from the Crusaders in 1187, Islam based on Egypt had been organized as an immensely powerful barrier between Asia and Europe. The extraordinary burst of energy, enthusiasm and zeal which had moved Christendom in the first three Crusades had come to naught, and the victory of Saladin, from the point of view of later history one of the most decisive in the world, had established Muslim predominance in the vital area of the Syrian and Egyptian coasts for centuries to come. That European statesmen were not unaware of this is proved by the fact that the fifth Crusade (1218–21) was directed against Egypt itself. Many great monarchs of Europe, led by Saint Louis of France, joined in a final attack (the seventh Crusade), but that also met only with defeat. Thus after 200 years of effort by the unified forces of Christendom, Egypt and the vital coast line remained firmly in Muslim hands.

The spice trade with the East, one of the great motivating factors of history and one which yielded the largest profits to merchants as commodities in universal demand, could only come from the Indian ports across the territories controlled by Muslim rulers. 'Pepper,' as a recent writer says, 'may not mean much to us, but in that age it ranked with precious stones. Men risked the perils of the deep and fought and died for pepper.' Mr G. F. Hudson in his learned study on *Europe and China* analyses the position in the following words: 'Spices which became more and more an essential for European cookery could not be obtained except from India and Indonesia and must come through Persia or Egypt; this indispensable and naturally monopolist trade came to be the chief bone of contention in the politics of the Levant and was the most powerful single factor in stimulating European expansion in the fifteenth century. The Tatar ascendancy in Persia, before the conversion of the Ilkhanate to Islam, allowed Italian traders to go direct to India and cut prices against the Egyptians, who were wont to raise them 300 per cent as middlemen between India and Europe; as a result Europeans knew where spices were produced and at what cost, so that when they were again cut off from the Indian market by a hostile Islam and by incessant wars in the Levant, they were well aware of the opportunities awaiting any Power that could find a new route to the "Indies where the spices grow".'

To this desire was added a new factor, the rivalry between Venice and

Genoa. By a combination of skilful diplomacy, adventurous spirit and far-sighted policy the Venetians had for long established powerful influence at Cairo and had made themselves the monopolist agents of Eastern trade in Europe. While their fortunes, so far as the land routes were concerned, varied with political changes in Byzantium, the Venetians were able to resist every challenge and to maintain their supremacy in the Red Sea trade. The continued preponderance of their hated rivals, in this the most profitable of all trades, was the reason of the never-failing urge of the Genoese to break out from the Mediterranean.

The rivalry between Venice and Genoa in the thirteenth and fourteenth centuries is a matter of singular importance in history. Venice was a mercantile State whose machinery of government served not the interests of the merchants but the commerce of the State. The 200 merchant families might build, as families, commercial empires in the Levant, but policy, appointments, war, the rules of commerce itself were strictly determined by the State. There were no private fleets, no private monopolies, but a State fleet, State monopolies, a whole economy directed by the State.

The case of Genoa was far different. Great families and factions captured the governmental machinery of the republic and turned it to private profit. When one faction came into power, it exiled its rivals. This individualism of the Genoese enabled them to become advisers and experts in every court, to perfect many commercial techniques, and to take the initiative in the great drama of oceanic discoveries, especially where these would help to break the monopoly that Venice enjoyed.

In the last decade of the thirteenth century the Genoese suggested to the Ilkhan Arghun of Persia a scheme by which the spice trade from Malabar could be diverted to the Persian Gulf and from there carried overland to the North Levantine ports where, under the patronage of the Paleolagi, the Genoese had supplanted the Venetians. The idea was that the Genoese should build a fleet on the Persian Gulf which would close the Red Sea to the Indian trade. The proposal did not materialize, but Genoa never lost sight of India. An all-sea route seemed to Genoa the only reply to Islam's power and Venice's monopoly. Hudson describes the previous efforts of European navigators to discover this route, the most interesting of which was the expedition of Ugolino de Vivaldo, who for the express purpose of discovering an ocean route to India sailed in 1291 from Genoa via Gibraltar down the African coast. Finally, through Spain and Portugal, the Genoese were able to break through Venetian monopoly and Muslim blockade, both by reaching the Indian Ocean by rounding the Cape of Good Hope and by reaching the Pacific across the American continent.

The result was, however, achieved only after over seventy-five years of intense effort in perfecting the technique of navigation and exploring the west coast of Africa. It was a co-operative effort and not the work of any one individual, though for over forty years the inspiration, guidance and funds for the comprehensive planning and sustained activity necessary for the success of the scheme were provided by an Infante of Portugal, Prince Henry, surnamed the Navigator.

Before we discuss the character and achievements of Dom Henry who stamped his spirit on an age, it is necessary to emphasize two further aspects of the question. The Iberian Peninsula, and Portugal especially, had become in a sense the heir to the Genoese tradition. In 1317, Manoel Pessanha, a Genoese noble, was made hereditary admiral of the Portuguese fleet and he undertook to provide experienced seamen to command the galleys of the king. Pessanha seems to have been a man of outstanding ability, for in 1319 the king bestowed on him vast estates including the town of Odemara. Many of Pessanha's captains were Genoese noblemen like himself. During the course of a century of association the Portuguese became not only thoroughly imbued with the spirit of Genoa's maritime adventure, but took over from her the unfinished mission of finding an alternative route to the East. For carrying on this work Portugal was geographically well situated. If the west coast of Africa had to be explored and charted and expeditions undertaken to round the Cape, there was no port in Europe better situated than Lisbon. Already in the fourteenth century Lisbon had become an entrepôt through which the African trade in ivory and dates passed to Europe.

If thus Portugal had become the heir to the Genoese tradition of exploration, she had also become in the fifteenth century the champion of Christianity against Islam. The spirit of the Crusades not only survived but flourished with added vigour in the Iberian Peninsula in the fifteenth and the sixteenth centuries. While to the other countries of Western Europe, Islam was but a distant menace, to the people of the Iberian Peninsula, to Castile, Aragon and Portugal, Islam represented something menacing, formidable and vigilant on the doorstep. Other countries became enthusiastic against the infidel by fits and starts; but the Iberian was a Crusader by necessity, every day of his life, for in the Peninsula itself Muslim kingdoms still existed and were flourishing. To a devout and patriotic Iberian, Spaniard or Portuguese, the fight against Islam was a stern imperative, a combination alike of religious duty and patriotic necessity. Islam was the enemy and had to be fought everywhere. Much of Portuguese action in Asia will remain inexplicable unless this fact is constantly borne in mind.

All these factors were compounded in the heroic figure of Prince

Henry the Navigator. Dom Henry (1394–1460) was the third son of John I. Brought up in the gallant tradition of Nuno Alvarez, the great national hero, whose victory over the Muslims gave to Portugal her independence, Henry imbibed early in his life a spirit of militant Christian mysticism to which was combined a bitter hatred of Islam. So great was his feeling against Muslims that while still young he organized an expedition against Ceuta, which he took by assault in 1415. This, it should be remembered, was the very first attack on the African base of Islam, the door through which Islam had entered Spain in 711. A second expedition against Tangier in 1437, where he hoped to repeat the success of the first adventure, ended, however, in disaster. Even before this time Henry had found his vocation. He became less and less interested in military actions of a limited character. His object from about 1417 was to plan the grand strategy which would turn the flank of Islam and take Christendom direct to the Indian Ocean. Henry's interest in India had grown with time. Azurara, his enthusiastic biographer, says that many Indians visited him and some even sailed in his ships. The idea of reaching India became almost an 'obsession' with him. In fact, according to Barros and other Portuguese historians, Henry believed that he had received the command of God for this purpose. In any case for so holy a purpose he utilized the immense revenues of the Order of Christ, of which he was the Grand Master. With such resources at his disposal, he collected around him in his castle on the Cape of Sagres mathematicians, cartographers, astronomers and even Moorish prisoners with knowledge of distant islands, and devoted himself seriously to the study of maritime navigation. Among those attached to him was one Jahuda Cresques, known as Master Jacome, an expert cartographer and maker of nautical instruments. Dom Henry realized early that the essential preliminary step for successful expedition to the East was the exploration of the African coast. To the south of Cape Bajador lay an uninhabited belt which no European navigator had passed. It extended for over many hundreds of miles and, until ships were able to find the land beyond the desert, there was no possibility of any expedition reaching the Cape of Good Hope, far less of sailing into the Indian Ocean. But the sailors showed an unsurmountable disinclination, fearing, it is said, that they would all turn black if they passed Bajador. Madeira was discovered in 1420 and the Azores in 1431. After fourteen successive attempts, one of his expeditions, led by Gil Eannes, passed Cape Bajador in 1434. Later his ships reached the coast of Guinea which at that time was a great mart for gold transported from Timbuctoo. Soon one of his captains crossed the Equator and reached territories which were no longer an extension of the Sahara Desert, forbidding, unoccupied and without signs of human life. This was indeed the greatest achievement of Portuguese navigation, for that alone made the rounding of the Cape and the sea route to India possible.

Up to Cape Verde the coast of Africa was effectively under Prince Henry's control, and Azurara, his chronicler, was not exaggerating when he observed: 'Of a surety I doubt, if since the great power of Alexander and Caesar there hath even been any prince in the world that had set up the marks of his conquest so far from his land.'[1]

The achievements of Henry the Navigator extended to many other fields, all having the supreme object of outflanking the hated Muslim power, which spread across North Africa and stood astride all routes connecting India with Europe. He established the first regular school for navigators and seamen, which in time became the Naval Academy of Sagres. There he recruited and trained adventurous spirits, ready to undertake in a crusading spirit the conquest of the seas. The latest scientific knowledge was imparted to the Portuguese mariners in this school. More, Henry realized that distant voyages could not be undertaken in the type of ships which were then in use. He perfected the caravel, a fast and light vessel but strongly built, capable of sailing very near the shore and of penetrating the lagoons. He also improved the galleons, heavily built, slow moving, but capable of carrying cannon.

In 1454 he received from the Pope Nicholas V the right to all discoveries up to India. The Bull, which is of fundamental importance and is the first of three which determines the Portuguese monopoly in the East, is quoted below:

'Our joy is immense to know that our dear son, Henry, Prince of Portugal, following the footsteps of his father of illustrious memory, King John, inspired with a zeal for souls like an intrepid soldier of Christ, has carried into the most distant and unknown countries the name of God and has brought into the Catholic fold the perfidious enemies of God and of Christ, such as the Saracens and the Infidels.

'After having established Christian families in some of the unoccupied islands of the Ocean and having consecrated churches there for the celebration of Holy Mysteries the Prince, remembering that never within the memory of man had anyone been known to navigate the sea to the distant shores of the Orient, believed that he could give God the best evidence of his submission, if by his effort the Ocean can be made navigable as far as India, which, it is said, is already subject to Christ. If he enters into relations with these people, he will induce them to come to

[1] In one of the slave-raiding expeditions along the coast after passing Cape Bajador, Croncalo de Sintara captured a negro chief by the name of Adlin who was in many ways a remarkable man. He had travelled widely and was able to speak the Moorish languages. It was he who told Dom Henry of the caravans that crossed the Sahara into the Sudan and on to the Red Sea.

the help of the Christians of the West against the enemies of the faith. At the same time, he will bring under submission, with the King's permission, the pagans of the countries not yet afflicted with the plague of Islam and give them knowledge of the name of Christ.

'It is thus that during the last twenty-five years that without the support of the armies of Portugal, but in the midst of the greatest perils and faced by the greatest trials, he in his fast caravels, searched without repose the meridianal regions to the Antarctic pole across the oceans, and after having traversed numerous seas reached at last the province of Guinea and from there pushed further to the mouth of the river commonly known as the Nile (*sic*).

'We, after careful deliberation, and having considered that we have by our apostolic letters conceded to King Affonso, the right, total and absolute, to invade, conquer and subject all the countries which are under rule of the enemies of Christ, Saracen or Pagan, by our apostolic letter we wish the same King Affonso, the Prince, and all their successors, occupy and possess in exclusive rights the said islands, ports and seas undermentioned, and all faithful Christians are prohibited without the permission of the said Affonso and his successors to encroach on their sovereignty. Of the conquests already made, or to be made, all the conquests which extend to Cape Bajador and Cape Non to the coast of Guinea and all the Orient is perpetually and for the future the sovereignty of King Affonso.'

On March 13, 1456, Calixtus III promulgated a second Bull confirming the grant to Nicholas V. Thus, Henry was able to obtain what in the fifteenth century was an absolute and incontestable legal title and, further, to proclaim both the political and religious objects of his work. The one thing that stands out most clearly in the Papal Bull, and which was to influence policy for a hundred years to come was the combination of the spiritual urge to conquer heathen lands for Christ, with the fanatical zeal to cut at the root of Islam by attacking it from behind.

The next stage in the mission of Portugal was the Treaty of Trodesilhas signed on June 9, 1494. By this treaty Portugal and Spain fixed a line 370 leagues west of Cape Verde Islands as the demarcation of their respective zones. This was confirmed by Pope Alexander VI and thus became the final line of division between the discoveries of the two Iberian States.

In the meantime, the naval expeditions on the lines set by Prince Henry were making progress. In 1487 Bartholomeu Dias had discovered the 'Cape of Tempests', renamed justly as the Cape of Good Hope, and had reached the Indian Ocean. The sea route to India lay open; and it was left to Dom Manoel, surnamed the Fortunate, to realize this dream.

The decision to undertake the grand expedition was taken only after much discussion. In the grand council which deliberated on the project, opposition was strong and persistent against a scheme which many leading persons argued was but a chimera, which was likely to ruin the finances of the State. It was Dom Manoel himself who decided in favour of the expedition and ordered that armed vessels should be fitted out immediately.

On July 8, 1497, four ships sailed from the harbour of Belem at the mouth of the Tagus. Vasco da Gama, a nobleman of the King's Household, was in charge of the expedition. The flagship *San Gabriel*, carrying twenty guns, and its consort *San Raphael*, commanded by Paul da Gama, the younger brother of Vasco, had been built six years previously by the greatest of all Portuguese navigators, Bartholomeu Diaz. The third ship was a fast caravel, while the fourth was a *navire de charge* under the command of Gonsalo Nunes, ordnance officer. The captain-general's ship flew at its mast a flag on which was painted a large cross of Christ and also carried cannon, symbols of the new power entering the East.

Little need be said here of da Gama's voyage. He had the assistance of navigators and mariners trained in the great school of Prince Henry. They knew the seas all the way down to the Cape. So far as the east coast of Africa was concerned, the voyage up to Mozambique presented no great difficulties. In the actual crossing of the Indian Ocean the captain-general was guided by an Indian pilot whom the King of Milindi had placed at his disposal. It should be remembered that the Indian Ocean, including the entire coast of Africa, had been explored centuries ago by Indian navigators. Indian ships frequented the East African ports and certainly knew Madagascar. Whether they had rounded the Cape and sailed up the west coast is not known with any certainty. Hudson mentions that Covilham was told that 'in those seas (Indian Ocean) there had been some knowledge of a passage to the western seas because the said doctors had said that they had found some memorial of that matter'. He further explains this by alluding to Fra Mauro's maps. 'Fra Mauro preserves the tradition of two voyages from India past the south end of Africa. He marks the southern cape with the name of Diab and says that an Indian ship in about 1420 was storm-driven to this point and sailed westward to 2,000 miles in forty days, without touching land. Fra Mauro had also spoken himself with a person worthy of confidence who said he had sailed from India, past Sofala to a place called Garbin on the west coast of Africa.' The Indian Ocean was therefore a charted sea whose routes were known, and as a navigation achievement Vasco da Gama's arrival at Calicut could not bear comparison either with those of the captains who first passed the desert coasts and crossed the Equator or of Diaz who reached the Cape. Yet it was the realization of the great dream, the crowning act of seventy years of achievement.

We have already discussed the urges behind the Portuguese effort, the grand strategy against the political strength of Islam, Christianization and the desire for the monopoly of the spice trade. These became from the time of da Gama's arrival the main springs of Portuguese policy in the East for nearly a hundred years. It is in terms of these objectives that the relations of the Portuguese with Asia should be viewed.

The arrival of the *San Gabriel* in the Indian Ocean introduced also another revolutionary factor – that was the ship carrying cannon. As we shall presently see, the armament of the Portuguese ships was something totally unexpected and new in the Indian seas and gave an immediate and decisive advantage to the Portuguese over their Indian opponents. The only non-European Power which had developed gunnery on the sea was the Ottoman Empire, and when the Portuguese arrived at Calicut the Turks had no navy in the Indian Ocean. By the time the Sultan awoke to this menace, Portugal had not only gained a foothold, but was in a position continuously to reinforce her navy which the Turk with his naval power concentrated in the Levant was unable to do. It is to this important aspect of the question we should now turn.

The Indian Ocean had from time immemorial been the scene of intense commercial trade. Indian ships had from the beginning of history sailed across the Arabian Sea up to the Red Sea ports and maintained intimate cultural and commercial connections with Egypt, Israel and other countries of the Near East. Long before Hippalus disclosed the secret of the monsoon to the Romans, Indian navigators had made use of these winds and sailed to Bab-el-Mandeb. To the east, Indian mariners had gone as far as Borneo and flourishing Indian colonies had existed for over 1,200 years in Malaya, the islands of Indonesia, in Cambodia, Champa and other areas of the coast. Indian ships from Quilon made regular journeys to the South China coast. A long tradition of maritime life was part of the history of Peninsular India.

The supremacy of India in the waters that washed her coast was unchallenged till the rise of Arab shipping under the early khalifs. But the Arabs and Hindus competed openly, and the idea of 'sovereignty over the sea' except in narrow straits was unknown to Asian conception. It is true that the Sri Vijaya Empire dominating the Straits of Malacca exercised control of shipping through that sea lane for two centuries, but there was no question at any time of any Asian power exercising or claiming the right to control traffic in open seas. It follows from this conception of the freedom of the seas that Indian rulers who maintained powerful navies like the Chola Emperors, or the Zamorins, used it only for the protection of the coast, for putting down piracy and, in case of war, for carrying and escorting troops across the seas. Thus during the hundred years' war between the Sailendra Kings of Sri Vijaya and the Chola Emperors, the reported battles are all on land, the Chola king carrying whole armies across to the Malayan Peninsula and fighting successive campaigns in the territories of the Malayan ruler. Naval fights on any large scale, in the manner of the wars between Carthage and Rome, seem to have been unknown in India before the arrival of the Portuguese. The Indian ships therefore were not equipped for fighting in distant seas.

Arab mercantile activity had never been political. The Arabs traded freely in all the Indian ports, sailed out to the Pacific and reached even the China coast. After the ninth century they seem to have entered into effective competition with Gujerati merchants for the spice trade of the Indonesian islands, for when Affonso Albuquerque arrived on the Malayan coast he noticed Arab, Hindu and Chinese merchants competing openly in the markets of that area.

From quite early times Chinese junks had also appeared in the Malayan waters and occasionally also in Indian ports. But systematic Chinese maritime expansion to the south began only in the Ming period. In the time of the Ming Emperor Yung Lo successive naval expeditions had been fitted out under a great captain, Cheng Ho, a full description of whose voyages in the southern seas has been left by the eunuch Ma Huan who accompanied the party as an interpreter. One of Cheng Ho's armadas consisted of no less than sixty-five ships, some of which were of very considerable size. In the Indian Ocean area he visited Ceylon and Calicut a number of times and even sailed up to Aden.[1] This outburst of maritime activity was only temporary and after Cheng Ho's death we do not hear of any further organized Chinese activity on the sea. The Ming Admiral's repeated visits to Malaya were, however, not without political consequences. For the first time the Malayan rulers became aware of the might of the Celestial Empire, and without presuming to challenge it they willingly became tributaries and accepted the suzerainty of the Emperor in Peking. This vassalage continued for a hundred years, in fact till the Portuguese warships arrived

[1] Sansom's statement about a Chinese factory in Calicut is wholly without foundation. He bases his statement on the account of a Nestorian priest who reported to Cabral that such a factory existed and that a Chinese armada came to Calicut and destroyed the city because the ruler had committed outrages against the factory. Sansom also draws the comforting conclusion that 'in point of priority the Portuguese must cede to the Chinese aggressors in India'. (G.B. Sansom, *Western World and Japan*, p. 44.) There was never any Chinese factory at Calicut, and Cheng Ho's fleets did not bombard the city. Nor is there any allusion to such action in Ma Huan's record of the journey.

off the coast and, as we shall see at the proper time, the conduct of the Portuguese authorities towards these Muslim potentates was destined to have far-reaching consequences for the relations of the Western Powers with the Chinese Empire.

At the end of the fifteenth century and indeed during the effective period of Portuguese power in the Indian Ocean (1499–1600) Peninsular India was organized under States of considerable power and internal stability. The area south of the Tungabhadra had been organized to resist the Muslim invasions in 1337. By the end of the century the Empire of Vijayanagar had consolidated itself and extended right up to Cape Comorin. Under Deva Raya II (1422–46) it became the most powerful State of the time in India and we have an authentic description of its power and resources in the accounts left to us by Nicolo Conti, the Italian traveller, who visited the State in 1420, and by Abdur Rezzak, the Persian Ambassador, in 1443.

At the time the Portuguese arrived in the Indian seas, this Empire, under Narashimha Raya, enjoyed undisputed supremacy in the entire area south of the Raichur Doab. It is important to note that the Vijayanagar Emperors had, in common with the Portuguese, the crusading spirit against the Mussulmans. Just as the presence of the Muslims in the Iberian Peninsula and their Empire across the narrow Straits of Gibraltar constituted a standing menace to the Portuguese, the presence of the Bahmini Sultanates on the borders of Vijayanagar provided that State with the powerful motive of safeguarding Hindu religion and culture in South India, and of upholding national independence against Muslim Powers. To both Portugal and Vijayanagar, Islam was the enemy, a factor of considerable significance, as we shall see, in the establishment of Portuguese authority in Goa.

To the north of Vijayanagar lay the Adilshahi Sultanate of Bijapur. Founded by Yusuf Adil Khan (1490), a son of Sultan Murad of Turkey, who had escaped to India and had taken service under the Bahmini King, the Kingdom of Bijapur extended to the Konkan coast. To the north of Bijapur was the powerful Sultanate of Gujerat with its capital at Ahmedabad. Founded in 1401 by Zafar Khan, the son of a Rajput convert, the kingdom, which controlled the major ports of Cambay, Chaul and Surat, through which the trade of North India flowed to the West, became immensely rich. Under Mahmud Begara, who ascended the throne in 1458 and reigned for fifty-three years (died 1511), the Gujerat Sultanate enjoyed the prestige and power of a major kingdom in India.

Three major factors about the political conditions in Asia, so far as they affect the development of relations with European nations, may be noted. The first, as we have seen, was the consolidation of the Hindu

Empire of South India, a movement of resistance to the expansion of Islam. The second was the supremacy that the Chinese under the Ming Dynasty had established over the southern area of the Asian continent up to the Sultanate of Malacca, and even to the islands of Indonesia. A recent historian of Indonesia describes the political results of the Chinese expansion to the south in the following words: 'The Ambassadors travelled from port to port explaining their mission politely and persuasively and requesting from local rulers a personal visit to the capital of China to present tribute. For a few years there was a rush towards Peking. The first to go was the King of Puni (either West Borneo or Brunei) who arrived at the imperial court with a remarkable request. He asked the Emperor, the overlord of all Eastern Asia, to release him from paying the tribute which he owed to Madjapahit, and allow him to pay it directly to China, a favour which was graciously granted. . . . The Raja of Malacca had the same success in Peking and obtained an imperial order to the King of Siam that he should leave Malacca undisturbed.'

Though with the decline of the Mings, Chinese authority in the islands and in Malacca had greatly weakened, it was still a political factor of significance. The Sultans of Malacca, Bitang and other Malayan States looked to Peking for protection and a shadowy *pax sinica* covered the whole of this area.

A third and no less important factor was the bitter struggle that was going on then between Islam and Hinduism in the Archipelago. Islam had entered Malaya and the islands from Gujerat. In the wake of trade it had made considerable headway in the ports by the middle of the fifteenth century. But the interior still remained strongly Hindu. The social organization of the Hindu structure in the islands had, however, been loosened and Hinduism, though it was still powerful and had a number of organized States on its side, was on the defensive.

The coastal tract at the extreme tip of the peninsula of India, separated from Vijayanagar by the impenetrable Western Ghats, was the only area where small princes held independent sway. This region, known as Malabar or Kerala, extending from Mangalore to Cape Comorin, was also 'the pepper country' *par excellence*, from which for a period of 2,000 years ships had sailed without interruption to the Persian Gulf and to the Red Sea, carrying spices, textiles and other products of India. The chief ruler in this tract was the Zamorin of Calicut, in whose capital Vasco da Gama arrived with his four ships on the fateful day, May 27, 1498. The King of Calicut, Zamorin, as he is known (the title still survives), though his kingdom was small, was a powerful monarch. For many centuries past Calicut had been the chief centre of the spice trade. Not only pepper and cardamon and other products from the Malabar coast, but spices from the islands of the Pacific passed through Calicut on their way to Europe. Numerous descriptions of the port of Calicut and its prosperity have come down to us from foreign observers. Abdur Rezzak, the Persian envoy, for example, noted that every ship from whatever place it might have come and wherever it might be bound for, when it put into this port (Calicut), was treated like other vessels and had no trouble of any kind to put up with. It was the direction of the monsoon that gave Calicut its special importance. It was ideally situated to take advantage of the monsoon winds from the Red Sea to the Indian coast and from India back to the Arabian shores.

The merchants of Calicut had their warehouses in Cairo, Alexandria and as far west as Fez. Close alliance had existed for at least four centuries between the Zamorins and the mercantile community which controlled the spice trade. As the major houses which were interested in this trade were Arabs, a very special relationship had grown up between this Hindu ruler and the Muslims, who, without political power in that part of India and unconnected with the Muslim sultans of the north, constituted no threat to Hindu authority. The political relations of the Arab merchants of the coast were with Egypt, Arabia and the Persian Gulf. This fact is of major significance in understanding the developments that followed. The Zamorin was fully aware of the policy of the Portuguese and, through the information he received from Muslim merchants, he soon awoke to the challenge to his own authority which the arrival of the Portuguese Navy signified. The hereditary dignity of the Zamorin of Calicut was 'the King of the Mountains and the Sea'. He also maintained a fleet powerful enough to enforce his authority along the western coast of India. It was at the capital of this King, the friend of the Muslims, and Monarch of the Seas, that Vasco da Gama landed.[1]

As the first voyage was only exploratory da Gama confined himself to a request for permission to trade, which the Zamorin freely granted. But the Portuguese captain's refusal to pay the customs duty was an indication of the troubles that lay ahead. Also da Gama had noted with surprise and alarm the presence of the 'Moors' in the city and the influence which they enjoyed at court. For this he had not been prepared. It should be remembered that the Bull of Nicholas V had proceeded on the assumption that the people of India were Christians. Da Gama even mistook a Hindu temple at Calicut for a Christian church. The presence

[1] For the events leading to the break with the Zamorin see my *Malabar and the Portuguese*, Bombay, 1927. The Portuguese point of view will be found uncritically in Danvers and with a greater sense of fairness in Whiteaway, *Rise of Portuguese Power in India*.

of the Muslims, their practical monopoly of trade and their influence with the Zamorin were, therefore, matters of unpleasant surprise, which went against the presuppositions of the Portuguese authorities.

After a formal exchange of compliments and the sale of the goods he had brought in exchange for spices, da Gama sailed back to Portugal to report the success of his expedition to his master. Dom Manoel and his advisers realized that in the Indian Ocean also they had come up against their mortal enemies, 'the Moors', and that without a prolonged and major effort the advantages of the discovery of an all-sea route to India would not accrue to them. The second expedition which the King ordered to be fitted out was on a much larger scale. It consisted of thirty-three ships and 1,500 men, with ample military equipment. It was a great naval expedition meant to assert the authority of the King of Portugal over the Indian seas. This powerful armada was commanded by Pedro Alvarez Cabral, a nobleman of distinction, and the officers of other ships were recruited from the flower of Portuguese nobility. The orders to Cabral were to sail directly to Calicut and to demand from the Zamorin, on threat of war, the right to establish a trading post and permission for five Franciscan fathers to preach the gospel. Of this armada of thirty-three, only six reached the Indian coast. The Zamorin was in no way displeased by the return of the Portuguese and sent a message welcoming Cabral to Calicut. But the Admiral was in no mood for friendship. He asked for an audience with the Zamorin, insisting at the same time that hostages should be delivered to him before he landed. The Zamorin agreed to this unusual proposal and the Portuguese envoy was received cordially and was allotted a place for trade. But the high-handed actions of one of Cabral's assistants, Correa, led to a popular outbreak, which cost the Portuguese many lives. Correa himself, who started the fight, was killed with fifty of his men. On this Cabral withdrew his ships and bombarded the city. The Zamorin fitted out a fleet of eighty ships carrying 1,500 men to avenge this act of barbarism. Cabral, however, sailed away on sighting the Calicut ships.

Though Cabral had sailed away, the Portuguese had not abandoned the Indian Ocean. On the contrary, Dom Manoel assumed for himself the title of 'The Lord of the Navigation, Conquest and Commerce of Ethiopia, Arabia, Persia and India' and fitted out an even stronger expedition with orders to enforce his claim to the supremacy of the Indian seas. It was Vasco da Gama himself who was appointed captain-major of this fleet. Since it was realized that there might be serious opposition a reinforcement of five vessels under Estavo da Gama was sent five months later.

The most impressive fact about this first and most decisive period of Portuguese endeavour is the remarkable manner in which the fleets in the East were kept reinforced by the Portuguese home government. Armada followed armada in unending succession under trained captains, and the Portuguese chiefs in the Indian waters knew that men and ships were on the way bringing succour to them. Even in the most difficult circumstances they could therefore hold out with the firm conviction that help was not far away. In this work, the Portuguese Government had the financial backing of the great merchant princes of Antwerp who, realizing the revolutionary change in trade that the Portuguese discoveries involved, had hastened to annex the benefits. The Weslers, for example, had invested in the Portuguese voyages of 1505, and the Lisbon Government had found it necessary as early as 1503 to open a depot for spices in Antwerp. To this system of continuous reinforcements, worked out by Dom Manoel with the assistance of Antwerp capital, must be attributed the success that attended the navies of Portugal on the Eastern seas.

Da Gama and his associates, even before they reached the coast of India, began to enforce the claim of his sovereign to be 'the Lord of Navigation'. Without any kind of warning he intercepted and destroyed any vessel he came across on his voyage. The following incident quoted in *Lendas da India* is typical of the policy of terrorism and piracy that he introduced into Indian waters. The Portuguese armada ran across an unarmed vessel returning from Mecca. Vasco da Gama captured it and in the words of Lendas, 'after making the ship empty of goods, prohibited anyone from taking out of it any Moor and then ordered them to set fire to it'. The explanation for capturing the vessel is perhaps to be found in Barroes' remark: 'It is true that there does exist a common right to all to navigate the seas and in Europe we recognize the rights which others hold against us; but the right does not extend beyond Europe and therefore the Portuguese as Lords of the Sea are justified in confiscating the goods of all those who navigate the seas without their permission.'

Strange and comprehensive claim, yet basically one which every European nation, in its turn, held firmly almost to the end of Western supremacy in Asia. It is true that no other nation put it forward so crudely or tried to enforce it so barbarously as the Portuguese in the first quarter of the sixteenth century, but the principle that the doctrines of international law did not apply outside Europe, that what would be barbarism in London or Paris is civilized conduct in Peking (e.g. the burning of the Summer Palace) and that European nations had no moral obligations in dealing with Asian peoples (as for example when Britain insisted on the opium trade against the laws of China, though opium smoking was prohibited by law in England itself) was part of the accepted creed of Europe's relations with Asia. So late as 1870 the

President of the Hong Kong Chamber of Commerce declared: 'China can in no sense be considered a country entitled to all the same rights and privileges as civilized nations which are bound by international law.' Till the end of European domination the fact that rights existed for Asians against Europeans was conceded only with considerable mental reservation. In countries under direct British occupation, like India, Burma and Ceylon, there were equal rights established by law, but that as against Europeans the law was not enforced very rigorously was known and recognized.[1] In China, under extra-territorial jurisdiction, Europeans were protected against the operation of Chinese laws. In fact, except in Japan this doctrine of *different rights* persisted to the very end and was a prime cause of Europe's ultimate failure in Asia.

Da Gama's barbarous acts of piracy reached the ears of the Zamorin even before his ships were sighted off the coast, and the Lord of Mountains and Seas was ready to meet the challenge. After Cabral's bombardment, the Zamorin had strengthened his naval forces, and these were reinforced by a fleet of heavier vessels belonging to Khoja Ambar, one of Calicut's leading merchants engaged in Red Sea trade. Though the Calicut fleet had the advantage of speed, it did not possess the fire power of the Portuguese ships fitted with heavy artillery. In the engagement that followed off Cochin, Khoja Ambar's ships suffered as a result of Portuguese fire, but the Zamorin's Admiral Kassim was able to manoeuvre his small ships so effectively that the Portuguese were unable to direct their fire against them. The Calicut vessels surrounded the Portuguese ships like wasps, and the result was that da Gama broke broke off the engagement and sailed away with his ships to Europe.

Though the honours of the battle off Cochin lay with the Calicut Navy, Kassim's inability to chase da Gama nullified the fruits of his victory. Near the coast it could meet the Portuguese fleet on more than equal terms, but the Calicut vessels were wholly unsuited for operations at any distance from their base. At the battle off Cochin the Portuguese discovered this secret and exploited it later to the fullest advantage.

Hardly had da Gama left the Indian Ocean when another fleet of fourteen ships under Lopos Soares arrived in Calicut waters. Soares was an experienced captain and in a surprise attack he destroyed a squadron of the Calicut force which under Mammali was lying at anchor off Cranganore. Then he proceeded to attack a mercantile fleet which had assembled in another port and dispersed it after a hard-fought struggle with its protecting convoy. The Zamorin now realized that against the heavily armed Portuguese caravels his own ships stood but little chance in ranged action. He invoked the aid of the Sultan of Egypt with whom

[1] For interesting sidelights on this problem in the twentieth century see Maurice Collis: *Trials in Burma.*

he was on friendly relations. An Egyptian fleet carrying no less than 1,500 men and equipped with the latest weapons sailed into the Arabian Sea under an experienced admiral, Mir Hussain, early in 1507. Mir Hussain's strategy was simple and sound. His first objective was the island of Diu which he decided to use as his base, and effecting a junction with the navy of the Zamorin, the combined fleet was to attack the Portuguese.

The Portuguese Viceroy at the time, Don Francesco d'Almeida, was a man of remarkable foresight and ability whose genius has been overshadowed by his rival and successor Albuquerque. A great nobleman with influence at court, he was definitely opposed to any policy of conquest, but he realized the necessity of an unchallenged control of the sea and knew well that all his master's schemes for a commercial empire in the East depended on achieving that control.

Hussain reached Diu immediately after the monsoon. The Zamorin's vessels joined him there and the combined forces moved south. The Portuguese Navy under Lourenço d'Almeida, the son of the Viceroy, sailed north from their base in Cochin to meet this new threat. The two fleets met at Chaul, halfway down the coast. It was mainly a war of artillery as the Portuguese attempts to board the Egyptian vessels failed. After two days of cannonading the Portuguese decided to flee, but the flagship of d'Almeida was hit and the captain himself was killed.

Disaster faced the Portuguese. An enemy who was equal in equipment and superior in seamanship had arrived on the Indian waters and at that moment the dream of Dom Manoel had almost become a nightmare. But the Viceroy, Don Francesco d'Almeida, did not lose heart. Collecting every available ship and all the arms he could lay hands on, he sailed north to meet the enemy. He had with him eighteen ships and 1,200 men. Reaching Diu on February 2, 1509, d'Almeida awaited the Indo-Egyptian forces. Here treachery favoured him. Malik Aiyaz, a European convert who was the King of Gujerat's Governor in Diu, secretly joined the Portuguese and deprived Mir Hussain of his supplies. The Egyptian Admiral had to fall back for his supplies on the 100 vessels that the Zamorin had sent. His own effective fleet, apart from the Calicut auxiliaries, consisted only of ten ships. In spite of these disadvantages Mir Hussain decided to give battle. On February 3, 1509, the opposing fleets met off Diu. Again as an engagement it was inconclusive. Neither side could claim victory, but the Egyptian fleet, disgusted with the treachery of the Sultan of Gujerat, sailed away shortly afterwards.

With the departure of Mir Hussain and the Egyptian fleet from Indian waters in 1509, the Portuguese may be said to have established their claim to be 'Lords of Navigation' in the Eastern seas. Though it is true that the Zamorin's naval power was unbroken and Calicut was able for another ninety years (till 1599) to challenge Portuguese authority in the coastal waters of Malabar and fought numerous successful actions against them, in the high seas the Portuguese established an unchallenged mastery which placed the seaborne commerce of India at their mercy for over a century and a half. The man who organized this maritime empire and carried it virtually to the Pacific was Affonso Albuquerque, undoubtedly one of the greatest names in the history of Europe's relations with Asia and the architect of Western domination in the East.

Albuquerque came out to the East, first in 1506, when he accompanied Tristan da Cunha on an expedition which had been sent out to attack the Red Sea traders and to blockade the entrance to that sea. This first cruise around Aden, Socotra and Ormuz gave Albuquerque the basic strategic conceptions of his oceanic policy. Socotra he seized and converted into a naval base, recognizing its importance for the control of the Red Sea trade. Acting on his own and without authority from anyone he demanded and obtained tribute from the King of Ormuz. It is also important to note that an Embassy from the King of Portugal to the legendary 'Prester John', King of Ethiopia, consisting of Joao Gomez and Joao Sanches with Sidi Mahmmed, a Tunisian Moor, as their guide, had accompanied the expedition and had been landed at Melinde to make their way to the Ethiopian capital. The party, however, reappeared after a year and presented themselves to Albuquerque who gave them letters in Arabic and Portuguese to the Christian Emperor. It will be seen from these preliminary activities that Albuquerque's vision had already embraced the entire Arabian and Red Seas when he actually assumed the Governorship of Portuguese possessions.

His first object was to establish an impregnable base in India from where he could enforce complete and undisturbed mastery of the Indian seas. The only Portuguese possession at the time was the fortress of Cochin situated on a small island, barely half a square mile in extent. Albuquerque decided that Cochin was unsuitable and it was to Calicut, still the great centre of the spice trade, that he turned. Previous failures in their encounters with the Zamorin rankled in the minds of the Portuguese, and Dom Manoel had sent out no less a person than the Grand Marshal of Portugal, Dom Fernando Coutinho, with express orders to reduce Calicut and destroy the power of the Zamorin. A surprise attack was decided upon. Two fleets, known respectively as the fleet of Portugal and the fleet of India under the separate commands of the Marshal and the Governor, appeared before Calicut carrying a large expeditionary force. A landing was effected without much difficulty. The Zamorin was away from the capital at the time, but the palace guard who engaged the Portuguese invaders found no difficulty in defeating them. In a sharp engagement the Portuguese forces were cut to pieces, the Grand Marshal along with seventy hidalgos losing their lives. Albuquerque himself received two wounds, one on the left arm and the other on the neck. A cannon shot felled him to the ground and he was carried unconscious to his ship. Thus ended in disaster the first attempt to challenge the power of an Indian ruler on land.

The defeat of the Portuguese under their greatest leader at Calicut had far-reaching consequences. For 230 years after this, no European nation attempted any military conquest or tried to bring any ruler under his control. Goa was no doubt occupied and converted into a great base, but this was with the help of Tulaji, the Hindu chief of the area, who joined with the Portuguese in order to weaken the Adil Shahi Sultan's authority in the neighbourhood. Also, it should be remembered that Goa was at an extremity of Adil Shai's extensive dominions and its conquest and fortification by the Portuguese were matters of great importance to the Hindu Empire of Vijayanagar in its campaigns against Islam. The Vijayanagar Emperors were quick to realize that Goa provided them an outlet to the sea, through which they could get not only arms and equipment, but the horses which they needed so much for their cavalry. Actually, therefore, the conquest of Goa was not the establishment of the Portuguese as a land power in India, but the creation of a suitable place for naval operations in the Indian Ocean.

Albuquerque reported to his master that he had put every Moor in Goa to the sword, adding 'wherever he could find them no Moor was spared and they filled mosques with them and set them on fire'. This bitter hatred of Islam brought the Portuguese into friendly relations with the Hindu monarchs of Vijayanagar, who had been carrying on relentless war against Islam for 170 years. In 1509 Krishna Deva Raya, the greatest ruler of the dynasty, and the inveterate enemy of the Muslim Rulers of the Deccan, ascended the throne of Vijayanagar. Not only did he welcome the occupation of Goa by the Portuguese, which enabled him to receive military supplies from abroad, but maintained cordial relations with them. In 1510, Albuquerque sent a mission to him soliciting permission for an establishment at Bhatkal and this was freely granted. The friendly relations between the Hindu Empire and the Portuguese authorities, united in their enmity to Islam, is a fact which is generally overlooked in considering how Portugal was able to maintain herself in Goa with little or no military power after the first fifty years of her appearance in Indian waters.

After thus settling the affairs of the Arabian Sea, Albuquerque turned his attention to Malaya and the Pacific. A major portion of the spice trade came from the Indonesian islands and this trade passing through Malacca and sailing well out into the sea, was being carried by the Arab merchants to the Red Sea ports. The complete control of the trade of the Indian Ocean was not possible without establishing authority in the Malacca Straits.

It should be remembered that Malacca at this period of history was a great international port. Its natural situation made it the key of the Pacific Ocean. As the main entrepôt of the trade of the Archipelago, of the rare spices that grew in Java, Moluccas and other islands, it was regularly frequented by ships from China and Japan in the east, India, Persia, Arabia and Egypt in the west. As Albuquerque himself notes: 'Every year there used to come to Malacca ships of Cambay, Chaul, Dubul, Calicut, Aden, Mecca, Shehr, Jidda, Coromandel, Bengal, of the Chinese, Gores and Javanese, of Pegu and all those parts.' As we have noticed earlier the Sultans of Malaya had, after Cheng Ho's expedition, accepted the suzerainty of the Chinese Emperor and paid regular tribute to the Son of Heaven in Peking. Malacca, therefore, had at that time an importance, as not only one of the commercial centres of the East, but as the connecting link between China and the countries of South and South-west Asia.

Albuquerque decided to go to Malacca himself. Assembling a fleet of eighteen ships he sailed from Cochin and arrived before Malacca in 1511. There as a preliminary to negotiations, presumably to impress the Sultan, he burnt the Arab and Cambay merchant vessels lying in the harbour, but spared the Chinese and non-Muslim ships. The captains of the Chinese ships in the harbour whom the Sultan appears to have maltreated previously offered to assist Albuquerque in the attack and he accepted some landing craft from them. The attack on Malacca took place on the festival of St James, the patron saint both of the Portuguese army and of a religious order of which Albuquerque was the commander. The religious fervour behind the Portuguese endeavour at this time and their conviction that they were carrying on in Asia the crusade against the Muslims is well brought out not only in this action but in what followed.

Albuquerque, in a speech to his men, drove this point home. He emphasized especially 'the great service which we shall perform to Our Lord in casting the Moors out of this country and of quenching the fire of the Sect of Mahomet so that it may never burst out again hereafter'. After service to God he alluded to the service to the King, 'for', he said, 'I hold it certain that if we take this trade of Malacca away from them (the Moors) Cairo and Mecca will be entirely ruined and Venice will receive no spiceries unless her merchants go and buy them in Portugal'. How well the two motives are blended.

The first attack was, however, a failure. The Sultan himself, riding a richly caparisoned elephant, led the defenders. But later, after a fiercely contested fight, the city was captured, though only after the Malayan Ruler and his army had withdrawn. The Muslims who survived the massacre that followed were sold in slavery, but the Chinese, Hindu and Burmese residents of the city were spared. The city was thoroughly sacked: the share sent to the King alone amounted to 200,000 gold cruzados.

The honours of the assault belonged to two captains, Fernand Perez d'Antrade and Antoine Abreu, both of whom became personages of considerable importance, for Albuquerque, realizing that the Pacific lay open to him, appointed d'Antrade the Admiral of the Chinese sea, while he sent Abreu with three ships to explore the islands of Indonesia, the legendary and inexhaustible storehouse of spices. The Portuguese had come into contact both with the great Empire of China indirectly and directly with the rich islands of the Pacific. By the conquest of Malacca not only did Albuquerque establish firmly his mastery of the Indian Ocean but opened the way for expansion into the Pacific. The town itself Albuquerque converted into a strong fortress and appointed to its government an able captain, Ruy d'Avio, before he returned to Goa.

With the conquest of Malacca, Albuquerque completed the structure of European maritime empire in Asia. He had set out to build up a commercial empire based on an unchallengeable position in the Indian Ocean. The major ports on the coast of Africa were already under Portuguese domination, but before his time there was in India only a small foothold in Cochin, and no strong points anywhere from which Portuguese naval authority could be enforced. By the annexation of Socotra, by political influence at Ormuz and by holding Malacca he established a system of control which remained unshaken as long as Portuguese naval power remained powerful enough in Europe. To enable this policy to be carried out successfully it was essential that there should be a territorial base in India functioning as the central pivot of Portuguese power. The conquest and partial settlement of Goa and its development as a metropolitan city with the complete paraphernalia of government constituted the foundation of all his schemes.

Abreu, whom Albuquerque had sent to the spice islands, reached Gresik, but the voyage proved difficult and only one of the three ships returned to Malacca in the following year. But the way had been opened. One of Abreu's officers, Captain Serrao, whose vessel was wrecked by storm, nevertheless reached Amboyna and there he established contact with local sultans. The conditions in Indonesia at the time were especially favourable to the Portuguese. A bitter struggle was going on in Java between the recently converted Muslim rulers and the old Hindu kingdoms, especially Kederi. The most important Muslim ruler was the Sultan of Demak whose help the dispossessed King of

Malacca had solicited. The Javanese ruler equipped a fleet of one hundred ships and sent it to Malaccan waters, but it was dispersed by the gunfire of Perez d'Antrade's caravels. By this victory the Portuguese established their maritime supremacy in the Java seas and they were able thereafterwards to set one ruler against another in the religious wars then prevalent in Java. But they had not made any considerable progress when in the spring of 1521 a European ship sailed into the harbour from the east. It was Magellan's[1] ship *Victoria* which had sailed across the Pacific from America. This alarmed the Portuguese who hastened to consolidate their political position by treaties with local rulers.

Perez d'Antrade's mission in the China seas and the attempts of the Portuguese to establish relations with the Ming Empire we shall discuss at a later stage. With their slow expansion into the islands and their appearance on the China coast, the first period of Portuguese supremacy in Asian waters ended and Portugal's monopoly of the spice trade was well established. One last effort, however, was made by the Turkish Sultan to expel the intruders from the Indian Ocean. Suleiman the Magnificent, of whose empire Egypt had become a part had come to realize the disastrous effects of the exclusion of the Arabs from the trade in the East. As we have seen, one of the major motives of Portuguese action in the Indian Ocean was the impoverishment of the hated Muslim. With the acquisition of Egypt the problem became one of direct concern to the Sultan at Constantinople. He entered into negotiations with the Zamorin of Calicut and the Muslim King of Cambay, the two sovereigns in India whose interests had been affected by Portuguese aggression, and reached an agreement for common action against the enemy. After the treaty was concluded the Sultan issued the following rescript to Suleiman Pasha Al Khadim, the Governor of Egypt:

'You who are the Begler Beg of Egypt, Suleiman Pasha, immediately on receipt of my orders will get ready your bag and baggage and make preparations in Suez for a holy war and, having equipped and supplied a fleet and collected a sufficient army, you will set out for India and capture and hold those parts, cutting off the road and blocking the way to Mecca and Medina, you will avert the evil deeds of the Portuguese and remove their flag from the sea.'

In obedience to these instructions Suleiman Pasha fitted out a great fleet and arrived in the Indian Ocean in 1538. He was, however, unable to effect a junction with the fleet of the Zamorin, for on February 20, 1538, when the Turkish fleet was approaching India, Martin de Souza, the Portuguese Governor, was able to force the Calicut admiral to fight

[1] About Magellan's interest in the Moluccas, etc., see Stanley's edition of his *Voyages for the Hakluyt Society*, p. 124.

an action and to disperse his ships. Suleiman, on receipt of this news, sailed back to Egypt after a futile cruise of the Arabian sea. Unchallenged, the Portuguese Navy ruled the Indian waters for the next sixty years.

We may at this stage consider why the aggrandizement of the Portuguese in the Indian Ocean and their activities in their coastal establishments did not create any widespread reaction in India, for the one thing that stands our most clearly in the relations of the Portuguese with the Indian Powers at this time is the general attitude of friendliness and tolerance towards the newcomers in the Hindu courts of the south with the exception of Calicut. As we have noticed, the great Hindu Empire of Vijayanagar maintained cordial relations with the Portuguese at Goa and permitted them to trade in its extensive dominions. With the rulers of Cochin, where the Portuguese had their first establishment, the Portuguese authorities maintained very cordial relations. With the smaller chiefs along the coast they traded freely and without political complications. In fact, it would not be incorrect to say that the Portuguese met with no hostility at the courts of Hindu rulers, except at Calicut.

The case of the Zamorin was very special. His State was the one considerable naval power on the coast and the Portuguese claims of supremacy on the sea conflicted with his own authority. For a hundred years the naval fight between the Zamorin's fleets and the Portuguese from Goa and Cochin continued without intermission, and it was only in 1599 that a treaty was signed between them. Also, it should be remembered that the prosperity of the Calicut State, for over 400 years, had been bound up with the activities of Arab spice merchants. The Portuguese attempt to displace them affected the basic policy of the Zamorins on which the strength of Calicut had been built up. The hostility of the Zamorin was therefore understandable and it was based on considerations which were particular to his own State.

For the rest, the activities of the Portuguese affected only the Muslim traders, and this was a part of their settled policy. We have noticed how at the conquest of Malacca, Hindu, Chinese aud Burmese traders were left unmolested by Albuquerque. The carrier trade in the Indian Ocean had become a monopoly of the Arabs and the determined Portuguese attempt to dispossess them of it did not affect Indian rulers or their merchants. It made no difference to Indian rulers whether their merchants sold their goods to the Portuguese or to the Arabs. In fact the Portuguese had an advantage in that they were able to sell to Indian rulers arms and equipment which they required. So far as the Indian merchants were concerned, very soon they worked out a system of permits by which they were able to carry on their trade without the competition of Arab merchants, and in that sense the Portuguese monopoly may be said to have helped them. The achievement of the Portuguese during the first period of their supremacy was to have swept the sea of Arabian traders and to have effectively extinguished the monopoly which they had enjoyed for so long. This was not unwelcome to the Hindus and does not seem to have been actively opposed by the non-Arab Muslim merchants of Cambay and Gujerat.

Also, after the disaster that their arms suffered at Calicut, the Portuguese seem to have divested themselves of any territorial ambitions which they might have originally entertained in regard to the mainland of India. The islands of Diu and Bombay and trading posts at different places on the coast, apart from the territory of Goa and the fort of Cochin, were all that they possessed and with these they seem to have been wisely content. Though the viceroys kept great pomp and style at Goa, and pretended almost to imperial dignities, they were realistic enough in their relations with Indian rulers. They exchanged embassies and missions, received and returned presents, and on the whole maintained the decencies of inter-State intercourse. They had in effect become a minor 'country power' – except, of course, on the sea where their claims were truly universal and their authority undisputed.

(ii)

With the appointment of Affonso de Sousa as Governor in 1542, begins the second period of Portuguese maritime supremacy in Asia. During this period they settled down to extract the maximum benefit from their trade monopoly, and for sixty years galleons sailed back to Portugal carrying the spices, gems and silks of the East. The servants of the Crown waxed rich and the life in Goa described by Camoens as the Babylon of the East witnessed a luxury and degeneracy which, if we are to believe the Portuguese authorities of the time, may well be considered unparalleled in history. Apart from a consolidation of their influence along the coastal tracts of Ceylon, extension of trade in the islands of Indonesia, and the establishment of limited relations with China and Japan, the period is politically unimportant. But a significant development took place in Portuguese policy in the matter of religion which may be alluded to here.

The missionary activities of the European Powers in Asia, beginning with Portugal, constitute a most significant chapter in the relations between the East and West and will be separately dealt with.[1] What we shall discuss here is the change that came over Portuguese policy with

[1] See Section VII.

Dom Joao III. Though Henry the Navigator had dreamed of conquering unknown lands for Christ and had indeed been directed to do so by Pope Nicholas, Portuguese policy in the age of discovery was only vaguely evangelistic. The spirit was one of destroying the infidel – the Moor – and not of converting the heathen. Dom Manoel and his representatives knew that they had not the power to enforce such a policy and they contented themselves by building churches and establishing bishoprics in the areas under their direct authority, Goa, Cochin and Malacca. With Joao III the position changed. The revival of religious zeal within the Catholic church, following the Protestant movement, had an immense influence on the Iberian courts. The movement known as counter-reformation found its stoutest supporters among the people of the Peninsula. Ignatius Loyala's Society of Jesus found its most devoted recruits there, and though the Society was founded by a Spaniard, it found a staunch supporter and champion in the Portuguese monarch. In the half-century that followed, religious philosophy witnessed a remarkable revival in the Portuguese seats of learning, especially Coimbra, under the inspiration of Jesuit teachers. This spirit of revived religious zeal was reflected in the policy of the Portuguese Crown towards Asia. It is noteworthy that some of the great figures in the history of Christian missionary activity in the East came to adopt Portugal as their second country. Francis Xavier came out as the Portuguese King's Inspector of Missions. Father Vagliano, an Italian, recruited in Lisbon forty-two missionaries of whom only six were Portuguese. To Ricci, another Italian, who completed his education at Coimbra and at Goa, Portugal was the spiritual home.

This was the background for the new orientation of Portuguese policy which in the time of Joao III preferred commercial profit to spiritual. In India, except of course in Goa, this policy had no very important results so far as the Hindu population was concerned, but for the local Christians of the Malabar coast it was an event of major significance. Elsewhere in Ceylon, in China, Moluccas and Japan, Portuguese commercial activity and evangelization become intermixed, leading to the exclusion of all foreigners from Japan at a later time and considerable trouble with the Chinese Empire in the seventeenth century.

The growth of Protestantism in Europe had a more important and far-reaching result in regard to Asia. It invalidated, so far as the Protestant nations were concerned, the Papal grant of monopoly to Portugal in the East. Also the balance of power in Europe began slowly to change. England under Elizabeth had challenged Phillip II's monopoly in the Spanish main, and after the dispersal of the invincible Armada it became possible for the maritime nations of Europe to enter the Indian waters.

It is also important to remember that the centre of spice trade had shifted from Lisbon to the great ports of the Lowlands during the century. The demand for spices was greater in the northern regions of Europe, and the importance of Lisbon in the beginning was mainly as the entrepôt for these essential goods. But the trade in Europe was in the hands of northern merchants, and from the beginning Antwerp had been a centre of this trade which it later on practically monopolized. The Dutch merchants who handled these commodities were no longer willing to pay the monopoly prices that Portugal demanded, especially as it became clear that the Portuguese power could easily be defied in Eastern waters. In 1592, at the meeting of the leading Dutch merchants at Amsterdam it was decided to establish a company for trading with India. In order to prepare for the voyage and to collect the necessary information the organization sent Cornelius de Houtman to Lisbon. The company had also the information placed at their disposal by Jan Huygen Linschoten who as secretary to the Archbishop of Goa had enjoyed exceptional opportunities for understanding the strength and weakness of the Portuguese position in the East. It should be remembered that the Portuguese had even in the time of Dom Manoel taken the greatest percautions to keep the route to India secret. In 1504 Manoel issued a decree forbidding the insertion on maps of any indication of the route beyond the Congo. Maps which had previously marked places beyond it were collected and the indications erased. The official cartographical service was treated by the Portuguese Government as a great mystery, and the Dutch therefore had to collect the necessary information from the reports of Linschoten and Houtman.

The first Dutch fleet to trade with Asia, consisting of four vessels commanded by Houtman, set out in 1595 from the roadstead of Texel. It reached the Indonesian islands and returned to Holland after an absence of two and a half years. Of the 259 men who left with him only eighty-nine returned, but the profits were ample. The sale of merchandise brought a profit of 80,000 florins.

The voyage opened the way for regular traffic and to the foundation of the United East India Company which was organized under the inspiration of the great statesman Oldenbarnevelt. By a charter dated March 20, 1602, the States General not only gave the Company the monopoly of trade, but invested it with wide sovereign powers to conclude treaties and alliances, to conquer territory, to build forts, etc. The first treaty that the Company signed was with that implacable enemy of the Portuguese, 'the Zamorin, the Emperor of Malabar' and was signed on behalf of the Company by Admiral S. Van der Hagen (1604), and the preamble declared that it was negotiated 'with a view to the expulsion of the Portuguese from the territory of His Highness and the rest of India'. But this was not possible so long as the defence structure of Albuquerque remained unbreached. Therefore the first attempt of the Dutch was to displace the Portuguese from the islands of Indonesia where the Portuguese hold was still weak.

The United Company declared its first dividends of 132½ per cent in 1610. It had, already in 1605, seized Amboyna from the Portuguese and soon in the Archipelago it was on the aggressive both politically and commercially. It was, however, only with the conquest and occupation of Jakarta on May 30, 1619, by Jan Pieterz Coen that the Company's position in the islands could be said to have been fully established. Reporting this event to his directors, Coen wrote: 'The foundations of the Rendezvous so long desired now has been laid. A large part of the most fertile land and the most prolific seas of the Indies is now yours; . . . Behold and consider what a good courage might accomplish and how the Allmighty has fought for us and blessed your Honoures.'

If Coen laid the foundations of Dutch power in the Indies it was Antony Van Diemen (appointed Governor-General, 1633) who built up the Empire and completed the downfall of the Portuguese. In 1641 he wrested from the Portuguese their bastion in the East, Malacca, and thereby breached Albuquerque's defence system. With this base in their possession it became possible for the Dutch to turn their attention to the trade of India proper which the Portuguese still controlled. Admiral Sebalt de Veert had already reported in 1603 that 'no place would be better for attacking the Portuguese (than Colombo) if we could only keep the King and the people of the country our friends'.[1] From Malacca the Dutch began to help the Sinhalese kings in their fight against the Portuguese, but Colombo was strong enough to withstand all attacks from the side of the land. In 1654 Van der Heyden after prolonged siege occupied the port and expelled Portuguese power from Ceylon.

After this, the downfall of the Portuguese commercial empire in Indian waters was rapid. Cochin, their first establishment, was occupied in 1660; other smaller trading stations fell one by one to the Dutch. From Colombo the Dutch captains engaged themselves in a systematic campaign of eliminating the Portuguese from the maritime trade of India.[2] Except Goa and the small islets of Daman and Diu (Bombay had been given in dowry to the British King in 1665) nothing was left of the great structure that Albuquerque had erected.

In the island of Java, Van Diemen had been successful in monopolizing the trade and to some extent in maintaining the Company's political

[1] Pieris – Documents relating to Dutch Power in Ceylon.

[2] The story of the destruction of the Portuguese power on the Malabar coast by the Dutch is told in the present writer's *Malabar and the Dutch*.

influence. By a system of advancing money to cultivators on harvests the Company had effectively dispossessed the people of the Banda islands, Amboyna and the Moluccas. It took possession of the land and proceeded to extirpate the clove trees outside its own territory, and when the population resisted they were put down by force. A Dutch historian describes the conditions that resulted in the Moluccas in the following words: 'The Company made them (the cultivators) change their clove gardens into rice fields and sago tree plantations. The small mountainous islands could not produce food enough and the inhabitants were obliged to buy a supplement of rice from the company. It sold this commodity to them at too high a price which made the situation still more desperate. Thus the economic system of Moluccas was ruined and the population reduced to poverty.'[1] We shall see later how this system, so successfully experimented in the Moluccas, was later extended to Java and the other islands when the Company had secured political authority over them.

By the middle of the century the Company's position in the islands was stabilized. The three great sultanates, those of Mataram in Java, Atjeh and Ternate maintained their independence with difficulty, and though the territorial possessions of the Dutch were still small, their political authority increased with the breakdown of the Indonesian State systems. The King of Macassar and the Sultan of Atjeh fought the Company's claims with determination and it took the Dutch many decades of hard fighting before they were able to establish their authority finally by about 1680. The campaign against Macassar was specially interesting, for the king of that country had developed a sea power which appeared menacing to the Dutch. A fleet of twenty-one ships with a European force was sent out against Macassar and it was only after two hard-fought campaigns that the Sultan was forced to sign a treaty by which the Company came to acquire sovereignty over the territory ceded by him.

With the trade of the Indies effectively in the hands of the Dutch, the sultanates of Mataram, Atjeh and other local sovereignties crumpled and lost their effective power. Bantam alone, under a remarkable king Sultan Abdul Fatah, showed signs of a revival, but the Dutch, taking advantage of the rivalry between the father and the son, brought that State also under subjection.

Though a political paramountcy in the interests of trade was thus established and the Dutch were the unchallenged masters of the wealth of the islands, the conquest of Indonesia had not yet been effectively accomplished or the direct rule of the Company extended to the interior. At this period, the object of the Dutch was not exploitation – except in

[1] Bernard H. M. Vlekke: *Nusantara*, p. 139.

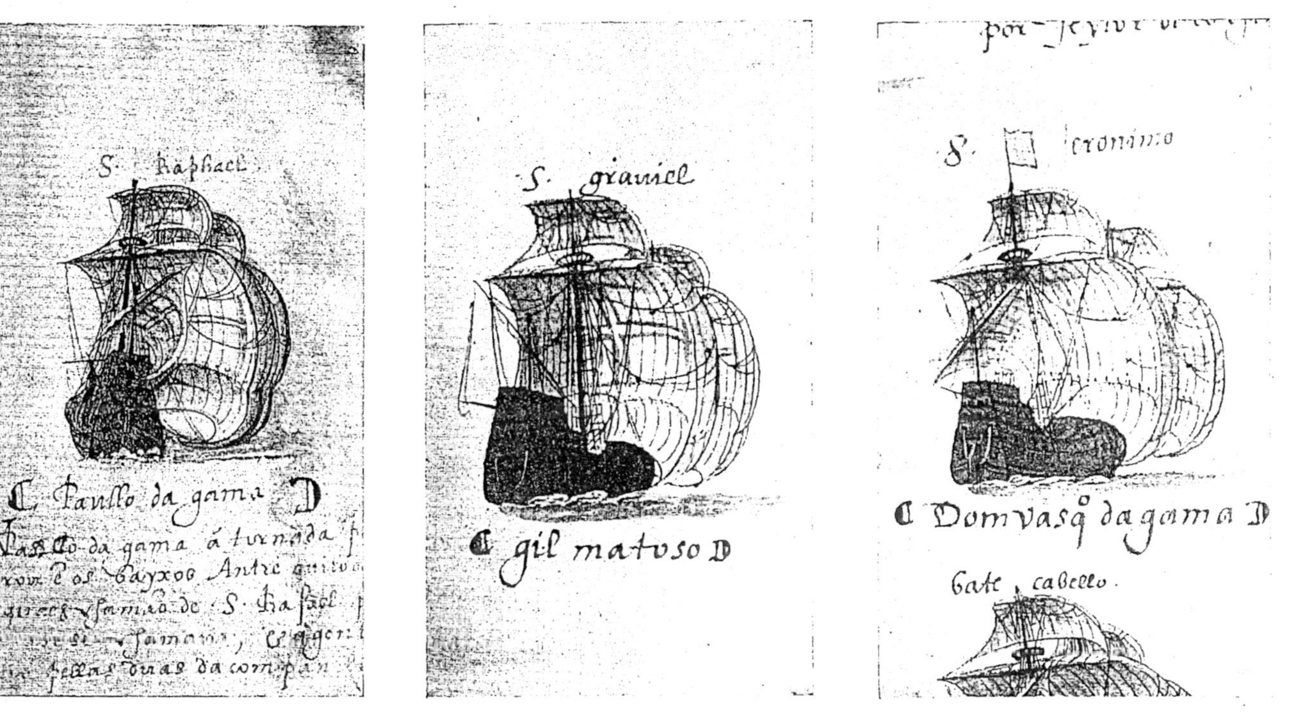

III SHIPS IN WHICH VASCO DA GAMA'S FIRST VOYAGE OF DISCOVERY WAS MADE

Contemporary drawings in the possession of the Portuguese Government

Photo: de Maria C. Cardoso, Lisbon

IV VASCO DA GAMA AT THE ZAMORIN'S COURT
(Painting by SALGADO 1898)

small isolated areas – but commerce. The directors of the Company were against the assumption of sovereignty. Writing to Rycklof van Goens, who had proposed the assumption of sovereignty over Ceylon, the Court of Directors declared frankly: 'This would be the work of a great and ambitious king and not one of merchants who only look for profits.' Later, however, this policy underwent a radical change when exploitation was found to be more profitable than commerce.

With the Pacific islands as their main bases of activity, the Dutch were advantageously situated for developing the trade with China and Japan. For a time their fleet occupied Formosa from which, however, Coxinga, a remarkable Chinese adventurer who supported the cause of the defeated Mings, expelled them. With the Manchu Empire they tried to open diplomatic relations, but with no success, though they were allowed to carry on a limited trade at Canton and in Fukien. Their commercial relations with Japan were most interesting and fraught with more signficant consequences, for they were permitted to establish and maintain a factory first at Hirado and later at Deshima under very strict supervision and control. Their trade with China was responsible for the introduction of tea in the West and their contacts with the Japanese had some influence in encouraging a desire for Western knowledge in the Island Empire.

(iii)

A year before the Dutch Company was established, the English East India Company had received from Queen Elizabeth the charter giving it a monopoly of trade in the East. To the English, spices were particullarly important at that time. 'The Elizabethans,' it has been said, 'lived on salt meat from autumn to spring, their fresh meat was of poor quality in general; for the good of the fishermen the law compelled them to eat fish more often than they cared about and with all this insipid food their craving for pungent flavourings was probably and naturally much stronger than ours. They liked heavily spiced drinks, moreover, for they had no tea.'[1] The Dutch, who were the chief middlemen of the spice trade in the sixteenth century, had supplied the northern countries with this essential commodity, but when in 1599 they put up the price of pepper from 3s to 8s a pound, the British merchants decided to enter the Eastern trade themselves.

The Company's first vessel sailed East under Captain Lancaster on January 24, 1601. It reached Achin in Sumatra and returned two and a

[1] Quoted in Thompson and Garret: *Rise and Fulfilment of British Rule in India*, p. 6.

half years later in November 1603 with a cargo of 1,030,000 lb of pepper. Other voyages followed mainly to the spice islands. But the Company's affairs did not progress very satisfactorily, for nothing was available in England to sell in exchange, and the export of specie was disliked intensely by the economists of the time. The Company's agents in the islands, however, discovered a suitable and satisfactory method. They reported that there was a great demand in the islands for Indian textiles, and if these could be brought and sold at Bantam and Moluccas, the spice trade could be financed from the profits. Thus it was to buy textiles that the British sought to establish a trading centre in India, and the place chosen for the purpose was Surat (1612).

In 1615, King James was persuaded to send out an ambassador to the Court of Jehangir. By this time the English had been forced out of Indonesia and their main commercial interest had become concentrated on the mainland of India. Again, the problem for the English Company was how to pay for the Indian trade, for payment in specie brought out from England was not to be considered. The Red Sea traffic seemed to offer an advantageous opening. But before their trade could develop, the Civil War in England made the position of the Company difficult, for Charles I had given a charter to a rival group of merchants to set up trade in India. This opposition did not prove serious and the East India Company embarked on a policy of cautiously extending their trading posts. They settled down at Masulipatam in 1641. In September that year they obtained from the Raja of Chandragiri, successor to the Empire of Vijayanagar, the right to build a fort at Madras. By 1647 they had twenty-three trading posts and ninety employees – not a very notable advance.

With the acquisition of Bombay in 1665 the position changed a little. Charles II transferred to the Company full rights of jurisdiction (1668) which they had always desired in their own settlements. The head-quarters of the Company's affairs were shifted from Surat, where they were under the shadow of Indian rulers, to Bombay, which the naval guns could easily defend. With the Restoration in England the affairs of the Company had begun to prosper or at least to attract public notice, for they came under the guidance of Sir Josiah Child – a truly astonishing man, grandiose, unscrupulous, arrogant and tempestuous, but gifted with a rare imagination. 'His appearance as a city merchant, instead of as the Emperor of China or the Great Mogul seems an error of Providence' so it was stated. Josiah Child was the advocate of a forward policy. He felt a deep contempt for everything Asian and even 'declared war' on the Mogul Empire. The result of this action was altogether ignominious. The Company's establishments in Bengal were occupied and what they had built up with so much effort was lost in one blow. The Company was forced humbly to sue for peace, to which the Emperor Aurangzeb agreed, after the English had promised 'to behave themselves for the future no more in such a shameful manner'. He also imposed a fine on the presumptuous merchants.

When the Company's factors returned to Bengal they settled in a fishing village on the River Hoogly (Calcutta, 1690), which they were allowed to fortify six years later. Thus by the end of the century there had come into existence Bombay, Madras and Calcutta, the three centres from which British power was able to penetrate into the interior a hundred years later. But at this time and for many decades to come, the Company had no political influence of any kind and the impression sedulously propagated by present-day historians that the Carnocks, Pitts, Oxendens and Yules who bought and sold and carried on trade were political personalities of consequence at the time is altogether misleading.

The entry of the French into the Asian trade may also be briefly noted here. The importance of keeping up with other European Powers in the Indian Ocean was realized by Henri IV, who tried to establish a French East India Company in 1601. Various exploratory voyages were made, but the preoccupation of France with European developments, and later the *fronde*, prevented the growth of a sustained interest in the affairs of the East till the time of Colbert. That statesman, who was anxious to establish the maritime greatness of France, took a direct interest in the incorporation of the East India Company (1664). In time, factories were established and the French, like other European nations, had their small trade settlements in India. The original idea of Colbert was to establish French authority in Ceylon, and a considerable fleet under Jacob de la Haye was sent out for that purpose in March 1670. The Dutch, however, were alert and prevented a French settlement on the island, and the only notable achievement of the expedition was the foundation of Pondicherry by Francis Martin who, with six others, had been left behind.

The picture that the East presented at the end of the seventeenth century was briefly as follows: the power of the Portuguese had been eliminated effectively from the Indian Ocean and from the Pacific, though their establishments at Goa, Macao, and Timor were left undisturbed. The Dutch controlled the coastal tracts of Ceylon and had a few trading establishments on peninsular India, of which the most important were Cochin and Negapatam. They occupied Malacca and controlled the trade of Malaya. In Indonesia they had built up an empire based on commercial monopoly and with China and Japan they carried on a profitable trade. The British, excluded from the Indonesian islands, had concentrated on India where they had built up an extensive trading organization. Last of all, the French had entered the Orient and staked their claims at Pondicherry. Except in island areas the European traders exercised no political authority, and when the Portuguese in 1633 and the British in 1689 came into conflicts with Indian rulers they were made to realize the folly of trying to challenge the authority of well-established States.

It is important at this stage to emphasize the great change that had taken place in the structure of Asian trade. As we have noticed, the European nations arrived in Asian waters in search of spices. In the sixteenth century spices dominated the trade between Europe and Asia. Even in the seventeenth century, so far as the Dutch were concerned, their main interest continued to be in spices. But with the total exclusion of the British from Indonesia and the growth of trade with the ports of China, the interest shifts to textiles, calico, muslin, silks, etc. This change was greatly helped by the revolution in economic conditions that had taken place in Europe. For a hundred years the wealth of America had flowed into Europe. The gold and silver mines of Central and South America had enriched the maritime peoples of the Atlantic coast. North American colonies of England and Holland had increased the prosperity of the mother countries. The spice trade of Asia had also contributed its quota. By the middle of the seventeenth century the Atlantic nations had reached a state of prosperity which only Venice had known before.

This economic prosperity created new demands. In England, France and Spain, the three great Powers at the time, the demand was for muslin and printed textiles from India, for tea and silks from China and for coffee from the Dutch East Indies. The spice trade continued, of course, to be very important, but with competition the profits became much less. The popularity of Indian textiles became a great political issue both in England and in France. Pamphleteers – notable among them that mercenary of letters, Steele – appeared on the scene to defend the virtue of British woollen goods. As early as 1677 Parliament felt called upon to prohibit all but woollen goods for winter use. By 1695 Indian textiles had displaced British goods so effectively that there was an insistent public demand for a total embargo on Indian textiles. The Spitalfields silk weavers demonstrated outside Parliament. Nor was the position any better in France. The Regency, under the pressure of textile interests in that country, attempted by successive pieces of legislation to stem the tide in favour of Indian and Chinese goods.

The Eastern trade, though it had shifted predominantly to textiles which because of their cheapness, durability, colourfulness and, above all, their washable quality had become irresistibly popular both among the rich and the middle classes in Europe, was not confined to them. Wallpaper, fans, porcelain and cabinet and tea from China, lacquered goods, shawls (cashmeres) and brocades from India had become important articles of trade. Opposition to the growing volume of this trade was vociferous. As Sansom observes: 'The root of the argument from which grew a tree of many branches was the old fear of the drain of gold. When the English pamphleteers professed to be shocked by the transparency of Indian fabrics, their care for the modesty of English females was a disguise, not less transparent than muslin, for the objections of those who on general grounds deplored sending gold and silver abroad or on particular grounds were anxious to protect domestic industries.'[1]

Essentially, till the nineteenth century the Asian trade was a one-way traffic. There was no large demand for European goods in any Asian country. The Empires of Asia being what Wittfogel calls 'the water works States', depending on land revenue, had, generally speaking, self-sufficient economies. Though the trade of India was large at all times, the economy of the country was not based on trade. This was true of China also, and the imperial government seems at all times to have discouraged the import of foreign goods into its territory. Also, Europe at the time had but little to offer to Asian economy. The story of the Amsterdam Company which exported to Siam a collection of thousands of engravings, of madonnas and biblical scenes, 'prints recording the stories of Livy and, finally, prints with a more general human appeal, a collection of nudes and less decent illustrations'[2] is not by any means strange or unique. Richard Cocke's letter from Japan complaining of the lack of interest in Biblical paintings may also be quoted here. 'They esteem a painted sheet of paper with a horse, ship or a bird more than they do such a rich picture. Neither will any one give six pence for that fair picture of the conversion of St Paul.'

The lack of demands for Western goods, until Manchester was able to provide cheap textiles and until manufactured goods could be expected, was a serious complaint. Even in the nineteenth century the demand for European goods fell far short of expectations, as we shall try to show later. Actually, therefore, at a period when economic nationalism, which begins with the Navigation Acts of the Commonwealth and is carried forward by Colbert, was seriously trying to protect national industries, develop export trade and safeguard the wealth of the country, it is nothing strange that the East India trade was looked upon with disapproval and was subjected to hostile criticism. But the views of the economists could not prevail against public demand, and the growth of wealth and luxury helped to maintain and even increase that demand.

The latter part of the first half of the eighteenth century witnessed

[1] Sir George Sansom: *Western World and Japan*, p. 154.

[2] Quoted in *Nusantara*, p. 198.

the great rivalry of England and France in the Indian Ocean. The changed political conditions in Europe which had pushed Portugal and Holland to back seats were reflected in the conflicts that developed between the European powers in the East. France and England alone remained in the contest. Neither the internecine quarrels of European nations nor their troubles with 'interlopers' concern us here; but it may be pointed out that the intermittent efforts of France (e.g. La Bourdonnais' naval actions in the Bay of Bengal) to interfere with the growing British naval power had very little significance in the development of events. So far as the Indian Ocean was concerned, the rivals to British commercial predominance had been eliminated, while so far as China and the Eastern seas were concerned, none of the Powers had so far developed anything more than limited trade. In Indonesia, the Dutch enjoyed a virtual monopoly.

MONGOLIA
Khingan Mts.
SINKIANG
Great Wall
Karakorum
TIBET
CHI
Delhi
Himalayas
MOGUL EMPIRE
BENGAL
BURMA
Chittagong
GUJERAT
Ahmedabad
Cambay
Surat
Champa
Diu (P)
Bombay (P)
WESTERN
BAY OF
BENGAL
PEGU
SIAM
ANNAM
Tungabhadra
Malabar
Goa (P)
Bhatkal
Mangalore
GHATS
VIJAYANAGAR
Coromandel Coast
CAMBODIA
COCHIN
Calicut
Coast
Negapatam
Quilon
C. Comorin
CEYLON
Kandy
MALAYA
ACHIN
Str. of Malacca
Malacca (P)
OCEAN
SUMATRA
Palemban
Bantam
Batav
JAV

CHAPTER 2

CHINA AND JAPAN

(i)

WITH the establishment of the Portuguese power in Malacca in 1511 the Pacific lay open to European ships. In the Malayan Peninsula there were many Chinese, mainly from Fu-kien, and from them the Portuguese heard of the vast riches and great commerce of the Empire of China. The first Portuguese to get to the China coast was Raphael Peresterello (1516), who travelled in a junk and returned after an adventurous journey. In the following year, according to George Philipps, Jorge Mascarehas visited the port of Chuang Chow and traded with the Chinese merchants. The information collected by Peresterello and Mascarehas convinced the Portuguese authorities of the desirability of opening up trade with China. An embassy was prepared and Thomas Pires, a pharmacist, carrying a letter from the King of Portugal, was escorted by Fernand d'Antrade up to Canton. D'Antrade was the chief of the Portuguese naval station in Malacca and he had brought with him a large cargo of pepper for which there was at all times great demand in China. The ambassador was well received and the Canton officials also permitted d'Antrade to sell his pepper and buy Chinese goods in exchange.

The emperor who was then reigning at Peking was Kang Te of the Ming Dynasty. Founded by a patriotic Buddhist monk, named Chu Yuan-chang, who organized the national resistance to the foreign Mongols, this dynasty was truly national and represented a revival of Chinese spirit. Under Chu Yuan-chang, who assumed the regnal title of Hung Wu, the Empire extended its authority even to Korea and the Ryukyu Islands and was accepted as suzerain by Burma and other outlying tributary States, while during the early Ming period Chinese suzerainty was freely accepted by the Japanese emperors.

As a national monarchy the policy of the Mings was generally one of a restoration of the spirit of Chinese culture. Hung Wu promulgated a code of laws, re-established the traditional bureaucratic organization of the Empire, and strengthened the mandarinate by restoring the system of imperial examinations. His successor, Yung Lo (1403-24), was also an emperor of great ability, who is now best remembered for the rebuilding of Peking in its present form, for the immense encyclopaedia which he compiled – the Yung Lo Ta Tien – and for the maritime adventures of his Admiral, Cheng Ho, who took a fleet of sixty-five ships into the Indian Ocean as far as the Arabian coast. But apart from these he has other claims to be considered one of the great rulers of China. He extended the imperial authority to Annam, Korea and Japan. Also through the naval expeditions of Cheng Ho he had converted the vague suzerainty which the Chinese had claimed over the southern regions into something like a system of tributary States. Over Siam, Java, Sumatra and Malaya, Peking for the first time began to claim the rights of a paramount Power.

Yung Lo's successors were not men of any marked ability, but it is worth while to emphasize that at the beginning of the sixteenth century and in fact well into the middle of the next, the Chinese Empire under the Mings enjoyed more or less unbroken peace and prosperity. The administration, as reorganized by Hung Wu and Yung Lo, continued to function normally, and considering the size of the empire it was reasonably efficient and capable of exercising its authority everywhere. In the time of Kang Te, when the Portuguese first reached China, the reorganized administration was working well, and the local viceroys and governors had sufficient initiative and ability to deal with matters that arose in the provinces. In fact, the outstanding feature of China's political structure, till the treaty of Tientsin (1858), was the loyalty and ability with which local viceroys carried out the policies of the centre, even when the government at Peking was weak, corrupt and inefficient.

The authorities in Peking were duly informed of the arrival of Pires and, after the inevitable delay, permission was received for him to travel to Peking. In the meantime information which was not altogether favourable to the Portuguese was reaching the Ming court. The Malay sultans, who as vassals claimed the right of protection, had been petitioning for help against the newcomers. More especially the Sultan of Bitang had sent a detailed report warning the Peking Government that the Portuguese, even when they came for trade, were planning conquest; he exposed Portuguese methods in the Indian Ocean. But the emperor, while suspicious, was not unwilling to receive the ambassador and orders were issued for Thomas Pires to be sent up to Peking. By the time Pires reached the capital the Portuguese themselves had proved to the satisfaction of the Chinese authorities that they were not to be trusted. Simon d'Antrade, the brother of the admiral who had first escorted Pires, sailed up to Shang Chuan and began to behave in the manner in which the Portuguese captains had been accustomed to do in Malaya. He landed a party and began building a fort. The Chinese fleet attacked him and he was driven off. When news of Simon d'Antrade's piracies reached Peking the Chinese Government naturally refused to receive the ambassador, who was sent back to Canton, where he died in prison in 1523.

It is necessary to emphasize that at this time the Chinese had no prejudice against the foreigners. The Ming Dynasty, though nationalist, and representing a revival of Chinese culture after the foreign rule of Yuan, was ready to welcome foreign intercourse. In fact, during the early years of the dynasty there was considerable maritime activity as we noticed, and Cheng Ho's voyages in the Indian Ocean and the contacts which the empire had established with Malaya and the southern islands showed clearly that China was not at that period moved by a spirit of isolation. Why, then, did the Peking court suddenly reverse its policy and refuse to have any dealings with the Portuguese? The answer is to be found in the political claims of the Portuguese and in their barbarous behaviour towards the people of Asia.

As we have noticed earlier the Portuguese king had assumed for himself the title of the Lord of Navigation and claimed 'sovereignty on all lands' discovered by his men. This claim, of course, the Portuguese could not enforce on land, and after Albuquerque's disaster at Calicut in 1511 it was quietly given up so far as land Powers were concerned. But where their ships could enforce it, that is, on islands like Ceylon and in Malacca, they did not abate their pretensions. Also on the seas they held firmly to the doctrine that they had the right of navigation on the Eastern seas with their exclusive monopoly as Lords of Navigation and the right of confiscating the goods of all who sailed the seas without their permits. Moreover, their method of trade, as developed in Malaya and in Cochin and other coastal areas of petty States, was to land at a suitable point, build a fort and hold it as their territory and trade from that base. This is what Simon d'Antrade tried to do at Shang Chuan, even while the ambassador was on his way to Peking.

It should also be remembered that the piracies of the Portuguese on the high seas were fully known to the Peking court. The Malayan Rajas, who were acknowledged vassals of Peking, especially the Sultan of Bitang, had reported to the emperor the outrages by the Portuguese along the coast, and had also warned him of the political ambitions of the Portuguese. Islam, then as now, was an international community and the activities of the Portuguese in Goa, Ormuz and on the Red Sea coast were not unknown to the Muslim rulers of Malaya. Through them the court had gained some information on the objects which the Portuguese had not cared to conceal in their relations with the smaller potentates of the Indian Ocean area.

It is no doubt true that after the Zamorin of Calicut had taught the too venturesome Portuguese Marshal the impossibility of conquering and holding territorial possessions, when sea power could not be used effectively, the Portuguese were content with the control of small islands and would not have ventured to challenge the might of China. But the Chinese emperors wanted no trouble and refused to have any further dealings with a people who recognized no international rights and who committed open and large-scale piracy on the high seas.

Though no political and diplomatic relationship was allowed to develop, the Portuguese carried on a flourishing trade with the southern ports. There was no special prohibition against trade and the local Chinese governors, it would seem, even encouraged commercial intercourse with the foreigners who brought such valuable commodities for sale. Jorge Mascerehas' visit to Chuang Chow had resulted in friendly relations with the commercial community, and a flourishing, though unofficial, trade came into existence with the connivance of the local authorities, especially at Chuang Chow and Ningpo. But the Portuguese temper and their extravagant claims to the lordship of the Orient brought them into conflict with the local population and with the viceregal government and they were driven out from both these settlements. Yet the trade had been profitable to both parties, and when the Portuguese had made ample amends for their misbehaviour and made suitable presents to the viceroy and other officials, they were allowed in 1557 to use a deserted promontory named Amakau as a place in which to land their goods and carry on trade. Amakau, or Macao as it has come to be known, is a tiny bit of a peninsula connected with the mainland by an isthmus.

A Chinese admiral chasing pirates had received help from a Portuguese ship, and the governor out of consideration for this had allowed the Portuguese to use Macao as a trading point. So it remained till 1887. It is necessary to point out that, till 1849, the Portuguese regularly paid rent for the land and the Chinese exercised both civil and criminal jurisdiction and fiscal authority over Macao. Chinese courts functioned there till 1690 and a special magistrate resided in Macao and exercised his authority. In the case of murder, the final judgment lay with the court at Canton and even houses could not be built in 'Portuguese' Macao till 1843 without payment of fees to the Chinese authorities. The generally prevalent idea that Macao was taken by the Portuguese and held against the might of China is, it will be seen, altogether untrue. In fact till the middle of the nineteenth century when the British and the French established European domination in China, the Portuguese were in Macao in the capacity of humble petitioners, not to the court of Peking but to a subordinate official at Canton.

The Spaniards were the next to come into contact with China. They had reached the Philippines early in the century and by 1571 the archipelago had been conquered and Manila founded. There they came into contact with Chinese vessels. The first Spaniards to visit China were two priests, Martin de Herrada and Geronomo Marin. Friendly relations were established with the authorities of South China and by the end of the century they were also permitted to trade at Canton. But the Spaniards met with no greater success than the Portuguese in trying to open diplomatic relations, though their commerce based on the Philippines seemed to have flourished. It was a strange kind of trade as the Philippines acted as an entrepôt of Mexico, and the trade with China from Spain was via Central America. 'The silver of American mines continued to be bartered from Callao and Acapulco for Asiatic textiles of cotton and silk, for spices and porcelain, cheating the treasury of their Catholic majesties.'[1]

Portuguese power in the Pacific declined by about the first quarter of the seventeenth century when the Dutch, after driving the Portuguese out of Amboyna in 1605, slowly excluded their rivals from the other areas of the Indonesian Archipelago. In 1619, the Dutch had established a factory at Jakarta which was renamed Batavia and, as the Dutch commander reported, by this act 'we have gained a foothold and Dominion in the land of Java'. Gradually the position of the Portuguese in the Eastern seas was for a time taken by the Hollanders. A Dutch captain arrived in 1662 with a fleet of fifteen vessels off Macao, and though he was unable to oust the Portuguese from the peninsula, his expedition had most interesting results as it led to the occupation of Formosa, which at this time had not been effectively colonized by the Chinese. The Dutch established themselves at Taiwan and built a fort. In view of the significance that this island came to assume in later history, it may be desirable to allude briefly to the course of events in Formosa before taking up the story of Dutch attempts to enter into relations with China proper.

The Dutch did not colonize Formosa but used it mainly for trade and as an intermediate port in their developing relations with Japan. But soon a major threat to their position arose, this time from a Chinese adherent of the fallen Mings, Cheng Chengkung, known to history as Koxinga. When the Manchus occupied North China and the partisans of the Mings were being slowly exterminated on the mainland, Cheng, who had held out stubbornly at Amoy, decided to establish his base in Formosa. With a force of 25,000 men he attacked the island, forced the Dutch to surrender after a prolonged siege of their fort and took possession of the island for the Ming Emperor. Koxinga held it against all

[1] Hudson, p. 241. See also Pere Henri Bernard: *Les Isles Philippines*, Tientsin.

comers and even harried the Fukien coast to such an extent that the Manchu Emperor had to order an evacuation of the coastal area of the province. Koxinga continued to rule over the island and, after his death, his son succeeded to the island territory and the Manchus finally annexed it only after the death of Koxinga's son.

The invasion of China by the Manchus is a major event in Asian history, as the dynasty which drove out the Mings continued to rule over China till 1911 and was thus on the centre of the stage in the 250 years of Europe's relationship with Asia. Their rise to power and the prestige and authority they gave to China for 200 years and their final collapse constitute a chapter of more than usual interest and importance.

The Ming Dynasty after Chang Te produced a succession of weak and effete rulers who became the playthings of court eunuchs and corrupt officials. Emperor Wan Li (1573-1620), a weak ruler who succeeded as a child, was a slave to his pleasures and conducted the work of the State mainly through his eunuchs and concubines. His chief adviser was the eunuch Wei Chenghsien, who has come to be regarded in China as the most infamous character in its long history. Wan Li's successor was murdered by the concubine of his father with the assistance of Wei. The next emperor was a weakling entirely under the control of Wei, who with the support of the foster-mother of the monarch ruled the State in the name of his master. Wei Chenghsien's actions were so monstrous and his defiance of public opinion and neglect of the welfare of the State so blatant[1], that the prestige of the dynasty was irreparably damaged. The next emperor, Chung Chen, had to reap the consequences of Wei Chung-hsien's misdeeds. Disorders broke out everywhere and the capital itself fell to Li Tzu-cheng, the rebel leader. The Empire was in a state of disruption, which enabled the growing power of the Manchus to step in.

The Manchus were a border race which at different times had accepted Chinese suzerainty, but never had actually been conquered by the Chinese. Organized in clans, they lived without any national unity, till a leader arose among them named Nurhachi (born 1559) who, moved by a desire for revenge for the murder of his father and grandfather by a Chinese official on the border, began organizing the Manchu tribes into a confederacy. The Chinese authorities endeavoured to placate him by making him a warden of the marches and conferring on him the title of 'Dragon and Tiger General'. This only increased Nurhachi's power and prestige which he used to strengthen his political authority over the tribes and to build up a powerful army. By 1586 his authority had been accepted by the different Manchu tribes and he was recognized as the

[1] These are summarized in sixteen counts in a remarkable memorial submitted to the Emperor by the Censor Yang Lien in 1624.

Ruler of Manchuria. Slowly he extended his authority also to Mongolia, over which the Chinese, under the effete rule of the later Mings, had ceased to exercise any effective suzerainty. As the Peking Government supported the Yehos in his fight to establish his authority over them, Nurhachi declared war on China in 1618. Though the Mings were then precipitately descending to their collapse, the Empire was not so easily to be defied and an army was sent to chastise the insolent Manchu. The campaign went on in a desultory manner for seventeen years with the power of the Manchus growing with each year. At Nurhachi's death in 1626 Manchu power extended up to the Liaotung peninsula, threatening the Empire itself.

Nurhachi's successor was known as Tien Tsung. It was he who established the suzerainty of the Manchus over the Korean State and over the Chahar Mongols and carried on the war into Chinese territory. In the time of his successor occurred in China the great rebellion of Li Tzu-cheng which made the last Ming Emperor commit suicide in Peking. This was the opportunity that the Manchus were waiting for. Joining hands with the Ming supporters in the north they intervened against the rebel, but after Li Tzu-cheng was defeated, the Manchu monarch claimed the Empire for himself and brought the whole of China under his rule (1645).

The substitution of the effete Mings by a vigorous new dynasty strengthened China at a very important time. The northern frontier tribes, like the Mongols, had in the later years of the Mings denounced the suzerainty of China. The Kalhkans, the Eleuths and other semi-independent tribes had also broken away, while the immense territory which was later to be known as Sinkiang was altogether independent. The Russians were moving into the vacuum in Siberia. Actually, therefore, when the Chings, as the Manchu Dynasty was known, began their reign in Peking the territory of China was limited to the area south of the Great Wall and did not include Sinkiang or Tibet. A succession of able rulers – and two of them Kang Hsi and Chien Lung were among the greatest monarchs in Chinese history – consolidated the Empire again, limited Russian expansion to the Amur, reconquered and brought under effective control the territory of Sinkiang and intervened with force in Tibet and established Chinese claims there also. The next 200 years saw the authority of China extended over the widest area, from the northern boundaries of Korea to Cambodia, from the Pacific to the Himalayas and the Karakorams.

From the end of the Ming period to the beginning of the nineteenth century there were in Peking a number of European priests who were employed by the court in different capacities. Though they were missionaries their work in Peking was mainly scientific, and the Emperor Kang

Hsi had an intellectual curiosity which was notable for a ruler of that period. China came to be known extensively in Europe, and the Chinese civilization and thought, conveyed to Europe by the translations made by these missionaries, had some effect on the thought and civilization of the eighteenth century, as we shall endeavour to show in a later chapter.

Attempts were made, mainly by the Dutch, to enter into diplomatic relations with the new Empire. They had rendered some assistance to the Manchus, and presuming on this they had suggested that they should be allowed to send embassies to Peking. But the interests of the Catholic missionaries clashed with the ambitions of Protestant Holland. A diplomatic mission headed by Peter de Goyez actually travelled up to Peking in 1655, as 'bearers of tribute'. They *kow-towed* before the vacant throne and were graciously given presents by the emperor. The only political result of this embassy was the permission by the Imperial Majesty to send such embassies together with four trading ships once in eight years. The next Dutch embassy, under Pieter Van Hoorn, reached Peking in 1665, and though he was also courteously received, in form as the head of a tribute-bearing mission, no political results followed from it also. The ambassador reported to Batavia that they had been conducted to Peking like spies and sent away from there like thieves.

Now the English also entered the China seas. The first English venture into this area was in alliance with the Dutch, then their mortal enemies in the East India trade. In 1619 a treaty was signed between the two companies by which they decided to occupy an island somewhere off the China coast and to force the Chinese junks to trade only with them. There was also to be a joint 'council of defence'. Article ten of the agreement provided: 'The defence shall be employed in the gaining of the trade to China. And to that end the fleet shall be sent to the Philippines, there to hinder and divert the Chinese that they shall not traffic with any others but with us.' This unnatural alliance failed because the Dutch, after fortifying the Pescadores with the help of the English, proceeded to monopolize the trade. The Dutch alliance having thus failed, the English merchants decided to approach the Portuguese. They sought and obtained a licence from the Portuguese Viceroy of Goa and fitted out several ships under the command of Captain Weddel. Their information about China was so meagre that Weddel considered it sufficient to bring some introductory letters from the Goa authorities to the Governor of Macao to enable him to trade with China. The 'miserable subjection' in which the Chinese authorities held the Portuguese in Macao, as the governor explained, did not permit them to render any assistance. So the English captain took it upon himself to force the issue. He fitted out a barge and pinnace with fifty men and sent them up the

Canton river. They were, however, stopped by the Chinese authorities and told to leave the river. The English as usual carried on with a high hand and 'demanded that they should be allowed to traffic freely as the Portugalls did and to be forthwith supplied with their monies, with provisions for their ships all of which the Mandarins promised to solicit the prime men resident at Canton: and in the meantime desired an extension of six days which was granted'.[1]

Naturally this attitude of a conqueror granting terms and demanding things 'forthwith' led to trouble. The ships landed a party of 100 men and occupied a small fort near the river and proudly displayed 'His Majesty's colours of Great Britain upon the walls'. They also committed various acts of piracy on the river. The Chinese showed great patience and two of the ship's officers were sent for to Canton where their petitions were duly received by the local officials. But no permission was received, and after Captain Weddel apologized for his conduct and undertook never to repeat the offence he was permitted to load his cargo and return to India.

In 1685, when under an imperial mandate the port of Canton was opened to trade, the East India Company, which had then the monopoly of British trade in the Asian waters, obtained the right to establish a factory at Canton. It also opened a trading post at Ningpo. After the voyage of the *Macclesfield* in 1700 this trade grew in importance and the vessels of the East India Company visited Canton each year. In 1715 a permanent factory was established in Canton and an agreement was formally reached with the Imperial Commissioner for trade, known in English as Hoppo, by which the trade was regularized. But this was only at Canton and even here business was conducted through a body called the Hong merchants, a monopoly guild of Chinese businessmen, who first enjoyed the recognition, if not the protection, of the Chinese officials. When its position was formalized later, the guild or Co Hong came to be 'armed with the full powers of the Government, acting as its agent and receiving its full support on the one hand and on the other serving as the channel through which was transmitted the stream of wealth in which the officials expected to share largely'.

The mechanism of this trade is of some interest, especially as it became a major factor in the political troubles in the nineteenth century. The Chinese attitude to foreign trade found its classic expression in a decree of the Viceroy of Canton. It declared 'the Celestial Empire appoints civil officials to govern the people and military ones to terrify evil-doers. The petty affairs of commerce are to be decided by the merchants themselves: the officials have nothing to hear on the subject'. On the Chinese side, the trade was controlled by the Hong merchants,

[1] *Embassy to China*, Vol. I, pp. 8 and 9. London. Balmer & Co. 1797.

who in their turn were under the authority of the Imperial Commissioner of Customs whose corrupted English designation was the Hoppo. The Hoppo alone had the right of issuing licences to trade, and through the Hong merchants kept a strict control over the entire business.

With the immense growth of the East India Company's power and resources in India the English came to have during the course of the eighteenth century the lion's share of China's trade. Tea was the main business of the East India Company in China. British interest was mainly in black tea grown in the province of Fukien, from where it was brought down to Canton and bought through the Hong merchants. In the evidence before the Select Committee of the House of Commons one of the witnesses stated: 'The Company have, I believe I may say, every leaf of black tea at their options: I mean every parcel of black tea of any value is first offered to the Company and is submitted to their inspection.' There was, of course, competition from other foreign buyers, but the investments of the other European buyers did not amount to a seventh of the British interest. Before the end of the eighteenth century tea had become a national beverage in England; and it was to pay for this immense investment that the Company encouraged the sale of opium which Warren Hastings had converted into a monopoly in India.

The Company had the largest number of Europeans resident in China, and yet no effort was made for a long time to send a diplomatic mission to Peking. The first ambassador chosen for the work was Colonel Cathcart, but he died before he could reach China (1787). Some years later the famous embassy of Lord Macartney bearing credentials from George III reached Peking. This was an unusual mission which started after elaborate preparations and with a numerous staff. The ambassador and his suite travelled up to Peking in great state, but with a banner bearing the inscription in Chinese 'Ambassador bearing tribute from the country of England'. Lord Macartney, however, behaved with great dignity and refused to *kow-tow*, agreeing only to present his credentials bending on one knee. Great courtesy was shown by Chien Lung to the ambassador, but the political and commercial results of the mission were altogether negative.

A later mission sent in 1816, under Lord Amherst, had to return from Peking as the Chinese insisted on the ambassador performing *kow-tow* and the ambassador with equal firmness refused to consider it. Thus the position continued till Britain, grown stronger by the conquest of India, determined to use force in order to compel the Chinese to trade.

(ii)

According to Antonio Galvano, Governor of Malacca, the Portuguese first reached Japan in 1542. The first to land on the islands, according to the same authority, were Antonio de Moto, Francesco Zimoro and Antonio Perota. At that time Japan was going through a period of feudal warfare in which the great Western Princes, headed by the Satsuma, had assumed territorial independence and had set at naught the authority of both the Mikado and the Shogun. It should be remembered that the Shogunate did not itself become a powerful machinery of centralized government till it passed into the Tokugawa family at the beginning of the next century, and the period between 1550 and 1600 was consequently one verging on feudal anarchy. From this chaos there emerged a military leader of genius, Oda Nobunaga (1534-82), who was able in time to hold in check the power of the great feudal magnates, the daimyos, and exercise supreme authority in Japan.

It was at this period, critical in the history of Japan, that the Portuguese arrived, displaying new and more efficacious weapons of war. The daimyos were not slow to realize the significance of the ships which were heavily armed and of soldiers who carried harquebuses. The western daimyos who were fighting for their local independence welcomed the intruders. In fact in 1551 one of these daimyos sent with Francis Xavier an envoy, and the hope was entertained by many feudal chiefs on the coast that they would be able to aggrandize themselves with the help of the Portuguese.

Fortunately for Japan, by the middle of the century Portugal had ceased to be in a position to exercise effective political influence anywhere, even on coastal tracts; but if it had been in the heroic period of Albuquerque they might have created a great deal of internal trouble and occupied some of the smaller islands. But with the 'sixty years of captivity' following the union of Crowns, Portugal had difficulty in maintaining her authority even where she had been firmly established for half a century, and soon was to be driven by the Dutch from her main island possessions. Also, with the growth and consolidation of Nobunaga's power the possibility of successful rebellion by local rulers became less and less a national menance. The danger was from the missionaries whose activities are treated separately elsewhere. The only point which may be emphasized here is the close relationship which the Portuguese captains maintained with the missionaries, arising from the historical connection of the Portuguese Crown with the evangelization of the East under *Jus patronatus* and the interests which the missionaries at that time had in the greatness and glory of Portugal. St Xavier had come to the East representing both the Pope – as a Legate – and the King as an inspector of missions. As missionary work was a State enterprise charged to the Crown's revenues in Portugal, this identification of national interests with religious activity should not be a matter of surprise.

The encouragement which the Christian missionaries received under Nobunaga might have thus turned disastrous to the State but for the widom and foresight of the great military leader who succeeded him. Hideyoshi was no ordinary general. He was a great patriot, a statesman of vision and an organizer of genius. Like Nobunaga he was at first anxious to keep on good relations with the Portuguese and their missionaries. But he was a keen-eyed observer. He noticed that the Portuguese had landed artillery to protect the area in which Christian converts lived. On a visit to a Portuguese vessel to see Father Coelho he observed that the ship, though small, was heavily armed. He was also well aware of the interest that the western daimyos were manifesting in the arms and equipment of the Portuguese and of their attempts to strengthen themselves by friendship with the foreigners. Hideyoshi acted with firmness and in 1587 the activities of the missionaries were prohibited throughout the length and breadth of Japan.

In the meantime the Spaniards had established themselves in the Philippines and conquered the main group of islands. With the Philippines the Japanese had commercial relations from the earliest times. Hideyoshi was not unwilling to enter into trade negotiations with the Spanish authorities, but an accident interfered with it. The commander of a Spanish galleon which was driven ashore spoke of Spanish power and recounted to the local daimyo, who had salvaged the vessel and claimed the cargo, the glories and prowess of the Conquistadores in a boastful manner. Hideyoshi's suspicious mind, already aware of Portuguese actions in the East, ordered the arrest of all Spaniards in the country and had them crucified in Nagasaki as spies.

Hideyoshi was succeeded by Ieyasu Tokugawa in 1600, and three years later he was installed as *Sheitai* Shogun, or the 'Barbarian subduing Great General'. The Tokugawa Shogunate lasted for 265 years, exercising *de facto* authority over the whole of the Japanese Empire, but preserving the form and dignity of the imperial title. While the Shogun was the actual ruler, he had to submit a report of his actions to the Emperor and inform and obtain his saction on matters of great national importance. Military power was vested exclusively in the Shogun, and the daimyos or feudal lords had to swear allegiance to each Shogun. Those who had fought against the Tokugawa Shogunate, known as the Tozama or the Outside Lords, were permitted to retain their fiefs but not allowed any share in the government of the country.

Though the Tokugawa Shogunate had thus restored central authority and established a dictatorship which lasted for over two and a half centuries, the feudal character of the regime, the unsubdued position of the Outside Lords and the great power of Princes like the Satsuma and other western territorial chiefs rendered Japan susceptible to external intrigue. Some of the Outside Lords, like the Choshu, who held thirteen out of the sixty-five provinces of Japan, and the Satsuma who held power in Kyushu, were in combination always able to challenge the authority of the Tokugawas. The Shogunate, always vigilant where the permanency of its own regime was concerned, realized the danger to the system they had established, which contact with foreign nations, powerful on the sea, would have meant, and the logical result was a decision to prohibit all foreign intercourse, except under official control. The policy of seclusion which the Shogunate enforced from 1637 had, therefore, both an internal and an external aspect. Internally it was meant to safeguard the security of the regime from revolts of powerful nobles, who might have formed alliances with foreign Powers, or at least have obtained superior weapons and arms. From the point of view of external policy it was intended to prevent direct contact between the foreigners and the people and to limit all unavoidable relations to the authorized representative of the Shogunate at a specified port. The Shogun had sufficient justification for his actions. Jacques Spex had explained to Ieyasu the methods of Spain and Portugal and in 1612 Henrick Brower presented to the Shogun a memorandum on Spanish and Portuguese methods of conquest. In the time of the second Tokugawa Shogun (Hidetada) the European nations were themselves denouncing each other's imperialist intentions. The Japanese converts had, as elsewhere, shown that their sympathies were with their foreign mentors and for this they had to pay a very heavy price. The Christian rebellion of 1637 in Shembara disclosed this danger to the Shogun. It took a considerable army and a costly campaign to put down the revolt which was said to have received support from the Portuguese. The Japanese were also fully informed of the activities of the Portuguese, the Dutch, the Spaniards and the English in the islands of the Pacific – especially in the Philippines, the Moluccas and Java – and these had taught them the necessity of dealing with the foreigners firmly and of denying them an opportunity to gain a foothold on Japanese territory. In 1615 the Japanese sent a special spy to the southern regions to report on the activities of the Europeans there. They were strengthened by the information that reached them in 1622 of a Spanish plan to invade Japan itself. By the beginning of the seventeenth century Spain had consolidated her position in the Philippines, where she maintained a considerable naval force. Japan was the only area in the Pacific which

Spain could attack without interfering with Portuguese claims or the Papal distribution of the world which in her own interests she was bound to uphold. It seemed natural to the Spaniards that they should undertake this conquest. The reaction of the Shogunate was sharp and decisive. All Spaniards in Japan were ordered to be deported, the firm policy of eliminating the converts was put into effect and a few years later the country was closed to the Western nations.

After the order of exclusion was enforced, the 'Bakufu' or the Shogun's government, which depended for its power on the military caste, developed a theory of life which it promulgated assiduously among its followers. Its ideology is contained in the *Legacy of Ieyasu*, the founder of the Tokugawa Shogunate. It is a philosophy of discipline, of the acceptance of hard life as the basis of national greatness. The Shogunate in fact was an attempt to organize the nation on a military basis, with the security of the country and, of course, the permanence of the Shogunate with which it was identified, as the first aim of every Japanese. It created a powerful central government and an administrative machinery capable of dealing with the complicated problems which were facing Japan. The Bakufu, developed into an organized bureaucracy, under a council of elders. Thus with the restoration of peace after a long period of internal strife, with a reasonably efficient administration and a strong central government, Japan was able to face the world without fear.

The exclusion edict did not, however, mean that all contact with the West was given up. In the time of Ieyasu the Dutch had already established a house at Hirado (1611), and the Portuguese were trading at Nagasaki.[1] The Daimyo of Hirado was profiting greatly by this trade. The English also arrived on the scene when the *Clove*, commanded by Captain John Saris and bearing a letter from King James I to the Shogun, arrived in Japan in 1613. Saris seems to have been received courteously and was granted permission to trade. An English house was also established. The competition of these different 'houses' was advantageous to the Japanese. There was, however, only one article in constant demand, cannon. It would appear that both the English and the Dutch used to cast ordnance at Hirado, but the Shogunate officials demanded cannon cast in England, as according to the Diary of Richard Cocks, the Japanese were aware of the difference in quality. The Dutch had in their intercourse made themselves generally useful and the order of exclusion

[1] The Dutch had sent tentative trading expeditions to Japan on different occasions beginning with 1594, but it was only when the *Liefde*, one of the ships of the fourth expedition, drifted to the coast that the Dutch as a nation came to be known to the Japanese. The survivors were treated with courtesy by Ieyasu. In 1609 the Dutch King sent an envoy to express his appreciation of the kindness shown to his subjects, and the Shogun was pleased as a result of this mission to allow the Dutch to trade.

did not apply to them. They were, however, removed from Hirado to a small islet of Deshima near Nagasaki. Merchants and seamen were not allowed to remain more than a year at a time. Annually they had to present themselves, like humble petitioners, before the Shogun at Yeddo. They were not allowed to bring their wives or other European women, and Japanese women other than prostitutes were not allowed to visit them. The Dutch were, however, not popular with the public. Takekoshi, a modern Japanese historian, remarks: 'Despite the Shogunate's policy of favouring the Dutch merchants, the Japanese in general were not friendly with them.'

All the same Deshima was Japan's window to the West. Its influence on the development of Japanese thought in the eighteenth century, through the *Rangakusha* or the Dutch group of scholars, will be dealt with in the appropriate place. Here it is sufficient to state that from the first the Japanese displayed great interest in military matters. It was in 1615 that Jacques Spex had cast a metal gun 600 lb in weight. In 1618 Spex was asked to teach the Japanese how to cast cannon, but though anxious to oblige he had no one at his disposal. But later experts were found, as we know that the Daimyo of Hirado had many pieces cast in his presence. In 1638 the Shogun sent a special commission to examine and report on the performance of a present of artillery pieces by the Dutch East India Company. The Dutch were not happy about the interest that the Shogun and his officers were showing in cannon and mortar. François Caron, their chief, said that for the future mortars should not be cast in Japan. His successor, Antonizoon Overwater, was even more frank. Writing to his superiors about the request for a mortar gunner Overwater said wisely: 'One may well ask whether it had not been wiser never to have taught this proud and haughty nation about them, but that now being past, we must resign ourselves thereto.' A mortar gunner named Jureann Schaedel was finally brought from Holland and he remained in Yeddo for six months (1650). The interest was, however, fitful, though it enabled Japan, even before the country was re-opened to the West, to have some knowledge of the problems of defence, and thus helped her to realize her own weakness in relation to European nations.

The Order of Exclusion continued till Commodore Perry's 'black ships' arrived off the Japanese coast in 1853. In the beginning of the nineteenth century, however, the contact with the outside world kept on increasing in spite of every effort on the part of the Shogunate to maintain and uphold its policy. The Russians had already reached the Pacific and were exploring the seas to the north. The British, after their authority had been firmly established in India, were also showing considerable impatience and a number of their ships on one excuse or another had sailed up the Japanese coast. Through the factors at Deshima the Japanese authorities kept themselves fairly fully informed, while a small but growing number of people, with strange persistence and almost heroic patience, kept on studying the Dutch language and familiarizing themselves with the scientific developments of the West. Deshima helped in the process of gestation which was destined to bear such remarkble fruit in the half century that followed the visit of Commodore Perry.[1]

[1] The extent of trade which the Dutch carried on from Deshima seems to have been insignificant. In 1700 only five ships were permitted to enter the port. In 1715 it was further reduced to two. Later, in the Kansu era (1789-90), only one Dutch ship every year was permitted and after that for several years no 'red-haired ships' entered Nagasaki. See Kuno, pp. 93-4.

BIBLIOGRAPHICAL NOTE TO PART I

The background of European efforts to reach India by a sea route is treated exhaustively in many books. Raymond Beazley's *The Dawn of Modern Geography* (London, 1906) and the same author's *Henry the Navigator* (N.Y., 1904) are authoritative. Zurara's *Chronicles of Guinea*, which is the main source for the activities of the Navigator, has been edited by Beazley and Prestage for the Hakluyt Series (1896).

For the economic background of this effort, *Les Hommes d'Affaires Italiens du Moyen Age* by Yves Renouard will be found interesting, while Professor Tawney's *Religion and the Rise of Capitalism* deals with the Antwerp interest in the Discoveries. A useful but authoritative summary is contained in Hudson's *Europe and China* (London, 1931).

On the period of Portuguese expansion English historians have, generally speaking, accepted uncritically the highly coloured and romantic versions of the Portuguese Chroniclers. The one exception is R. S. Whiteaway's *Rise of Portuguese Power in Inda.* An early monograph by the present writer on *Malabar and the Portuguese* (Bombay, 1928) may also be consulted.

Henri Cordier's *L'arrivé des Portuguais en Chine*, Toung Pao, 2nd series, Vol. XII, is well documented and Chang Tien-tse's *Sino-Portuguese Trade from 1514 to 1644* (Leyden, 1934) is also interesting.

About the early activities of the Dutch in the Indian and Pacific Oceans there is very little authoritative literature in English. Peiris' *Dutch in Ceylon* and the present writer's *Malabar and the Dutch* deal with limited areas. John Nieuhoff's book on the *Embassy of Peter de Goyers and Jacob Keyzer to Peking* is available in an English translation by John Ogilby. Professor C. R. Boxer's *Jan Compagnie in Japan* provides very interesting sidelights on the relations of the Hollanders with the Japanese Empire.

Part II

THE AGE OF CONQUEST

1750–1858

CHAPTER I

INDIA AND THE ISLANDS

(i)

IT would have required supernatural vision for an observer in 1750 to foretell that in the course of fifty years a European nation would have conquered a third of India and would be preparing to contest with the Marathas for a position of paramountcy over the rest; for after 250 years the position of European nations in India was substantially the same as it had been after Albuquerque in 1515. The Portuguese ruled over their territories in Goa, Daman and Diu, the sport of every Power on the sea, and they counted for nothing in the political struggle that was soon to follow. The Dutch had a few minor settlements, the most important of which was Cochin, half a square mile of fortified beach situated on an island, from which they carried on a flourishing pepper trade. The French 'India' consisted of the establishments at Pondicherry and a few minor trading posts, Karikal, Mahe and Chandernagore, then under the governorship of the flamboyant and intriguing Dupleix. The British, whose trade had greatly increased during the first half of the century, had establishments at Surat, Madras, Masulipatam and Calcutta, besides smaller trading posts in Bengal. The island of Bombay they held in sovereignty, as it had been transferred to the King of England by the Portuguese and by him to the East India Company to be held 'in free and common soccage as the manor of East Greenwich on payment of the annual rent of 10 pounds in gold, on the 10th of September each year'.

It is necessary to remember that nowhere outside the island of Bombay did the East India Company claim territorial sovereignty and the Fort St George (Madras) was confined to the beach. Just next to it, barely a mile and a half away, was the Portuguese settlement of St Thome. In 1700 a Mogul governor had appeared in Madras, and had to be bought off with an immense gift and a banquet which included 600 dishes, followed by an adequate supply of dancing women. The visit of the Nawab became almost an annual affair. The township of Madras as part of the Company's settlement came into existence only in 1708, when the Central Government at Delhi made a grant of five villages adjacent to the fort. In Bengal also the position of the English was in no way different. The Viceroy of Bengal continued to be addressed by them in the most cringing terms. In addressing the Emperor one of the English Presidents described himself as 'the smallest particle of sand, John Russel, President of the East India Company with his forehead at command rubbed on the ground'. The Company had the right of free trade in Bengal and were allowed to rent two villages near Calcutta. But the Mogul Government denied them jurisdiction and the activities of the Company were restricted to the legitimate business of trade. They continued to maintain this humble attitude not only to the throne at Delhi and the Mogul viceroys and governors, but to local potentates, for no dream of political power or empire had come to possess them as yet.

Nor was their power adequate for any serious political intervention. The previous experiences of the Portuguese, the Dutch and the British had shown that the Euopean nations were not yet in a position to enforce their claims even against minor rulers. The Dutch came up against the Raja of Travancore in 1739, and though their power in neighbouring Ceylon was considerable, the battle ended in a disaster for the Netherlanders, whose landing party, including over a hundred Europeans, had to surrender ignominously. The attempt of the British to extend their authority to the villages near Madras had led to their forcible eviction by the local authorities at the beginning of the century. Even on the sea, as late as 1722, Kanoji Angria had defeated and put to flight a combined attack of the British and the Portuguese. In 1738, the British naval authorities on the West coast reported: 'Our strength is not sufficient to withstanding him (Sambhaji Angria) for I assure Your Honour that he is a stronger enemy than you and a great many others think.' In fact, for well over a quarter of a century after Plassey, British military power was not so serious a factor as later historians have been inclined to think.

What, then, enabled these trading establishments and the East India Company in England to gain political and military power within a period of fifty years, enabling them to fight the Maratha power and crush it on the field of Assaye (1803)? What forces, political, economic and social helped to bring about so mighty a transformation? An explanation of this change is fundamental to the understanding of Europe's position generally in Asia in the nineteenth century, for undoubtedly it was the India-based strength of Britain, as a great Asiatic Power, that enabled it to force open the doors of China, establish European predominance in the Yangtze Valley, reduce the power of the Great Manchus, and help to convert the rest of Asia into a European dependency. It is the military conquest of India which, though completed only in 1858, had given to the British an unshakable foundation by 1818, that enabled the industrially revolutionized Britain in the post-Napoloeonic period to project her political and economic power into the Pacific. An analysis of the factors that led to this transformation is therefore necessary at this stage of our study.

The picture that India presented in 1748 was one of extreme complexity. In the continental area, extending from the boundaries of Mysore in the south along the western coast to the gates of Delhi, including within it the fertile areas of Gujerat, Malwa and the vast central tract between the Ganges and the Vindhyas, the Marathas had established a powerful empire which was centrally controlled and directed from Poona. This constituted at the time the only indigenous dynamic political force in India, animated, as the Duke of Wellington noted, by a spirit of national patriotism and guided for another half century by policies of national preservation. The Maratha Empire, with its capital at Poona, had not yet come to look upon the merchants in Bombay, Madras and Calcutta as possible rivals to the Empire of Hindustan and its main interest at the time was to consolidate its conquests in Malwa and Central India and take over the heritage of the Moguls. It is, however, interesting to note that not only in 1803 and 1818, but in 1858, it was the Maratha power that challenged Britain, for such organization, military ability and political direction that the war of 1857-8 displayed on the Indian side came from the Marathas under Nana Sahib, the last Peishwa, Tatya Topee and the Rani of Jhansi – all remnants of Maratha power.

Apart from the Marathas, there was no clearly defined political authority which evoked loyalty or allegiance anywhere else in India. A number of Mogul war lords had usurped authority in different provinces. The great area of the Deccan had been taken over by Asaf Jah, a disloyal and ambitious viceroy, who by tortuous diplomacy supported by large payments to the Marathas, was able to maintain himself in Hyderabad. When he died in 1748, the Delhi Emperor, unable to nominate an official of his own choice, allowed the succession to be ought out. There was no local loyalty or allegiance involved, for the succession was *to a post* and not yet *to a throne*, and there was no dynastic claim or rights based on tradition, custom or popular acceptance. The Carnatic – the Mogul province to the south of the Deccan, which nominally extended to Cape Comorin, but where the Mogul had never exercised any authority whatever – was under a nawab who claimed to administer his *suba* from his headquarters at Arcot. It should be remembered that there was not even a tradition of Muslim rule in the area, and the nawab and his mercenaries were only titular representatives of a titular emperor in Delhi. His power was negligible and he controlled no administration worthy of the name. The rich and fertile province of Bengal was under a capable viceroy, Aliverdhy Khan, in 1750, and he also had made himself more or less independent.

In the major areas where the foreign companies had their trade, the war lords had taken over from a fast dissolving centre, a position analogous to that in China after the Manchu Empire disappeared. The situation appeared reasonably stable so long as the original governors, appointed by legitimate authority, conducted the administration. Thus, Asaf Jah in Hyderabad was not merely a powerful potentate, but in the public mind he symbolized the central power. But his successors, fighting among themselves, represented no political authority or principle. In the Carnatic it was even worse. Anwar Din – the Nawab – was no more than a subordinate official, appointed by the Nizam, himself a servant. It was no principality, no hereditary dominion that Chanda Sahib and Mohammed Ali claimed, but merely a nominal post which they desired to be conferred on them by the Mogul court. So far as the authority of the nawab over the Carnatic was concerned, how nominal it was would be evident from the fact that in 1740 a Maratha general had laid the country waste, killed Dost Ali, the governor, and had exacted a tribute of ten million rupees from his successor! So when Anwar Din died, the claim to any legal authority – if it ever existed in the Carnatic – had vanished.

A similar position arose in Bengal when Aliverdhy Khan died in 1756. Aliverdhy had himself become the viceroy by a successful rebellion against his predecessor. At his death the succession to the viceroyalty became a matter of family intrigue. His grandson, who finally became the Nawab Nizam, or viceroy, no doubt received the Mogul authorization, but as events were to demonstrate clearly he had no claim on the loyalty of anyone, least of all of the members of his family whom he had ousted. In fact, the basic factor in the political situation which developed in Hyderabad after the death of the Nizam Asaf Jah, in the Carnatic after the death of Anwar Din and in Bengal after the death of Aliverdhy was the same – the extinction of political loyalty as a result of the attempt *to convert an official post into a heritable princedom* – thereby not only creating confusion by the extinction of legitimate authority which people accepted and to which people in general were still loyal, but reducing authority to naught by the unavoidable civil wars in which different parties at court supported different candidates. Chanda Sahib and Mohammed Ali fought in Arcot: Muzaffar Jung's succession to the Deccan viceroyalty, confirmed by the Emperor, was challenged by Nasir Jung; Sirajud-Doula's claims to the Bengal viceroyalty were opposed by Ghasiti Begum, and her son Shaukat Jung at one time had even received the firman of the Emperor.

This war-lordism in the Mogul territories and the consequent breakdown of local authority, following attempts to secure family successions, enabled the merchants groups in the ports to intervene on the side which promised the most liberal rewards or the greatest concessions. Dupleix, whose imagination outran his wisdom, saw great possibilities of making a fortune for himself by intervening in the interests of the legal claimant, Muzzafar Jung, in Hyderabad, and of Chanda Sahib at Arcot (1749). The English East India Company in Madras thought that the time had come for them also to intervene, and they naturally threw their weight on the side of the rival candidate to the Suba of the Carnatic, Mohammed Ali. This individual, one of the vilest characters in history, achieved a remarkable eminence by the amount of his debts (mostly created by collusion), by the corruption he introduced in *British* politics where through pocket boroughs he maintained no less than six members of Parliament at one time, and finally by being the subject of an eloquent denunciation by Edmund Burke. But apart from these claims to glory, Mohammed Ali is also entitled to remembrance as the first Indian official to invite British intervention and with foreign help to convert the governor's chair into a princely *gaddi* (throne). The East India Company gained by little by this intervention, except the discomfiture of the French - no doubt satisfactory to the national pride of the British - and a doubtful ally from whom, when their power became more substantial, they were able to extract greater and more valuable concessions.

The intervention in Bengal was a little more fruitful. The British had cautiously supported Ghasiti Begum and her Hindu bankers against Siraj-ud-Doula, and when that personage assumed the position of viceroy they were naturally marked out for his displeasure. The British, who were illegally erecting fortifications at Calcutta, were ordered to pull them down. On their refusal he marched against Calcutta and captured Fort William (June 20, 1756). But if the East India Company could not fight against Sirajud Doula they could intrigue against him, and they were past masters in the game. As emphasized before, Sirajud Doula had no claim to the loyalty of anyone. He was not a legally appointed nawab nazim, which title properly belonged to Shaukat Jung. Against him there was therefore a powerful group of Muslim nobles, led by Mir Jafar. More important was a new force which began to manifest itself in these struggles.

With the establishment of European trading centres in the main coastal areas of India, there had developed a powerful Indian capitalist class closely associated with the foreign merchants, and deriving great profits from trade with them. In Surat, these merchants had established a pre-eminence to which the Company's early records bear full witness.

Their influence in political affairs had also been considerable, for they had mediated for the Company with the Mogul governors as early as 1662. The Ananagaranga Pillais (the Dubash of Dupleix) and the Pachiappa Mudaliars of Madras were men of great power and influence. During the eighteenth century, as a result of the growth of Bengal trade, the commercial community of North India had flocked to Murshidabad and Calcutta. The Marwari millionaires of Bengal had become the equivalent of the comprador classes of Shanghai of a later period. While the nawabs and generals were able to squeeze them occasionally, there was no doubt that effective power in the form of control of the economic life of the province had passed from the decrepit Mogul nobles to the *bania* capitalists who fawned on them in their *durbars* but held their purse strings tightly.

The emergence of this powerful class, whose economic interests were bound up with those of the foreign merchants and who had an inherited hatred of Muslim rule, was a factor of fundamental importance to the history of India and of Asia. It meant a change of tremendous significance in the political and economic structure of Asia. As we have pointed out before, India's economy had been agricultural, i.e., based on the produce of land, and the industrial production of the country had been mainly for consumption. Such a system had contributed to the power of the landed classes and of a military aristocracy – *jagirdars* – based on land. This traditional system had for over two centuries been subjected to the influence of a commercial economy, based on oceanic trade. In the sixteenth century, as this trade was mainly in spices, it did not affect the economy of continental India; but in the seventeenth century there was a change in the structure of India's trade. India's manufactured goods, calicoes, muslin, etc., and also commercial crops like mustard seed and hemp became the main items in demand. The produce of the rich Gangetic Valley flowed down to the ports of Bengal, through the agency of Marwari merchants, who, with their offices all over North India, soon became the wielders of effective power. In the courts of provincial viceroys they backed those who paid the largest interest on loans and helped them in their business. In Bengal especially their power had waxed greatly under the leadership of Jagat Seth, a veritable Croesus, the stories of whose wealth have become legendary in India. Jagat Seth had been insulted in public by Sirajud Doula, and the revenge he took on the nawab was to enter into negotiations with the East India Company at Calcutta to create a palace revolution.

Plassey, which was the result, was a transaction, not a battle, a transaction by which the compradors of Bengal, led by Jagat Seth, sold the nawab to the East India Company. The nawab's generals, already in league with the Hindu merchant princes and their British allies, did not fight and the treacherous general, Mir Jafar, received, as the price of his betrayal, the Nawabi of Bengal. But it would be a mistake to think that Plassey either gave the province of Bengal to the Company or made the Company a military power of any significance. All that it did, in form, was to make the Company *a Zamindar* – the landlord of the district known as twenty-four *Pargannahs*. In effect, it placed the governor under the Company's thumb, a pitiful figure who could be squeezed by the greedy servants of the Company and from whom every kind of concession could be exacted. The Nawab's Government broke down utterly as his authority now depended entirely on the Company's authorities at Calcutta. In quick succession the nawabs were changed. The Mogul court at Delhi now thought that the time had come for it to intervene in the affairs of Bengal, but its attempted intervention proved ineffectual and at Buxar (1764) the Emperor, after an engagement in which his forces were defeated, granted to the Company the *Diwani*, i.e., the right of revenue administration, over the rich territories of Bengal, Bihar and Orissa.

It is unnecessary for our pupose to go into the sordid details of the Company's early administration of their *Diwani* of Bengal. In brief, it may be stated that for a decade the whole power of the organized State was directed to a single purpose – plunder. It was a robber State that had come into existence, and Richard Becher, a servant of the Company, wrote to his masters in London on May 24, 1769, as follows: 'It must give pain to an Englishman to have reason to think that since the accession of the Company to the *Diwani* the condition of the people of this country has been worse than it was before. . . . This fine country, which flourished under the most despotic and arbitrary government, is verging towards ruin.' In a remarkable document, some of the leading landowners of the country petitioned the Council and stated: 'The factories of the English gentlemen are many and many of their *gumastas* are in all places and in every village, almost throughout the province of Bengal. They trade . . . in all kinds of grain, linen and whatever other commodities are provided in the country. In order to purchase these articles, they force their money on the ryots and having by these oppressive methods bought the goods at a low rate, they oblige the inhabitants and the shopkeepers to take them at a high price, exceeding what is paid in the markets. . . . *There is now scarce anything left in the country*.'

A new State, based on a merciless exploitation of the people, had come into existence in India, and that State had an unchallenged mastery of the sea, which enabled it to concentrate its strength anywhere on the coast. But again it would be a mistake to think that the Company had already become anything like a powerful competitor for authority in India. In 1769 Hyder Ali, who had usurped the government of Mysore, was able to dictate peace at the very gates of Fort St George in Madras. An attempt by the Bombay Government to repeat the success of Clive in Bengal by challenging the might of the Marathas led to the humiliating convention of Wadgoan in 1779. But after 1772, Warren Hastings was steadily building up an administration in Bengal which in a few years' time was to convert the robber State of Clive into a powerful and organized government. Also, Hastings realized that it was beyond the power of the Company to challenge Maratha authority and therefore set himself to detach the more powerful feudatories, the Raja of Nagpur in Central India and Scindia who controlled Maratha interests in the north, from the central government at Poona.

Two decades of settled administration under Hastings and Lord Cornwallis, and the complete exclusion of the French Navy from the Indian Ocean following the withdrawal of Admiral Suffren, gave to the British at the end of the century a superiority of strength, which, though not yet decisive, was sufficient to give them a dominant influence with the lesser States of India. The Carnatic passed under their control: the Nawabi of Oudh had been reduced to a tributary. At the end of the century only three Powers faced the Company in India: the Maratha Empire covering the west and central parts of India, the Nizam of Hyderabad, whose territories covered the tablelands of the Deccan, and Tipu Sultan, who ruled over Mysore in the south. That was the position when Lord Mornington (later the Marquis of Wellesley) came out as Governor-General in 1798. The history of the British in India is not illumined by many outstanding names, but Warren Hastings, Wellesley and Dalhousie have claims to be considered among great statesmen. Though he was vain, pompous, intolerant of opposition and capable of chicanery and meanness, Wellesley had from the first a very clear vision of what he set out to achieve. That was to destroy the power of the Marathas and make the English Company supreme in India. For this purpose it was necessary to gain control of Mysore, so that the Maratha homelands could be attacked from the south, to neutralize the Nizam, so that the threat from the powerful force which the Frenchman Raymond had organized could be eliminated, and above all to weaken the central government of the Marathas by sowing seeds of dissension in Poona. In a short and swift campaign, Wellesley, with the active assistance of the supporters of the Hindu Dynasty of Mysore, whose power Tipu had usurped, destroyed the power of the Sultan and pushed the Company's forces to within striking distance of the Maratha homelands. By a determined *coup d'état* in Hyderabad, the French-controlled forces of the Nizam were disbanded and the Nizam himself reduced to the position of a dependent prince. Wellesley now felt himself to be in a position to challenge the Marathas. He signed a treaty with a traitorous

VI IEYASU TOKUGAWA, 1542-1616

V HIDEYOSHI, 1536-98

pretender to the headship of the Maratha State, which his more brilliant brother, Arthur Wellesley (later Duke of Wellington) described as 'a treaty with a cypher', and under the cloak of supporting the legitimate authority of the Peishwa attempted to bring the Maratha Empire within his system of subordinate alliances.

In the war that followed, the genius of the future Duke of Wellington destroyed Maratha military power at the field of Assaye (1803) in the Deccan, and Lord Lake routed Scindia's northern forces at Laswari. But though great victories were won, the Marathas could not be disposed of in the manner that Tipu had been dealt with, or the Nizam brought under subjection. The successive failures of Lord Lake before Bharātpur and the chasing of Colonel Monson's forces up and down Central India by Holkar showed that British military power, while it had achieved superiority on the field, was yet unable to conquer and hold India. The effort was given up, to be renewed twelve years later. Then the Company, under the Marquis of Hastings, destroyed the Maratha power at Poona and annexed the Peishwa's territories to the Bombay presidency and reduced the power of Scindia by detaching from him the Rajput principalities and in general extending their sway up to the Sutlej.

In 1818 the English Company had become 'the paramount power' in India, holding as its direct territory the Gangetic Valley up to Delhi, the Maratha homelands in the Deccan, the littoral of the Arabian Sea and the coastal strips extending from Bengal to the south. The interior of India was still under protected princes, one of whom, Scindia, was then considered an independent State. Across the Sutlej, in the meantime, had grown up the formidable power of the Sikh kingdom extending up to the Khyber Pass on the west, to Gilgit in the north and to Sindh in the south. The Company watched the growth of this powerful empire, to challenge which they did not yet feel strong enough. The disastrous experience of the Afghan campaign (1838-42) – as unblushing an act of aggression as any in history – had taught the British not to over-estimate their military strength. But the existence of an independent Indian kingdom was an eyesore and the same strategy that Wellesley had followed with regard to the Marathas was repeated with the Sikhs. As a preliminary step Scindia's large forces were demobilized (1843) as the Nizam's had been in 1799. Sindh was conquered (1844) for the same reason that Mysore had been conquered by Wellesley, to enable the British to strike the enemy from behind. The most powerful personality and military commander in the Sikh Empire, Raja Gulab Singh of Jammu, was bribed by the fair province of Kashmir (for which the Company later unfairly insisted on a cash payment also). When these steps had been taken an excuse was found to declare war on the Sikhs, and after two bloody campaigns the last Indian kingdom was conquered and annexed (1848).

From the Indus to the Brahmaputra, from the Himalayas to Cape Comorin, the British had, in the course of a hundred years of warfare, established their unchallenged authority. Such kingdoms as had been permitted to exist, like Kashmir, Gwalior, Hyderabad, Baroda, Travancore and the Rajput States, apart from minor principalities set up or detached from the major States, had been turned into dependent territories, isolated from each other, and powerless individually against the authority of the British. The Company felt itself to be the undisputed master of India, and under Lord Dalhousie set itself to the task of building up a modern unified administration. But the Indian people though conquered had not yet been subdued. They made one last effort, under the leadership of the Maratha Peishwas, still using the name and authority of the Mogul Emperor, to throw off the foreign yoke. The great outbreak of 1857-8 – known in British history as the Indian Mutiny – was the last determined but ineffective attempt of the old ruling classes, the Marathas and the Moguls, to drive out the British. It was put down with a heavy hand after eighteen months of desultory fighting and in 1858 the East India Company, which had built up the Empire of India, ceased formally to exist. The British Government, in that year, took over the direct administration of India.

Once British rule was firmly established on the land mass of India, with no serious challenge to its authority, it began to disclose imperial ambitions towards neighbouring States. Previous Indian empires, except the Cholas (850-1150), never having possessed the command of the seas, had not ventured to look across the oceans as suitable areas of imperial expansion. With the British the position was naturally different. Also, when the Napoleonic wars had forced the Dutch Republic into an alliance with the French, the British Government was able to utilize its position in India for pursuing an aggressive policy in the East. From India a policy of imperial expansion was planned, and the British Government of India was set on the perilous road of conquest and annexation in the East for the benefit of Britain, but of course at the expense of the Indian taxpayer. Malacca was taken originally in 1795 and again in 1807. Java was conquered from the Dutch but returned to them after the treaty of Vienna. These were only the beginnings. It was only after 1818, after the Maratha power had been finally crushed, that the British authorities in India began to look upon themselves as an empire on the march. Lord Hastings encouraged Raffles to acquire from the Sultan of Johore the island of Singapore[1] for the East India

[1] It was almost accidentally that Singapore was selected as a settlement. In the postscript of a set of directions from Lord Hastings to Raffles was the sugges-

Company. The idea behind it is explained thus: 'You have only to glance at the map . . . our station completely outflanks the Straits of Malacca and secures a passage for our China ships at all times and in all circumstances. What Malta is in the West, Singapore may become in the East.'

Burma bordered on India, and that was a sufficient reason for British interest in her affairs. In 1784 the Burmese conquered Arakan and since that time there had been occasional frontier incidents. One such incident in 1823 provided the occasion for a trial of strength. The British attempts to invade Burma from the land side ended in failure, and Maha Bandula, the famous Burmese general, gained some victories against the Company's troops. But the British fitted out an expedition and occupied Rangoon and began an advance on Ava. A peace was patched up under which the Burmese King surrendered Arakan and Tenasserim and paid a heavy indemnity. But the Company's thirst for conquest was not quenched. Twenty years later another and even more frivolous excuse was found. The captain of a British vessel, Captain Lewis, put forward a claim for Rs.9,200 as compensation for indignities and fines inflicted on him by authorities at Burmese ports. Lord Dalhousie, who was then the Governor-General, took it up with the court of Ava, and in order to give force to his representation about a debt of £920 sent to Rangoon a fleet of six naval vessels under Commodore Lambert. The Commodore, an impatient empire builder, and in Dalhousie's own words 'too combustible for negotiations', forced the issue by seizing a vessel flying the King's flag. The incidents leading up to the Second Burmese War may best be described in Richard Cobden's words:

'Lord Dalhousie begins with a claim on the Burmese for less than a thousand pounds: which is followed by the additional demand of an apology from the Governor of Rangoon for the insult offered to our officers; next his terms are raised to one hundred thousand pounds and an aplogy from the King's Ministers: then follows the invasion of Burmese territory, when suddenly all demands for pecuniary compensation and apologies cease, and his Lordship is willing to accept the cession of Pegu as a "compensation and reparation" for the past whilst

tion that if the Sumatran coast had already been occupied by the Dutch, then Johore might not be a bad substitute, and to enable Raffles to take action Hasting had forwarded a complimentary letter to the Sultan. Writing to his friend Marsden a week later Raffles said: 'My attention is principally turned to Johore and you must not be surprised if my next letter to you is dated from the site of the ancient city of Sinhapura.'

In his note to the authorities in Calcutta he declared: 'Its position in the straits is even more commanding than even Rhio for our China trade passing down the straits of Malacca and every native vessel that sails through the straits of Rhio must pass in sight of it.'

at the same time he pens long minutes to prove how calamitous it will be for us to annex that province to our Indian Empire. . . . Ought we not to advertise in *The Times* for a Governor-General who can collect a debt of a thousand pounds without annexing a territory which will be ruinous to our finances?'[1]

The war ended rather informally by the masterful Lord Dalhousie annexing Pegu by a proclamation. No treaty was signed with the Burmese king; there was no formal cessation of hostilities and even the debt of £920 was forgotten in the expenditure of millions which the Indian treasury had to bear. And the Burmese were duly warned that Britain had not finished with them. In his proclamation Dalhousie added ominously that aggressions if persisted in 'must of necessity lead to the total subversion of the Burman State and to the ruin and exile of the King and his race'. Of course the lamb continued his aggression and thirty-three years later, as we shall see, the prophecy was duly fulfilled. The Burmese State was subverted and the king and his race were exiled.

(ii)

Up to the time of Van Imhoff (1743-50) the Dutch rule in Indonesia was confined to the administration of scattered establishments and forts, from a central point, Jakarta (renamed Batavia by Coen). The great State of Mataram and the Sultanates of Atjeh and Ternate and numerous lesser principalities remained nominally indepedent, though greatly weakened as a result of internal troubles and the operation of economic forces. In Bali and Lambok, Dutch influence had not penetrated. In Sumatra the Sultanates of Palembang and Jambi were vassal States of Batavia, but the rest of the territory was politically independent, though the Company had the monopoly in regard to the export of spices. Dutch authority hardly touched the immense island of Borneo, and it was only in 1756 that the Company was able to conclude a satisfactory treaty with the Sultan of Banjermasin in the south-east corner of the island.

The Dutch had appreciated quite early the cheapness of the system of 'indirect rule' and its effectiveness from the point of view of unhampered exploitation. The sultans were allowed to fight among themselves, to oppress their peoples and do whatever they liked so long as the trade was monopolized by the Company, and under the cover of the sovereign authority of the sultans the Dutch were able to exploit the resources of the island. But as was inevitable under such a system of indirect government, the States through which it worked began soon

[1] Richard Cobden: 'How wars are got up in India.' *Political Writings of Cobden*. London, 1867, Vol. II (pp. 25-106).

to disintegrate and it became necessary for the protecting Power to prop them up by direct intervention. From 1705 it was the definite policy of the Company to uphold monarchical authority in Mataram; the condition of Dutch support being the obligation to deliver *all the rice that the Company may demand at the price fixed by them.*

This unnatural system of political independence and economic vassalage led to an inevitable breakdown of the State administration. Mataram was not only at war continuously with the Balinese chiefs, but also had to struggle against rebellions led by members of the royal family and vassals who had to be fleeced in order to meet the ever-increasing demands of the Dutch. This state of affairs led to continuous interference in support of the rulers where the rulers were friendly; and against them, where they were not subservient to Dutch policy; justifying the celebrated observation of Abbé Raynal that the Dutch 'armed the father against the son and son against the father. The claims of the weak against the strong and of the strong against the weak were supported according to circumstances. One day they sided with the monarch, the next with the vassals.'

The policy of direct territorial acquisition and reduction of the political independence of the Sultanates was first inaugurated by Van Imhoff in 1743. In that year the Company had acquired all the coastal districts on the north side of Java, the exclusive control of all the seaports and also the territory of the kingdoms of Balambangan. Next, they turned to Mataram itself. A civil war was promoted in that kingdom in which the Company, after first supporting the legitimate ruler against his rebellious relatives, finally partitioned the State. The new rulers were only sovereigns in title. To their courts were attached Residents who effectively controlled the administration. In 1755, apart from the territory directly held by the Company, Java was divided into five small States – Bantam, Cheribon, Djokjakarta, Surakatra and Mangkunagara. In Bantam alone a spirit of independence had remained. There a remarkable lady, known to us as Ratu Sjarija, had acquired great influence over the Sultan, but a rebellion had broken out against her led by a holy man, Kiai Tapa, who seems to have exploited the surviving Hindu feelings of the local population. The Dutch intervened, in this case, against the Sultan's authority. They were soon able to get the old Sultan deposed and install in his place someone who accepted a position of dependence.

By 1760 the Dutch position in Java had thus been consolidated, but in Sumatra and in the 'outer' territories, the Company's interest continued to be solely one of trade. The Sultanate of Atjeh in Western Sumatra maintained a separate, if precarious, existence. In the 'outer' areas the political authority of the Dutch was still nominal and the Company insisted only on the monopoly of trade. But a central territory having come into existence, the gradual penetration of all areas became inevitable and within the course of the next few decades the Dutch became not only the monopolists of the Indonesian trade but the effective masters of the island territories.

What forced the pace and completed the change was not so much the political ambition of the Dutch as the intervention of the British. In 1795 the Netherlands had followed the wake of France and opted for revolution. The authorities in Batavia were alarmed about the application of the revolutionary principles in colonial countries. Liberty, fraternity and equality at home, but exploitation in the colonies – this was the slogan of revolutionary Holland. But revolutions could not be easily controlled. In 1798 the Company's charter was abrogated and Indonesia became a State colony of the Netherlands. But though the Government in Holland continued to profess revolutionary principles they added the rider that 'the doctrines of liberty and equality . . . cannot be transferred to nor applied to the East Indian possessions of the State so long as the security of these possessions depends on the existing and necessary state of subordination' (of the Indonesians). Nor was the Government prepared to abolish slavery, being content with the pious statement that the reform must wait 'until a higher order of general civilization will permit the amelioration of their fate'.

It is difficult to speak with restraint about the Dutch system in Indonesia. In the words of a Dutch historian: 'Destruction, resistance and reprisals were the monotonous story of the Moluccas.' An English writer, sympathetic to the Dutch and an apologist of colonial rule, J. S. Furnivall, describes the effect of the Dutch system as follows: 'Amboyna could produce more cloves than the whole world could consume and the Dutch therefore encouraged the King of Ternate . . . to continue his war against Tidore so that his people could be diverted from the cultivation of cloves. In Banda, they substituted slave labour for free cultivation by peasants, and by cutting off the supply of rice from Java they reduced the people from a diet of rice to a less nutritious diet of sago. On this food many died and more slaves were required. These were imported from so far afield as Arakan, but the Archipelago itself was the main source of supply, and islands which grew no food raided neighbouring islands to capture slaves to exchange for rice.'

Coen, the founder of Batavia, who according to Dutch writers of the time 'carried on in such a criminal and murderous way that the blood of the poor people cries for revenge',[1] laid down the principle on which Dutch policy was built up later. 'May not a man in Europe,' he asked,

[1] *Report of some people who have returned from the Indies*, 1662. Kroniek, pp. 321-39.

'do what he likes with his cattle? Even so does the master here do with his men, for everywhere, these with all that belongs to them are as much the property of the master, as are brute beasts in the Netherlands. The law of this land is the will of the King and he is King who is strongest.'[1]

Armed with a convenient theory of this character, the Dutch had no occasion to pretend that they had any moral obligation towards the people of Java. In fact, it must be said to their credit that the avowed purpose of their presence in the Indies was to make maximum profits by every method, moral or immoral, open to them. The cry of 'Mission Interrupted' is only a recent pretence and the Dutch themselves never considered the claims of the population till international events at different times forced them reluctantly to do so.

Till the beginning of the eighteenth century the trade in spices had yielded them the largest profits. The profits of the clove trade in the sixteenth and seventeenth centuries were phenomenal. Magellan's ship *Victoria*, which had taken a cargo of cloves from Moluccas, had sold it at a profit of 2,500 per cent. But by the beginning of the eighteenth century these profits had begun to dwindle, as the Dutch by their monopoly had forced other countries to encourage the cultivation of cloves, in India and elsewhere. Then it was discovered that coffee had a large market in Europe and would be a very profitable trade. About 1660 coffee had been introduced into Europe and had soon become a popular beverage. The demand for it appeared to be inexhaustible. In Java the plant was introduced from Malabar in South India at the beginning of the century and in a few years it became a major product of the island. As it fetched high prices in the world market, this crop might have restored the prosperity of the peasants of the islands, but this the Company did not desire. 'The Javanese might become too rich' was the fear most commonly expressed in the documents of the period, and to prevent Javanese prosperity and to gather as much of the wealth of Java into their own coffers were the simple and openly declared aims of the Dutch.

The Company therefore followed a threefold policy, an arbitrary reduction of coffee prices in Batavia, a restriction of plantations and an open system of cheating under which the producers were forced to deliver 240 to 270 lb for the price of 125 lb, of which also, after deductions on various accounts, only the price of 14 lb went to the Indonesian cultivator. Thus cheated out of their profits and denied even a fair price for their produce, the peasants were not willing to cultivate coffee. The 'Regents', who were the Indonesian agents of the Company, also showed no enthusiasm. The Dutch, therefore, decided to force both the regents and the peasants to cultivate coffee and to deliver it to them at a fixed

[1] Gongrijp – quoted in Furnivall, p. 44.

price. The theory of the Company was simple. They had inherited the sovereign rights of the sultans and therefore they had the right of absolute property over the land; the right of exploitation belonged to them wholly. The regents and peasants were merely their agents. In fact, in the eyes of the Company Java had become a vast coffee estate owned by them, and the sovereignty which they exercised was meant only to give the planter—in this case the Company—the right, on legal pretext, to deprive the Indonesian even of reasonable wages for his labour.

Coffee had been previously made an article of monopoly. By about 1760 the regents were made responsible for the cultivation, and were placed under the supervision and control of a Dutch official. A number of minor officers, known as Coffee Sergeants, were appointed to see that the regents and the peasants did not neglect coffee cultivation. In fact the whole business was planned systematically as in an estate, and the coffee thus cultivated was collected and sold by the Company.

It was a silent but far-reaching revolution that the plantation system introduced in the Dutch-Indonesian relations. Previously the Dutch had only been merchants buying the spices and rice that the country produced and selling them at profit. True, they used their power to establish a monopoly, but beyond this the trading activities of the Company did not interfere with the life of the people. But the change-over into a plantation economy involved the actual exploitation of labour, a control of the economic activity of the population and an effective supervision: in fact 'estate management' over a whole country. The island of Java became a plantation of the Company, and the relations between the sovereign, which the Company now claimed to be, and its subjects were in substance those of planter and coolie, in which the former was not merely the employer of labour, but also the authority invested with the rights of life and death and the wielder of the machinery of comprehensive oppression that only a legal system enforced with the authority of the ruler can devise. The latter was not merely a coolie, but one without even nominal rights against his employer, against whom he could not appeal either to the judiciary or to the executive. There is no parallel in history where a whole people was thus converted by the exercise of sovereignty into a nation of estate coolies, with their own natural aristocracy reduced to the position of foremen and superintendents, through whom the work was exacted and the oppression carried out. The Incas of Peru no doubt were ruthless and equally systematic in their exploitation of the people, but they at least lived in the country and the profits were spent there. Here on the other hand the profits were sent to a distant land to enable the masters to live a life of luxury far away from the scenes of toil.

The regents, who were the instruments through whom the Dutch worked this cruel and heartless policy, were appointed by the Governor-General, though the position was considered hereditary and the Dutch authorities took into consideration and generally respected hereditary claims. Though appointed by the Dutch they 'considered the peasants as well as the soil as their personal property' and exacted forced labour on coffee plantations from all. That the regents themselves were not allowed to grow rich is demonstrated by the fact that the Commissary for Native Affairs, the dignitary under whose directions the regents worked, had usually to give them loans at usurious rates in anticipation of coffee deliveries, and the debts became so heavy that after a short time the coffee delivered was not sufficient to pay the interest. Thus neither the poor Indonesian, who by a system of *corvé* was forced to work in the fields, nor the regents, who supervised the labourer, received any profit. The policy of preventing the Indonesians from becoming rich was carried out with the utmost thoroughness.[1]

From the miserable degradation to which the people of Java were reduced they were saved by the virile inspiration of Islam. We have already seen how, at the time of the arrival of the Portuguese, Islam had only been established at the great trading centres and at some of the courts of the rulers. The attempt of the Portuguese to convert the Hindu population of the interior met with no success, and by the end of the sixteenth century most of Java and Sumatra had accepted Islam. The pressure on them was continuous, and when the kingdom of Balambangan in East Java fell in 1639 to the attack of the Sultan of Mataram, organized Hinduism ceased to exist in Java. Slowly the character of Islam itself began to undergo a change. Introduced originally from India by Gujerat merchants, it was, until the middle of the seventeenth century, no more than an Islamic layer on the old Hindu beliefs. But in the case of a religion like Islam, whose solidarity, orthodoxy and rigidity are maintained by the annual pilgrimages to the holy cities and by a constant diffusion of learning through maulvis and preachers, such a situation could not last for any length of time. Returning Javanese hajis brought learned men with them. Also it should be remembered that in the seventeenth century the world position of Islam was represented by Turkey, whose menacing power in the Middle East, in the Levant and along the entire African littoral of the Mediterranean still made Europe tremble. Nor was the Mogul Empire in India a factor which could be

[1] Apart from this utterly depressed position of the people it should be remembered that under the Dutch law the evidence of non-Christians was not admitted in courts. After 1633 their testimony was admitted 'in some cases in which no Christians were involved'. With a judiciary established on this basis, the Indonesians, even if any rights had been accorded to them, would have found it impossible to get them enforced.

overlooked in Eastern politics at the time. A great pride in the international position of Islam, the privilege of belonging to a mighty world community was always a sustaining force with Muslims everywhere even when their political position appeared weak or depressed in any particular area. With the arrival of sheikhs, hajis and maulvis from Mecca and the Middle East, a major transformation in religious, social and political conditions began to take place in Indonesia.

The period of intense missionary activity, starting with 1630, witnessed in its religious phase the intensification of Islamic beliefs, the establishment of the authority of religious leaders and a general approach to the Muslim outlook on life. Its object was both to wean the Indonesians away from persistent Hindu traditions as well as to organize resistance to Christian religious aggression. Socially, the Mecca influence was directed towards Islamic conformity – in marriage, laws of inheritance, etc., which are governed in most Muslim countries by the *shariat*. Politically, the movement represented a spirit of resistance. An Arabian sheikh is said to have conveyed to the Ruler of Mataram the title of sultan on behalf of the Khalif's Governor of Mecca. The other sultanates, especially Atjeh, situated nearest to the mainland, began also to enter into relations with the Muslim Powers in the Middle East.

It should not be understood that there was no local reaction in Java itself against the influence of Mecca-educated priests. Sultan Amang Kurat I, for example, is said to have put to the sword a large number of mullahs and their families because they had tried to assume authority over the people. He also deprived the priests (*kadis*) of all the jurisdiction that his father Sultan Angung had given them.

The strengthening of Islam led to a great intensification of resistance against Dutch aggression in the islands. The resentment of Muslims at the missionary efforts of the Dutch in Amboyna led to war in the Moluccas. The leading officials of the Company at the time, like Rycloff Van Goens, were convinced that religion was one of the main causes of the continuous wars against the Dutch in the Archipelago, which constituted a marked feature of history in the latter half of the seventeenth century.

Of course the Dutch took no interest in the education of the Indonesians. This afforded an opportunity for Islam to consolidate its position. Education became the effective monopoly of the Muslim priesthood, and mosques were the natural centres from which Islamic learning influenced the masses. Continuously reinforced from Mecca and India, Muslim teachers were able to keep the spirit of the people alive. The parsimony and shortsightedness of the Dutch thus helped the Indonesians to save their soul.

Dutch policy under Daendals (1808), the Jacobin Governor-General, brought the problem to a head. He set himself to reorganize the administration and to strengthen the defences of the country, but the opposition of the local Dutch was so great that he had to be withdrawn. Soon afterwards a British expedition with a fleet of a hundred transports and carrying 12,000 soldiers arrived before Batavia. In six weeks the campaign was over and the Dutch signed the capitulation on September 18, 1811. The British became for a period of fourteen years the masters of the Dutch Empire.

The British interlude in Java is the real dividing line between the Company's rule and the Dutch State imperialism in the nineteenth century. The indirect system of rule which had yielded large profits to the Dutch without the trouble and worry of government was practically abolished. Raffles deprived the princes of the rights of management. Bantam was annexed, the Sultan voluntarily resigning his government in consideration of an annual pension of 10,000 Spanish dollars (1813). Cheribon was taken over in 1815. In Surakarta and Djokjakarta the sultans promised to regulate the conduct of the affairs of their States according to the advice tendered to them. Thus Raffles, in a short time, destroyed the old system and substituted for it the direct administration of the colonial power. In this he was merely completing the policy that Daendals had himself inaugurated.

Whatever the merits or demerits of Raffles' reforms – they were undoubtedly humanitarian, far-sighted and meant to give rights to the Javanese cultivators and therefore subject to hostile criticism by Dutch historians and by apologists of colonialism like Furnivall – there is no denying the fact that they put a stop to the inhumanly oppressive plantation system. When the colony was returned to the Dutch they had no option but to accept the principle that Indonesia should be governed for the sake of its own people. The aim of the King, now restored to his throne in Holland, was proclaimed to be to promote the interests of all his subjects without exception.

Holland's policy after the restoration was one of intense exploitation of Java and portions of Sumatra (Padang and Palembang) and abstention in the Outer Territories. The Dutch authorities were absolutely frank as to the reason of this neglect of the immense area outside Java and Sumatra. The development of the outer areas would have required the utilization of the surpluses of the Java administration which had to be sent to the mother country. Known as the 'favourable balance' policy, it judged administration by the amount of net profits that the Java administration could send to Holland.

It is true that the Portuguese in their relations with the Moors, at least during the first half of the century of their arrival in the East, were cruel and without a sense of humanity. This could at least be explained as being a continuation of the bitter fight between Islam and Christianity in Europe. They were also for a time fanatical in the enforcement of Catholic conformity and persecuted the non-Christians in Goa and their other possessions. The British for a short period of fifteen years in Bengal established a robber State where, without reference to the rights of others, they freely plundered and looted under the cover of their 'rights', but even during that period the Indian merchants were not interfered with and the public had the right even of protesting in public as we have already seen. The Dutch alone of the European nations in the East carried out a policy which systematically reduced a whole population to the status of plantation labour, without recognizing any moral or legal obligation to them. Cringing and *kow-towing* in China, humble and reverential before Japanese officials, they were tyrannical beyond belief to the people from whom they derived their greatest profit. Lacking the spiritual enthusiasm of the Portuguese, or, generally speaking, the wide human interests of the British, at least in areas where they exercised direct political authority, or the sense of cultural mission to which the French laid claim, the Dutch held firmly to the theory of possession and expliotation, without accepting in the least degree any obligation for the welfare of the people over whom they had acquired control. When they were forced to change their policy during the course of the next century, it was not out of any conviction, but by the strength of the movements outside Holland and Indonesia.

NOTE

The literature about the Dutch in Indonesia in English or French is not very extensive. The following books are, however, of special interest:

Amry, Vandenbosch: *The Dutch East Indies*. University Press, California, 1942.

Angelino, A. D. a de Kat: *Colonial Policy*. London, 1931.

Angoulvant, G.: *Les Indes Netherlands*, 2 vols., 1926.

Chailley Bert, J.: *Java et ses Habitants*, 1900.

Coupland, Sir R.: *Raffles*, 1926.

Furnivall, J. S.: *Netherlands India*. London, 1944.

Raffles, T. S.: *Memoir on the Administration of the Eastern Islands*, 1819.

Raffles, T. S.: *Substance of a minute recorded in February* 1814.

Raffles, Lady: *Life and Public Services of Sir T. S. Raffles*. London, 1830.

Schirke, Dr B.: *The effect of Western Influence on Native Civilizations in the Malaya Archipelago*, 1929.

Vlekke, Bernard H. M.: *Nusantara – A History of the East Indian Archipelago*. Harvard University Press, 1943.

CHAPTER 2

CHINA

With Britain established as a major land Power in South Asia, an overflow of British commercial interests into the Pacific was clearly an unavoidable development. The position of European nations in China in the first quarter of the nineteenth century was in many ways similar to their position in India before 1748. They had a few trading stations on the coast, but political influence or military power they did not possess. They were interested solely in trade in competition with other European nations in a spirit of rivalry. They did not desire to penetrate into the interior and were content to deal with middlemen who waxed rich on the profits of the trade. But there were two important differences between the position of Europeans in India and in China. In India the trade was encouraged and had, in fact, become an integral part of the country's economy. The coastal areas to which financial and economic power had shifted from the interior depended for their prosperity on this trade. The rulers of the coastal tracts were, many of them, directly interested in its maintenance. Thus Hyder Ali of Mysore considered Mahe, the small French settlement on the French coast, as a matter of vital interest to him. The Governor of the Carnatic, the Raja of Tanjore, and the other minor potentates of the east coast, looked upon Madras and Pondicherry as their natural outlets. In fact, India, with age-long traditions of maritime commerce, did not consider the foreign trade centres as anything objectionable. The position in China was different in this respect. The Chinese Government was not interested in maritime trade. When Chien Lung wrote to George III that his Empire possessed all 'things in prolific abundance' and desired nothing from outside, he was voicing a well-established Chinese tradition which looked upon exchange of commodities with foreign countries as unnecessary and against the prestige of China.

A second difference of political significance between India and China was that, while China even in the days of her weakness maintained a political unity, and the Emperor was able to enforce his authority in the most distant provinces and the viceroys 'trembled and obeyed', in India by 1740 the Imperial authority had completely broken down. In the great coastal provinces, where the European trading communities were established under the protection of forts, the local authorities had become in fact independent of the Emperor and were moved mainly by dynastic considerations, that is, of transforming their governorships into hereditary princedoms. In China, the issue therefore had to be fought out in every case with the central government, while in India the British and French companies dealt with local governors, viceroys and princelings, and were therefore able to exercise pressure on them.

The political situation in the world had also changed radically in the first half of the nineteenth century. Apart from her unchallenged position in India and on the oceans everywhere, Britain, after the Napoleonic wars, had become the colossus of the world. She enjoyed a political, economic and moral predominance in the world such as no country before or since has enjoyed.

The pioneers of maritime empires, Spain, Portugal and Holland, had fallen back in the race. Portugal still had its tiny possessions in Asia, but the successors of Vasco da Gama and Albuquerque, though still enjoying the same titles, had become mere historical anachronisms. Spain continued to hold the Philippine Archipelago, but it had not taken any part in Asian developments. The position of Holland was peculiar. During the Napoleonic war, Britain had divested the Netherlands of her colonial possessions. But in 1816 the Indonesian islands were generously returned by Britain with the gesture of a medieval emperor reinstating a rebellious vassal in his fief after mulcting him of some portion of his estate (Ceylon) to be resumed again at will in case of trouble. From that time the Dutch were happy to concentrate themselves on a systematic exploitation of their rich estate, without political ambitions or imperialist pretensions. Thus apart from Russia, the whole of Europe was represented in the East in the era between 1815-48 by the overwhelming power of Britain.

Economically and financially also Britain's position was supreme. The Industrial Revolution of the eighteenth century had placed her far in advance of her rivals. Her expanding economy and her dominant position in shipping gave her a position which no Power or group of Powers was in a position to challenge. It was therefore to be expected that the restrictions which China had so long enforced would no longer be acceptable to a country whose commerce required new and expanding markets. The conditions of foreign trade in Canton were indeed humiliating. The following were typical of the attitude of the Chinese. Women, as we have already noticed, could not be brought into the factories; so late as 1830, the Chinese authorities threatened to stop the trade to force some women to return immediately to Macao. Foreigners could not employ Chinese servants; foreigners could not use sedan chairs, but must walk. Foreigners could not make representations, but might only present petitions through their Chinese guarantors. In 1831 a concession was made in regard to this. If the Chinese Hong merchants would not forward representations 'then two or three foreigners might go humbly to the city gate (but not enter the city) and leave their petition with the guard of the gate'.

It was not to be expected that Britain, in the pride of her dominant position in the world, would continue to allow her merchants to trade under such humiliating conditions. The East India Company had for over a hundred years accepted this position, though with occasional grumbling, because the trade was profitable. As Sir John Pratt has pointed out, 'it is the profitable nature of the trade that made the foreign merchants consent to endure the humiliations which the Chinese officials in their arrogance delighted to heap upon all foreigners'. As long as the East India Company, through their *taipan*, dealt with the Chinese authorities the system worked fairly satisfactorily. But in 1833 the monopoly of the Company was abrogated by Parliament. This brought to the South China trade a large number of adventurous merchants who, in their pride of race, were not prepared to accept any restrictions and almost 'itched' for a fight.

Also, the theory was gaining increasing acceptance that there was a divine right to trade everywhere: that it was unnatural for governments to close their countries to the free flow of trade. In an era of expanding economy such an attitude is perhaps natural; and no one could then have foreseen that England herself, in less than a hundred years, would be enforcing quotas, prohibiting imports, and regulating trade by every conceivable method. In the thirties of the nineteenth century all such ideas seemed to the English merchants reactionary and against the rights of peaceful trade. If the Chinese Government did not desire to encourage foreign trade she must be made to do so, in the interests of peace, prosperity and progress.

China trade had long been a one-sided affair, the European merchants buying immense quantities of silk, tea and rhubarb and selling but little. The difficulty had always been to find something for which there was a demand in China. The adverse balance had in the past been adjusted by the export of bullion to China. A new method of payment was discovered in the growing popularity of opium. The credit for this discovery goes to the Portuguese. In 1729, opium, however, was prohibited by Imperial decree. After a time, not much notice was taken of this prohibition, but the trade was not very considerable. In 1773 Warren Hastings made the sale of opium a monopoly of the Company in India, and in 1797 it assumed the monopoly of the manufacture of opium. The East India Company thus came to have an immense interest in the promotion of this trade both for filling its coffers in India and as a payment for its trade with China. In the first quarter of the century the sale of opium on a large scale became the most flourishing part of the European imports into China. In the sixteen years from 1818 to 1833 opium jumped from 17 per cent to 50 per cent of the total British imports into China.

Though this trade was strictly illegal, especially after its total prohibition in 1800, the Company had worked out a system by which, though its own ships did not carry the drug and the Hong merchants officially did not deal with it, an immense quantity of opium reached China through 'country ships', sailing under the licence of the Company, which sold direct to 'outside' merchants. With the abolition of the Company's monopoly, this system could not be maintained, as the private merchants were no longer under the control of the Company. Anticipating the confusion that would prevail if private traders were not controlled, the Viceroy of Canton asked the Hong merchants to inform the Court of Directors of the East India Company that as hitherto 'it will be incumbent on them to deliberate and appoint a chief who understands the business to come to Canton for the general management of commercial dealings'. The British Government recognized the desirability of such a step and appointed Lord Napier as the 'Chief Superintendent of the trade of British subjects in China'.

Lord Napier came out to China (1834) prepared 'to stand no nonsense'. Though his appointment was not that of an envoy, but merely as a superintendent of trade and had not been notified to the Chinese authorities, he proceeded to Canton without permission. On reaching Canton he insisted on communicating direct with the Viceroy, a strange demand on the part of a commercial superintendent, whatever his personal rank might be. It was as if a non-diplomatic minor trade official of a foreign government insisted on writing to the Viceroy of India. He refused to deal with the Hong merchants who were, according to the Chinese regulations, the sole channel of communication for foreign traders with the Chinese Government. The Viceroy, while refusing to receive any letter from the Chief Superintendent of Trade and insisting on the responsibility of Hong merchants, was conciliatory and showed every inclination consistent with the rights of his government not to force the issue. But Lord Napier, whose name, translated into Chinese, meant 'Laboriously Vile', would agree to no compromise. The Chinese authorities then took the only action open to them. After issuing a proclamation drawing attention to the stupidity and obstinacy of the English, the Viceroy ordered the withdrawal of servants and porters from the factory, prohibited the local population on pain of death to sell

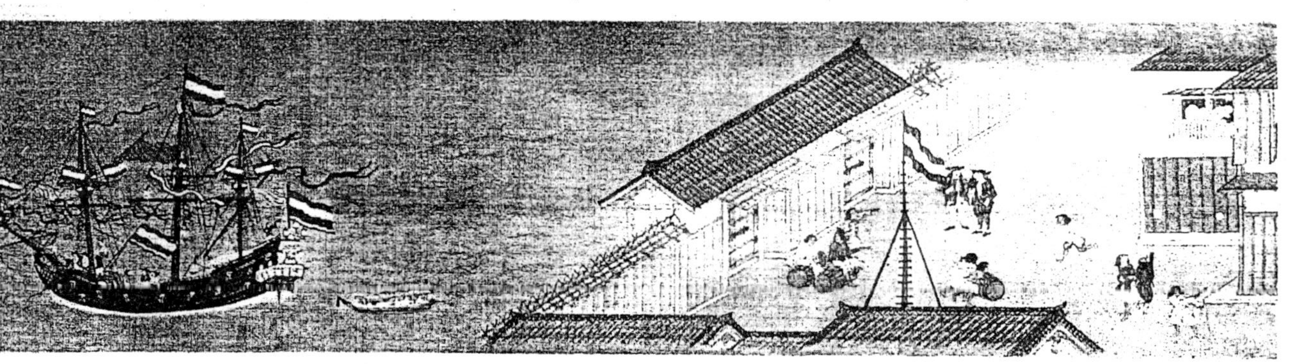

VII DUTCH HOUSE AND SHIP AT DESHIMA, NAGASAKI

From a MAKIMONO painted in 1690

provisions to the British and warned other foreigners against supplying goods to them. He also sent troops to the factory to see that these orders were obeyed.

Lord Napier, who had previously thought that, in view of Britain's overwhelming prestige, he had only to show firmness and determination for the Chinese to go down on their knees, now felt that his honour demanded satisfaction, and ordered the frigates under his command to force the passage of the Bogue and landed marines as a guard to the factory. This violation of Chinese territory and authority called forth an immediate warning from the Viceroy followed by effective preparations to surround the area and to isolate the British. Lord Napier now realized that he had gone too far and reluctantly agreed to return to Macao, taking his frigates with him. He died there two weeks after his hasty and rather humiliating return.

The attitude of the British could best be judged from Napier's letters to Lord Palmerston. These documents are interesting because of their arrogance, refusal to understand the Chinese point of view and the firm conviction that nothing that the British desire can be wrong. Though it was clearly Napier who had acted against established procedure, had even forced an entry for his frigates and landed marines, his letter speaks of 'chastising' the Viceroy and he recommends to Palmerston the policy of always negotiating with the Chinese under the threat of force. This was also the view of the British merchants in China. Since the monopoly of the East India Company had come to an end in 1834, the free merchants had become the most powerful element and they were spoiling for a fight. In fact an article in the China Repository signed by 'a British merchant', which was generally considered to have been written by Jardine, advocates the benefits of 'private and untrammelled enterprise', and speaks eloquently of England's economic power and her industries crying out: 'Obtain us but a sale for our goods and we will supply any quantity.' How is it to be done? The 'British merchant' had an easy answer. 'Nor indeed should our valuable commerce and revenue both in India and Great Britain be permitted to remain subject to a caprice, *which a few gunboats laid alongside this city would overrule by the discharge of a few mortars* (italics added).... The results of a war with the Chinese could not be doubted.'

The 'British merchant' spoke for his community, for indeed the situation had become intolerable. The whole system of Hoppos, Hong merchants and Eight Regulations, with their numerous restrictions on merchants and impositions on trade, could no longer be maintained against a country whose power was so overwhelming.

Indeed the system had for at least two decades become a make-believe, for the trade with China had gone out of formal and official channels. From Canton, where these regulations existed and were enforced, shipping had been diverted to the anchorage of Lintin, an island at the mouth of the Canton river. There the foreign merchants, with the connivance of Chinese officials, defrauded the imperial treasury, defied the authority of the Hoppo and the Viceroy and ignored alike the Eight Regulations and the Hong merchants. In 1831, while the official foreign trade of Canton was valued at only seven million dollars, the trade through Lintin carried on by private firms amounted to seventeen millions out of which eleven millions were accounted for by opium alone.

It was therefore clear, as Jardine had foreseen and expressed with clarity and vigour, that a radical change in the system which provided for the equality of nations and for facility of trade had become urgent. It was also clear that such a change could not be brought about except by the use of force. A war was perhaps unavoidable under the circumstances. What shocked the world and created misunderstandings for the future was the excuse and the method: for the excuse was opium and the method was piracy. The extraordinary increase in the volume of opium trade has already been alluded to. Though the East India Company was not directly exporting it to China, the opium which was carried by private traders was sold by the Company at the Calcutta auctions. The method of its sale was by smuggling at Lintin and by piratical actions along the coast. The great firms engaged in the trade used armed ships and operated in defiance of Chinese laws along the coast to sell the poisonous drug to the people of China. That it was by Chinese, British and international law clear piracy for ships to be armed without licence from any government and to carry cargoes of prohibited goods, cannot be doubted.

The Imperial Government was fully aware of these activities. The Emperor especially felt gravely concerned at this deliberate attempt to force opium on his people and he now decided to take effective measures to stop this traffic. For this purpose he appointed as special Imperial Commissioner a man of proved integrity, honour and patriotism, Lin Tse-hsu, who was then Viceroy of Hu Kuang. Lin was invested with almost unlimited powers, including those of Imperial Commissioner and High Admiral, which placed him above the Viceroy of the two Kwangs. It is said that on hearing the news of his appointment, the Viceroy fainted. Lin's programme was a simple one: he desired to continue and even encourage legitimate trade; but he was determined to eradicate root and branch the traffic in opium by every means at his disposal. There is no evidence at all to support the view that he was unfriendly to the foreigners or aggressive in his action except where the maintenance of law was concerned.

He demanded and secured the surrender of the chests of opium with the merchants (20,000 chests) and to everyone's surprise destroyed them at a public ceremony. Then he obtained from the merchants bonds that they would not carry on this nefarious trade, contrary to the laws of the Empire. Though the British merchants signed up, they did so with mental reservation, as the most important British firm, Jardine and Matheson, was planning at the same time to carry on coastal smuggling through armed vessels based on Manila. So far matters had gone well. A few weeks later trouble arose when a party of drunken British sailors killed a Chinese on the mainland. The British superintendent of trade refused to surrender the criminal. Lin, realizing that the authority of his sovereign was being questioned, issued a peremptory order for the surrender of the sailor and demanded that the British ships at the mouth of the river should either enter or sail away within three days, failing which he would take action to enforce his authority. The High Admiral followed this up with a concentration of war junks. The British on their part brought up two frigates, the *Volage* and the *Hyacinthe*, and, without waiting for negotiations, started firing on the junks and sank them. Thus began the first Opium War.

Lin had made two miscalculations. He was under the impression that the British Government was not a party to the smuggling of opium, which like an honest man he thought was the activity of unscrupulous traders and of depraved and barbarous pirates. This is well brought out in the letters which he addressed to Queen Victoria. 'We have reflected,' he said, 'that this noxious article is the clandestine manufacture of artful schemers under the dominion of Your Honourable nation. Doubtless, you the Honourable Chieftainess have not commanded the growing and sale thereof.' Lin pointed out that in Britain itself 'people are not permitted to inhale the drug. If it is admittedly so deleterious, how can you seek to profit by exposing others to its malific power to be reconciled with the decrees of Heaven?' Here he was in the wrong. The Queen's Government, as the Committee of the London East India and China Association emphasized, was fully and knowingly in it. A memorandum by that body said: 'When we find the growth of opium within the territories of the East India Company is a strict monopoly, that the drug is sold by Government of India at public sales, and that its destination is so well known that in 1837 the East India Company's Government actually directed by public notice a large sum of money to be given as a bonus to shippers to China of the season; when we observe that the Committees of the Houses of Lords and Commons have inquired minutely into the subject of the growth of opium, the amount it contributed to the Indian revenue and with a full knowledge of the place of its ultimate destination have arrived without hesitation at the conclusion that it did not appear advisable to abandon so important a source of revenue.

. . . When we know, moreover, that the India Board, over which a Cabinet Minister presides, has an effective control over the East India Company and might prevent what it did not approve, we must confess that it does seem most unjust to throw any blame or odium attaching to the opium trade upon the merchants, who engaged in a business thus directly and indirectly sanctioned by the highest authorities.'

Indeed the British Government was committed up to the hilt in this illegal and depraved traffic and in the piracy which went along with it. This Lin did not and could not be expected to know, especially when his own view of the State, as a true Confucian, was a moral one, where the Emperor under a mandate of Heaven upheld the proprieties. His second mistake, which flowed naturally from the first, was his conviction that the British Navy would not intervene to protect the malefactors. He, of course, had no proper idea of the might of Britain on the sea, and as Lord High Admiral of War Junks he had the complacent belief that he could enforce his authority against the clippers, merchantmen and even the frigates of the British. These miscalculations affected the result, but they did not alter the legal rectitude of Lin's action. Nor could they be held to justify the action of Elliot in forcing a war on the Chinese and giving his Government's moral authority to a commercial system based on illegal traffic in drugs enforced by organized piracy.

The details of the war do not concern us here, but it is necessary to note that as soon as war began the British claimed compensation for the opium surrendered and for surrender of islands! Also the British were determined to push the war to a conclusion, for the chimera of a great Chinese trade, the sale of British goods to the most populous nation in the world and practically in terms of a monopoly, had begun to operate powerfully on the imagination of the British. Here was the greatest single country, so far untapped, which would provide an inexhaustible market for British goods. So it was argued. That was the chimera which was to drag Britain deeper and ever deeper into the quagmire of China. The British forces occupied Shanghai on June 13 (1842), penetrated the great central line of China's life, the Yangtze, and preparations were made for an assault on the great city of Nanking. There the treaty of Nanking was signed (August 29, 1842).

One strange act, which was precursor of many such in Chinese history, may be noted. The Chinese Repository, XI, 680, records: 'Sept. 3. A party of British officers and others acting the barbarian in right good earnest visited the porcelain tower. They went (so the Abbots testified) with hatchets and chisels and hammers and cut off and carried away large masses doing no inconsiderable damage.' A Chinese observer of this desecration noted that 'the English barbarians frequently ascended the pagoda . . . took away several glazed tiles, which is indeed detestable in the extreme'. William Dallas Barnard even excuses this act of desecration as 'a not unnatural desire to possess specimens or relics'. This inveterate tendency to desecrate and destroy was repeated again and again in European relations with China, in the Summer Palace in 1860, in Tientsin in 1870, and in Peking itself in 1900.

Apart from the annexation of Hong Kong, the main clause of this treaty, on which the entire structure of relationship of China with the Western Powers was to be raised, was the clause opening five ports for trade 'where the foreign merchants with their families and establishments shall be allowed to reside for the purpose of carrying on their mercantile pursuits, without molestation or restraint'. It was also provided that 'consular officers' or superintendents should be allowed to reside and that a fair and regular tariff and customs duties would be established at these ports.[1] Similar treaties were signed with the Americans at Wanghia (July 3, 1844) and with the French at Whampoa (October 24, 1844); and in Macao the Portuguese claimed authority which they never had at the height of their power.

The treaty of Nanking is the basic act in the imposing but unstable structure of international relations which governed China for a hundred years. Its main purpose was forcibly to break down China's isolation and to compel her to trade with European nations and also to teach the Chinese that far from being superior to all other nations of the world she was actually inferior. The treaty ports were at the mouth of the Yangtze and along the coast, Shanghai, Ningpo, Foo-chow, Amoy and Canton. There foreign merchants had the right of direct trade. A warship was to be stationed at each of the five ports and the French and Americans demanded and obtained the right that the ships of war 'cruising for the protection of commerce should be well received in any of the ports of China at which they might arrive'. The French in their treaty added a clause, which led in time to the undoing of all efforts to build up friendly relations between China and the West – the championship of Christian religion. By this act, the European nations identified themselves with a religion which they and their missionaries desired to impose on the people of China.

The merchants who had so long been cooped up in their factories breathed freely. The golden dream was about to be materialized. They had now freedom of trade in the great ports of South China. In Shanghai, England, America and France had their settlements. Shanghai was

[1] One curious aspect of the British treaty, which histories by European writers gloss over, was the exaction of 'ransoms' for towns which had not been occupied. This was supposed to be compensation *for not plundering the city*, which the soldiers would have done had they occupied it. For the city of Yangchow alone a sum of 500,000 dollars was demanded and so for others also.

organized as a foreign commercial port, with its own municipality, land regulations, etc. The great British firms moved up to a port which seemed to provide unlimited markets in the interior of China. But the golden dream somehow did not materialize. The value of British exports to China in 1850, in spite of the special privileges of the Treaty ports, showed no increase over that of 1843. In 1854 it was even less. The correspondence of the China firms at this period speaks invariably of 'depression', of the 'unpromising aspect of things', the 'wretched position of your (China) markets'. There was a market for opium; but for other goods none. Jardine and Matheson, the most powerful firm in China trade, reported in June 1850: 'Our last monthly advices informed you of the unfavourable turn our markets had taken for imports. This we confirm and advise serious fall in cotton yarn and shirtings, vessels with further goods causing glut that for a long period will not be easily got over.'[1]

The dream not only did not come true but was turning into a nightmare. The China merchants could not understand this. To them it seemed clear that if the market of 300,000,000 Chinese did not appreciate the quality of Lancashire goods, there must be hidden reasons for it. The opposition and obstruction of Chinese officials and the weakness of British consular representatives were put down as the reasons for this failure. Matheson in his evidence before the Parliamentary Select Committee on commercial relations with China (1847) complained that 'where an Englishman gets into trouble in China, the British authorities . . . almost invariably take the side of the Chinese'. The British commercial community had a simple remedy consisting of three elements to meet their difficulties. These were extension beyond treaty ports, consuls to be given the right to use force to redress grievances and direct dealings with provincial authorities to the exclusion of the Central Government. 'Our trade with China,' declared the Manchester Chamber of Commerce, 'will never be fully developed until the right to sell and purchase is extended beyond the ports to which we are now restricted.'

The chimera was beckoning. Now it was not in the treaty ports, it was in the Yangtze Valley. Excuses were not wanting for a further advance. There had been numerous riots and cases of violence occasioned generally by the unruly and overweening conduct of the foreigners. An instance may be quoted. An Englishman named Compton felt annoyed by the cries of a hawker in the street, took the law into his own hands and drove away the hawker and damaged his property (July 4, 1846). Soon after another hawker was beaten in the street for a similar reason by a

[1] A comprehensive study of British-China trade and its political bearings is contained in *Old China Hands and the Foreign Office*, Nathan Pelcovits King's Crown Press, N.Y., 1948, and George Allen & Unwin, London.

friend of Compton. The result naturally was a riot. The Chinese authorities protected the foreigners but the result was strange. While neither Compton nor Church who assaulted the Chinese hawkers were punished, the British authorities called upon the local administration to punish the rioters. A ship of war was to be stationed in Canton to protect the merchants and no doubt to enable them to kick the cane hawkers with impunity.

A study of the correspondence at the time clearly demonstrates two things: first, the anxiety of the Chinese Government to fulfil the terms of the treaty and to avoid trouble if possible, and secondly, the overweening pride of the foreign merchants who in the words of Inglis' evidence in court 'never paid any attention to any law in China'. The merchant traders were desirous of extending their privileges and authority by a constructive interpretation of the clauses which ensured the rights of foreigners in China. The result was also two-fold—intense hatred of the foreigner on the part of the Chinese and a continual weakening of the Government's authority by displays of the mailed fist of the British Navy. The local authorities were forced to yield even on the most unreasonable demands against most determined popular opinion.

It was clear that the treaty of Nanking had only unsettled things and the situation had not been stabilized. The British authorities especially were under constant pressure to reopen the issues and effect a definitive settlement by force. Negotiations for treaty revision were taken up in 1854 by British, French and American representatives. These were to be directed towards the achievement of four main objects: free access to all parts of the Empire, free navigation of the Yangtze, the legalization of the opium and 'pig' (Chinese labour) trades and direct diplomatic relations at Peking. It was known to the envoys that these objects, two of which, the navigation of the Yangtze and the legalization of opium and 'pig' trade, could not have been agreed to by any Power except after an overwhelming defeat, would be resisted by the Chinese.

The excuse for a war was found without difficulty. A ship named *Arrow*, owned by a Chinese, Ssu Ah-cheng, but claiming British registration (actually its certificate of registration had expired some time before), arrived in Canton, carrying on board a notorious pirate, Li Ming-tai, who had been implicated in many acts of piracy. The Viceroy and High Commissioner of Kwantung, Yeh Ming-chin, ordered the vessel to be boarded and the wanted persons arrested. The British authorities found in this action the excuse they were looking for. An apology was asked for and redress demanded, which the Viceroy, feeling himself to be within his rights, refused. The British entered on a studied course of coercive measures, but the Viceroy, a man of determination, refused to be intimidated. If he had agreed, some other excuse no doubt would have been found, for treaty revision had been decided upon and this could be effected only by force.

If the excuse for the first Anglo-Chinese war was opium, that for the second was the protection which the British authorities extended to illegal activities of Chinese whom they had taken under their wings. The course of the second war was not very different from that of the first. The French, who under Napoleon III were being taught anew the benefits of *La Gloire*, were also anxious for a share in the spoils of the East, and joined the war now on the excuse of the murder of a French priest.

It thus became an Anglo-French war, and though the Americans did not associate themselves with the conflict, the United States Government also showed itself in complete sympathy with the objects which the Anglo-French associates were pursuing. As the war in India (1857–58) intervened, operations could not proceed effectively. However, in 1857 Canton was taken, the Viceroy Yeh being arrested and taken to India. The representatives of the Powers now demanded direct negotiations with Peking. If Peking refused, the navies were to take possession of the Taku forts guarding Tientsin. The Viceroy of Tientsin offered to negotiate, but that did not satisfy the Allies. They were determined to break down once and for ever the pretended superiority of China and to negotiate with imperial plenipotentiaries and sign the treaty at the capital of the Empire. The Emperor refused to admit the foreign envoys to Peking. On this the admirals occupied the Taku forts, the troops protecting the fort offering no resistance. Seeing that resistance was hopeless the court now agreed to negotiate and appointed imperial plenipotentiaries.

The Tientsin treaty, of course, gave to the Western nations what they had been fighting for for the past twenty years, the right of navigating the Yangtze, the addition of eleven more ports for the residence and trade of foreigners, including the more important Yangtze ports up to Hankow, the exclusion of Europeans from Chinese jurisdiction and freedom for Christian missionaries, and in the case of France protection for apostates to Christianity. Foreign Powers were to have the right of resident envoys. The British, however, were bent on humiliating China further. Elgin, who was appointed the first Minister, had instructions to take with him 'a sufficient naval force' to Taku while proceeding to Peking to exchange ratifications: he was to insist not only on proper reception at the capital but at Taku and Tientsin. The Russians and the Americans had exchanged ratifications, but the British insisted on attacking Taku forts on the ground that their warship was not allowed to enter the river. The French under Napoleon III were anxious to demonstrate their friendship for Britain by joining in every act of aggression, and the Anglo-French allies opened hostilities again. But the attack on Taku failed, though the next year the forts were taken and Tientsin occupied.

Attempts were made to reopen negotiations, but the British and the French were obdurate, insisted on proceeding to Tung Chow with a considerable military force. Either through misunderstanding or through bad faith or through both (there was bad faith on both sides; Canton had not been evacuated by the British) the Chinese made prisoners of three officials who went to them under a flag of truce. On this the Allies decided to force their way to Peking. When they reached Tung Chow on the outskirts, negotiations were again opened through Prince Kung, the younger brother of the Emperor, who was destined to become the leading statesman of the Manchus during the critical period to follow. As the preliminary negotiations failed, the Allied armies advanced to the Summer Palace, the beautiful residence on the lake built by Chien Lung. There the Allied soldiery and their chiefs repeated the vandalism which we noticed in regard to the Porcelain Pagoda at Nanking. The Palace, which according to the French Commander Montauban 'was of a character that nothing in our Europe can give any idea of such luxury', was systematically plundered by the officers.

Not satisfied with this, after entering Peking, Lord Elgin ordered the burning of the Summer Palace 'whose splendours' the conquerors themselves had 'found it difficult to describe'. This action Elgin in his ignorance had imagined would impress the Oriental and leave a lasting fear of the European in the Chinese mind. By a strang process of reasoning, the Europeans have, throughout their relations with Asians, convinced themselves that acts of savagery and inhumanity will increase their prestige[1] in the eyes of Asian people.

The event did create a lasting impression, one of burning hatred mixed with unspoken contempt of the character of the 'barbarians'. The burning of the Summer Palace has not been forgotten and the present writer was told by a high official of the Central People's Government in 1951 that the account is still left open and awaits settlement. The Elgins have been unfortunate in their historical imagination – whether it be in respect of Greek marbles or Chinese palaces.

By the Convention of Peking, which brought these unedifying incidents to a close, the Emperor was made to express his 'deep regret' for the breach of friendly relations. The foreign Powers were permitted to establish legations in Peking, higher indemnities were exacted, Tientsin was added to the list of treaty ports, and Britain, of course, gained something for herself again. China was made to cede Kowloon in perpetuity

[1] A recent example of this was a suggestion by American representatives at a conference in 1943 of which the present writer was also a member, that the Imperial Palace in Japan should be destroyed as a symbolic act. It met with widespread support and only the opposition of a British Member of Parliament, Captain Gammans, and a few others persuaded the conference to drop it.

to the British Crown, and France, it would appear, surreptitiously and without knowledge of the Chinese, added a clause to her own treaty making it lawful for French missionaries in any of the provinces to lease or buy land and build houses, in the hope that thereby she would be able to extend her spiritual domination over the Celestial Empire.

The treaties of Tientsin, together with the convention of Peking, opened a new chapter in Sino-European relationship. That it should have been inaugurated by a gross breach of international faith and by an act of unparalleled vandalism and an unnecessary humiliation of the Emperor was to have unfortunate results for the future. The European nations continued at all times to be suspicious of Chinese faith, and proceeded invariably on the assumption that international morality had no bearing on their relations with China and that European nations should act together diplomatically as one body in matters affecting their interests.[1] The Chinese on their part have never been able to forget or forgive the crude and uncivilized barbarism which considered the destruction of a beautiful national monument as an act ensuring political prestige.

[1] This continued till 1895.

BIBLIOGRAPHICAL NOTE TO PART II

The literature relating to this period of Chinese history is very extensive. A comprehensive bibliography of Chinese works relating to the first Anglo-Chinese war has been published by Feng Tien-chao in the *Yenching Journal of Social Studies* (October 1940).

The *Fu I Jeh Chi-Diary* of Chang Hsi, one of the officials connected with the negotiations at Nanking (1842), has been translated and annotated and published by SSu Yu-teng, University of Chicago, 1944.

In English, *The Chinese Repository*, Vols. IX-XII, contain many contemporary accounts and interesting documents.

The following descriptive books will also be found useful:

Bernard, William Dallas: *Narrative of Voyages*, 2 vols. London, 1844.

Day, John Francis: *China During the War and Since the Peace*, 2 vols. London, 1852, based on Chinese documents.

Lane Poole, Stanley: *Life of Sir Harry Parkes.*

Nye, Gideon: *Peking the Goal.* Canton, 1873.

Lin Tse-hsu's life is the subject of a study by Gideon Chen, Peking, 1934.

British records are dealt with in:

Costin, W. C.: *Great Britain and China*, 1833–60. Oxford, 1937.

Fairbank, K. J. K.: 'Chinese Diplomacy and the Treaty of Nanking, 1842', *Journal of Modern History*, XII No. 1.

Fairbank, K. J. K.: 'The Manchu Appeasement Policy of 1843', *Journal of the American Oriental Society*, LIX, No. 4, 1937, pp. 469–84.

Keo Ping-chia: *A Critical Study of the First Anglo-Chinese War, with documents.* Shanghai, 1935.

The Opium Question in all its aspects is dealt with in:
David Edward Owen: *British Opium Policy in China and Japan*. New Haven, Conn., 1934; and in H. B. Morse: *The Trade and Administration of China*; also in Maurice Collis: *Foreign Mud*, Faber and Faber, London, 1945.

Books relating to the period between 1842–60, see especially:
H. Cordier: *L'expédition de Chine de* 1857–8.
Davis, Sir J. F.: *China*. London, 1857; *China During the War and Since the Peace*. London, 1852.
Leavenworth, C. S.: *The Arrow War with Chinese*. London, 1901.
Oliphant, L.: *Lord Elgin's Mission*, 1857, 1858, 1859.
Parliamentary Papers: China, 1859.

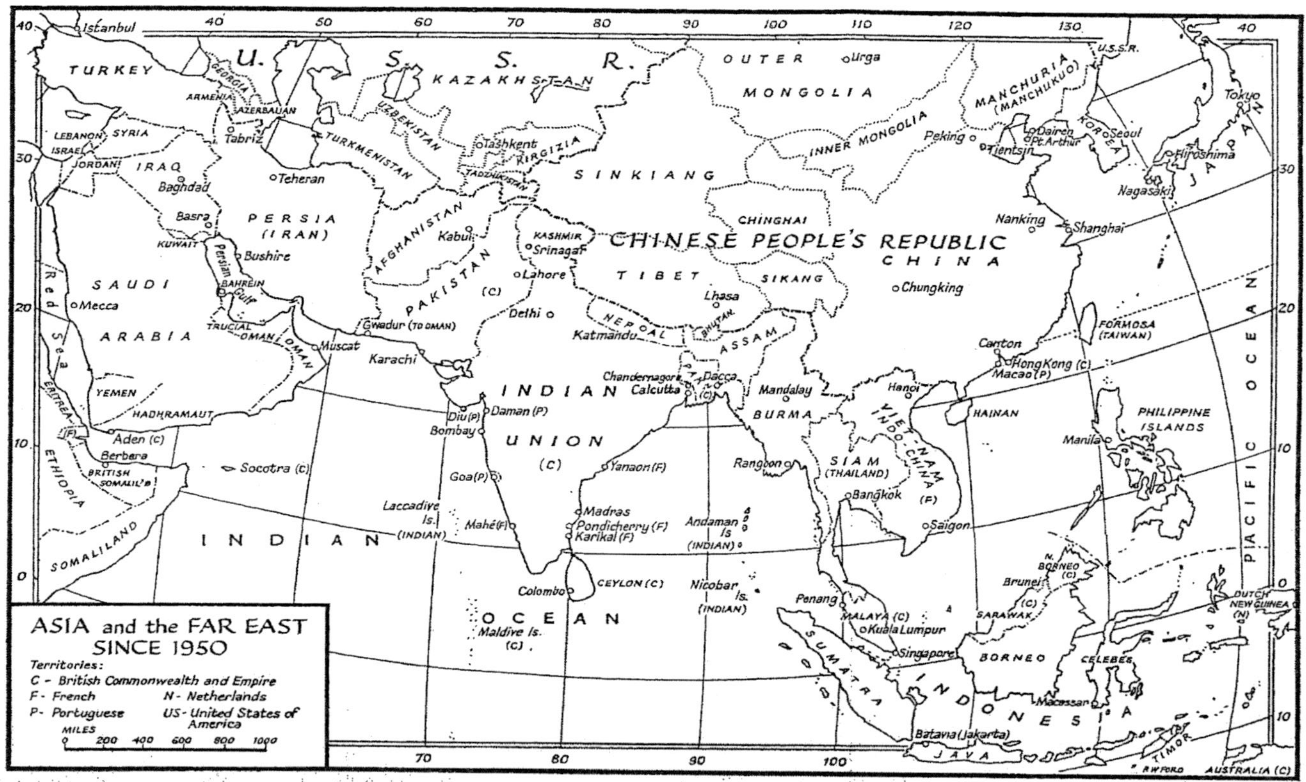
ASIA and the FAR EAST
SINCE 1950
Territories:
C - British Commonwealth and Empire
F - French
N - Netherlands
P - Portuguese
US - United States of America
MILES
0 200 400 600 800 1000
U. S. S. R.
TURKEY
Istanbul
GEORGIA
ARMENIA
AZERBAIJAN
KAZAKHSTAN
UZBEKISTAN
TURKMENISTAN
KIRGIZIA
TADZHIKISTAN
Tashkent
Tabriz
Teheran
LEBANON
SYRIA
ISRAEL
JORDAN
IRAQ
Baghdad
Basra
KUWAIT
PERSIA
(IRAN)
Bushire
Persian Gulf
BAHREIN
SAUDI
ARABIA
Mecca
TRUCIAL OMAN
OMAN
Muscat
YEMEN
HADHRAMAUT
Aden (C)
Red Sea
ERITREA
(F)
Berbera
BRITISH SOMALIL'D
ETHIOPIA
SOMALILAND
Socotra (C)
AFGHANISTAN
Kabul
PAKISTAN
(C)
Gwadur (TO OMAN)
Karachi
KASHMIR
Srinagar
Lahore
Delhi
INDIAN
UNION
(C)
Diu (P)
Daman (P)
Bombay
Goa (P)
Mahé (F)
Laccadive Is.
(INDIAN)
Madras
Pondicherry (F)
Karikal (F)
Yanaon (F)
Chandernagore
Calcutta
Dacca
(C)
CEYLON (C)
Colombo
Maldive Is.
(C)
INDIAN
OCEAN
Andaman Is
(INDIAN)
Nicobar Is.
(INDIAN)
NEPAL
Katmandu
BHUTAN
ASSAM
TIBET
Lhasa
SINKIANG
CHINGHAI
SIKANG
CHINESE PEOPLE'S REPUBLIC
CHINA
Chungking
OUTER
MONGOLIA
Urga
INNER MONGOLIA
Peking
Tientsin
MANCHURIA
(MANCHUKUO)
Dairen
Pt. Arthur
KOREA
Seoul
U.S.S.R.
JAPAN
Tokyo
Hiroshima
Nagasaki
Nanking
Shanghai
FORMOSA
(TAIWAN)
Canton
Hong Kong (C)
Macao (P)
HAINAN
Hanoi
VIET-NAM
INDO-CHINA
(F)
Saigon
BURMA
Mandalay
Rangoon
SIAM
(THAILAND)
Bangkok
Penang
MALAYA (C)
Kuala Lumpur
Singapore
SUMATRA
PHILIPPINE
ISLANDS
Manila
N. BORNEO
(C)
Brunei
(C)
SARAWAK
BORNEO
CELEBES
Macassar
INDONESIA
Batavia (Jakarta)
JAVA
TIMOR
DUTCH NEW GUINEA
(N)
AUSTRALIA (C)
PACIFIC OCEAN
R.W. FORD
40
50
60
70
80
90
100
110
120
130
30
20
10
0

Part III

THE AGE OF EMPIRE

1858–1914

CHAPTER I

INDIA

THE last sovereign independent State in India, the kingdom of the Punjab, was conquered and annexed in 1846–8, and with it British authority extended from Kashmir to Cape Comorin and from the Hindu Kush to Assam. Though the kingdoms and States of India were thus annexed or reduced to dependence, the people of India made one last effort on a national scale to recover their freedom. The Great Rebellion of 1857–8 was a desperate attempt led by the former ruling classes, who found themselves dispossessed and bereft of all their power. The Rebellion was put down after fifteen months of fighting. It was the last gasp of an old and dying order, and though it evoked the loyalties of the past and called forth the enthusiasm of the masses over wide areas, it had not the idealism, organization or strength to build up and sustain a State which could at that time have taken over from the British. From 1858, when the Rebellion was crushed and the last Mogul Emperor who was its titular head was banished to Rangoon, up to the Montagu-Chelmsford Reforms, 1919, there was no serious threat or challenge to British rule. Till 1947, that is ninety years from the Mutiny, the Union Jack flew over the Mogul fort as the symbol of British authority.

The history of India during this period of imperial domination is especially significant for the unseen transformation that the British rule underwent as a result of economic, political and geographical factors. Starting from the status of a 'possession' and a colony, British India, by slow stages, developed into an 'empire', no doubt subordinate to the authorities in London, but claiming to be heard in its own right, and often forcing the home government into policies with which it was not in entire agreement. The size, importance, resources and geographical position of India began slowly to assert themselves, and the interests of the British Empire in India soon became a major factor in shaping imperial policies. As we shall see, many aspects of British policy in China, Persia and Afghanistan were determined by considerations of India's safety or what Britain then considered to be the interests of India. This transformation, which of course had but little to do with the people of India, during the period of imperialism became in the succeeding period, when Indian nationalism began to assert itself, a highly significant fact in the shaping of the new Asia.

During the first part of this period (1858–1914) India was, in fact no less than in name, a British possession: a country 'owned' by the British people and governed primarily in their interests. The authority over India after 1858 was vested in the British Parliament, which, through a Secretary of State responsible for it, supervised, directed and controlled the Government of India. Till 1946 the Government of India was in every sense an agent and instrument of the British Cabinet, though after 1919 the British Government accepted certain limitations to its own authority in regard to financial matters. All-important decisions had not only to be referred to London but were actually taken there, or at least they had to secure the Secretary of State's approval. The contracts of superior appointments in India were with the Secretary of State, and officers of the 'Covenanted' service had the right of appealing to him even in matters connected with their service conditions. The Viceroyalty of India conferred immense prestige and high honour, but the authority of the incumbent was strictly limited and, as against the Secretary of State for India, he was no more than a subordinate whose voice no doubt was entitled to weight, but was not in any way to be considered decisive. The Government of India was what Lord Curzon, himself a celebrated Viceroy, described it to be—a subordinate branch of Government.

Under the 'Imperial' or Central Government of India there were the provincial administrations, again with authority delegated from the centre. The administration of India was conducted by a Civil Service, a regular mandarinate, recruited in England by open competitive examination. The curriculum of the examination was so arranged as to place a premium on candidates from the two metropolitan universities of Oxford and Cambridge, with their preponderance of public school students, thereby ensuring both the 'class composition' of the services and the imperial tradition. In the first quarter of a century after assumption of direct government of India by the Crown (1858) there were hardly any Indians in the Civil Service. Though from the end of the century a number of Indians continued annually to secure admission to this service, their proportion was not considerable till after 1919, that is, during the whole period of imperial supremacy. The Civil Service not merely administered, that is, collected the revenues, maintained law and order, and formed generally the magistracy over the entire country, but also participated in higher judicial work, a proportion of the judges of the Provincial High Courts being drawn from the administrative service.

Below this practically 'all white' service was a large Indian bureaucracy recruited on a provincial basis and strictly controlled and supervised in its functions by the former. It was through this subordinate or provincial service, exclusively Indian in personnel, that the authority of the Government penetrated to the masses. The control, however, was for a long time solely in the hands of European officials. A similar system was also evolved for the police, the all-Indian or superior cadres of which were recruited in England, while a provincial police service recruited locally did the less important work.

The defence of India was under a commander-in-chief appointed directly from England. The forces consisted of a 'sepoy' army whose commissioned ranks were open only to Europeans, and this force was stiffened by contingents of British troops posted in India. The great Indian army, which was the main instrument of British authority in the East and whose prowess in battle became famous in three continents, was thus in man-power Indian, but during the period under review officered wholly by Europeans. After the experiences in the Great Mutiny, the British Government took every precaution to respect the sentiments of the troops in religious matters and this is one of the major reasons why the Indian Government gave no official encouragement to missionary propaganda. More, it provided priests for their respective religions for Hindus, Sikhs and Muslims in the army, a matter of considerable importance in safeguarding India from the proselytizing aggression of Western missionary bodies.

The policy of depending on a 'sepoy' army had other political results. It became one of the primary concerns of British authorities to ensure that those from whom they recruited their armies did not get infected by political ideas. It became necessary, therefore, to confine recruitment to well-defined groups, who could be shown special favour, flattered and kept in good humour. Thus was developed the famous theory of martial and non-martial races, which overlooked that the sepoys, who had originally fought and conquered for the British, came from classes which were later declared non-martial. Also the Marathas, who had shown outstanding military ability and valour, ceased to be counted as being martial as they had a marked sense of nationalism and could not be isolated from the rest of the community. The Sikhs, Rajputs and Jats, the Punjab Muslims, Baluchis, Dogras and other favoured communities became in this manner the special reservoir for recruitment. The policy of 'divide and rule' was nowhere more clearly practised than in the concessions shown to these classes who were made to believe for a long time that they were the special favourites of the Empire.

By conquest Britain had acquired only three-fifths of the territory of India. Two-fifths of the entire area were still under Indian rulers, some of whom, like the Maharajas of the chief Rajput States and of Mysore, Travancore and Cochin, represented the survivals of older dynasties, while the more important ones like Hyderabad, the Maratha States and Kashmir were, as we have seen, but the territories of 'war lords' who had made peace with the growing power of the East India Company. Slowly, the British rulers, after their authority had been established firmly in the areas under their direct rule, inaugurated a policy of reducing the 'independence' of these rulers by systematic intervention in their affairs. In 1875, the Maharaja of Baroda, one of the most powerful of Indian rulers, was deposed. By entrusting the 'Residents' or diplomatic officers at the court with greater powers, by appointing direct administrators, and sometimes even by restricting the authority of the ruler, these States were one by one brought into the same pattern[1]: a system of indirect rule which imperial authorities elsewhere, e.g., France in Indo-China, Japan in Manchukuo, etc., began in time to imitate. In this way both British and 'Indian' India became in effect a single, immensely powerful political entity under the control of the authorities in London.

The economic control of India during this period was completely in British hands. India provided a monopoly market for Britain during the expansive period of her industrial life in the second half of the nineteenth century. The Lancashire cotton industry, which as a result of the Industrial Revolution had become the greatest supplier of the world's cotton goods, seemed to have an unlimited market in India till the rise of the Indian textile industry, and even then British vested interests were able to impose, through the dictation of Whitehall, a countervailing excise duty to deprive it of the protection of a small customs tariff. Railway construction in India was entrusted to British firms with guarantees of interest on capital. Large-scale plantations of tea, rubber, coffee and indigo were financed by British capital, and areas like Assam, portions of Bihar and the hill territories of South India assumed the aspect of a colonial regime, with planters exercising a local authority and often dominating the policy of the Government. In the planter's regime that was established in these regions, the Indian labourer was no more than the chattel of the plantation owner. Labour contract was enforced by criminal law. Murders by plantation managers went unpunished, and the small European colonies assumed and enforced their own authority within the plantations.

The Government of India after 1858 encouraged European settlers in these areas. Lord Canning made the acquisition of land easy for Europeans by issuing a special law entitled 'Waste Land Rules', under which large areas of hill land were alienated to Europeans in the hope

[1] See *Indian States and the Government of India* by the present author.

of getting them to settle down in milder climates and of building up large-scale plantations. In Assam and the Nilgiris this process led to enormous plantation colonies. European indigo planters had been imported from the West Indies and settled in Bihar. There they established a semi-feudal system of land holding. 'They were a lawless set,' says Edward Thompson, 'who combined some of the worst features of the eighteenth-century *Zamindars* (landowners) with the tenacity of the Indian moneylender. Very few grew indigo themselves. They obtained their raw materials by advancing money to cultivators and gradually getting them completely under control.'[1] As the Official Indigo Commission's Report stated: 'It matters little whether the ryot took his original advance with reluctance or cheerfulness: the result in either case is the same. He is never afterwards a free man.' In fact, in the plantation areas conditions amounting to slavery were re-established by the planters with the acquiescence of the Government.

Some idea of the misery to which the population of these areas was reduced by this system of merciless exploitation in the interests of British capital may be gained from the Bengal Indigo Commission's Report and from some of the literature of the period. *Nil Darpan or the Mirror of Indigo*, a Bengali drama, created a sensation by throwing a little light on this dark corner of Britain's action in India, and the reaction in official circles was so great that a European missionary, Mr Long, who translated and published it in English, was fined and imprisoned. During the whole of this period, in fact till the rise of nationalism after the Great War, conditions in plantations were of a kind which showed the worst features of European relations with Asia.

British monopoly interests in India were not primarily based on plantations. They rested on shipping, banking, insurance and the control of trade inside the country through the machinery of distribution, because Indian capitalists, realizing that they had little chance of independence, adjusted themselves to the position of being agencies of British firms. In the early decades of our period British interests did not develop the idea of establishing industries in India. Raw jute went to Dundee, and it was only when it was felt that, with cheaper labour and no welfare laws in practice, the industry would yield greater profits in India that the Dundee firms opened their factories on the Hoogli. The exports from India were raw materials, and in the nineteenth century India continued to be thus not only a market for British goods but a leading supplier of raw materials for British industries.

That India was becoming poorer as a result of the drain of wealth from the country was one of the favourite themes of Indian publicists and economists of the time. *Poverty and 'un-British' Rule in India* was

[1] Thompson and Garret: *British Rule in India*, p. 474.

the name of a detailed study on the subject by Dadabhai Naoroji, an Indian nationalist leader who became a Member of Parliament in England. Whether the British Government consciously drained India of her wealth or not and whether unjust payments were exacted from India or not, there is no doubt that during the second half of the nineteenth century British capital exploited Indian resources without competition and drew enormous profits and in this process was helped by the economic policies approved by the British authorities in London. This was perhaps natural and not a matter one need complain about, but has to be stated as fact, against which many offsetting factors have perhaps also to be stated.

One other aspect of British authority in India at this period was the conviction held by every European in India of a final and enduring racial superiority. Seton Kerr, a Foreign Secretary of the Government, explained it as 'the cherished conviction of every Englishman in India, from the highest to the lowest, by the planter's assistant in his lowly bungalow and by the editor in the full light of the Presidency town – from those to the Chief Commissioner in charge of an important province to the Viceroy on his throne – the conviction in every man that he belongs to a race whom God has destined to govern and subdue'.[1] Many equally authoritative statements of this point of view, from persons in the highest official position in India, could be quoted to show how universal this conviction was during the last century and indeed up to the time of the First Great War. One further quotation may, however, be permitted, as it throws light on the attitude of the army. Lord Kitchener, a most distinguished Commander-in-Chief of India, declared: 'It is this consciousness of the inherent superiority of the European which has won for us India. However well educated and clever a native may be, and however brave he may have proved himself, I believe that no rank we can bestow on him would cause him to be considered an equal of the British officer.'

This frank racialism permeated all the services and constituted the distinguishing characteristic of British rule in the East in the nineteenth century. Its effects were widespread. In the army no Indian could hold a King's Commission. In the Civil Service, though Indians could enter by open competitive examination, no appointments above a certain rank were open to him and the most distinguished Indian administrator of his day, R. C. Dutt, had to resign because, on the ground of his race, he was not promoted to the post of a commissioner. Social life was, of course, exclusive, and from hotels and clubs and even from certain parks unwritten rules excluded Indians. Also Indian life was held cheap. Rudd, a planter's assistant who committed an unusually brutal and

[1] Quoted in Thompson and Garret, p. 536.

cowardly murder, became, on his conviction, a martyr and the European public carried on agitation for his reprieve. Even Lord Curzon, the apostle of imperialism, became unpopular for a time because he punished a regiment which, it was alleged, deliberately sheltered a murderer. In fact, during this entire period and for a short time afterwards also, it was impossible to secure criminal justice against a European, and more than one Viceroy had to face public odium from his own community for making known his views on this subject.

It was the agitation in regard to the Ilbert Bill that made everyone realize how deeply rooted this feeling of racial superiority was among Britons in the East. The Bill was meant to remove the disability which prevented Indian magistrates from trying Europeans. It was introduced by the great jurist, Sir Courtney Ilbert, in order to place British and Indian magistrates in the Civil Service on a position of equality. The agitation that European non-officials, numbering at that time less than 2,000, organized was exceptional in so far as it was directed against the highest authorities of the British Government itself. Defence Leagues were formed: money was collected and a furious campaign was set on foot against the Viceroy himself. Irate *Sahibs* wrote to the papers asking what right Indians had in India! If India is not a white man's country and if once it was accepted that Indians had any right at all, where would it all end? The whole idea was considered an insult to the British race, and English women wrote home reminding people of the outrages of the Mutiny days and protesting against the inconceivable degradation to the entire white race which would follow if Europeans were tried by Indian magistrates. In England, Florence Nightingale, shocked by the violence of this exhibition of racialism, quietly informed Queen Victoria of the dangers of the situation and calmed the sovereign's conscience.[1] But the Europeans in India realized what was at stake—it was the principle of race supremacy on which the Empire in India rested. The Europeans won for the time and the Viceroy had to yield to their pressure. Racialism continued to be the official doctrine, though with lessening strength for another forty years.

If race was the basis of government, then it followed that the 'prestige' of the race should be maintained at all costs and an elaborate code, formulae and ceremonies had to be devised to keep up the authority of the white man. The British authorities went into this question systematically. Their assumptions were unfortunately fallacious. They held the view, and cherished it almost as a superstition, that the 'natives' were impressed by pomp and circumstance, and the prestige of the European required him, 'even the planter's assistant in his lowly bungalow', to live in state. Mackrabie, as quoted in Busteed's *Echoes of Old Calcutta*, talks

[1] See Cecil Woodham Smith: *Florence Nightingale*. London, 1950, pp. 550–1.

of 110 servants to wait on a family of four people. In the anonymous *Letters from Madras*: 'Every horse has a man and a maid to himself – the maid cuts grass for him and every dog has a boy. I inquired whether the cat had any servants, but I found she was allowed to wait upon herself.' At the end of this period in 1913, Olive Douglas remarked: 'It seems to me that I go about asking "why" all day and no one gives me a satisfactory answer to anything. Why, for example, should we require a troop of servants, living as we do in a kind of hotel?'[1] This kind of living in style was supposed to be necessary to keep up the prestige of the *Sahib*.

An elaborate code laid down what language should be used to the different classes of natives, where they should be received and with what shades of courtesy or discourtesy they should be treated; who should be seen only in the courtyard, who on the veranda and who could be allowed to enter the drawing-room; who should be offered a seat and who should not. Indeed *kurzi nishan*, the right to be offered a chair, was raised to the position of an 'honour' given personally or in heredity for services rendered to the administration. The European believed that his prestige was kept up by these rules and regulations and the native was impressed by the shades of discourtesy shown to him. How foolish this belief was and how much it contributed to the dislike of Europeans and contempt for their manners, they in their isolation did not know.

Another favourite superstition, again bearing on the doctrine of 'prestige', was the belief that Indians as a whole were impressed by grandeur. Every collector, therefore, held his *durbar*, every Commissioner a bigger *durbar* with even more elaborate ceremonies, while the Governors and Viceroys felt it to be a part of their official life. 'Imperial *durbars*', in the grand style of Lytton and Curzon, with jewelled princes, elephant processions and the rest of the magnificence of Oriental courts were one thing. The routine *durbars* of officials were in another category. It was presumed that these occasional doses of ceremony would keep the memory of the *Sahib's* dignity and authority green in the minds of all. The imperial *durbars* were the extensions of this principle on a national scale. It was meant to impress the princes and peoples of India with the might, majesty and magnificence of the British Empire.

Undoubtedly, the Indians, like all other people everywhere, love *tamashas*, festivals of gorgeous colour with processions, crowds and great displays. But anyone with normal vision could have told them even in 1877, when Lytton held his first imperial *durbar*, that generally in India what conferred prestige was neither rank nor power, but the reputation for goodness and holiness. In fact, Indian reaction to British

[1] *Olive in India*. London, 1913.

officials should have also told them this. Lord Ripon, because he was considered 'good', and Lord Irwin (Halifax) later for the same reason, impressed Indians, and the same was true of lesser personages like Munro whose 'good works' and religious faith earned respect, while *durbar*-holding and prestige-worshipping viceroys and officials made themselves only ludicrous in the eyes of the people.

As a result of this doctrine of prestige and race superiority, the Europeans in India, however long they lived there, remained strangers in the country. An unbridgeable chasm existed between them and the people, which was true till the very end of British rule in India. Penderell Moon, an officer of the Civil Service, writing in the forties of the present century, emphasized this fact, but in the period of imperial domination this was so obvious that it required no explanation. They lived in two countries, Anglo-India and India, and the two never met. The one governed the other. It is in the field of administration that Britain was able rapidly to demonstrate her ability and proclaim to the world her achievements. Great codes of law were promulgated, and enforced, from one end of the country to another. An imposing judicial machinery, suitably graded with its apex in the different High Courts, but with appeal to the Privy Council, was established to dispense the laws thus promulgated. Lands were 'assessed and settled' and a uniform system of taxation introduced. Large irrigation schemes, at least in the Punjab and the Gangetic Valley, provided water to the cultivator. A system of roads was constructed, no doubt originally for strategic purposes, but it connected vast areas and helped the development of commerce. Railways, telegraphs and a national system of cheap postal communication gave India the apparatus of a modern State. Universities, technical institutions like the Roorkee Engineering College, institutions for medical and other studies were opened in India. These, it should be noted, were the results of Government activity.

Politically also, though in a lesser degree, similar developments were taking place under Government auspices. In 1861 the Indian Council's Act provided for the inclusion for legislative purposes of non-official members. Among those nominated in 1862 were also three Indians. In the provinces also similar councils were established. The principle of indirect election for representation in these councils was established in 1892, with the right of discussing the budget and of asking questions on matters of public interest. This reform, though very modest, gave opportunities of public criticism of Government measures and a share in the making of laws. In 1909 a further step was taken. The Indian Legislative Council was given a majority of non-official members, twenty-seven of whom were to be elected, some by special constituencies like landowners and chambers of commerce and others by the provincial legislatures. The Central and Provincial Cabinets also were to have Indian members for the first time. The Minto-Morley reforms were not the inauguration of parliamentary government, but they represented a principle of associating Indians with the government of their own country. India was undergoing a process of transformation.

Two further facts may be noted on the political side: the development of local self-government institutions and the deliberate introduction of the vicious principle of separate electoral rolls for Muslims—the precursor of the doctrine of two nations. It is Lord Ripon's name that is associated with the first, the reform which laid the foundation of popular government in India by establishing a system of district boards and municipal authorities in which the popular element had the first real experience of administration. It is the existence of these institutions that enabled the provincial legislatures to function smoothly, for they formed the electorate which chose members to the provincial bodies. The growth of local self-government institutions familiarized the rural population with the machinery of representative institutions and thus became the cornerstone of Indian democracy in the period that followed.

The institution of separate electorates for the Muslims was the first expression of the pernicious two-nation theory, which ultimately resulted in the foundation of Pakistan. Published documents fully establish the fact that this was created by deliberate policy as an effective method to keep the Hindus and Muslims apart. Lady Minto, the wife of the Viceroy who was reponsible for this piece of political Machiavellianism, noted with glee that her husband had by this act ensured for a long time the authority of the British in India. The system of separate electorates was a simple device. It provided that Muslims should be represented only by Muslims, elected only by Muslim voters and, further, that no Muslim could represent a Hindu constituency or vice versa. By this expedient the Muslims in India from Cape Comorin to Kashmir became a separate political entity, perpetually at odds with the Hindus and judging all issues from the point of view of a religious community. As the Muslim candidates to the legislatures had to depend on a religious franchise, their views and policies came to be moulded by considerations of religious fanaticism. India took over forty years to be rid of this vicious system and that, too, at the terrible cost of a partition.

It would be clear from the preceding analysis that the twin doctrines of 'possession' and 'racial supremacy' underwent a subtle but far-reaching change during this period. True, both these doctrines persisted well into the twentieth century, but their transformation was real enough, and the edge soon wore out of the doctrine of 'possession', and even the sense of racial superiority lost much of its political, though not its social, content even before the nineteenth century came to a close. How this transformation was effected is a subject of the utmost importance for a proper understanding of the evolution and ultimate success of Asian nationalism.

The emergence of India under the British as a powerful State, with an efficient administration, was the work of a bureaucracy, carefully recruited, elaborately organized and maintained with dignity and prestige. The British bureaucracy in India was not merely an officialdom. It was a governing corporation, holding all but four or five of the most important posts in India, the Viceroyalty, the Governorships of Bengal, Bombay and Madras and the Law Membership in the Central Cabinet. In the judiciary also they were adequately represented. They, therefore, had the preponderant share in the making of Government policies and constituted the sole machinery of putting those policies into practice. Soon, they developed a common tradition, an *esprit de corps*, doctrines of political integrity and a general attitude towards India. India as the country where their career began and ended and as the country they were 'serving' became their exclusive concern. True it was not the India of the Indians, but a special India of their own conception. To that India they developed a sense of loyalty. They visualized it as a country whose millions of inhabitants were entrusted to their care. Thus developed that strange identification of themselves 'with the masses' of which the counterpart was a deep distrust of the educated classes who questioned the right of the Civil Service to govern.

The most important result of the development of the Civil Service tradition was the conflict which grew out of it between the Secretary of State, representing the British Government's policies, and the authorities in India representing the Civil Services. Before the development of nationalism and the consequent conversion of British politicians, beginning with the time of Edwin Montagu, to the view that Indians were best represented by Indians themselves, the Civil Services fought the case of *their* India against the dictates of Whitehall. The doctrine of 'the man on the spot', the man who knew local conditions and was therefore best able to judge, became the slogan of the Civil Service, against the policies decided under parliamentary or financial pressure in London. An important characteristic of the Civil Services was its open refusal to be influenced by commercial and industrial interests in India. The classes from whom the Civil Services were recruited helped to form this idea. Sir Bartle Frere, writing to Lord Goderich, had insisted that it was 'of more consequence to the natives that he (the British Civil Servant) should be good on the cricket field, and on horseback, popular with the servants and the poor, and the champion of the bullied fags' than that he should be intellectually superior. Russell, the famous

Correspondent of *The Times*, noted that though 'a successful speculator or a merchant prince may force his way into good society in England . . . in India he must remain for ever outside the sacred barrier, which keeps the non-official world from the high society of the services'. There was thus no alliance between the Civil Service and big business, and the British Indian bureaucracy was not interested in the exploitation of India. In fact it could legitimately be said that the services championed 'their India', the India of the dumb masses, against British businessmen and capitalists, except where these had become powerful vested interests in rural areas, like tea plantations in Assam and indigo plantations in Bihar.

The continuous struggle with Whitehall, which in some cases even assumed a public and political aspect, as when a distinguished Viceroy resigned rather than enforce a policy clearly in the interests of Lancashire and against the interests of India, led to the public enunciation by successive Secretaries of State of the doctrine of the absolute subordination of the Government of India to the authority of Whitehall, but it was a difficult doctrine to enforce against a permanently entrenched Civil Service, holding not merely secretariat and executive posts but Cabinet positions in respect of all major departments. Gradually, in a very large sphere, the Indian Government began to exercise an effective authority, which led to the formulation of independent policies based on what the Civil Services considered to be the genuine interests of India.

An even more important cause of this transformation was the realization in England of the position of India as an imperial structure, a great land Power from which Britain's authority radiated to all parts of Asia. The transformation of the Government of India into an Empire was not merely one of name or title. Even before 1858, India under Britain had begun to play some role in the affairs of her neighbours, Afghanistan, Burma, etc., to which we shall revert later. But with the firm establishment of the Indian Government, British statesmen began gradually to realize that they had now a vast storehouse of power and resources and, with a great army and an efficient administrative machinery, it was possible for them to exercise a dominating voice in the affairs of Asia. India's part in the first China war has already been noted. In the period under study British authority based on India began to penetrate into Sinkiang during the rebellion of Yakub Beg, and into Afghanistan which, as we shall see presently, was sought to be reduced to the position of a protectorate. It also annexed Burma, tried to intervene in Persia and generally established a supremacy on the Arabian coast and in the Persian Gulf. In fact from 1875 India became an Imperial State, the centre of a political system in South Asia.

Lytton, a poet and the son of a famous novelist, may claim to be the founder of Imperial India not only in the literal sense that he held the great *durbar* to announce the imperial title which the Crown of England had assumed and thereby conferred a status on the country different from that of colonial possessions, but by his fanciful vision of 'bequeathing to India the supremacy of Central Asia and the revenues of a first-class Power', in fact a revived Mogul Empire. Lytton annexed Baluchistan, occupying Quetta in 1877, thus stepping out of Indian boundaries. From 1863, the Indian Government had taken a sporadic interest in the affairs of Afghanistan, but with the extension of Russian power in Central Asia, it began to feel that it should play a greater role. Lord Lytton, as Viceroy, began a series of manoeuvres meant to reduce Afghanistan to the position of a protectorate. He bagan by asking Sher Ali, the Afghan monarch, to receive a mission to announce the assumption of imperial title. Sher Ali politely declined it on the ground that the Russians might also demand the same right. After fruitless negotiations, the object of which was clear to the Afghans, Lord Lytton decided on intervention. In a letter to Lord Cranbrook he declared: 'I am persuaded that the policy of building up in Afghanistan a strong and independent State, over which we can exercise absolutely no control, has proved by experience to be a mistake. If by war, or by the death of the present Amir . . . we should have the opportunity of disintegrating and breaking up the Kabul power, I sincerely hope the opportunity will not be lost by us.'[1] Soon the opportunity which Lytton was hoping for arrived and, in violation of instructions, he decided on war in the hope of dismembering Afghanistan in the interests of his Indian Empire. He forced the issue over the head of the authorities in London. On trumped-up pretexts war was declared. Three Indian armies marched into Afghanistan. The Amir, failing to secure the assistance of Russia, fled the capital, and his son, Yakub Khan, signed a treaty under which Afghanistan agreed to the control of its foreign policy by the Indian Government. But this quick success was illusory. The British Resident, appointed under the treaty, along with his staff was attacked and killed by the Afghans, and Lytton's political structure across the Hindu Kush crashed overnight. Writing to Beaconsfield he complained that 'the web of policy so carefully and patiently woven has been rudely shattered. We have now to weave a fresh and I fear a wider one from undoubtedly weaker materials'.[2] It was the firmness of the imperial structure in India which made it possible for the Viceroy, in spite of the military disaster, to think in terms of weaving wider webs. The notorious General Roberts marched again at the head of an army, occupied Kabul and indiscriminately began hanging and burning villages so that the Afghans might

[1] Lord Lytton's *Indian Administration*, p. 247.
[2] Lord Lytton's *Indian Administration*, p. 358.

know what it costs to resist the British. But the Afghans refused to learn. They fought and made the position of the British invaders intolerable, so that finally a political settlement had to be reached. The army which had marched into Afghanistan with the hope of a cheap success withdrew, at least with no credit to itself. Abdur Rahman, the founder of modern Afghanistan, established himself on the throne, and though he agreed to receive a British envoy and not to enter into relations with other Powers the independence of Afghanistan was saved.

It should be noted that the Afghan campaign was an utter military failure and cost India an immense amount of money by increasing her public debt. The political system established after the war, however, continued practically undisturbed till 1919. The Afghan kingdom remained an independent buffer State where the influence of the Indian Government, though not visibly exercised, was dominant in the country's political relations. But India also discovered that her status as an empire cost her money, for all the wars in the East were debited to her account.

The intervention in Burma was more successful, though it was a crude and brazen instance of commercial imperialism. We have already seen how in the time of Dalhousie, Lower Burma had been annexed on the pretext of collecting a petty debt. Upper Burma, however, continued to be an independent State. This was an eye-sore to British commercial interests, who, for some time past, had been interesting themselves in the possibilities available in that rich and undeveloped country. A pretext was found in the action which the Burmese Government took in imposing a heavy fine on the Bombay-Burma Trading Corporation, a timber company, in which among other highly placed persons some of the relations of the then Viceroy of India had a financial interest. A political excuse was also found in the influence that France was building up in Indo-China and Siam and reportedly in Burma itself through the activities of her Minister. In 1885, Lord Dufferin sent an ultimatum to King Theebaw and, when that was rejected, a force was sent to Mandalay which concluded the 'campaign' in fifteen days, and captured the King. Again the expenses were charged to India; but it could at least be said that the influence of the Imperial State had now been carried to the borders of Siam, Indo-China and Yunnan!

To the west, British Indian authorities had from the beginning showed considerable interest in Persian affairs as Sir John Malcolm's mission in the 1830's shows. This interest became keener when the authority of Russia became more firmly established on the northern border of Persia. There, of course, the issue was not purely Indian, as the rivalry between London and Moscow and Britain's interests in the Middle East were also important factors. In the words of Sir Reader Bullard: 'The dispute, which began early in the nineteenth century, as to whether HM Government or the Government of India should be responsible for diplomatic relations with Persia, lasted for nearly half a century. The difficulty resulting from the presence of Malcolm representing India and Harford Jones representing Home Government was solved for the moment by the appointment of Sir Gore Ousley as sole envoy to Persia, but the question of principle was not settled until 1860, when it was agreed that diplomatic relations should be in the hands of the Foreign Office and the Government of India should contribute towards the cost of the diplomatic establishment in Persia.'[1]

If Persia was a divided responsibility, the intervention in Tibet was undoubtedly in the alleged interests of India and was exclusively the outcome of the policy of the Imperial State. As early as the end of the eighteenth century attempts had been made to open up trade with Tibet, but they had not been successful. In 1886, the Tibetans made an incursion into Sikkim, over which State they claimed some authority, but the Government of India, who had also established relations with the ruler, intervened and drove out the invaders in 1887. Later the boundary was marked by a Sino-British Commission in 1890 and, though an agreement on trade was also concluded at the same time, the Tibetans were able to prevent it from being brought into effect. However, with Lord Curzon the situation began to change. It seemed to him that the isolation of Tibet and the refusal of the Dalai Lama to permit free intercourse with the outside was almost an insult to British power in India, for he felt that such a desire did not go well 'with proximity to the territories of a great civilized Power at whose hands the Tibetan Government enjoys the fullest opportunities both for intercourse and trade'. The Imperial State wanted its unique position recognized by neighbouring courts, the old doctrine of *Samrajya* in India and of the universal empire in China.

An excuse was soon discovered. It was put out, as it is now known with hardly any truth, that Russia was trying to gain influence over the Dalai Lama. A Buriat Buddhist monk by name Dorjieff, whose later history as a dispenser of wisdom at Fontainebleau is interesting, reached the high office of the Grand Almoner to the Dalai Lama. Dorjieff was a Russian national and wrote letters to high officials in St Petersburg, which gave Curzon his necessary pretext for discovering Russian intrigue in Lhasa.[2] In 1902 the Viceroy, thirsty to play an imperial role, pressed the Secretary of State to agree to the dispatch of a mission to Lhasa. Though at first the British Government in London objected, Lord Curzon was able to force the issue by putting forward impossible

[1] Bullard: *Britain and the Middle East*. London, Hutchinson, 1951, p. 90.
[2] For an authoritative statement see Bell: *Biography of the Dalai Lama*.

demands to the Tibetans and, on their refusal, claiming that the Tibetans had shown unfriendliness and were being provocative. An expedition crossed the frontier, shot down Tibetans armed with antiquated weapons, to the use of which they were not trained, marched into Lhasa, to earn the glory of having captured the veiled city, but only to find that the Dalai Lama had fled to Mongolia. A treaty was forced on the Regent, but even the London Government was shocked by this exhibition of unprovoked imperial expansion. Also the international position forced a withdrawal of troops from Tibetan territory and an agreement was reached with Russia that both Powers recognized the suzerainty of China over Tibet. The Tibetan expedition was the high-water mark of the 'Empire State' in India.

If Lord Lytton was the originator of the doctrine of the Empire State, Lord Curzon was its most outstanding representative, almost the personification of the idea of the British power in India, as a great Empire shedding its greatness and glory on the neighbouring States. It is significant that even before Curzon was appointed Viceroy he had prepared himself for the task by extensive travels on India's borderland. As Viceroy, he pictured himself, as Lord Morley remarked with reference to the Tibetan expedition, as the Grand Mogul running an imperial policy of his own. To him, as Viceroy, India was the centre of the world around which everything rotated. He visited the Persian Gulf, tried to increase, with only a moderate measure of success, the influence of the Indian Government in Afghanistan and in Nepal, and generally claimed for India a position of importance in South Asian affairs as if it were an independent country.

Actually, as a distinguished English observer has noted, the Indian Empire at that time was a 'continental order', a political structure based on India and extending its authority from Aden to Hong Kong. 'Its spread', says Mr Wint, 'was the result of Indo-British partnership, of Britain and India, of the emigrants of the British middle class and of Indian man-power which they had organized. India could not have established the Empire without Great Britain, nor could Great Britain without India. All the principal actors who conceived the expansionist policies were Englishmen; but the Empire which they built was based on Indian, not British, needs. Except for the sake of Indian security what interest would Great Britain have had in the Persian Gulf, Tibet or Sinkiang, in all of whose affairs it began to intervene? Indian emigrants, not British, swarmed into the new provinces and, while British capital built the railways, mines, plantations and new industries, Indian moneylenders acquired the land. The fact that in their activities in Asia the British were in part doing India's business and acting as servants of the Emperor of India rather than of the King of England explains much about the past and present of the Empire which is otherwise obscure.

'The Indian Empire is to be thought of', Mr Wint continues, 'as consisting of a kernel which was the rich lands directly administered and of a protective rind; this rind was made up partly of minor and more or less primitive States, such as Bhutan and Nepal and part of mountain and desert territories, inhabited by people tribally organized . . . Over both these groups the Indian Government exercised a control whose form varied . . . but whose common purpose was to prevent or restrict their relations with other countries or at least to ensure that they could not be used by them for hostile purposes.

'Still further afield, and as a sort of open ground in front of the outworks, the Indian Government formed a ring of neutral States, Persia, Arabia, Tibet and Afghanistan, and even for a time a part of Sinkiang. On one side the limit of India's interest was in general the Arabian Desert between Baghdad and Damascus, which forms the true division between the countries which look towards Europe and those which look towards Asia and which was once the boundary of the Roman Empire. . . . On the other side the interest extended to Indonesia and Indo-China, though for various reasons it was less keen and alert than on the Western side.

'A corps of specialists in the Indian Army and the Foreign Office of the Indian Government, inconspicuously and at times with the sense of carrying on a conspiracy or an esoteric rite, secured the continuity of policy. Round it grew up a romance, a vision of the seas swept by the British Navy, the 3,000 miles of mountain frontiers of Northern India, the lands beyond, supposed in the imagination of the classically educated officials to be so much like the barbarian territory beyond the *limes* of the Roman Empire, the mysterious Central Asia in which the forces might one day collect and coalesce for a descent on the tropic lands of the south, the small frontier forces whose wars with tribesmen (if heard of at all) seemed such amusing anachronisms to the outside world, but which protected millions of peaceful peasants, the secret agents who, like the associates of Kipling's *Kim*, flitted through the mountain lands disguised as traders or Lamas, loaded with silver rupees and measuring rods.'[1]

Thus this period witnessed the growth of an 'overseas India', a large-scale emigration of Indian people into the tropical areas of the Empire, where they carried with them not only their agricultural and labour skills but a modified Indian social system, India's religious, temples and festivals. In South Africa, in the British Colonies of East Africa and in the distant lands of British Guiana, Trinidad and Jamaica, flourishing Indian colonies came into existence which were not without significance

[1] Guy Wint: *British in Asia*, pp. 21–3.

for the internal life of India. Though the status of India did not improve, as she remained a very minor partner in this grandiose development, the status of the Indian Empire improved and became that of a major Power in Asia.

CHAPTER 2

CHINA

We have seen in an earlier section how the treaties which the Anglo-French allies compelled the court of Peking to sign established the doctrine of extra-territoriality. This included the freedom of missions to propagate religion in every part of China and protection for missionaries and their converts. Tientsin was added to the treaty ports, and envoys of treaty Powers were allowed to open Legations and remain permanently in Peking. By these treaties the court of Peking, which had so far maintained only a distant relationship with foreign governments, became subject to the daily pressure of diplomacy in the capital when it was least prepared to meet such an attack. The British and French Legations reached Peking in March 1861, the Russian envoy in July of the same year; the American, Mr Anson Burlinghame, who was destined to have a romantic career later, reached Peking in 1862 after a leisurely journey from Canton. Thus China opened a new chapter in her long history, the main feature of which was her subordination to and dependence on the representatives of the Powers who had forced themselves on her. Under the treaties, these now claimed rights, privileges, dignities and prerogatives, which by a liberal interpretation, backed by force, developed within a period of fifty years into a special corps of international law controlling practically every aspect of Chinese life. How the treaty system was used to 'chain the dragon', and how under its cover a system of imperialist exploitation of the resources of China was built up steadily and systematically, and how the proud Empire of the Hans, Tangs, Mings and Chings was reduced to the position of complete impotence when areas under her flag were quietly snatched away and the Powers virtually partitioned her vast territories into 'spheres of influence', is a story which has no parallel in history.

During this entire period the destiny of China, by an unfortunate turn in the wheels of fortune, was placed in the hands of an ignorant, corrupt and unscrupulous woman, Yehonala, known to history as Dowager Empress Tzu Hsi or, familiarly, as 'the Old Buddha'. From 1860, when she became one of the Regents, to her death on November 15, 1908, this woman ruled China as undisputed autocrat, except for a short period when the Emperor tried to assert his authority. She had three outstanding characteristics. Yehonala was a dominating personality, a truly imperious woman, a person who was born to command. She had a remarkable capacity for court intrigues, an almost feline sense of danger and an ability to spring unexpectedly and strike down her enemies. Thirdly, she had no conscience and no scruples. Nothing restrained her, neither family bonds nor human relationships, except perhaps in the case of Jung Lu, her early and devoted lover. National interests she equated with her own whims and caprices.

Yehonala (born 1835), the daughter of a Manchu nobleman, was merely one of the concubines of Emperor Hsien Feng till 1856, when on the birth of a son to her she was raised to the rank of a first-class concubine. From this time, as the mother of the heir-apparent, she came to have considerable influence on the Emperor, which she used to encourage the Emperor in the policy of resisting the Anglo-French demands. On the death of the Emperor at Jehol, she, with the assistance of Jung Lu, the Commander of the Guards and the friend of her early days, put down a conspiracy of leading Manchu princes to establish their authority, and assumed full powers in association with the Empress Consort, a colourless and ineffective lady, who yielded in everything to her masterful 'junior sister'.

The first problem that Yehonala, now known as Tzu Hsi, or Motherly and Auspicious, had to tackle was the Taiping Rebellion.[1] This strange movement was itself in a measure the outcome of foreign impacts. Primarily it was the weakness of the Manchu Government, laid bare by the aggression of the West, that opened the eyes of the patriotic societies which joined forces with Hung Hsu-chuan, the Celestial King, and made the rebellion the serious affair that it became. Secondly, Hung himself, the professed younger but more meritorious brother of Jesus, was the product of a misconceived Christian teaching. It was a strange version of Christianity that he preached, a doctrine under which Hung himself, as the Son of God, represented his Father in Heaven and claimed to rule the world as the Celestial King.

The defeat of the Chinese forces in the first serious clash with the West had, as we saw, a profound influence on Asia as a whole. The leaders of Japan were themselves thunderstruck that the Celestial

[1] For a history of this rebellion, its religious theories and the way it was put down, see especially Hail: *Tseng Kuo-fan and the Taiping Rebellion.* Yale Historical Publications, XVIII, New Haven and London; and *Events in the Taiping Rebellion,* Egmount Hake, London. Allen, 1891.

Empire could so easily have been beaten. Fantastic stories gained currency about the might of the foreigner and many equated it with the Christian religion. In China itself, especially in the south, the defeat of the imperial forces served as an eye-opener to all the discontented elements in the Empire, especially the anti-Manchu Secret Societies which had always been active in those areas. The teachings of Issachar Roberts may not have given Hung any real idea of Christianity, but the future Celestial King, when he came away from the missionary's house, was deeply convinced of the doctrine of a Messianic incarnation to save the world and, having been persuaded by numerous visions that he himself was the new Messiah, announced the fact to the world and established a church called the Society of the Supreme. Not only did Hung claim divinity for himself but also for his son. In an edict of 1860, quoted by Hail, Hung claimed: 'The Father and the Elder Brother (Jesus) have descended upon earth and have established the heavenly kingdom and have taken me and the junior Lord (Hung's son) to regulate the affairs pertaining to this world. Father, Son and Grandson are together Lord of the New Heaven.'

Hung describes his ascent to heaven in the following poem:

He returned to heaven
Where the great God
Gave him great authority.
The celestial mother was kind
And exceedingly gracious,
Beautiful and noble in the extreme,
Far beyond all compare.

The celestial elder brother's wife
Was virtuous and very considerate,
Constantly exhorting the elder brother
To do things deliberately.

HAIL (p. 93)

Thus the two elements mingled, Christian fanaticism and anti-Manchu nationalism, and the mixture produced a revolutionary force of great vitality which spread over vast regions of the Empire and all but engulfed the dynasty.

From the provinces of Kwangtung and Kwangsi the rebels spread to Hunan and, striking along the Hsiang river, captured the cities on the way till they reached the great city of Changsha, where they met with organized and determined action by an official who was on leave, Tseng Kuo-fan. He was fated to be the most distinguished figure of the century in China. Though checked at Changsha, the rebels moved north and, without meeting serious opposition, reached the great Wu Han cities (Hankow, Wu Chang and Han Yang) almost along the same route and with the same ease as Chiang Kai-shek's armies did in 1926. In 1853 they captured Nanking, the southern capital. The Celestial King made it his headquarters and continued to reign there for full ten years.

In 1860, when the Anglo-French War was concluded and Empress Tzu Hsi took over as effective Regent on the return of the court from Jehol, the Taipings were still in control of the Yangtze Valley and the Celestial King was ruling from his palace in Nanking. His principal assistant at the time was a man named Li Siu-ching, known to history as Chung Wang or the Faithful King. This man was a soldier and administrator of genius. He had enlisted with the Taipings as a private and had taken part in practically every action of importance from the beginning of the movement. After a notable victory in 1856 he had been put in command of an army and had later been raised to the position of a king. His autobiography, translated by Walter T. Lay, and said to have been edited by Tseng Kuo-fan himself, is a document of primary importance.[1] Chung Wang maintained the authority of the rebel chief over large areas to the south of Yangtze. Faced by this grave menace to the regime, the Regent showed her determination in organizing an effective campaign against the rebels. Nanking fell in 1864 to Tseng Kuo-fan, and the Celestial King joined his Father in Heaven by committing suicide. His son, who was proclaimed his successor by Chung Wang, had but a brief reign and in July both he and the usurper were caught and executed.

The successful campaign against the Taipings brought to national prominence three statesmen, who between them dominated the Empire for the succeeding forty years and saved the Manchu Dynasty from internal collapse and as far as possible maintained its position under the most difficult conditions in the face of increasing foreign pressure. Tseng Kuo-fan, the eldest of them and the leader and *guru* of the other two, Tso Tsung-tang and Li Hung-chang, was primarily responsible for the defeat of the Taipings. Later he became the Viceroy of Chihli, the great strategic northern province, and it was mainly because of his pre-eminent influence at court that the relations with the foreign governments were maintained in a satisfactory manner. To Tseng Kuo-fan's credit also stands the establishment of the ironworks at Shanghai, which later became the Kiangnan Arsenal. He it was who supported Yung Wing in building the first modern ship in China. Tso Tsung-tang,[2]

[1] A detailed analysis of this autobiography, with numerous extracts, is available in Mr J. H. Teesdale's article on the Faithful Prince in the *Journal of the Royal Asiatic Society, North China Branch*, 1926 (pp. 92-109).

[2] There is an interesting biography of Tso Tsung-tang by W. L. Bales. Kelly and Walsh. Shanghai, 1937.

another distinguished official who had taken part along with Tseng in the suppression of the Taipings, was by no means a favourite of Tseng, who disliked him as a militarist. Tso's services were, however, remarkable. He was responsible for suppressing the Nienfei Rebellion. But his greatest achievement was that he put down the Muslim Rebellion which for another period of fourteen years, from 1864–78, devastated the provinces of Shensi and Kansu. Sinkiang, under a leader of ability, Yakub Beg, became virtually independent and began to enter into relations with foreign Powers. The situation that faced the Manchu Empire was in many ways more critical than the one caused by the Taiping Rebellion. The Taiping movement was a revolt of the Chinese. Its success would only have affected the dynasty. The Muslim Rebellion of the north-west was, on the other hand, a revolt against China. The British in India and the Russians in Central Asia had begun to show an interest in what was happening near their borders. For a time it seemed that the work of Kang Hsi and Chien Lung in bringing this great territory within the Chinese Dominion would be undone. From this dismemberment Tso Tsung-tang saved the Empire. He moved slowly into the area, pacifying as he went and making careful preparation before advancing. Showing extreme resourcefulness, tact and statesmanship, and, when required, unequalled ruthlessness, Tso penetrated into Sinkiang and destroyed the new State that Yakub Beg had founded. In 1878 Kashgar and Yarkand surrendered and the Chinese were again masters of Sinkiang.[1]

With Li Hung-chang's[2] work, which was mainly in the diplomatic field, extending from the time of the Tientsin incident in 1870 to the Boxer Protocol in 1901, we shall have to deal as we proceed with our own narrative. Here it is sufficient to say that, like his senior and protector Tseng, it was by independent and patriotic action against the Taipings that Li Hung-chang came into prominence. On receiving information of this action, Tseng Kuo-fan took him under his own command. It was Li who was associated, first, with the American adventurer Ward and, later, with Gordon in the organization of a Western-style army. Thus, early in his official career, he came into contact with the foreigners, an experience which was to stand him in good stead during the three decades of tortuous diplomacy in which he had to be the chief negotiator of the weaker and often defeated side.

From the defeat of the Taiping and Nienfei Rebellions (1865) to the

[1] In 1876, when Tso was putting down the rebellion, the British Foreign Office even suggested to the Chinese envoy, Kung Sung-Tao, that it would be in the interest of China to set up a Muslim kingdom in Central Asia under Yakub Beg, to which Tso replied that if Britain wanted a Muslim State, she should furnish the territory in India (Bales, pp. 360–1).

[2] There are four biographies of Li Hung-chang: the best is J. O. P. Bland's, 1917, London. Also see R. K. Douglas, *Li Hung-chang and Mr A. Little*, 1903.

Sino-Japanese War in 1895 the Empire had an appearance of great prosperity. Peace reigned from one end of China to another and, after the failure of the Sinkiang Rebellion, even in border areas. There was a great revival of trade and the finances of the State appeared to be sound. A band of experienced officials, the last generation of great mandarins, administered the country with a fair amount of efficiency. Internally, the prestige of the dynasty and of the Empire stood high. There were no serious complications with foreign Powers, though the Tientsin incident and the French action that followed gave a preview of what was to happen.

But during this period the foreign Powers were building up the structure of relationship which was to reduce China to impotence and render it a helpless prey to their aggression. Under the cover of the clauses of the treaty of Tientsin, the Western Powers, and especially England, were quietly and unostentatiously forging political, commercial and economic fetters which limited the sovereignty of the Central Government, undermined its authority in the provinces and established over wide areas an economic influence which converted them into British 'protectorates'. At the same time, the United States and France were putting into effect a planned spiritual aggression, which in one case was meant to conquer China for Christ and American trade, and in the other case for the Catholic church and French political influence. The methods used by the Powers which within twenty years brought them much political profit and converted China to the position of a semi-colonial area are worth close examination.

Under the treaties at the ports opened to trade, foreigners had been permitted to reside and do business. The ports—the most important of which were Canton, Swatow, Amoy, Foochow, Ningpo, Shanghai, Tsingtao, Chefoo and Tientsin—were spread over the entire coast of China from Canton in the south to Tientsin in the north. But apart from the ports on the coast, many towns on the Yangtze from Chinkiang to Chungking, including Nanking and Hankow, for a distance of nearly 1,000 miles in the interior, were considered treaty ports. At these ports the foreigners, on the basis of the clause permitting them to reside and trade, began slowly and quietly to build 'settlements' and claim the right to set up municipal establishments and courts. Thus, at Hankow, many hundred miles up the Yangtze, there came into existence British, French, German and Russian settlements. Since the foreigners enjoyed extra-territoriality, they set up courts in these places. In a few years, spread all over China were small bits of territory, from which Chinese authority and jurisdiction were ousted and which in some cases became the centres of every kind of illegal traffic.

Besides these 'settlements' there were the concessions, the most important of which were the International and French concessions in Shanghai, the British, Italian and German (later Japanese) concessions in Tientsin and the British and French concessions at Canton. The story of the rise (and fall) of the International concession at Shanghai, a fascinating romance of adventure, commercial spirit, Western co-operative methods of administration, police and business management, together with international sharp practice, aggrandisement at the expense of the weak and toleration of vice and malpractices of all kinds, will serve to epitomize this chapter of Western relations with China. Shanghai, in 1842, was a small, walled city at the mouth of the Hwangpu River, which joins up with the Yangtze at its mouth. Its importance arose from its position at the mouth of the Yangtze Valley and in the treaty of 1842 it was included in the list of five ports open to foreign residence and trade. By agreement, the British, French and later American Consuls acquired from the local authorities 'settlements', i.e. areas marked out for the residence of their nationals. Consulates came into existence and along with them the agencies of the firms engaged in China trade. There was no question of any jurisdiction over the territory, but the British consular officials immediately set about establishing an embryonic municipality, which body also set up committees for various affairs. During the next twenty years they consolidated their position and in 1869 the Municipal Committee on its own authority issued what were called the Land Regulations under which they assumed to themselves the right to levy rates and taxes and the control of sanitation and police. This was the so-called self-created charter of Shanghai which Mr Justice Feetham with a curious and peculiarly South African form of logic declared as possessing the sanctity of a treaty.

Under the Land Regulations the Shanghai Municipal Council had claimed the right to construct roads leading out of the settlement. This provided cover for an extension of the 'rights' claimed by the municipality. Thus larger territorial claims were gradually advanced. Briefly, within the first twenty years after the Treaty of Tientsin, in the period between 1860 and 1880, 'the international settlement' of Shanghai developed into a sovereign city State, independent of China, where the Chinese police were not allowed to function, where Chinese courts had no jurisdiction even over its own subjects, where Chinese laws did not apply and, what is worse, where the Chinese were treated as members of an inferior race with no rights and a prominently displayed notice announced that 'Chinese and dogs were not allowed inside a park'. The American and British settlements had been amalgamated and what was known as the international city had arisen, housing many thousand foreigners and a large Chinese population.

The growth of this financial and commercial megalopolis had a profound, if imperceptible, effect on China. By a process similar to the one we examined in India at the end of the eighteenth century, the economic life of the country, which had for centuries been land-based, began now to flow into the coastal cities of China especially to Shanghai. The comprador economy of this city soon produced a class of merchants, middlemen, bankers and agents of foreign firms whose financial power when allied to the old merchant guilds became immensely powerful in relation to the internal conditions of China—as indeed in similar circumstances the Seths or merchants of the port cities of India had become in relation to the Mongul Empire in India. Shanghai in fact became a rival capital to Peking.

Apart from this development of concessions and settlements dotted all over China, the foreign Powers began at this period also to exercise authority over the great internal waterways. The Treaty of Tientsin (Article 52) provided that British ships of war, coming for no hostile purpose or being engaged in the pursuit of pirates, should be at liberty to visit all ports within the dominions of the Emperor of China. Overriding the Chinese point of view that this clause gave to the British warships only the right to visit ports which were open to foreign shipping, the British authorities, and following them the other Great Powers, maintained fleets of gunboats to patrol the Canton River and the Yangtze. The area from Chungking to Shanghai, a distance of 1,500 miles right across the centre of China, was thus made subject to the control of foreign navies. Nothing could make it clearer how grossly the Western Powers abused their treaty rights than this singular extension of what was meant to be a right to visit ports. Britain even maintained an officer with the curious title of Rear-Admiral Yangtze, and it may help us to understand the Chinese point of view if it is recalled how angry Britain was when Wilhelm II styled himself Admiral of the Atlantic, though that ocean had never been claimed to be an inland waterway. The fleet of gunboats that cruised up and down the Yangtze was a standing temptation for the local representatives of the Great Powers to give point to their often unreasonable demands by a demonstration or the threat of a bombardment. Many instances could be given of this kind of 'gunboat diplomacy' in the interests of missionaries, private debtors and even ordinary Christian converts.

Apart from cases involving only local intervention, in two notorious cases gunboat diplomacy in the interests of Christians and missionaries was also utilized for the assertion of political authority. In 1867, when the missionaries opened a house in one of the interior towns, Yangchow, the local population rose against them and rioted in the city. The mission house was burnt down, though none of the missionaries was killed. On this, after some attempt to browbeat the officials, the British Consul at

Shanghai, Medhurst, went to Nanking escorted by four ships of war and threatened the Viceroy and secured the dismissal of the magistrate of the locality where the riot had occurred. Christ had been vindicated and the power of the British gunboat demonstrated.

France was not to be outdone. French bishops began assuming authority and writing directly to the Tsungli Yamen – the Chinese equivalent of the Foreign Office – about the interests of their missions. On the excuse of the pillaging of two mission houses far in the interior Comte de Roche Chouart, the French Chargé d'Affiaires, visited the Viceroy at Nanking escorted by two warships sailing up the Yangtze.

The structure of foreign rights in China was based on extra-territoriality of the nations of the treaty Powers. In the settlements and concessions the Consuls made the most extravagant claims of jurisdiction, the British Consul in one place claiming without success to exercise police authority even on American nationals resident within a British settlement. Police jurisdiction meant constables, jails, courts of appeal, etc., and the British, of course, maintained the entire paraphernalia with a supreme court in Shanghai. But many of the other Powers did not have these facilities. Appeals from other consular courts were to the capitals in Europe. All the Consuls of the Great Powers claimed a kind of fiduciary interest in the trial of Europeans who had no extra-territorial rights. All this might have been overlooked, as it was confined to limited areas, but for the position that the missionaries arrogated to themselves in the interior and the protection that the converts claimed. Under the treaties, missionaries had only been given the right to reside and acquire property anywhere they liked. But the French had inserted a clause into their treaty without the knowledge of the Chinese, by which France claimed a general right of protection over Catholics including Chinese converts. In any case, it was claimed that the clause in the treaties with the other Powers that Chinese converts should not be persecuted gave the right to foreign Consuls to intervene in litigation in which Chinese Christians were parties. This question will be dealt with in some detail in a later chapter. What is important to emphasize here is that between 1865 and 1885, not only the Catholics and the China Inland Mission but numerous other sectarian bodies had penetrated into the farthest corners of China taking with them their own extra-territoriality and their claims to protect the Chinese Christians. Actually this proved to be a greater violation of China's sovereignty and her authority over her own people than even the 'concessions', settlements and territorial aggrandisements.

Also during this period, the Powers started on the policy of detaching from China states which had accepted her suzerainty. Cambodia and Annam were the first to go. In 1886, Upper Burma was annexed. China was forced to agree to both these changes. The pressure on the periphery was to continue till China recovered her full sovereignty after the Second Great War, but it is perhaps desirable to emphasize in view of the foreign criticism of Japanese action in Korea, Manchuria and Mongolia, that the pattern of aggression on outlying territories and their gradual detachment from China was originally set by France in respect of Cambodia, Annam and Tongking and followed by Britain in regard to Burma.

The attitude of the Powers to China at this time can be best understood in the light of the incident known as the Tientsin massacre. The first of these is important as it is the real prelude to the attacks on China's authority which every Power was to try later with success.

On the site of a temple in Tientsin, which was also an imperial palace, the French, without any legal title, erected a Roman Catholic Cathedral in 1869. The behaviour of the French authorities in general during the ten years they were established in Tientsin before the incident is tersely described by the American historian Morse: 'It is not too much to say that at Tientsin, the French nation and the Catholic missionaries as a whole were detested.'[1] At Tientsin was also established an orphanage by a Catholic sisterhood. These sisters arranged for the payment of a sum for every child brought to the orphanage, that is in plain words established a kind of purchase system, encouraging the less scrupulous Chinese middlemen to kidnap children. Payments were also made for children to be baptized in the last stages of illness in the no doubt pious belief that death immediately after baptism would ensure safety of the soul. Naturally the Chinese public was greatly agitated by this procedure which incited people to kidnap children and also the system by which immediately after baptism so many children died and were buried in the Christian cemetery. At this time an epidemic also visited the orphanage and many children in the orphanage died. The Imperial Commissioner, to whom the matter was represented, took it up with the Consul. An agreement was reached that a committee of Chinese should inspect the institution. But here the French Consul, feeling that his authority was being infringed, interfered and opposed any idea of inspection. Public resentment ran high and the following extract from the report of the Imperial Commissioner will show the temper and attitude of the Consul. 'On going out to receive him (the Consul) I saw the Consul, whose demeanour was furious, had two pistols in his belt and that a foreigner who accompanied him was armed with a sword. They rushed towards me and as soon as M. Fontainer came up to me he began talking in an indecorous manner, drew a pistol from his belt and fired it in my presence. The shot fortunately did not take effect and he was seized. To avoid a personal collision I withdrew.' The impetuous Consul while

[1] See Morse and MacNair, *International Relations*, p. 404.

returning from the Yamen fired on the crowd and was murdered. Following this, the crowd set fire to the cathedral and the Christian institutions were destroyed. On June 21, 1870, the crowd went out of hand and took vengeance on the French.

The occasion was utilized by the Powers to present a collective note to the Peking Government. This was followed by the arrival in Tientsin of a French admiral with men-of-war, soon joined by ships of the British, American and Italian Navies. The Western Powers had lined up. The French demands, which the other Powers supported, included death by decapitation of the officials concerned, and if that demand was not acceded to the French Consul threatened that he would hand over the charge of the situation to the naval authorities. War had just been declared between France and Germany and the French envoy, like his masters in Paris, was hoping for a victory which would re-establish the pre-eminence of France. The Chinese, while refusing to decapitate the officials without trial, offered to execute twenty rioters and banish the officials. The representatives of Prussia (then at war with France), England, Russia and America sent again a collective note saying this offer was unsatisfactory! Li Hung-chang, who in the meantime had been appointed Viceroy of Chihli and in that capacity was responsible for the negotiations, stood firm and a settlement was effected mainly because France lay stricken after the German war. Now China realized that the Powers were united against her.

This brief analysis will show that the twenty-five years, beginning with the suppression of the Taiping Rebellion, were the most crucial in the history of China's relations with the West. The apparent prosperity of the country was deceptive. While the treaty ports were flourishing, the internal economy of the country was moving towards a collapse. True, China had no debts to pay, but actually during this period Chinese authority had been so undermined and the prestige of the Government with its own people so completely destroyed that it may well be said to have prepared the ground for the Walpurgis night of imperialism, which was witnessed in the decade following the Sino-Japanese War in 1895.

One major complication which rendered diplomatic relations between China and the Western nations, led by Britain, extremely difficult was the attitude of the British mercantile community. The chimera of inexhaustible trade had drawn them into the interior. The central highway of China, the Yangtze, had now been opened. 'Settlements' and trading establishments existed in every important city. But for some reason the results were bitterly disappointing. The fabulous China trade did not materialize.

The mercantile community attributed their failure to the opposition of the Chinese officials and to vexatious imposts. Their remedy, pressed on the British Government through every source open to them, was for the exercise of compulsion on China to buy British goods. Their cry was 'treaty enforcement', of direct dealing with the Chinese consumers. Their openly expressed desire was that the whole country should be enlarged into a vast treaty port, with all authority vested in local officials, in dealing with whom the Consuls were to be given the right of calling up the gunboats as a final argument. They pleaded frankly for the establishment of a protectorate at least over the Yangtze Valley and promised in that case that Lancashire would have an unlimited market, and that 'all the mills of Lancashire', as Pottinger said, 'could not be making stocking stuff sufficient for one of its provinces'.

That this was nothing but vain and foolish optimism, experienced consular officers did not fail to point out. Mitchell, the Assistant Magistrate at Hong Kong, made a remarkable analysis of the Chinese commercial prospects which explained to the Foreign Office the absurdity of the mercantile claim. After pointing out how strange it seemed that ten years after the restrictions were removed China did not consume one-half of what Holland consumed, Mitchell explained: 'When we opened the seaboard provinces of this country to British trade ten years ago, the most preposterous notions were formed as to the demand that was to spring up for our manufacture. Our friends in Manchester and their counterpart on the spot here . . . seem to have all gone mad together upon the idea of an open trade with "three or four hundred millions of human beings".'

One of the Consuls, after an experience of ten years, reported that, 'with the exception of our own domestics I have never yet seen a Chinaman wearing a garment of our long cloth, who had to get his daily bread by his daily labour'. Other consular officials warned the British Foreign Office regularly against 'any hope of supplanting the sturdy household thrift of the Chinese', but the treaty port merchants thought otherwise. Their conviction was that the ordinary Chinese were being prevented by the mandarins from buying freely, and that if they, the merchants, could be given a free hand, one province of China could consume all that Lancashire could produce and more.

Though the Foreign Office was ultimately persuaded of the correctness of the view put forward by their own consular officers, the pressure of mercantile opinion was sufficiently strong at all times to make compromises necessary. But the failure of the commercial dream remained an unpleasant factor till the beginning of the railway age, when investment rather than trade became the object of British financial interests.

An unexpected result of the extension of foreign business into the interior was the growth of a powerful commercial Chinese class. In 1869, Sir Rutherford Alcock drew attention to the fact that the distribution of trade in the interior was being taken over by the Chinese merchants. The diversion of foreign trade at Amoy to Chinese merchants was noted by the Consul, and at Foochow it was reported that 'owing to superior knowledge of language and markets and lower overhead charges, the Chinese were almost monopolizing the business of distribution'. A similar position, it will be remembered, had existed in India from the very beginning, and after British authority was established it was the Indian merchants who handled the distribution of British goods. The growth of this powerful commercial class, not only in the coastal areas but along the entire Yangtze Valley, was a social revolution of major significance, as we shall see later.

There is another aspect of this question which requires mention before we leave this period, and that was the establishment of the Chinese maritime customs service. The Rules of Trade attached to the Treaty of Tientsin had laid down that at the open ports customs duties should be levied on a uniform basis, and that foreigners should be appointed at the discretion of the Chinese to assist in this administration. In 1860, under the convention of Peking, when the indemnities exacted from China were made a charge on the customs revenue, the foreign representatives came to have a direct interest as mortgagees in the customs administration. In 1863, Robert Hart, an Irishman, was appointed to the post of Inspector-General of the maritime customs service, a department nominally belonging to the Chinese Government, but administered almost exclusively by foreigners belonging to every nationality in the West. That the service was honest and efficient is recognized, but that it constituted a visible limitation of Chinese authority is too often forgotten.

It is, however, important to note that the British mercantile community looked upon this service, administered by foreigners themselves, as a major obstacle to the growth of their trade. In numerous communications, the action of the customs authorities in enforcing laws was held up as unpatriotic, anti-European and generally as something which the Powers should oppose. The Shanghai and Hong Kong merchants even proclaimed the view that smuggling was not an offence against Chinese laws, but only against the treaty and that Chinese customs authorities therefore could not deal with such offences without consular approval.

The attitude of Europeans in general towards China and the Chinese may be judged from the development of what is known as the 'Pig Trade'. From 1847 Chinese labourers were illegally, and against the protests of the Imperial Government, being shipped to mines, estates and plantations in the colonies in place of slave labour. To San Francisco alone 108,471 Chinese labourers had been taken before 1863. The Portuguese and Spanish possessions and Australia and California were the main receiving areas. The recruitment of labourers was through contractors who received a capitation fee for every person brought to the depot, and once the miserable labourers were within the premises of the depot nothing could save them. They were transported in ships known as 'floating hells' and the rate of mortality among the passengers was often as high as forty-five per cent. This system of semi-slave traffic where the recruiting was based on abduction and kidnapping (in 1859 the Viceroy at Canton decapitated eight convicted kidnappers) led to incalculable scandals. When the Chinese authorities insisted on enforcing some kind of regulation as a condition of repealing the decree prohibiting emigration, the trade was transferred to Macao, from which microscopic colony in a single year 5,207 Chinese labourers, kidnapped from China, were shipped to Cuba, and 8,417 to Peru.

It was also during this period that China finally took the decision of establishing diplomatic missions abroad. The first step taken in this connection was the curious Burlinghame Mission. Anson Burlinghame, who had been American Minister at Peking, was, on his retirement, appointed as a roving ambassador for China and accredited to all the courts of the West. Burlinghame first reached America with an impressive retinue and was well received. He negotiated there a treaty on the basis of equality. It also contained clauses upholding the territorial integrity of China and providing for reciprocal rights of trade and residence. Burlinghame, having been the American Minister himself, knew the methods of Western diplomacy in regard to China, and while in London he asked for assurances that undue pressure would not be exercised to secure rights which infringed China's sovereignty. Unfortunately, before his mission could be completed, Burlinghame died in St Petersburg. His mission was important from two points of view. In the first place he was able to secure assurances both from America and England that they would deal only with the Central Government at Peking, and the danger that existed at one time of the Powers directly negotiating with viceroys and thus securing a dissolution of the central authority on which British mercantile opinion was insistent was avoided. The Shanghai merchants' refrain at this time was 'when will the Foreign Office realize that China was a confederation of many States?' Secondly, the Chinese Government realized the necessity of establishing permanent diplomatic missions abroad; though it was only a few years later that the Peking authorities finally decided to open legations in Western capitals.

Thus the Empire continued, with its moral authority shattered, its hold on its own people weakened, and its diplomatic machinery abroad not firmly established, when a new chapter in her relations with the West was opened as a result of the Sino-Japanese conflict. It is unnecessary for our purpose to discuss the relations between Japan and China, except in so far as they affected the relations of either with Europe. Korea was a State over which China had exercised a general kind of suzerainty. The Emperor of Korea had willingly accepted the protection of, and paid his annual tribute to, the Peking court for over 300 years. Various European nations had tried to intervene in Korea, the French Chargé d'Affaires at one time (1866) even notifying the Chinese Foreign Office of the intention of his country to annex that kingdom. An invasion was actually carried out and after an indecisive campaign France was compelled to abandon her schemes. Thereafter the Koreans resisted the attempts of all Powers to force them into friendly relations. The only serious effort was the one made by the Americans in May 1871, when an American admiral, receiving no response to a demand opened fire, captured the coastal fortifications and killed a few Koreans, but finding that this action had not created the impression he had hoped for withdrew in disappointment. The only effect of the American action was a formal appeal by the Korean Government to the Chinese Emperor for effective protection.

It is at this time that Japan stepped upon the stage. She had also some claims on Korea, as it had been customary for the Korean monarchs to send missions on formal occasions bearing tributes to the Japanese Emperor. A mission which Japan had sent in 1868 had been treated rather unceremoniously; and similar treatment was meted out again two years later. This led to a demand in Japan for a punitive expedition to Korea and, though feeling ran high, the Emperor decided in favour of peace. In 1876, however, Japan was able to force a treaty on Korea, under which it was stated that Korea was completely and absolutely independent, thereby opening the door for Japanese action later.

The Koreans, however, continued to recognize China as the Sovereign State, and after the establishment of foreign legations in Seoul an intense diplomatic struggle began in the capital. By 1890 the Japanese were getting ready to force a decision, if necessary, and the occasion presented itself in a revolt staged by an anti-foreign society which seemed to be particularly directed against Japan. The revolt, however, soon became a rebellion which the Korean Government was unable to put down. The Seoul Cabinet therefore appealed to China as the protecting Power. The Chinese responded to the appeal by sending a small force. The Japanese also sent their marines. After a short period of preliminary negotiations Japan announced her decision to 'reform Korea'. The Korean Government, itself anxious to maintain the right to be protected by China, was not agreeable to this forced reformation and the Japanese attacked the palace, seized the royal family and confined them in the Japanese Legation.

The war that followed was short and swift. Both on land and on sea the Chinese were defeated decisively. After defeating the land forces in Korea, the Japanese crossed the Yalu River and invaded Manchuria, while the fleet moved into Dairen and invested Port Arthur. The Chinese now offered to negotiate, but the Japanese, desirous of settling other issues also, declined the intervention of the Powers. The Chinese fleet, shut up in Wei-hai-wei, surrendered and the mainland of China itself was invaded. Realizing that foreign intervention would not help her the Peking Government sued for peace, and Li Hung-chang was sent as special ambassador to negotiate the terms. The outcome was the Treaty of Shimonoseki, under which China recognized the independence of Korea, ceded Formosa and the Pescadores and the Liaotung Peninsula in Manchuria, besides agreeing to an indemnity of 200,000,000 taels. Japan also insisted on being given all the privileges, including extra-territoriality, which the European Powers enjoyed. It would appear that Li Hung-chang, before his departure for conducting peace negotiations, had already been in contact with the Russian Ambassador and had received some assurance from him of intervention in case Japan demanded territorial concessions in China.[1] Before he signed the treaty he had also received assurances from Detering, his agent in Berlin, that Russia had persuaded the German Foreign Office to support her action. In any case eight days after the treaty was signed, Russia, France and Germany joined in a demand that the Liaotung Peninsula be returned to China, a demand to which Japan yielded reluctantly.

The Treaty of Shimonoseki is a turning-point in the history of China's relations with the West. The territorial loss to China was not very great. The suzerainty over Korea was no doubt important, but the Chinese had not previously attached much significance to it. They could have overlooked the loss of Formosa and the Pescadores, but what was infinitely more serious than all this was the irretrievable damage inflicted on her international position from which she did not recover fully till half a century later. It was clear to all that corruption had eaten into her vitals (actually the navy had an insufficient supply of ammunition and could not therefore fight and battleships had to be used as transports); that her administration had become altogether inefficient; that the court, immersed in its pleasures and dominated by ignorant and debased eunuchs, was unable to give any leadership to the country; that the old classes had lost much of their prestige and authority as a result of the commercial economy of the ports; finally, that China was totally helpless before any kind of foreign aggression.

A new complication which was to be the undoing of the country was introduced by the treaty with the Japanese. An immense indemnity had

[1] See J. O. P. Bland: *Li Hung-chang*. London, 1917, pp. 179–80.

to be paid. The extravagance of the court and the expenses of the war had left the treasury empty. A loan was therefore negotiated in which French and Russian banks, under the guarantee of the Tsarist Government, agreed to advance the money. Other Powers, especially England and Germany, protested and insisted on lending money to China, nominally for reconstruction also. These loans were charged to the customs, and the salt and likin revenues of the Yangtze Valley were also pledged to cover the debt charges. This ushered in the period of control by loans.

The pattern of events that followed is difficult to delineate in detail, but easy to describe in general outline. Every European Power, great and small, began to press Peking for concessions. Railway construction was the first programme. We have already seen the shattered dream of commercial expansion. An easier way of profit, with at least limited political control, now seemed to open with the prospect of railway concessions. Even in the 'nineties the China market had shown no notable expansion. In 1894, for example, the intake of Lancashire goods in China was less than twenty per cent of that of India. The big business interests, led by the Hong Kong and Shanghai Banking Corporation, were therefore turning to the export of capital as the most profitable business in China. The French in the south (Yunnan and the three southern provinces), the Belgians (Peking-Hankow), the Americans (Hankow-Canton), the Russians (Manchuria), the British (in the Yangtze Valley and under the cover of an Anglo-Italian syndicate in Shansi) – all these, within the three crucial years of 1896–9, parcelled up the Chinese territory under the control of various European States, Germany, at this time the most powerful country in Europe, felt left out in all this loot and scramble and decided to carve out an empire for herself in China. On the classic pretext of the murder of two German missionaries (1892) by bandits, the Germans landed troops, expelled the Chinese garrison from Tsingtao, and occupied the port. Later, the German Minister presented the demands of his Government which, apart from indemnity, punishment of officials, erection of tablets and other recognized Western formulae, asked for the sole right to construct railways and open mines in Shantung and for the lease of Kiaochow as a naval station.

Other Powers immediately followed with demands of a similar nature. France first thought out and enunciated what may be described as the doctrine of 'soldering'. The idea was simple. Indo-China being a French possession, France demanded that the areas adjacent to it should be 'soldered' to her. The great province of Yunnan was to be connected to Tongking by a railway. In 1899, Kwangchow Bay with its dependencies was taken over as a naval base. Kwangsi, Yunnan, Kweichow and

Szechuan, in fact over one-fourth of the total area of China proper was to be 'soldered' to Indo-China. French imagination saw a greater empire than that of the British in India in the making. The British were naturally alarmed. The China Association of London in a letter to Lord Salisbury declared: 'Holding the opinion that these several railways are so many political stakes driven into regions, which an endeavour will be made one day to encircle by a cordon, the Association has noted with great regret the admission of French interests in a province which is the hinterland of Hong Kong.' The British merchants looked upon South China as a privileged area of political influence and trade, a mere hinterland of Hong Kong.

The doctrine of the 'spheres of influence' was formally recognized by Britain in 1899, she herself claiming wide and exclusive authority in the entire Yangtze Valley. With what high-handedness Britain upheld this claim may be seen from the action she took in the matter of the Peking-Hankow railway concessions. The Chinese Government had agreed to allow a Belgian company to build this line. When the British Minister was informed of this he demanded that his country should immediately receive 'the concessions which she had demanded on terms identical with those of the Peking-Hankow agreement'. Otherwise, it was threateningly added, the Chinese Government will be considered as having shown deliberate hostility against this country and 'we shall act accordingly'.

Thus began a series of manoeuvres the object of which was to stake claims for the future. This was secured by what was described as a declaration of non-alienation. The French again started the ball rolling by asking that China should declare that she would not alienate the island of Hainan to any other Power, Britain asked for a similar assurance in regard to the Uangtze Valley, and Japan asked for the Fukien coast, opposite Formosa. Russia occupied Port Arthur and Britain countered it by occupying Wei-hai-wei. Claims were also put forward for permanent national rights in regard to the headship of the customs and salt administration. Italy, feeling that she had been left out of the scramble, demanded a naval station in Shamen Bay in Chekiang, but this time China refused and declared that she would resist by force any further violation of her territory.

Thus within three short years after the treaty with Japan, China was effectively parcelled up for economic activity, for political influence and for railway development. Briefly, Yunnan and the area bordering on Indo-China were claimed to be a French sphere: Canton and the Yangtze Valley and the large area in between were claimed by the British; Russia was established in Manchuria, Germany controlled Shantung and Japan looked to Fu-kien. Foreign controlled railways intersected the country. In the coastal and inland waters foreign shipping operated freely.

The 'spheres of influence' for which the British merchants had been pressing for so long a time had at last materialized. A further doctrine of the 'Balance of Influence', by which it was meant that if one Power obtained an extra concession others should be given something equal to balance it, was also promulgated. Unfortunately for the West this programme of breaking up China met with a sudden check by the declaration of the United States of what came to be known as the 'open door' policy. By the acquisition of the Philippines, the United States had become a major Power in the Pacific, and when the scramble for concessions was at its highest the American Secretary of State demanded formal assurances from all interested Powers that the claim of 'spheres of influence' would not affect the treaty rights of other nations, that the collection of customs duty everywhere be by the Chinese authorities, that no preferential harbour dues or railway charges should benefit the subjects of any Power'. This was frankly a policy meant to safeguard American commercial interests in China in areas which were fast passing into the exclusive influence of other Powers. But, indirectly, it helped to maintain the unity of China, especially the provision that the collection of customs duty everywhere would be by the Chinese. The far-reaching consequences of this declaration were not recognized immediately, for no one in 1899 foresaw the leading role that America was destined to play in the Far East during the next half-century.

The danger of partition was apparent to all and even the court finally woke up to it. The viceroys of provinces were specially directed to be ready to repel aggression. The presence in Chinese waters of Italian cruisers as well as the building up of a considerable German force in Kiaochow had alarmed the authorities. Peking showed a brave front all through 1899, and the old Dowager seemed to have gained new strength. A Reform movement of Kuang Hsu having failed, the Empress had by a *coup d'état* assumed the full authority which she had only nominally renounced. All the reactionary forces gathered round her, but the Powers knew that the court was helpless and that the administration could be moulded to suit the policies of foreign Powers. But what the foreign dignitaries under-estimated was the patriotism and temper of the Chinese people. The countryside arose in frenzied anger and out of the dark recess of uneducated and superstitious but intensely patriotic minds was born the movement known as the Society of Harmonious Fists (Boxers) which began to show itself in the provinces. The anger of the people was primarily against the missionaries who swarmed the countryside and their converts. The missionaries were looked upon as the advance agents of imperialism and the Christian converts as a fifth column. The history of twenty years, the French aggression following the incidents in Tientsin, the British attempts to wrest concessions after the Margary murder and the continuing pressure on the Peking court for concessions of all kinds—and, above all, the facile assumption of the Powers that China was there to be divided up had aroused the patriotism of the common man. The movement first showed itself in Shantung. 'Cherish the dynasty, exterminate the foreigner' was the motto of the Boxers—the same policy which the pure Shinto sect had preached in Japan in the period prior to the Meiji restoration. The movement, which was essentially based on popular feeling, found support among some of the higher officials who were not in direct contact with foreigners, especially Yu Hsien, Governor of Shantung, and the patronage of the Manchu princes Ching and Tuan. The Empress also finally veered round to their side. By January 1900, the Boxer movement had not only gained immense popular strength but the support of the Empress herself.

That the Boxer movement was essentially a national and patriotic reaction, though viewed by Westerners as fanatical xenophobia, can hardly be doubted. Even Jung Lu, who was convinced of its unwisdom, in a letter confesses that the northern Boxers were not inspired by lust of plunder but by a religious frenzy. The Viceroy, Li Hung-chang, in his Memorial to the Throne protesting against the encouragement given to the Boxers, says: 'Craven would be the man who would not seek to improve our defences and shameless would be he who would not long for the day of reckoning. . . . Needless for me to say how greatly I would rejoice were it possible for China to enter upon a glorious and triumphant war.'[1] The Diary of His Excellency Chang Shan, a day-to-day record of events and impressions by a distinguished scholar and high official, clearly shows that orthodox Chinese opinion viewed the movement with sympathy as a genuine patriotic outburst.

The strength of this national movement alarmed the Powers, who now went to the extent of demanding the suppression of the Boxers, it being suggested that an imperial decree should be issued distinctly stating 'that to belong to either of these societies or to harbour any of its members is a criminal offence against the laws of China'. It was then even sought to make popular opposition to foreign aggression and missionary work an offence. But this unfortunate move, instead of weakening the Boxers, only made it all the more clear to them that the foreign Powers were bent on destroying China. The court, faced with the united opposition of foreign Powers, issued orders to the Viceroy of Chihli and the Governor of Shantung to suppress the movement. The Viceroy of Chihli did in fact issue such a proclamation. But this did not

[1] Bland: *Li Hung-chang*, p. 306.

satisfy the European envoys. They ordered a naval demonstration in the Gulf of Chihli to overawe the court. But it was not the court they were dealing with, but an infuriated people.

In May the Boxers began to take matters into their own hands and swarmed into Peking. Their attention was directed mainly against Chinese converts or, as they called them, 'the secondary barbarians'. The foreign diplomatic missions sent for guards and military forces. The British landed a naval force at Tientsin. The situation both in Peking and in Tientsin grew steadily worse, but the activities of the Boxers were directed mainly against the unwelcome missionaries. The representatives of the Powers felt that the time had come for action, and the admirals in Tientsin occupied the Taku forts by assault. After this act stray hostilities began in Tientsin and Taku, and in Peking the legations were besieged. The foreign community defended itself with heroism behind hastily erected barricades, but outside the legation quarter heavy toll was taken, especially of missionaries and Christians. In the interior also, except in areas where the viceroys were showing enough strength to put the movement down, mission buildings were pillaged and the workers massacred.

If the ignorant Chinese Boxers displayed cruelty in their treatment of missionaries and converts and committed outrages and atrocities, the behaviour of the European Powers at the time of their triumph was marked by an equally disgraceful exhibition of extreme vindictiveness. According to authenticated reports at the time, the troops of the allied Powers turned freebooters in Tientsin. 'Military raids,' writes one chronicler, 'were made in all directions and it is certain that the three shortest of the ten commandments were constantly violated on an extensive scale.' In Peking it was worse. The soldiers of the European Powers in the capital of China showed themselves in their true colours, shorn of even the veneer of civilization. Even Daniele Varé, a former Italian envoy and a staunch champion of imperialism, is forced to confess that 'the citizens of Peking suffered only a little less than if the town had been sacked by the Taiping rebels'.[1]

Peace was again negotiated by Li Hung-chang. The Powers exacted heavy penalties, and a cruel and humiliating peace, known as the Boxer Protocol, was forced on China. Apart from the punishment of offenders and the erection of a monument for the foolhardy German minister, the main clauses of this document provided for the suspension of the official examinations for five years in towns where the foreigners had been molested – a device meant to give a chance to the missionary-educated young men and Christians to be employed in service; prohi-

[1] Daniele Vare: *The Last of the Empresses.* John Murray, Albemarle dition, p. 205.

bition of the importation of arms and ammunition for two years; the payment by China of an indemnity of 450 million taels, approximately a little over 100 million pounds in annual instalments which were to end in 1940; reservation to foreigners (to the exclusion of Chinese) of the legation quarter and its defence by the legations themselves, with the right of stationing troops thereby in Peking itself; and the demolition of the Taku forts. The indemnity was to be secured on the revenues of the maritime customs, salt tax and the native customs; the Powers supposed that they could thereby ensure control by foreigners of this major department of administration. The humiliating clauses, like the erection of tablets, expiatory monuments in cemeteries, etc., were intended to increase the prestige of the foreigner.

The settlement bore witness to the double character of the Boxer uprising – the anti-missionary sentiment and the resentment against the Powers for the humiliations inflicted on China. The missionaries were amply provided for in the settlement. They were to receive a share of the indemnity, and the imperial examinations against which they had so long complained as the main obstacle to their intellectual domination were abolished for five years. The Powers were able to convert a portion of Peking into an armed camp and there, in the heart of the capital and overlooking the Forbidden City, they were able to lord it over the Chinese. But few foresaw that these extreme conditions carried the seeds of their own destruction; for it is to the Boxer Protocol that we can trace the extreme bitterness which characterized Chinese relationships with the West during the next fifty years.

The Dowager Empress who, when danger threatened Peking, had ignominiously fled in disguise to Sian, now returned by slow stages to reside once again in the Forbidden City. She had made up her mind that for the rest of her days she would not have any trouble with foreigners. She, the autocrat of China, was prepared to flatter the wives of diplomatists, even to receive missionary ladies, and generally be pleasant to everyone and pretend as if nothing had happened to disturb friendly relations. Indeed, the next few years added a sunset glow to her long reign. Though the Empire maintained only the semblance of sovereignty and was saddled with an enormous debt, it recovered sufficiently to have an air of prosperity. Also, the Far East soon became the centre of a great conflict – the Russo-Japanese War, which gave China a respite from the unwelcome attentions of the Great Powers. The Empress died in 1908 and was succeeded by Pu Yi with the regnal title of Hsuan Tung, but the dynasty, though it lingered on for three years before revolution overtook China, had ceased seriously to count.

The ten years between the Boxer settlement and the downfall of the Manchus constitutes the heyday of Western authority in China. The missionaries had practically established a monopoly control of education. The coastal areas where the foreigners held sway became the centre of a new life. Canton, Shanghai and Tientsin became the seats of financial and economic power, which was predominantly in European hands. The Yangtze was policed by foreign gunboats. The foreign consulates, lords and masters not only in their own territory but in territories larger than European States, felt a glow of satisfaction that by their prestige they were able to afford protection to all who sought it. But underneath all this a profound change was coming over China. New classes of Chinese, associated with European capital and enviously viewing the opportunities the foreigner enjoyed in their own country, had become a factor of importance in the economic life of the concessions. The growth of Chinese capitalism had been remarkable. In 1865 the Kiangnan shipyard had been established. In 1872 the China Merchants Steam Navigation Company was organized to compete with the monopoly that the foreigners were trying to establish in the coastal and river waters. Silk filatures, cotton mills, match factories and flour mills began to spring up in Shanghai and other coastal towns. These merchant leaders, though representing a comprador economy, disliked the privileges that the European businessmen enjoyed and were inclined to support the nationalist claims.

Revolutionary groups took advantage of the political freedom in the settlements. A powerful nationalist movement, unconnected with and indeed hostile to the reactionary imperial court, had shown signs of vigorous growth in these areas and had spread from there into the interior. Boycotts began to be used as a powerful weapon in political matters. In 1905 the Chinese in Canton started a large-scale boycott of America to protest against the treatment of the Chinese in the United States. In 1908 an even more vigorous boycott was enforced against the Japanese, which should have opened the eyes of the imperialist Powers to the strength of China's new nationalism. Groups of young Chinese students also had begun to go abroad for study, and the victory of Japan against the might of Tsarist Russia had finally and decisively broken the prestige of the European in Asia. Thus, when the Revolution started as a mutiny in Hankow and Wuchang on October 10, 1911, and the Manchu Dynasty fell without even striking a blow, few Europeans realized that what had fallen so ignominiously was not merely a monarchical system, rotten to the core, but the elaborate structure they had erected by force, fraud and cajolery over a period of seventy years. The ineffectiveness of the first few years of the Revolution concealed its effects for a time, but before a decade had elapsed the European system in China also began to crumble in the same manner as the Manchu monarchy had done, without resistance and without fight.

BIBLIOGRAPHICAL NOTE

The bibliography on China for this period is extensive, but one-sided. The following is fairly representative from the Western point of view:

Ballero, E.: *Overture de la Chine a l'influence française an cours des XIXe et XXe siècle.*
Brine, L.: *The Taiping Rebellion in China.*
Gros, Baron: *Negociations entre la France et la Chine en* 1860.
Hail, W. J.: *Tseng Kuo-fan and the Taiping Rebellion.* New Haven, 1927.
Parliamentary Papers: *The Taiping Rebellion.*
Colquhoun, A. R.: *English Policy in the Far East.*
Documents Diplomatiques: *Affairs en Chine.* Paris, 1885.
Jenkins, E.: *The Coolie, His Rights and Wrongs.* London, 1871.
Letters regarding the Tientsin Massacre. Shanghai, 1870.
Wheeler: *The Foreigner in China.* Chicago, 1881.
Williams: *Anson Burlinghame and the First Chinese Mission to the Foreign Powers.* N.Y., 1912.
Japan, 1853-64. Translated Satow. Tokyo, 1905.
Satow, E. M.: *Japan.* Cambridge Modern History.
Vladimir, F. J.: *China-Japan War.* London, 1896.

For the history of the Taipings see Hail: *Tseng Kuo-fan and the Taiping Rebellion.*

Lindlay, A. F.: *The History of the Taiping Revolution.*
Vizetelly, H.: *The Chinese Revolution,* 1853.
Li Hake (Egmont): *Events in the Taiping Rebellion.*
Bland, J. O. P.: *Li Hung-chang.* London, 1917.
Douglas, D. K.: *Li Hung-chang.* London, 1895.

The Boxer Rebellion is the subject of numerous books but there is no work which presents the Chinese view. The nearest approach to it is the *Diary of His Excellency Ching Chan* included in:

Bland and Buckhouse: *China under Empress Dowager.*
Beresford: Lord, C. *The Break-up of China.* London, 1899.
Clements, P. N.: *The Boxer Rebellion—A Political and Diplomatic Review.* N.Y., 1915.
d'Herrison: *Loot of the Imperial Palace.* Smithsonian Annual Institute Report, 1900.
Hart, R.: *The Peking Legation.* Shanghai, 1900.
Hewlett: *The Diary of the Siege of Peking Legations.*
Weale, Putnam: *Indiscreet Letters from Peking.*

The following books are also interesting about special aspects of China's relations with the West at this time:

Bau, M. J.: *Open Door Doctrine in Relation to China.*
Barry, A. J.: *Railway Expansion in China.* London, 1910.
Bland, J. O. P.: *Recent Events and Present Policies in China.* London, 1912.
Liu, S. S.: *Extraterritoriality: Its Rise and Decline.* N.Y., 1925.
Reinsch: *World Politics at the end of the Nineteenth Century as Influenced by the Oriental Situation.* London, 1900.
Stiger: *China and the Occident.* New Haven, 1927.
Wellington Koo: *Status of Aliens in China.*

CHAPTER 3

JAPAN

WE have already seen the efforts made by Russia, Britain and other Powers to enter into trade relations with Japan and the success with which the Shogunate had warded off these attempts. The conquest of California in 1844 brought the USA to the Pacific littoral and the report by the Committee of Naval Affairs of the Congress stated: 'The acquisition of California presents facilities of trade and commerce with China which should not be neglected.' By the middle of the century the American authorities decided that the time had come to force open the door that had for so long a time been effectively closed against the Westerners. Japan, of all Eastern nations, had greater knowledge about the intentions of the Western Powers and a fairer appreciation of their strength. As we have seen, there was a steadily increasing group of people who were interested in Western knowledge and who had applied the knowledge they had acquired with so much persistence and difficulty to the problems of national defence. The defeat of China in the war with Britain especially opened their eyes to this danger, and in the period following the Treaty of Nanking (1842) there was intense activity in Japan to strengthen the island's defences and to safeguard national independence. The Japanese knew that an effort would soon be made to open relations with them. In fact the Dutch king, in numerous personal letters to the Shogun, had urged on him the desirability of opening the country to foreign trade.

It was on July 8, 1853, that Commodore Perry with four men-of-war arrived before Uraga.[1] The Commodore had with him a letter from President Fillmore. The letter was sent on to the Shogun with expression of friendly intentions, but with a veiled threat that the Commodore would return next year with a larger force when he expected to receive a satisfactory reply. In his letter he said ominously: 'Many of the large ships of war destined to visit Japan have not yet arrived in these seas, though they are hourly expected; and the undersigned, as an evidence

[1] The most interesting account of Perry's expedition will be found in Arthur Wallworth's *Black Ships of Japan*, 1946.

of his friendly intentions, has brought but four ships of the smaller ones, designing, should it become necessary, to return to Yeddo in the ensuing spring with a much larger force.' Japan was to be opened by force to the 'American way of life'. The threat proved effective, for the Japanese knew their weakness and had also learnt the lesson of the Chinese War. Ii Kamon no Kami, the most far-seeing adviser that the Shogunate had at the time, pointed out in a memorial the impossibility of resisting the Western barbarian and suggested compliance till Japan by learning the secrets of the West was able to deal with them on terms of equality. So when Perry returned as he promised with a stronger force, he received the favourable reply he expected and a treaty was signed on March 31 which opened two ports to American trade where consular representation was also allowed. Great Britain, Russia and Holland followed in quick succession and signed similar treaties and received similar privileges.

By this agreement the Shogun had, however, weakened his own position. The nobles and the Samurai were almost unanimously against the policy of opening the country to the foreigners, and the Imperial court was also hostile. At this critical time the Shogun, under whose authority the treaties were negotiated, died, leaving no direct male heir. But before the confusion that the Shogun's demise had caused could be resolved, the first American envoy had arrived in Japan demanding an extension of the agreement with Perry. The Shogunate was in no position to resist, and the treaty concluded at Nagasaki contained the provision for the residence of Americans in the two treaty ports and the acceptance of the vicious principle of extra-territorial jurisdiction. The chain had been slipped on the Japanese as it previously had been on the Chinese. It should be added that the Japanese agreed to these provisions only after Townsend Harris had threatened the Japanese with serious consequences and drawn attention to the plight of the Chinese at Canton. The British and the French arrived on the scene almost immediately and demanded similar treaties by which these Powers and others who followed obtained the rights of diplomatic and consular representation and extra-territorial privileges.

The Conservatives and others who saw the independence of their country infringed in this manner looked now to the Throne to withhold the consent to these humiliating treaties. The Shogunate was thereby placed in an extremely awkward position, for anti-foreign and anti-Shogun feeling were mounting in the capital and the Emperor proved unexpectedly obstinate in withholding his approval. The cry of 'reverencing the throne and expelling the foreigner' resounded through Japan, and the Emperor agreed to ratify the agreements only on the understanding that the foreigners would be driven away within a few years. Between 1857 and 1863 public opinion became so excited that attacks on foreigners became frequent. The Shogunate, having agreed to a date for the expulsion of foreigners – June 24, 1863 – found itself caught between the devil and the deep sea, for the daimyos in the provinces, taking seriously the date fixed for the expulsion, began attacking foreign ships while the Shogun's Government was endeavouring to placate the foreign representatives. Responsible opinion, influenced to some extent by those who had returned from foreign missions, like Ito Hirobumi – the future Prince Ito – had come to realize that the old ideas based on closing the country to the barbarians were no longer valid, and a change of policy was necessary if Japan was to deal with the menace of foreign domination. The country became divided on this important issue, and the Shogunate, after an ineffective attempt to re-establish its authority, collapsed leaving the way open for the Meiji restoration (1868). Sansom well summarizes the position at the time in the following words:

'As seen by foreign students the history of the years between Perry's arrival and the Restoration of 1868 is concerned chiefly with the struggles of the Western Powers to induce Japan to emerge from seclusion. It is partly for that reason that a foreign writer can hardly avoid stressing the deceitful stratagems of the Japanese Government and the general atmosphere of xenophobia which pervaded the country in those days. But examined from a different viewpoint, these aspects are of incidental rather than primary importance. The true interest of the events related emerges when they are studied as evidence of the way in which a society can decay and renew itself without changing its essence. The arrival of foreigners demanding admission brought to light and even resolved certain conflicts latent in Japanese political life, and in that respect Western influence was clear and decisive.'[1]

The Meiji Restoration was intended as a clean break with the Shogunate and its policies, and yet it is significant to note that the Shogunate had in its last period sent abroad for study selected young men, and these when they returned formed the hard corps of the reforming sections. Again, the restored court had to depend a great deal on the officials of the Shogunate. Actually it was more of a political revolution which, by restoring the Emperor, gave to the new forces a greater freedom of operation and an unassailable source of authority, from behind which it was possible for those who were planning the new Japan to act with decisive effect. The leaders of the clans which displaced the Shogun had these advantages, and it is to their credit that they were able by cautious steps and careful planning to break the chains that had been placed on Japan.

[1] Sansom: *The Western World and Japan*, p. 325.

The position in Japan was not in theory different from what it had been in China after the Treaty of Nanking. Foreign settlements had been established in towns, ports had been designated by treaty as open to foreign traffic, and in Nagasaki the British even used force to secure proper facilities of navigation and docking in the interior. The records of the British Consulate published by Pakse-Smith show that the foreign officials had begun to take an aggressive attitude towards local authorities and had also quietly begun to bring in their own military guards. Municipal organizations were set up on the lines of those in Chinese treaty ports, and the foreign communities cherished the expectation that, with civil wars then raging inside Japan and with the Shogun's power daily declining, Japan would fall into the general pattern of Asian countries.

The Restoration and the policies pursued by the leaders of Japan in the twenty-five years from 1868-1893 had, however, the unexpected result of breaking Japan's chains completely and placing her in a position of total independence of European nations. The recovery of Japan is dealt with separately along with the movements of general Asian recovery. Here we shall deal only with the political and other transformations her leaders effected in order to remove the restrictions which had been placed on her sovereignty.

Soon after the Restoration the Emperor issued a decree (March 26, 1868) in which he announced to his people that it had been decided to have relations with foreign Powers and that the Imperial court would direct those relations and would fulfil the treaties in accordance with international law. 'It is therefore ordered that the whole nation do obey His Majesty's will and act in accordance therewith.' The Emperor also warned 'that all persons in future guilty of murdering foreigners or of committing any acts of violence towards them will not only be acting in opposition to His Majesty's express orders and be the cause of national misfortunes, but also committing the heinous offence of causing the national dignity and good faith to suffer in the eyes of the Treaty Powers with whom His Majesty has declared himself bound by relations of amity'.

It is clear that Japan had deliberately taken the step of maintaining friendly relations with the foreigners and was from the beginning anxious about national dignity. Many foreign observers had noted even at the time the difference between the Chinese and Japanese approaches to the West. 'One result,' Lord Elgin wrote, 'of the difference between the habits and the mode of feeling of the Chinese and the Japanese is undoubtedly this, that whereas the Chinese are steadily retrograding and will in all probability continue to do so until the Empire falls to pieces, the Japanese, if not actually in a state of progressive advancement, are in a condition to profit by the flood of light that is about to be poured into them and to take advantage of these improvements and inventions which the Chinese regard with contemptuous scorn, but which the Japanese will in all probability, when they come to know us better, be both able and anxious to adopt.'[1]

There is no doubt that the Japanese were alert and more fully informed of conditions in Europe than the Chinese were for a long time. They had a full appreciation of their own political and military weakness. Also they analysed early the causes of that weakness as backwardness in scientific and technical skill and ineffectiveness of political organization. These two they set themselves to remedy, and for that purpose they welcomed Western assistance and whole-heartedly devoted themselves not merely to the acquisition of Western technique but to an understanding of the scientific background necessary for material advancement. But apart from this objective, it is a mistake to which Western writers were prone, especially in the period before 1930, to think that Japan was impressed by the civilization of the West, or accepted its moral superiority. In fact, as we shall see in a later chapter, the Japanese leaders, while they were zealously and industriously adopting from the West the military, naval and other organizations and building up a State on modern lines, were at the same time taking every precaution to see that Western ideas did not penetrate into Japan. In fact, they were simultaneously building up a race theory, a political ideology and a national morality based on a denial of the basic principles of Western life.

Having, however, taken the decision that the Empire was to live in association with other States, Japan reconciled herself for the time to the limitations placed on her sovereignty and started on a career of reformation, the objects of which were in the first place to convince the Powers that the Japanese were in fact as good as the Westerners and had become civilized and were no longer 'native'; and, secondly, to build up the armed power so that she could at the first opportunity demonstrate her own strength. The first was the contribution of the Meiji reformers, acting on the advice of the astute observers whom they had sent to the West. The second had been recognized as urgent by the Shoguns themselves, who had begun with the advice of the Americans and the Dutch to reorganize their navy, and with the advice of the French to reorganize the army. Thus on April 18, 1868, a few months after the Restoration, Emperor Meiji was able to review the Japanese Navy which then consisted of six vessels and was commanded by Admiral Seigoin-no-Miya. It is interesting to note that apart from the flagship, *Tenriyo Maru*, and

[1] Quoted in *Western Barbarians and Japan* by M. Pakse-Smith. J. L. Thompson & Co. Kobe, 1930, p. 140.

another which had a Japanese name, the others had foreign names – the *Cosmopolité*, the *Gerard*, the *Coquette*, etc.[1]

Japan's desire to acquire Western knowledge, especially of a scientific and utilitarian character, was genuine. The devoted efforts of the Rangakusha – the group of scholars (Japanese scholars of Dutch) who with extraordinary persistence and industry kept up an interest in Western sciences – and the quite considerable information they collected and disseminated, show that at least a section of the Japanese intelligentsia, unlike the Chinese, had no prejudice against 'European' learning, and had come early to the conclusion that national security demanded the cultivation of Western sciences. C. R. Boxer in his *Jan Compagnie in Japan*[2] has brought together impressive evidence to show that in the fields of cartography, geography, military arts, medicine, botany and astronomy the Rangakusha had collected and disseminated much information. Therefore when the Emperor in his Charter Oath ordered his subjects to seek knowledge from everywhere, there was an enthusiasm for Western learning which was truly remarkable.

The Charter Oath of 1868 was the beginning of a great change. It is a short document of five clauses which reads as follows:

(i) An Assembly widely convoked shall be established and thus great stress shall be laid on public opinion.

(ii) The welfare of the whole nation shall be promoted by the everlasting efforts of both the governing and the governed classes.

(iii) All subjects, civil and military officers, as well as other people, shall do their best and never grow weary in accomplishing their legitimate purposes.

(iv) All absurd usages shall be abandoned: justice and righteousness shall regulate all actions.

(v) Knowledge shall be sought for all over the world and thus shall be strengthened the foundation of our imperial polity.

The concluding phrase, 'the strengthening of the foundation of imperial polity', gives the clue to the whole of this truly historic development. The statesmen of the Meiji era set themselves to the task with a wisdom, caution and vigour which were truly remarkable. Technical experts of every kind were invited and made welcome. Men of eminence in many fields came as advisers, teachers or as officials of departments. Over five thousand foreigners were employed at one time, not less than thirteen hundred of them being in high official positions. What Japan sought earnestly to learn from these experts of different nationalities was how to become a powerful nation able to claim equality with the strongest in the world. Educational methods and social organizations

[1] Pakse-Smith: *Western Barbarians and Japan*, pp. 280-1.

[2] The Hague. Martinius Nijhoff, 1936.

were no less important than military arts and scientific technique. Industrial production, improved agriculture, the mechanics of international trade, modern communications and shipping – these were undoubtedly of the greatest urgency and importance; but the Japanese realized that they must also have modern laws, courts and a political system in conformity with modern conditions.

All this they set about to create, and within a generation Japan was modernized in appearance. The primary object was to convince the Great Powers that Japan was approaching their own standards, in fact that in all except colour the Japanese were Europeans. If in order to convince the foreigner of this fact it was necessary to discontinue the 'top knot' and take to Western hair style, or to adopt foreign dress for court and official ceremonies (1872) or for the Emperor himself to make it known that old style costumes were not appropriate for the time, the leaders of new Japan had no objection to do so. In fact, during the period of intoxication many strange things were done, all meant to insist upon the modernity of Japan and upon its effective Westernization. Sansom, who discusses these tendencies with great discrimination, comes to the conclusion: 'It is not too much to say that the problem of securing new treaties on a footing of equality with other Powers overshadowed all other problems and influenced not only foreign but also domestic policy throughout that period. The attitude of the authorities towards adoption of Western institutions and customs was to a great extent shaped by their anxiety to show to the Western nations that the Japanese people had assimilated enough of Western culture to justify their claims to be treated as members of a civilized modern State.'[1]

To secure the revision of treaties the Japanese were prepared privately to suffer much, even to accept in public that the Western civilization was superior. They even worked out a constitution which sought to reconcile the sacred and inviolable Emperor with a parliamentary system, and when the constitution was promulgated in 1889 they felt that they had become entitled to be considered among the progressive nations. They were a little doubtful still about Christianity, but if the price of treaty revision, as Japanese observers sent abroad reported, was freedom for Christian missionary activity, the Empire was glad to include in the constitution a clause by which complete religious toleration was to be the law in Japan.

The main difficulty that the Japanese faced in their efforts to secure the modification of the unequal treaties was the solidarity of European diplomatic representatives in Far Eastern capitals. It was at that time a recognized principle, which Russia alone did not fully accept, that in their dealings with Asian courts the Powers should give support to each

[1] Sansom: *The Western World and Japan*, p. 401.

other's claims and should in no case follow a policy at variance with their general rights. Thus when in 1873 Japan negotiated a treaty with Italy under which Italian nationals were allowed to travel in the interior and Italy for her part agreed to a modification of the privileges of extra-territoriality, the other Powers protested and prevented a ratification! The American Government, which at this time looked upon the efforts of Japan to modernize herself with sympathy, also signed with her a convention which recognized Japan's equality and thereby aroused much resentment among other Powers. Actually, however, it was Russia that helped Japan in her fight to gain a status of equality. The island of Sakhalin had been for some time a bone of contention between the two empires. By the treaty of 1855 it had been left for later settlement, but negotiations had dragged. Finally, in 1875, the matter was settled by a treaty by which in exchange for a recognition of her rights over the Kurile Islands, Japan gave up her claims on Sakhalin. The treaty was signed as between two equal Powers and it was the first international agreement which placed Japan in the category of a Power standing on a footing of equality with the Great Powers of the world.

The political system of Japan also began to take a different shape, which helped the Imperial Government in its fight for the recognition of its status. The defeat of the Satsuma Rebellion (1877) had finally eliminated the feudal clan government, at least in form, and the first steps towards representative institutions had also been taken. In 1881 the Emperor issued an edict promising to establish a parliament on Western models which was to be the coping stone of the new system. Ito Hirobumi, after a comparative study of political institutions in the leading countries, suggested the steps by which in gradual stages the paraphernalia of parliamentary government under a monarchy was to be established in Japan. The first step in this direction was the creation in 1885 of a cabinet to administer the country. This was followed by the establishment of a privy council composed of distinguished personages and statesmen of experience modelled on the British institution of the same name. And finally, in 1889, a constitution was promulgated with due ceremony, announcing to the world that Japan had taken her place in the comity of civilized nations.

To reconcile the position of the Emperor with a parliamentary system of government was more difficult; but Ito and his collaborators found no contradiction in it. The first article of the constitution laid down:

'The Empire shall be reigned over and governed by a line of Emperors unbroken for ages eternal.' The third article says that 'the Emperor is sacred and inviolable'. Ito himself commented on these clauses as follows:

'The sacred throne was established at the time when the heavens and

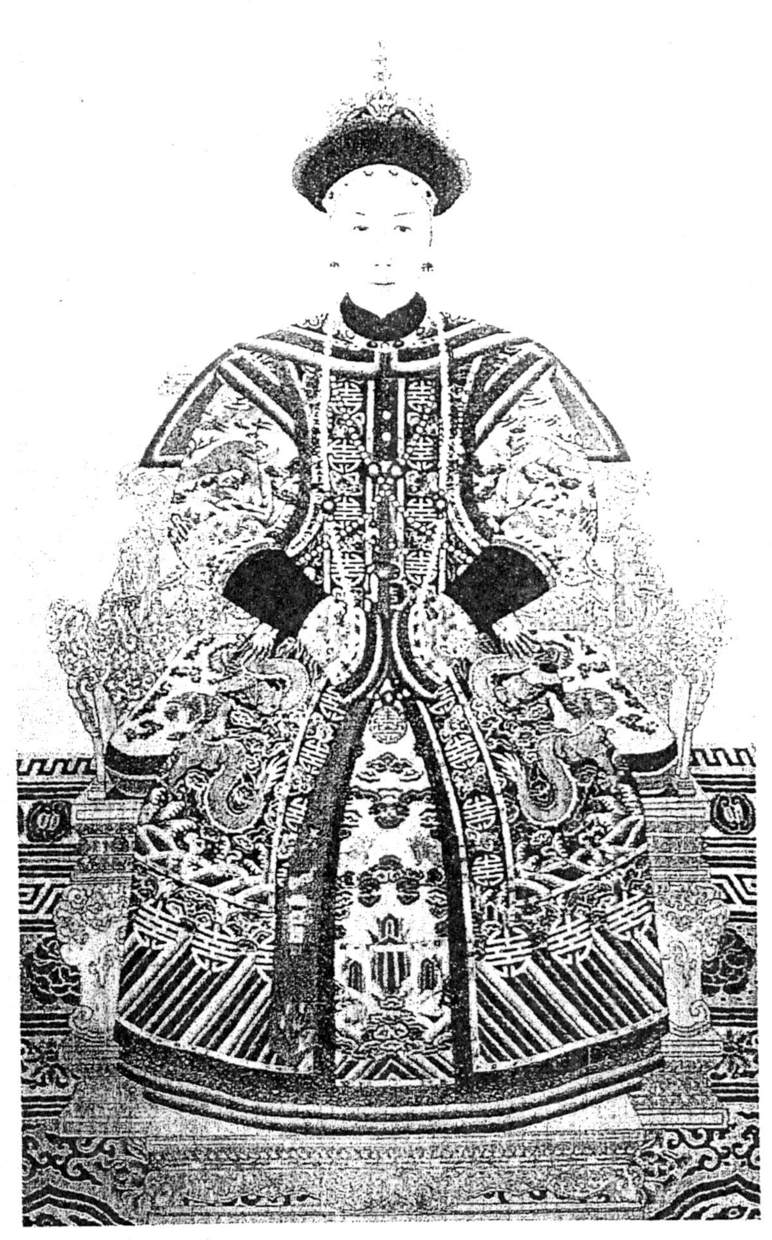

VIII 'OLD BUDDHA'
The Dowager Empress of China, TZU HSI

the earth became separated. The Emperor is heaven descended, divine and sacred. He is pre-eminent above all his subjects.'

With a divine Emperor who not only reigned but governed there can be no parliamentary responsibility. The Cabinet was to be responsible to the Throne, and the Diet was meant only to enable the Emperor to ascertain his people's wishes. In the constitution of the Diet, Ito followed the British model of a House of Peers and a House of Commons.

The increased prestige resulting from these actions was utilized by the Imperial Government for furthering its immediate object of obtaining the revision of unequal treaties. The main opposition to this had come from Britain, and the Japanese deliberately set themselves out to court and flatter that Power. It was fashionable then for Japanese to allude to themselves as the British of the East. The study of the English language was specially encouraged, and in fact every attempt was made to convey the impression that the Japanese were great admirers of the British and were anxious to be considered their disciples.

So far, though continuous negotiations were being carried on by successive foreign ministers, most notably by Count Inouye (1879-1887), nothing substantial had been achieved. But Japanese propaganda in Britain, combining subtle flattery of the British with a presentation of the Japanese point of view in most favourable colours, had the desired result. Lord Granville gave cautious approval to Japan's claims. In 1886 a conference was opened in Tokyo for the revision of treaties. Before it met, Japan had been able through careful diplomacy in Western capitals, to secure the support of America, Britain and Germany. The negotiations resulted in a compromise which among others included a provision that Japanese courts trying foreigners should have foreign judges associated with them. Also the proposals in regard to tariff did not concede the complete freedom of Japan. When these came to be known there was an outcry in the country, as Japan was in no mood to be satisfied with half-measures. The spirit of the country found expression in a memorial by General Viscount Tani, a document of considerable significance, in which the policy of flattery and dependence was exposed and attacked with merciless logic. 'Laying aside the principle of dependence, improve our internal Government affairs, make our country secure by military preparation . . . and then wait for the time of the confusion of Europe which must come eventually.' As a result of this agitation the Inouye proposals were dropped.

After the constitution was promulgated and the Diet convened, the movement for treaty revision became irresistible. The Diet was uncompromising in its demands, and Japan, giving up the policy of collective negotiation, decided to concentrate her attention on England. In 1894 a treaty with Britain was signed which provided for the termination of extra-territoriality in five years and restored tariff autonomy to Japan. Other nations followed and, when Japan had won her war in Korea and emerged as a military Power, there was no more any question of treating her as an inferior country or one in which any privileges could be claimed. Japan had broken her chains, and by the conclusion of the Anglo-Japanese Alliance in 1902 stepped on the international stage as a Power of some consequence.

CHAPTER 4

SOUTH-EAST ASIA

WE shall see later on the attempts of France over a period of a hundred years from 1747 to 1850 to gain control of the Peninsula of South-east Asia through missions, fraud and force. After the romantic efforts of the martial Bishop Pigneau de Behaine, France's position seemed in nowise to have improved. The successors of Gialong whom the Bishop restored to the throne were even more against French domination than their predecessors. Failing in all their efforts, France under Napoleon III decided to use strong-arm methods and establish for herself an empire in Asia. The excuse was as usual to protect the church. In a communiqué published in *Le Moniteur Universal* of November 14, 1858, Louis Napoleon announced that 'the ruthless persecutions of our missionaries have brought our warships on more than one occasion to the coast of the Annamite kingdom, but their efforts to enter into relations with the Government have been futile. The Government of the Emperor cannot allow its overtures to be spurned. Therefore an expedition has been planned.' The Spanish authorities in the Philippines co-operated, their commander-in-chief emphasizing the necessity 'to avenge the insults to our sacred religion and our pious missionaries'.

The campaign was not as easy as the French had expected. The local Christians failed to give any support. It was only after five months that the French were able to force the river mouth and take the fortress of Tamane which guarded the peninsula. In February 1859 Saigon was attacked and captured, but the Annamites under an able commander, Nguyen Tri-phuong, laid siege to the town and placed the French garrison in a very precarious position. The siege, however, was raised when fresh troops arrived after the China campaign under Admiral Charner. The Admiral, after raising the siege, made advances to the King of Cambodia who showed a more friendly attitude. A treaty was signed with Cambodia on August 11, 1863, which reduced it to a protectorate, placing its foreign affairs under the exclusive authority of France. The other conditions of the treaty were: the nomination of a

French Resident to supervise the affairs of the kingdom; freedom of travel; the right of French missionaries to carry on religious activities; the right of France to exploit forests. The influence of the Indian system of government through local kings, which was reaffirmed after the Mutiny, is clearly noticeable in these arrangements, except for the provision regarding missionaries necessitated by the excuse for aggression in the Peninsula. A later treaty with Siam (July 16, 1867) gave to France the right to navigate the Mekong and Tonc-Sap rivers where they bordered on that kingdom. By a further convention (January 15, 1869) all the river area of Mekong passed to the French, restricting the Annamite kingdom to the coastal strip.

The Annamite kingdom was not yet brought into the system. The Emperor Tu-Duc had signed the treaty in 1862 which gave France only the eastern part of Lower Cochin China. French aggression and Annamite resistance continued for a period of fifteen years. In 1873 French troops marched into Hanoi and also conquered all the area in the delta of the Red River. Tu-Duc now appealed to his suzerain in Peking, and though the Chinese Government fully realized its impotence in the face of French aggression, it privately ordered its troops to go to the assistance of its vassal. The French in Hanoi suffered a defeat, but the action led to a definitive settlement by which France recognized the sovereignty of the Emperor of Annam and promised him 'protection' against all foreign foes. Tu-Duc on his part agreed to be guided by France in matters of foreign policy, to cede Cochin China to France and to open the Red River to French commerce. This treaty of March 15, 1874, brought into existence the political structure of Indo-China with its separate areas of Cochin China, the Empire of Annam, the Kingdom of Cambodia and the Principality of Laos.

Though the treaty regularized the French position in the Peninsula, it did not immediately settle the issue. The Chinese, whose suzerainty had never been questioned, were in no mood to accept the position. In Indo-China itself local bands of patriots with the help of the Chinese Black Banners were carrying on a policy of systematic harassment. Finally, at the request of the Annamite court, the Peking authorities sent an army to pacify the area. This afforded an opportunity to settle the issue of Chinese suzerainty. Marquis Tseng, the son of the great viceroy, who was envoy at Paris, took up a bellicose attitude. The French, however, took no notice and began extensive military operations in 1882. When the Chinese Foreign Office protested, the French reply took up the position that China had no *locus standi* in the matter. 'We have given instructions,' declared De Freycinet, the French Foreign Minister, 'to the Government of Indo-China to apply fully the treaty of 1874, which concerns only the two signatory Powers. We have no explanations to furnish the Chinese Government.' Li Hung-chang negotiated an agreement with the French Minister, Bourée, by which Tongking was divided into two zones of influence and the French further agreed to respect the sovereignty of Annam; but this was repudiated by the Quai d'Orsay. In the hostilities that followed, the Black Banners surrounded and cut up Commander Rivière's force on May 19, 1883, which forced the French to organize a major expedition under General Bouet and Admiral Courbet. There was no actual rupture with China, and hostilities were carried on only in a haphazard manner for some time. An attempt was made by Li Hung-chang to close the matter by negotiation, but he was disowned and the Chinese Army began to march into Tongking. The French failed to stem the advance, Colonel Dougenne meeting with defeat at Bacle on June 23.

The French now realized that the situation had become serious, and proceeded to extreme measures. Regular hostilities broke out and Admiral Courbet, after destroying the Chinese fleet, proceeded to blockade the Yangtze. On this the Chinese entered into negotiations through Duncan-Campbell. By the final settlement China abandoned her authority over Tongking and her suzerainty over Annam (April 25, 1886).

From 1861 to 1876, which may be described as the period of conquest, French authority was for the most part vested in a succession of admirals who were advocates of the policy of force. The 'Home Authority' (in Paris) of the territory was vested alternatively in the Ministry of Marine and the Ministry of Commerce; and these two bodies, without adequate experience of territorial administration, failed to bring any kind of understanding to bear on the problem of government. The mandarinate and the lesser officialdom in Indo-China followed a policy of non-co-operation from the beginning, with the result that from 1862 to 1882 the local areas were directly administered by the French Inspector of Native Affairs. The entire social system broke down under the impact of foreign authority. The Indo-Chinese legal and political system, highly developed, complex and fully understood by the people, was set aside. In its place the policy of 'assimilation', of forcing the system prevalent in the metropolitan country, was attempted with persistence by the French Colonial authorities. The result was, as anyone with imagination could have expected, a breakdown of social authority. The first civilian Governor of Indo-China, Le Myre de Vilers, analysed the situation correctly in 1885 in the following words: 'We have destroyed the past and nothing has taken its place. We are on the eve of a social revolution which began during the conquest.'[1]

Also the French, anxious to maintain their prestige, on which, as they

See *Des institutions civiles de da Cochin Chine*. Paris, 1908.

learnt from their British friends, depended the authority of the European in the East, developed an attitude of racial superiority. This attitude is well described in a pamphlet of Phan Tsu Trinh. After noting the contempt for the Indo-Chinese, which the Frenchman in the Colony did not consider even necessary to conceal, the writer says:

'In your eyes we are savages, dumb brutes incapable of distinguishing between good and evil. You not only refuse to treat us as equals, but even fear to approach us as if we were filthy creatures. . . . There is a sadness of feeling and shame which fills our hearts during the evening's contemplation when we review all the humiliations endured during the day. Caught in a machine which saps our energy, we are reduced to impotency. This explains why beggars only dare show themselves in the offices of the French.'[1]

The French went on with their administration, with the construction of roads, dams, telegraphs, telephones and railways. But the population was not reconciled to French authority. In Annam, Tongking and Cambodia revolts and local outbreaks were frequent. Under a leader of ability and standing, Prince Si Vattha, the Cambodians carried on a devastating war for eighteen months. It took five years to put down the Rebellion of Detham, while in Tongking the Regent himself revolted in 1884, leading to the massacre of the Christian population supporting the French. The plain fact was that the policy of pacification had not succeeded; the Indo-Chinese, heirs to a proud civilization, were not prepared to be 'assimilated'.

The 'assimilation' policy began to be tempered soon by an 'associative' one. The beginnings of the associative policy are to be found in the Council of Notables established by Bert in 1886. Chailley, the admiring eulogist of British methods in India, praises this scheme as the first effort to win over the 'native' to French rule. Paul Bert was undoubtedly a man of vision, and his ideas were to limit French authority and leave local administration to Annamites. His policy in some respects was a repetition of that of Lord Ripon in India. As Resident General in Annam and Tongking he proclaimed the new policy which he explained in numerous speeches. He told an assembly of Tongkingese notables: 'You will know that France has but one desire, namely, to give the people prosperity under her moral guidance. We do not desire to take over the direct administration, which events have forced us to do in Lower Indo-China. The class of scholars, so strongly established because it is not a closed class, will remain in power so long as it is loyal. It will continue to be the centre of authority and the source for the selection of all officials. I have confidence in these races of the Orient to whom we have pointed the way

[1] Dépêche Coloniale, August 1909, quoted in Innes' *French Policy in Indo-China*, p. 61.

towards a brighter tomorrow. I can foresee only a magnificent future resulting from this meeting of Europeans and Asiatics.'[1]

After Bert's death the only one who tried the policy of 'association' seriously was de Lanessan, who was, however, recalled because it was felt he was moving too fast. Anarchy and confusion again raised their heads. Under Paul Doumer, the most successful of France's Proconsuls in the East, Indo-China, however, enjoyed a period of sound administration. But Doumer, like his contemporary Lord Curzon in India, thought in terms of imperial glory. In an appreciation of his own work Doumer declared in words which could have been uttered by Curzon: 'Her (Indo-Chinese) strong organization, her financial and economic structures, and her great power are being used for the benefit of French prestige. In five years commerce was more than doubled. The public projects undertaken have no parallels in Asia . . . she has paved the way for a future which should make France a great Asiatic Power.'[2]

But in making France a great Asian Power, by centralizing the administration and by imparting greater efficiency into the Government of Indo-China, Doumer, like Curzon, again had only intensified the animosity of the Annamites. The Annamites found themselves increasingly governed according to French conceptions of administration, and the bitterness of the population led to the gradual development of nationalist parties armed with modern methods of agitation, propaganda, etc. The rise of Japan and the victory which an Asian country gained over one of the great Powers of the West, both on land and on sea, had an immense effect on Indo-China. Organizations began to be formed in Japan where many students had gone for study. Propaganda literature began to penetrate the masses. One such declared: 'I, your humble servant, an obscure student, having had occasion to study new books and new doctrines, have discovered in a recent history of Japan how they have been able to conquer the impotent Europeans. This is the reason why we have formed an organization . . . We have selected from young Annamites the most energetic, with great capacities for courage, and are sending them to Japan for study . . . several years have passed without the French being aware of the movement . . . our only aim is to prepare the population for the future.'[3]

It is interesting to note the growth of extreme nationalism in the Far East in the period following the Japanese victory. In India, under Tilak, Lajpat Rai and others, nationalism assumed a more aggressive form. A militant group organized widespread terrorism and, generally

[1] Quoted by Mager, p. 150.
[2] See Doumer: *L'Indo-Chine Française* for a description of his own administrative achievement.
[3] Quoted in Ennis: *French Policy in China*, p. 178.

speaking, the movement became revolutionary in its outlook. A similar tendency was noticeable in Indo-China. Students trained in Japan led an agitation openly for throwing the French out of Indo-China. The movement became so widespread that France was able to maintain her authority only by large-scale arrests of leaders and dependence on her troops.

It is, however, essential to remember that in the first decade of the new century France, along with other Western Powers, was satisfied about the perpetuity of European domination over Asia. There was not the least recognition, even among thinkers considered 'advanced' at the time like Lord Morley, that the time was fast approaching when Europeans would cease to exercise political authority in Asia. Not only 'old China hands' and sun-dried Anglo-Indians and French Colonials, but informed and intelligent opinion in London, Paris and The Hague felt satisfied that, by firmness tempered with conciliation, European authority could be indefinitely prolonged. They planned their administrative, political and economic policies on this basis. Albert Sarraut, who succeeded Klobukowsky, was a notable champion of this policy in Indo-China. During two periods as Governor-General with an interval as the Minister for Colonies he took in hand large-scale reforms, reorganized and extended sanitary and medical work, improved the harbours of Saigon and Haiphong, reformed the departmental organizations. His successors also undertook major public projects. In fact, during the first three decades of the century, French administration of Indo-China was as well run and as efficiently organized as the best colonial governments and created a vast system of roads, railways and other communication facilities, provided the public with the full apparatus of a modern government, and undertook economic measures meant to benefit large numbers. It also showed a great interest in the history and culture of Indo-China, preserving with care the monuments of the past and maintaining a famous institution of Oriental studies.

But unfortunately all these well meaning and highly desirable activities seemed to impress the Indo-Chinese no better than the previous regimes based on force. The feeling against the French kept on growing. France began reluctantly to realize that good government was no substitute for self-government, and that civilization in an alien clothing had no attraction to those held in subjection. Various schemes of reforms were tried. Maurice Long, disciple and successor of Sarraut, tried to placate the 'young Annamites' by establishing elected Communal Administrative Councils. Indo-Chinese representation in the Colonial Council of Cochin China was increased (1922). But all this was merely tinkering with the problem of national rights. A glimmering of this truth is seen in the Socialist Governor-General Alexandre Varenne's speech on December 21, 1925, before the Council.

'Both men and ideas, and Asia herself, are being transformed. The Orient today stands upon the path leading to the higher forms of modern civilization. Indo-China cannot escape from this movement for emancipation. Our lessons have been carried to her. Indo-China is thinking about them. She questions the future and seeks to determine her destiny. What will the future hold? If peace is preserved for us, if Indo-China is able to develop freely, she ought to aspire to a more independent higher life and become some day a great nation.'[1] Brave words, indeed, but Varenne was forced by opinion at home to modify his ideas. Pierre Pasquier, Governor-General from 1927–34, realized that some conciliation of nationalist opinion was necessary if France was to maintain her position in Indo-China. The Great War had shaken the moral position of Europe and events both in India and in China were moving fast. The partial reforms of 1919 in India had changed the structure of government; in the provincial governments they had introduced, to a limited extent, the rule of Indians. But instead of satisfying the public, these changes had only led to the great non-co-operation agitation of 1920 which, after twenty years of struggle, took the country to the inevitable climax of the 'Quit India' movement.

More important than even the Indian movement in its influence on affairs in Indo-China was the emergence of the Kuomintang in China and the development of its revolutionary policy in 1924–7. We shall discuss at the appropriate place the influence of these factors on the growth of nationalism in Viet Nam. Here it is of importance only to see in perspective the 'reform' attempts of Pierre Pasquier. He reorganized the Council of Notables and a so-called Chamber of the Representatives of the People. How the 'reformed' chambers were constituted may be seen from the composition of the electoral college which consisted of chiefs and assistant chiefs of cantons, pensioned officials, pensioned non-commissioned officers of the army, navy and militia, officials and notables, nominated by the Résident Supérieur, etc. Besides, in these chambers the expression of political opinion was prohibited.

In brief it was a combination of the two policies of 'bribing the bribable'—the so-called notables—and of camouflaging colonial rule by a façade of representation. The most noticeable feature of French policy even in its most 'advanced' periods was an utter distrust of democracy, a refusal to share power with the people. The utmost the French would do was to associate the 'mandarins' with their administration, in the strange illusion, shared by all colonial administrations, that 'men of position' carry influence with the people against what the public vaguely recognizes as its national interests. The mandarins and pensioners in

[1] Quoted in *L'Asie Française*, March 1926, pp. 108-13.

the chambers in fact counted for no more than the knights and rajas in India when it came to a question of public agitation against foreign rule.

The French calculations went awry even before the Japanese invaded Indo-China in 1941. They had argued that with increasing 'association', nationalist movements would die down and a policy of co-operation with France would replace the barren opposition of the extremists. The nationalist movements inside the country had been organized on the basis of a recovery of complete independence and the exclusion of French authority in any shape or form. From centres outside Indo-China, from Paris, Bangkok, Hong Kong, Canton and Tokyo the movement was directed effectively to give it a unity of purpose and a strength of organization which made it clear that France had to face the issue of the national independence of Indo-China.

The development in Indo-China after the Great War, and the fight between Viet Minh and the French forces, need not concern us. But the exclusion of France from effective political authority in the Far East has become an accomplished fact.

CHAPTER 5

SIAM

Till the defeat of the Chinese forces and the establishment of European domination over the court of Peking, Siam's relationship with Western nations had been in every way satisfactory. Captain Burney's treaty of 1926 had expressly provided that English subjects who visit a 'Siamese country must conduct themselves according to the laws of the Siamese country in every particular, that is to say that British subjects would be rendered liable to be punished by a capital penalty in case of homicide, by whipping, fine or imprisonment for other offences and by immediate expulsion from the country for the use of disrespectful language towards any Siamese officer'. A similar treaty was also signed with the Americans in 1933. But this position underwent a change as a result of the changed position in China. Sir John Bowring, who negotiated the treaty of 1855, was able to secure the principle of extra-territoriality for British subjects, permission to build churches and *exemption of all duty for imports of opium.* The British annexation of a part of Burma had also rendered the Siamese Government nervous of the frightening presence of the leviathan on its borders.

A new menance soon developed on its northern border. In the reign of Louis XIV French troops had been allowed to occupy Bangkok (it was not then the capital) with the connivance of a Greek adventurer, Constantin Phaulkor, who was at that time the 'Superintendent of Foreign Trade' in the Siamese court. But the arrival of foreign troops roused bitter opposition in court circles. Phaulkor was killed and the French troops left Bangkok and, after suffering great hardships, managed to reach Pondicherry (1688). After the failure of that abortive experiment, Siam had not been troubled by the French, though the activities of her adventurers and missionaries in Annam in the succeeding periods were vigilantly watched by the court at Bangkok. But after Napoleon III's intervention in 1858 and the establishment of French authority in Cambodia by the treaty of August 11, 1863, the problem became one of immediate importance to Siam. Siam had claimed a vague suzerainty over Cambodia. When the French began to press the Cambodian king, he turned to the court of Bangkok for help and signed a secret treaty with Siam on December 1, 1863. A diplomatic tussle followed, as a result of which an agreement was reached between France and Siam by which Siam withdrew her claims over Cambodia in exchange for the provinces of Angkor and Battambang. France also received the right of navigating the Mekong.

This latter concession was the subject of further complication. From at least the beginning of the century a stretch of territory on the left bank of the Mekong going up to the mountainous boundary of Annam had belonged to Siam. It was the secret object of France to take over this area and open the field for aggression against Siam at a later and more convenient time. Soon after the treaty was signed an expedition was fitted up under Doudart de Lagrée[1] and François Garnier.[2] France immediately began putting forward claims to Angkor and Battambang, recognized as Siamese by the treaty of 1863, and for other territories belonging to Siam. In view of France's own troubles in Indo-China and with the court of Peking over Tongking, nothing effective was done, though diplomatic and other pressure continued to be exercised at Bangkok. A proposal to neutralize Siam made by the French in 1885 failed owing to the opposition of Britain, whose expansionist ideas in the Shan and Malayan borders of Siam had not yet been realized. When at last the 'pacification' of Indo-China was completed in the last decade of the nineteenth century, France was free to turn her attention to Siam. A pretext was soon found in a border incident in 1893, when some French lives were lost in an incident typical of the excuses which imperialist nations found in the past while dealing with weaker countries. Under the threat of bombardment of Bangkok, France demanded all territory to the east of the Mekong together with the islands in the river, withdrawal of police and military forces on the west side to a distance of fifteen miles, and a heavy indemnity. Nor was this all. France was to be given the right to open consulates with extra-territorial jurisdiction wherever she pleased.

Under the arrangements of this treaty (1893) Siam would have shared the fate of Annam, especially as the right of extra-territoriality, under a curious extension, named *ressortissants*, was to be applied not only to Frenchmen, but to the Asian subjects of France and even to the Chinese who registered themselves in French consulates. It is said that in three years the number of people entitled to French protection jumped from 200 to 30,000. But Siam was saved from the dangers that threatened her by two factors. The first was the determination of

[1] See Doudart de Largrée: *Explorations et missions*. Paris, 1863.
[2] Also Garnier: *Voyage de l'exploration en Incochine*. Paris, 1863.

Britain not to have a common boundary with France. British policy in Asia required buffer States, and Siam therefore had to be maintained in that position. The second factor was the wisdom, tact and ability of King Chulalankorn who was able to steer clear of further complications. British intervention against French expansionist policy in Siam, primarily meant to prevent France from reaching the Burmese border, led to the Anglo-French convention of January 15, 1895. This convention neutralized Central Siam, but the position of the eastern and southern sections of the country was left ambiguous. Britain hoped to encroach on the Malayan and Shan areas, and France in the area of the borders of her colony. This convention gave King Chulalankorn the respite he required. He was indeed a remarkable monarch. He was widely-travelled, had visited Western countries, and had noted their sources of strength. He introduced a series of essential reforms including the abolition of slavery. Also the State Government was reorganized. In 1895 a legislative council and a cabinet of ministers and the paraphernalia of modern government came into existence. In fact, during the next ten years King Chulalankorn did much to modernize his State, by building railways, telegraphs, telephones, reforming the coinage, establishing a modern postal system, etc. A new penal code was drafted, and though it went into effect only in 1908, the administration of law had so far improved that in 1899 the Siamese Government had negotiated with the British an agreement limiting the jurisdiction exercised under extra-territoriality.

These changes were by no means welcome to France since the ambition which the French Government openly cherished was to bring the whole of Siam within her protection, or if that were not possible to obtain as large a slice of Siamese territory as possible. British opposition had rendered such a policy difficult, but the deterioration of the situation in Europe forced the British and the French to settle their rivalries. This gave to France a limited freedom of action in Siam, and the French Government took full advantage to force the Bangkok court to cede her territories and make further concessions. Thus in 1904 France extended her territorial authority over a large tract and a 'neutral zone' was created. By a further revision of the treaty in 1907, Siam was forced to cede the neutral zone, and the only consideration that she received was that extra-torritoriality with regard to French Asian subjects was to be abolished in ten years' time.

Britain agreed to this annexation as she herself had designs on the southern area. The States of Kelantan, Trengganu, Perlis and Kedah were the compensation that England received for permitting French annexation in the north. Between them, these two nations had, without even an excuse, deprived Siam of 25,000 square miles of territory. But at that price Siam was enabled to live, not so much because the imperialist wolves had become lambs but because even before the new areas could be digested and a new phase of aggression planned retribution had overtaken Western nations in Europe itself in the Great War of 1914–18. Siam under King Rama VI was able to utilize the respite to strengthen her position further. Realizing the changed international situation, she even declared war on Germany in 1917, thereby assuring her own place at the Versailles Conference.

Part IV

RUSSIA AND THE FAR EAST

CHAPTER I

BEFORE THE REVOLUTION

In studying the relations of Russia (whether under the Tsars or under the Soviets) with China, it is necessary to remember that both had been under the rule of the great Mongols. Their liberation from foreign yoke, following the expulsion of the 'Yuan' Dynasty in China and the breakdown of the Golden Horde in Russia, were practically at the same time. The result was that the area from the Urals to Mongolia was a political vacuum in the fifteenth century, when the Mings were establishing themselves in China and Grand Prince Ivan III (1462–1505) was proclaiming himself as the Tsar of all Russia. It was only in 1480 that Ivan refused to pay tribute to the Khan of the Golden Horde From 1483 we see the Russians spreading themselves into Siberia. By 1555, the Khanate of Sibir, belonging originally to the fief of Ogotai, fell under Moscow's authority, and the flood began to flow eastward. The areas bordering on the Urals were slowly colonized and the vacuum was systematically occupied. Using the great river systems of Siberia, the Muscovites controlled the vast and forbidding steppes. In a hundred years after the fall of the Khanate of Sibir, Moscow had stepped into the inheritance of the great Khan and reached the Pacific.

While the northern area was thus being occupied by the Russians, a similar process was being followed by the Chinese from the south. The homeland of Jinghis and of the tribes which had conquered the world passed quietly under Chinese occupation. When Manchu expansionism replaced the decrepit Mings, the Peking Government had brought under its authority the Eulaths, the Kalkhas and other tribes within its reach. The Amur region had passed effectively under Chinese authority. Thus Moscow and Peking shared between them the inheritance of the great Khans; the two great vassals had stepped into the authority of the suzerain.

The partition of the Empire of the Khans between the Empires of Moscow and Peking brought the Caesar of the Third Rome and the Son of Heaven face to face. The two great land Powers claimed large areas of disputed territory, which historically belonged neither to China nor to Russia. Originally it was the Manchus and *not* the Chinese who expanded across the Amur. In 1616 the Manchus had crossed the Amur River and in 1636 they had reached the Sea of Okhotsk. To the west their claims extended to Nertchinsk. The Russians also reached the Amur at the same time, a party crossing the river in 1636. In the meantime the activities of the Manchus had been diverted to the conquest of China. This prevented them from further expanding northwards, but the claims of the Manchus were now reinforced with the prestige of the Chinese Empire. This set a limit to Russian expansion.

While Manchus were consolidating their authority south of the Great Wall, the Russians, especially under Yarka Pavlov Khabarov, were systematically and by successive expeditions bringing the Amur tribes under control. The Russian method was to permit adventurous individuals to take up this work by organizing 'private expeditions'. The Ching Dynasty, once well established in Peking, was able to turn its attention to the changes taking place in the north. Under Shung Chih in 1652 the first expedition was sent to deal with the intruding Russian adventurers, but the Chinese had under-estimated the strength of the Russians in the area. In 1653 the forces met again. After a desultory campaign Onufria Stepanof, who led the 'Russian expedition' along with his small force, was defeated and the majority slain in battle. The Chinese records relate these incidents in the following words:

'In the 12th year (regnal) General Ming set out with his forces from Peking. He attacked them (the Locha-Russians) at Ku-mar and other places with some success, but soon retreated owing to lack of provisions. In the 14th year (1657) Sarguda, Defence Commissioner, defeated them. Next year again he defeated them. . . . In the 17th year Bahai, son of Sarguda, scored an overwhelming victory over them.' The Chinese records, however, add that though successful in battles, 'our troops withdrew without subjecting the Locha who continued to make their appearance intermittently'.[1]

With the reign of the great Emperor Kang Hsi a new chapter opens. Kang Hsi established a system of frontier posts under a senior commander. The Russians, who had temporarily withdrawn, also realized that they had come up against a military Power and therefore the period of unofficial expeditions was over. They began by founding two towns, Nertchinsk and Albazin, which were fated to figure prominently in later history. Built at the mouth of the River Nertcha, in 1656, the town of Nertchinsk was a fortress of some strength. Kang Hsi took up the matter in earnest and, after adequate preparations, including the establishment of military farms, postal communication, construction of river

[1] *Shuo fang pei shung*. Introduction, p. 5.

transports and a dockyard of Kirin, Kang Hsi started on his expedition to punish the intruders. Albazin was captured in 1685 and the fort was destroyed. The Russian Government now woke up to the situation and, wisely treating the whole thing as a border incident arising from the foolishness of private adventurers, nominated envoys to discuss and settle the problem of the Amur frontiers with the Government at Peking.

It is, however, interesting to note that both parties, the Russians no less than the Chinese, at this period were equally ignorant of the strength and resources of their opponents. The Tsar, with only vague notions of what the Chinese Empire was, called on the Son of Heaven to accept his suzerainty. Kang Hsi, looking upon the Northern Barbarians as only another and more powerful tribe like the Eulaths or the Kalkhas, expected as a matter of course that the ruler of Moscow should send tribute to Peking. He claimed even that previously (in 1655) the Tsar had sent a tributary mission to Shun Chih. This mission of Theodore Baikoff had actually arrived in Peking, but no agreement could be reached on procedure, the Ambassador refusing to *kow-tow* and to give his credentials to anyone other than the Emperor. The mission proved a failure and retured to Moscow without entering into any negotiations or even presenting their credentials. The next Ambassador, Ivan Pulilieff, seems to have been received by the Emperor and, according to Baddley, the Russian report states that the Chinese replied: 'The tribute thou didst send we have accepted and in return we send thee out gifts and favours.'[1]

After this, it is a little surprising that in 1670 the Tsar should have, in his letter to Kang Hsi, demanded that the Emperor of China should become his vassal. The following is the text of the letter (as translated):

'There are Tsars and Kings who own allegiance to the Great Lord and Grand Prince Alexei Mikhailovich, Autocrat of all the Russias, Great, Little and White and the Great Lord graciously deigns to extend to them his royal gifts and favour.

'The Bogdoi Tsar (Chinese Emperor) should seek likewise the favour and presents of the Grand Prince Alexei Mikhailovich, Autocrat of all the Russias, Great, Little and White and place himself under his Tsarial Majesty's protection.

'And the Grand Prince Alexei Mikhailovich, Autocrat of all the Russias, Great, Little and White and lord and possessor of many kingdoms, will in that case send the Bogdoi Khan gifts and keep him in his gracious royal care and protect him from his enemies. At the same time the Bogdoi Khan would come under His Tsarial Majesty's high hand

[1] Baddley: *Russia, Mongolia and China.* Macmillan, 1919. London. Mission of Pulilieff and Abbu, pp. 167–8.

for ever without fail and present to him, the Great Lord, tribute and allow the Great Lord's people and his own, on either side, to trade freely.

'And what the Bogdoi Khan decides, let him forward to His Tsaria Majesty by these same envoys.'[1]

The purport of this letter does not seem to have been communicated, for the envoy of 'His Tsarial Majesty' and Great Lord himself *kow-towed* before the Son of Heaven and was duly admonished for the troubles on the frontier. The mission returned without achieving anything. The next embassy (May 15, 1675) was led by Nikolai Sparthary and among other things it desired that forms of address between the two emperors should be settled and that some Chinese bridge builders should be sent to Russia.

Again the negotiations broke down during the preliminaries because the question which interested the Chinese, the Amur dispute, was not included in the subjects of discussion, and also because among other things the ambassador had 'been disobedient, refusing to accept the gifts for your sovereign on your knees'.

The pretensions of the Tsar received a shock after the destruction of the fort of Albazin. The Russian court, realizing that China could not be dealt with in the same manner as the other States with which it had so far come into contact, decided to send a proper embassy and, if possible, arrange matters by negotiation. Theodore Alexeivich Golovin, the ambassador selected by Peter the Great, arrived at Selezinsk in August 1689, and the Chinese mission led by Prince Songo-tu and other officials of high rank with the Jesuits, Gerbillion and Pereyra, as interpreters, arrived almost at the same time. The conference dragged on, each side putting forward demands which the other considered inadmissible, but after the Chinese had shown their determination and strength an agreement was concluded (August 27, 1689).[2] This was the Treaty of Nertchinsk. Under its terms the boundary between the two empires was fixed along river lines, from the source of the Argun northward into the Amur, to the Outer Khingan Mountains, to the source of the Udi River. The Valley of the Udi lying between the Inner and Outer Khingan Mountains was declared neutral territory. The Russian fortress at Albazin was destroyed.

This important treaty, which was the first to be signed between China and a European nation, remained in force for 150 years and limited

[1] John Dudgeon: *Historical sketch of the ecclesiastical, political and commercial relations of Russia with China – Drawn chiefly from original sources.* Peking. 1872.

[2] Much of the credit for the success of these negotiations goes without doubt to Gerbillion who constituted himself an adviser to Prince Songo-tu, the chief Chinese representative.

Russian expansion to the south. A cautious beginning was, however, made by the Russians at this time for establishing trade relations with Japan. With a base established in Okhotsk (1649) the Russians began exploring the area, and in 1700 Altasov reported to Moscow the existence of the Kurile Islands near Japan. This group was visited in 1713–14 and a Russian landing on Sakhalin took place in 1714. The amazing adventure of Count Benyowski[1] was an interesting interlude, but it was of some importance because the Pole warned the Japanese of the expansionist policies of Russia. In 1792 the Russian Governor Zaberia sent out a mission, but again without success. But these sporadic activities awakened Japan to the seriousness of the problem of coastal defence, and the Shogun and his Government were on the alert against movements from the Siberian side.

After the Treaty of Nertchinsk the relations of Russia with China remained on the whole friendly, though at different times the question of Russian navigation of the Amur was brought up. Thus according to Chinese records in 1757 'Russia requested the privilege of transporting her provisions through the Amur. The Emperor (Chien Lung) deemed it a violation of treaties and refused the permission'.

The decisive step in Russian Far Eastern policy was taken only in the time of Tsar Nicholas, who in 1847 appointed Nikolaevitch Muraviev, at the age of thirty-eight, as Governor-General of Eastern Siberia. Muraviev had the ambitions of a Wellesley and the ability of a Dalhousie and may well be considered even more than those two proconsuls a maker of Asian history. The establishment of Russian authority on the Amur was his first objective. With this end in view he sent an officer named Vaganov down the Amur. He was, however, not heard of again. Muraviev, who had large views, had in the meantime decided to construct a naval base at Petropavlovsk, and the Amur seemed to him essential for its safety. In conjunction with Admiral Nevelski, who had been commissioned to explore Sakhalin, the straits and the mainland near it, he decided on the acquisition of the mouth of the Amur. The authorities in Moscow did not approve of this, but Nevelski ignored the

[1] Benyowski, a Polish nobleman who had been captured in the war in Europe and imprisoned by the Russians in Kamchatka, escaped to Japan, taking with him the daughter of the local governor. He seems to have been on quite friendly terms with the Japanese but his restless spirit carried him further on to Taiwan or Formosa where he tried to establish himself as the ruler. Failing in his attempt he sailed away and reached Madagascar where he managed to get himself elected king. In this royal capacity he visited the United States and offered to enter into treaty relations with the new republic. He returned to his kingdom but was killed some time afterwards, fighting the French (in 1786). His career seems to have attracted considerable attention in Europe as Kotzebue wrote a play about it in German which was translated into English by the Rev W. Render (1798).

instructions and planted the Russian flag at the mouth of the Amur on January 13, 1850. Nesselrode, the Russian Prime Minister, was angered by this defiance and demanded punishment, but the Tsar, whose personal views were different, supported Muraviev and Nevelski. China's claim to the mouth of the Amur was shadowy at best. At the height of her power, under Kang Hsi, she had only limited Russian authority and not extended her own effective control over this area. In fact, the Chinese court remained for a time ignorant of the action taken by the Russians. It was the Russian Government itself in May 1851 which informed the Chinese of what had taken place.

After this Russia began an effective consolidation of its position in the Transbaikal area. The Peking Government was at that time not only facing the Taiping Rebellion, but had been rendered impotent by the pressure of England and France. It was, therefore, unable to press its own imperialist claims when the homeland itself was being attacked. In 1845, Muraviev had forced his way down the Amur, but had been careful enough to ask for Chinese permission to pass through what was definitely Chinese territory. He was tactful and accommodating and informed the Peking court that 'all military preparations and necessities have been supplied by ourselves, without causing China any damage in the least'.[1] It is interesting also to note that Muraviev emphasized the benefits to China of effective Russian defence of her Siberian territories.

Muraviev's intentions to strengthen the hold on the Amur in view of British action in the Pacific during the Anglo-Russian War was, however, a matter of grave concern to Peking as this affected the Manchu homeland. Negotiations were taken up for a determination of the boundaries. After protracted discussions the Chinese finally conceded the legal title to the area on the north bank of the Amur by the Treaty of Aigun. This was supplemented by the Treaty of Tientsin, which provided for the appointment of a minister plenipotentiary and for the right of maritime trade at ports opened to other Powers.

A new envoy, Pierre Perofski, arrived in Peking in 1859. The Russians, now anxious to enlarge their overland trade, asked for caravan rights to Kashgar, Kalgan and other areas, but nothing came of this because of Chinese objections. Perofski's mission was followed by the embassy of Ignatiev, who reached Peking at a time when the Anglo-French allies were forcing their way through Taku. The exhibition of Western vandalism in burning and looting the Summer Palace gave the Russian ambassador an opportunity to emphasize the friendship of Russia for China and to dissociate his country from the barbarous action of the Anglo-French allies. It was the first of the long series of acts by which

[1] *Yi Wu Shih Mo*, Vol. 8, p. 46, quoted in Fang Chih-chien's *Eclipse of Manchuria*.

Russia showed that she had a greater appreciation of the psychological reaction of the Chinese than the Western Powers. The Russian ambassador offered to mediate and seems to have benefited by his role in getting the boundary dispute settled, giving Russia the Ussuri country up to the border of Korea. (Additional Treaty of Peking, 1860.)

It is now necessary to take up the thread of Russia's relations with Japan for this agreement brought her into an area where her interests were bound to clash with those of the Japanese Empire, and in 1732 a Russian ship visited Nemuro and asked for trade privileges. In May 1739 Russian ships appeared near the coast of the Awa district within a hundred miles of Yeddo. In 1785 it came to be known that the Russians had established posts in the Kuriles. In October 1804 a Russian man-of war, the *Nadiezhada*, carrying Rezanov, an envoy accredited by the Tsar, entered the harbour of Nagasaki. Rezanov tried to open negotiations with the Shogun's Government but without success. In 1807 Captain Golowsien, who was exploring the Kuriles, was captured and held as a prisoner, but was later allowed to be taken away by his own warship the *Diana*. For over forty years after this nothing further was done till Muraviev advised Nesselrode to open up friendly relations with Japan and for this purpose an embassy under Admiral Putiatin was sent by the Tsar Nicholas in 1852. Admiral Putiatin arrived in Japan on the *Diana*. An earthquake and tidal wave so damaged the warship that it was practically lost. As there was no other way to return to Siberia, the Admiral arranged with Japanese shipbuilders to build two schooners for him. Thus was the first modern dockyard constructed in Japan. This enforced stay enabled Putiatin, who had developed friendly relations with the Japanese, to negotiate a treaty by which, apart from providing for the establishment of diplomatic relations, the boundary in the Kurile Islands was settled but the problem of Sakhalin was left to be decided at a later date. At this time, and in fact till the weakness of China led to the scramble for Manchuria, it is certain that Russian policies did not seriously conflict with the interests of Japan. The question of Sakhalin itself was taken up for negotiations in 1875, and it is significant to note that the treaty signed that year at St Petersburg determining this question was as between two equal Powers. Russia in fact showed from the beginning that she did not share the European feeling of superiority in her relations with Asian peoples.

After the Treaty of Aigun and the supplementary treaties, the relations between the Russians and the Chinese developed normally without any serious incident. During the Rebellion of Yakub Beg in Chinese Turkestan, Russia temporarily occupied Ili, on the express understanding that when order was restored it would be returned to the Chinese Government, and though China was in no position to enforce her demand, it must be said to the credit of the Tsar's Government that after some hesitation the area was returned on payment of expenditure incurred for occupation.

What brought Russia again into prominence in Chinese affairs was the question of Korea and Japan's manifest ambitions in regard to that kingdom, which has been discussed earlier. After the Treaty of 1876, Japan was treating the Land of the Morning Calm as an independent country where she had special rights. The Chinese authorities had also begun to move and Li Hung-chang had nominated von Mollendorf to reorganize the Korean administration and had sent Yuan Shih-kai as Amban or High Commission to Seoul. Mollendorf suggested to the Russians to send officers to reorganize the army and the Tsarist Government responded readily, receiving as compensation the use of Port Lazareff on the east coast of Korea. The Japanese found not only that their designs on Korea had been frustrated but their own security threatened by the acquisition of an ice-free port by Russia. They felt that the time had come for them to act. Russia had at that time developed no special interests in regard to Korea which made it necessary for her to deny China's suzerainty over that country. They took no further interest, but Japan, whose leaders had been manifesting an increasing sensitiveness to the conditions in Korea, embarked on the policy which forced on China the option of either disclaiming her rights and interests in that kingdom or of upholding them by force. The Sino-Japanese War, discussed earlier, was the result.

The course of that war and its results have been dealt with elsewhere. What followed the defeat of China was of immense consequence to the development of Sino-Russian relations. As we have seen, Britain and America declined to mediate and bring about a satisfactory conclusion of hostilities, in spite of repeated requests by China. The Peking court was therefore compelled by the Treaty of Shimonoseki to surrender the Liaotung Peninsula so vital to her security. The Chinese Government felt itself betrayed by its friends.

But strangely, again it was Russia that came forward to protest and demanded the restoration of the territory to China. From 1895 begins a new chapter of Sino-Russian relations, of which the governing factor is not China itself, but the known ambitions of Japan to control Korea. The attitude of Russia in respect of the surrender of Liaotung had converted Li Hung-chang, who had so far been an advocate of collaboration with the United Kingdom and the United States, into a friend of Sino-Russian co-operation. In 1896 Li Hung-chang went to Russia to represent his Emperor at the coronation of the Tsar. There a secret treaty was signed which provided for mutual assistance on sea and land in case of Japanese aggression. Under Article IV of the treaty Russia was given the right to take the trans-Siberian railway line across Northern Manchuria direct to Vladivostok. A joint Russo-Chinese Bank was to construct and operate the Eastern Chinese Railway. It is significant that the railway agreement reserved China's right to redeem the lines (except, of course, the trans-Siberian) in thirty-six years, and that in any case it was to revert to China at the end of eighty years. In 1904, before the Russo-Japanese War, the total length of Russian railway lines in Manchuria was 1,596 miles and if, as Li Hung-chang and Count Witte foresaw, the menace to China was from the side of Japan, the treaty could not be said in any way to have been an aggression against China. In fact, Li Hung-chang was convinced that the safety and security of China lay in the construction by Russia of these railway lines and that Japan could be resisted only with Russian assistance. But from 1897 onwards a new attitude dominates Russian policy, mainly as a result of the influence of Wilhelm II of Germany; his policy was reflected in the Hamburg speech in which he had vaingloriously declared that the 'German Michael has firmly (!) planted his shield with the device of the German Eagle upon the soil of China. Should anyone essay to detract from our just rights or to injure us, then up and at him with your mailed fist.' Russia was privy to German plans and had herself decided as her share a lease of Port Arthur and Dalny. But here again it is significant that the two conventions of Peking (March 27) and St. Petersburg (May 7), 1898, expressly reserve China's sovereign rights. Port Arthur, which was to be a naval base, was closed to all but Russian and Chinese vessels, and Dalny (or Dairen) was to be a trading port. Russia received also the right to connect the two ports with Harbin.

During this period of seven years, from 1897–1904, Russia became an active participant in the policy of the Western nations to take full advantage of the weakness of China. She claimed the inclusion in loan arrangements, pretended to special rights in railway construction and was prepared to join with others in putting pressure on China. She began to expand her authority on the Manchurian railways, and while no territorial claims were put forward in respect of Manchuria itself, there was a noticeable tendency to consider that area as being within the Russian sphere of influence, perhaps for the reason that in view of the proximity of her own frontiers she desired to exclude from it British influence which Russia feared ever since the abortive attempts of British naval authorities in the North Pacific during the Crimean War.

Russia's dream of a naval base in an ice-free port and an outlet to the sea free from British control seemed at last to have been realized, but by this act she had challenged the maritime powers and come up against the ambitions of Japan; and also alienated China. The Russo-Japanese War, in which Japan had the moral support of Britain, was the result;

and by the Treaty of Portsmouth, Russia was excluded from Manchuria and her rights in that territory passed to the victor. After this time the Tsarist Government was inactive in Chinese affairs. Before she had recovered her position in the East, the world war had started, bringing with it the Great Revolution. The influence of the Revolution on the people of Asia will be considered presently in some detail. Here it is sufficient to say that in July 1919, Karakhan, the Assistant Commissar, announced to the world that the Soviet Government voluntarily renounced her rights of extra-territoriality and was prepared to restore to China the unfair rights acquired by the Tsarist Government.

We may pause here to consider the special features of the Tsarist expansion in Siberia and the marked differences between Russian policy and the policy of the maritime Powers, especially England and France.[1] The position of America was at all times different from that of the Western European States, except in the matter of religious aggression and educational activity. Germany and Italy, though anxious to play a part and the former to take a leading role, were late comers in the Far Eastern field and did not have sufficient time to work out a consistent policy. Germany, it is true, occupied Kiaochow and acquired extensive rights, but these were meant to give her a position in the sun along with the other Great Powers and a share in the loot. The policy of the Western nations was patterned on the historic tradition developed by Britain and France. From this the Russian policy differed in the following essential respects.

Alone among the great European States, Russia, during her 300 years of contact with the Chinese, never had to resort to war. While on the excuse of opium or of missionaries, England, France and Germany actually carried on wars or war-like operations, Russia ostentatiously kept aloof. She did not resort to coercive measures to acquire rights.

Secondly, as we have pointed out earlier, her expansion (till the 'Manchurian issue' developed) was in the disputed area where the Chinese themselves were trying to expand. While Britain, after the first Chinese War, occupied Hong Kong and France later annexed Tongking, both integral parts of the historic Chinese State, the expansion by Russia to the coast and her occupation of the north bank of the Amur were of territory which the Chinese no doubt claimed to be under their protection, but which was not actually under their occupation. This is demonstrated by the fact that till Russia notified Peking, the Chinese authorities were not even aware of the action of Muraviev and his colleagues. The attitude of the Chinese towards these two sets of acqui-

[1] Russian expansion in Central Asia followed a different pattern from that in Siberia. In Central Asia, the expansion was by conquest, Russian imperialism was much more like the imperialism of Western countries.

sitions is fundamentally different. In the case of territories occupied by the Han race, the Chinese feeling is as if China has been deprived of a part of her own body: in the case of the trans-Amur territory, it is the limitation of a claim which was never very effective and in any case one which did not affect to touch China's own home territory.

Even in regard to Manchuria, where undoubtedly Russia was carrying out an aggressive policy, the Tsarist Government was careful enough not to offend the sentiments of the Chinese and took pains at least in form to safeguard the sovereignty of Peking.[1]

More important than these two considerations was the fact that Russia was at no time concerned with the two policies – the forcing of opium on China and the trade in human flesh – which both the people and Government of China resented and which brought her untold humiliation. In opium traffic, which caused so much degradation, misery and loss of face to the Chinese and was the direct cause of her military defeats, the main offender was Britain. In the 'pig trade' – that is, the forcible transportation of Chinese workers to plantations and mines – again, in defiance of the orders of Government and of the protests of the people – in this new slave trade, where sometimes forty per cent of those transported died on the way, all Western Powers including America were deeply involved. Russia, for whatever reason, was no party to it. It was these two, the 'poison trade' and the 'pig trade', that made the iron enter the soul of the Chinese and made them bitterly anti-foreign.

Again Russia had no significant part or lot in the attempted religious conquest of China. We shall in a later chapter examine the effects of the misguided enthusiasm which led the Western nations, especially America, Britain and France, to invade China spiritually, undermine her social and ethical traditions, and try to impose under the authority of imperialism and extra-territoriality a religion which the Chinese as a whole unequivocally rejected.[2]

Finally, it is necessary to emphasize that the Russians ostentatiously dissociated themselves from the crude acts of vandalism, such as the burning and looting of the Summer Palace in 1860; and even during the Boxer incident, when the Western allies were carrying out the announced German policy of giving no quarter, the Russian envoy and the troops withdrew from Peking. When expeditions were being sent out in April

[1] Russian imperialism was none the less a reality. Its penetration of Manchuria was comprehensive and effective. Its instruments were the Chinese Eastern and South Manchuria railways. These were ruled by the St Petersburg Ministry of Finance.

[2] In Central and West Asia, Russia's record was less good. In the eighteenth century, the Tatars of the Volga valley were persecuted for religious reasons with special savagery.

1901, the Russians took no part in them. Though the Russian representative after a period of hesitation co-operated with other Powers in relieving the Legation at Peking and in exacting reparations, it is noteworthy that Russia took up an independent attitude. In fact, it was a matter of complaint at the time that the Russians withdrew their troops before the treaty was signed; and during the negotiations for the peace protocol it was well known that the Russian representative maintained direct contact with the Chinese negotiator, Li Hung-chang, whose house was guarded by the Cossacks. The attitude of the Russians was considered from the Western point of view to be 'indecent'. The Russian minister, it would seem, moved heaven and earth to get Li accepted as 'Negotiator Plenipotentiary' in spite of the opposition of the British representative. The Russian envoy in fact became the friend and adviser of the Chinese negotiator.[1] Also after the peace was negotiated, while others were seeking revenge and pressing for punishment, Baron de Giers on behalf of Russia did all in his power to help to evade the 'punishment edict' and to give official protection to numerous Chinese. Also, it should be remembered that Count Lamsdorff, the Russian Foreign Minister, declared to the British Ambassador in St Petersburg that his government 'took no interest in missionaries' and would not therefore associate itself with other Powers in demanding punishment of those who had attacked missionaries.[2] This deserves to be contrasted with the demand persistently made by the Western Powers for the execution of those against whom they preferred the charges of attacking missionaries.

It is no wonder that in these circumstances, in spite of Westernized education of Chinese leaders and the influence which America and Britain exercised with successive governments, the attitude of the Chinese people towards Russia was never particularly hostile, and she suffered but little from the anti-foreign feeling which swept over China at different times.

[1] Daniele Varé: *The Last of the Empresses.* John Murray, p. 208.
[2] Bland: *Life of Li Hung-chang*, pp. 205–9.

CHAPTER 2

ASIA AND THE RUSSIAN REVOLUTION

THOUGH the effects of the October Revolution on the peoples of Asia are outside the scope of this study, a brief analysis of the forces generated by that historic event is necessary for a proper appreciation of the relations between Europe and Asia in the vital period between 1918 and 1948. This period marked the end of Western authority on the Asian continent and as the national movements in the countries of Asia which finally won their freedom were influenced, and in some cases inspired, by the existence of the Soviet State and the growth of Soviet power, it is necessary to understand in what way this influence worked. The question is therefore discussed here only to the extent of trying to discover what influence the October Revolution and the ideas it generated had on the relations of Asia with Europe.

Before we proceed to examine in general the influence of the Soviets in Asia, it is necessary to describe in outline the character of the former Russian Empire in Asia. The Russian moves towards Central Asia, as Mr Wint points out in his study,[1] were 'little more than the acceptance of the transfer of the allegiance of Muslim princes from the Mongol to the Russian Empire'. The principal nomads in the routes to Central Asia, the Kazakhs, were divided into two hordes, one of which voluntarily asked for Russian protection; and gradually without any serious military operations the vast area between Siberia and Jaxartes passed under the authority of the Tsar. The only effectively organized States in Central Asia were the Khanates of Khiva, Bokhara and Khokand, famed in Islamic history as the centre of Timur's Empire and the seats of learning and culture. Khokand was in due course annexed, but Khiva and Bokhara maintained a formal autonomy under their own khans. Thus the Russian Empire reached the frontiers of Afghanistan and Persia and had even before this extended to the Pacific.

The character of the Tsar's Empire, which differentiated it from the imperialism of Britain, is well described by Owen Lattimore in the

[1] *British in Asia*, p. 137.

following words: 'The Russian Empire was built by an incorporative process differing from the accumulative process (of Britain). All its holdings lay within one vast unbroken expanse of land. . . . People were incorporated as well as territories. The ordinary Russian was himself a subject, rather than a citizen. Non-Russian peoples were elevated to the status of the Russians themselves. . . . A part of the ruling class of each people was assimilated to the status of the Russian ruling class. . . .'

This difference became more and more marked with the rise of nationalist movements. The growth of nationalism was hastened in the British and other empires of Western nations by the racial exclusion and the resentment of what had been or would have become the ruling classes. In Tsarist Russia, on the other hand, as Lattimore emphasizes, 'any form of revolution including nationalist revolution, was bound to affect both Russians and non-Russians who lived side by side or inter-mingled with each other'.[1] Naturally the ruling classes, Russian and non-Russian, in Tsarist Russia were allied together. Therefore when the Revolution broke out, it seemed at first, as when Enver Pasha tried to organize a Muslim rebellion in Central Asia, that with the disappearance of the Tsar the Asian territories might break away from Russia.

This did not happen. True, the Asian nationalists made a bid for power. But in the Volga region, in Azerbaijan, in Bokhara and in Georgia they were quickly suppressed by the Bolsheviks. Russia's Asian Empire was maintained intact.

On the whole, Bolshevik Russia had little further trouble in defending its authority. It was able to enlist for the cause of the revolution a part of the Asian peoples themselves.[2]

Also it should be remembered that the Revolution had a well-defined national policy which had an irresistible appeal to the struggling dependencies, colonies and semi-colonial countries in Asia. The Declaration of the Rights of the Peoples of Russia, over the joint signatures of Lenin and Stalin, proclaimed the equality and sovereignty of the peoples of Russia, and the right of the peoples of Russia to freedom of development of national minorities. This was indeed an explosive statement and all the nations of Asia, struggling for freedom, heard it with a new hope. This emphasis on national self-determination and ethnic separateness of minorities had an immense effect in shaping opinion in Asia during the next quarter of a century.

From the first the Soviets also announced their support for the struggle for independence in India, China, Indonesia and Indo-China, not only as a Revolutionary slogan, but on the ground that imperialism

[1] Owen Lattimore: *Situation in Asia*, p. 17.

[2] Where it did encounter resistance, Russia suppressed it ruthlessly. The fate of the Kazalh people is an example.

is in itself the summation of capitalism and its destruction by bourgeois nationalist movements is a progressive stage in evolution. It therefore deserved support. There is no doubt that the nationalist movements in all Asian countries gained moral strength by the mere existence of a Revolutionary Russia. In countries where the nationalist movements had already been in existence for a considerable time, like India, the Communist theory gained but little support; but in Indonesia and Indo-China, where the movements for independence became effective in the period after the Russian Revolution, the Communists became a major factor in the forces working for liberation. In each one of these countries Communist parties came into existence in the period between 1920–23. In Indonesia they were able to gain considerable influence by 1926, when their hand was suspected in the widespread disturbances directed against the Dutch, which broke out in Java in that year. In Indo-China also it spread quickly among the nationalist groups.

In China the Communist Party was founded in Shanghai in 1921. But the small groups which established the party were no index of the wide influence of the Revolution on the progressive national leaders of the time. This could be judged from the fact that Sun Yat-sen, the Father of the Revolution and the spokesman of Chinese nationalism, stated publicly after he became fully aware of the attitude of the Western Powers and of America towards a strong and rehabilitated China: 'We no longer look to the West. Our faces are turned towards Russia.' The Soviet leaders also began to realize that the main stream of national awakening in China was represented then by Sun Yat-sen and his party, and following a report by H. Maring, who visited China to study the problem on the spot, the Soviet Government sent Adolphe Joffe to establish contact with Sun Yat-sen. The discussions between the two leaders, conducted in the safety of the international settlement at Shanghai, led to a joint statement regarding Sino-Soviet co-operation. In this famous document the Soviet representative gave expression to the view that 'China's paramount and most pressing problem is to achieve national unification and full national independence'. The support of Asian nationalism by Revolutionary Russia was thus publicly proclaimed.

Even more important than the added strength that the nationalist movements received was the change in the character of nationalism itself which is to be attributed mainly to the doctrines of the Revolution. Before the October Revolution, the nationalist movements in India and China were liberal and exclusively political. The issue was solely one of freedom from foreign domination. Such political content as the nationalist movements had was based on parliamentary liberalism, and on representative government. The movements had neither a defined social nor an economic objective, and were in that sense vague and Utopian. The Russian Revolution altered all this. The San Min Chu I, the Three People's Principles, confused though they may appear, formulated an economic doctrine, the central point of which was Land to the Tiller. The Indian Congress Party put in the forefront of its programme the abolition of untouchability – itself a revolutionary measure of immense significance. Also national movements thought in terms of 'planning'. The achievements of the successive five-year plans gave an impetus to all Asian countries to organize their economy for production in order to take them out of colonial systems which had made them weak, disorganized and dependent. The attack on the West came where it touched Europe most – in the sphere of economic life. The Asian countries were no longer content to be markets for Europe's industries; and the way a 'backward' country like Russia had in a few years of planned production emerged as a leading industrial country gave to the peoples of Asia the hope of industrial regeneration and economic independence.

The intellectual domination which the West had so long exercised was also undermined effectively by the Russian Revolution. In the first two decades of the twentieth century, philosophers like Dewey and Bertrand Russell, Bergson and Croce, political thinkers like Laski and Cole and intellectual leaders like Shaw, D'Annunzio, Anatole France and Pirandello had the greatest vogue. But by the end of the 'twenties new movements had begun to develop in Asia reflecting the revolutionary trends which had their origin in Russia. Progressive writing became not merely a fashion but a movement. With the emergence of Lu Hsun in China and Prem Chand in India the century-long reign of Western Letters may be said to have come to a close.

That the Russian Revolution quickened the pulse of the peoples of Asia no one would deny. That it also helped to awaken the masses, to create doubts in the minds of thinking people about the validity of many things which they had accepted without question from the West, could not also be doubted. Equally it would be accepted that its general effect was to weaken the hold of the West on the peoples of Asia. But beyond all this there is one significant point: and that is, it affected different people differently. In countries like India, where social reorganization had to some extent taken place and the old tradition broken down as a result of a hundred years of reform, the message of the Russian Revolution did not have the same force as in China and Indo-China where, owing to the historical factors previously analysed, the West had only helped to undermine the old society without helping to build anything to take its place. In the social and ethical anarchy thus created, the doctrines of the Russian Revolution had a dominant influence which they failed to secure in India. In countries like Iran and Afghanistan, where the social structure, however reactionary, had held together and was not subjected to the same pressures as in China and in India, its direct influence has been even less. Thus we have the significant phenomenon of Communism moving in to fill a vacuum in China and in Annam, while in India, where the vacuum had been previously filled by a partial readjustment of society and a reform of religion, Communist thought has been mainly an intellectual development, helping to oust the hold of the West. And, finally, in independent countries like Iran, Afghanistan and Siam, where there has been but little social or religious aggression, Communist thought has on the whole failed to have any appeal.

The case of Japan stands in an entirely different category. The October Revolution instead of raising any hopes in Japan caused it the greatest alarm. Japan had joined the ranks of 'aggressors' and her interest naturally was that any revolution in Asia against the West should be solely for national independence and not for radical changes in society. Therefore the Russian Revolution with its appeal to the proletariat and with active encouragement of 'the exploited classes' was a threat as much to her as to the Western nations. She was among the most vociferous advocates of intervention in Russia, and unsuccessfully tried to separate Eastern Siberia from Soviet territory. While the other Asian countries, even the most conservative of them, were inclined to see in the new Russia a possible ally in their struggle against the West, Japan saw in her the most dangerous enemy to her national greatness. It is this feeling, together with the sense of suffering injustice at the hands of Britain and America, that forced her to join Germany and Italy in the anti-Comintern Pact.

Part V

EUROPE IN RETREAT

1918–1939

CHAPTER I

THE EUROPEAN CIVIL WAR AND ITS EFFECTS

The Great War of 1914-8 was from the Asian point of view a civil war within the European community of nations. The direct participation of Asian countries, during some stages of this conflict, was at the invitation and by the encouragement of one of the parties, the *entente* Powers, and was greatly resented by the Germans. It is necessary to emphasize this internal character of the European conflict to realize its full significance on the development of events in Asia.

We have already noticed that at the beginning of the twentieth century the European nations, in the enjoyment of unprecedented economic prosperity and political prestige, remained unshakably convinced that they had inherited the earth, and that their supremacy in Asia was permanent and was something in the nature of a predetermined Divine Order. It was the age of Kipling and the white man's burden, and it seemed the manifest destiny of the white race to hold the East in fee. But though the edifice seemed impregnable two cracks had already appeared. The first was, as we noticed, the ambition of the new German Empire under Wilhelm II for a place in the Asian sun. Contradictions and rivalries of a kind which never existed before, when Britain's authority in the East was unchallenged, developed within the ranks of colonial Powers. The partition of China, at least into spheres of influence, was the great objective and seemed to be on the point of realization when the rivalries of territorial and non-territorial imperialists clashed, and China got a welcome and, as it happened, a decisive respite. America, which at that time disclaimed all territorial interests and was concerned with the policy of deriving maximum benefits from privileges granted to others, constituted a non-territorial imperialism whose claims could not be reconciled with a territorial partition of China. The old system, therefore, felt the strain of a double attack by the newcomers among the imperialists, Germany and Japan, who desired to gain control over territories and by America who desired that all parts of China should be equally open to her.

The second crack in the European hegemony was the growth of Japan as a Great Power in the Far East. From 1895, Japan had declared that she would line up with the European Powers, that in effect she would follow the same policies and expected to be treated in the same manner as the European Powers. Though in form Japan had therefore joined the forces arrayed against China, it was clear from the beginning that she was only utilizing the machinery of collective European action against China for the purpose of aggrandizing herself with the object of excluding European influence wherever possible in the Far East.

The immediate result of the European war was to effect an irreparable breach in Western solidarity in Asia. The major scene of action in this matter was, of course, China. Though at the very beginning, on August 3, 1914, China asked that her neutrality should be respected and no hostilities should take place in Chinese territories leased to foreigners, the Powers wantonly disregarded it and refused to respect her territorial integrity. A Japanese force, assisted by a British contingent, landed on Chinese territory, attacked and reduced Tsingtao and took over the Kiaochow Peninsula. The extraordinary course that the Japanese authorities followed and the Twenty-one Demands made on China will be discussed elsewhere, but the point necessary to emphasize here is that by this act one major European Power in Asia was for the first time driven out by an Asian Power and excluded from further influence in Asian affairs, and this was done with the active assistance of Britain, whose general, it will be remembered, fought under a Japanese commander-in-chief, General Kamio.

Secondly, as time went on and the war situation became more and more critical, Britain and France, in a frenzy of anti-Germanism, instigated a reluctant Chinese Government on one pretext or another to take over German properties and to eradicate all German influence in China. Britain especially was anxious to get control of German ships interned in Chinese ports. Under French pressure, German industries in China, banking and commercial houses and other enterprises, were closed. The concessions were taken over and, of course, extra-territorial rights denounced. A precedent of great future value to China was thus established. Finally, China was encouraged to declare war on the Central Powers.

In 1914, when the German invaders had reached the Marne, divisions of the Indian Army under British officers had been rushed to France and had helped at the critical moment to stem the German tide. Later, they were extensively used in the defence of the Suez Canal and the Middle East and in campaigns elsewhere in Africa. In 1917, Siam declared war on Germany. An Indo-Chinese labour force had been recruited and was working in France. On August 14, 1917, China also joined the Allies.

Thus all the nations of Asia were brought into the European civil war. However, opinion in India, China and even in Japan was at the time more pro-German than pro-Ally. In India, except among the ruling princes, there was no pro-British feeling, and public opinion rejoiced at every report of German victory and felt depressed when the Allies were winning. China declared war only with the greatest reluctance and for the express purpose of checking Japanese plans of aggression. In Japan itself, after the Shantung campaign, feeling against the Allies was most marked, and a Press campaign of great virulence was conducted against Britain at the end of 1916. Actually, though the Asian countries fought on the side of the Allies, public opinion in the East looked upon the conflict as a civil war in which neither party had a claim to the friendship of the peoples of Asia, and if any party could appeal to the sympathy of Asians it was the Germanic alliance which had no tradition of Asian conquest and was allied with the chief Muslim Power, Turkey.

But the participation of Asian people in the war had far-reaching consequences.

The Indian soldier who fought on the Marne came back to India with other ideas of the *Sahib* than those he was taught to believe by decades of official propaganda. Indo-Chinese Labour Corps in the South of France returned to Annam with notions of democracy and republicanism which they had not entertained before. Among the Chinese who went to France at the time was a young man named Chou En-lai, who stayed on to become a Communist and had to be expelled for activities among the members of the Chinese Labour Corps.

More important than these influences was the fact that the French and British administrations in Asia had to appeal to their subjects for moral support. To ask Indians and Indo-Chinese to subscribe to war loans for the defence of democracy and to prevent the world being overwhelmed by German *Kultur*, would have sounded as strange and callous irony unless accompanied by promises of democracy for themselves and freedom for their own cultures. When, besides subscriptions for war loans, Indians and Indo-Chinese were pressed to join up and fight to save democracy, the contraditions of the position became too obvious even for the colonial administrators. In India the demand was made openly by the nationalist leaders that prior agreement on political problems was necessary before support of the war could be considered a national programme.

Politically, a further weakening of the colonial and imperialist position came about as a result of President Wilson's declaration of fourteen points. In 1917, the doctrine of the 'self-determination of peoples' had the ring of a new revelation. Whatever its effect was on the suppressed nationalities of Europe, in Asia it was acclaimed as a doctrine of liberation. As every Allied Power hastened to declare its faith in the new formula of Wilson (and it was soon raised to the position of an accepted 'war aim' in the propaganda campaign against the Germans), the colonial Powers found it difficult to oppose openly or resist publicly the claims of Asian nations based on this formula. It became difficult to proclaim self-determination of peoples as a great ideal for the establishment of which Asian peoples should co-operate with Europeans and fight and lose their lives in distant battlefields, but which, however excellent, could not be applied to themselves. Self-government for colonial countries had thus to be accepted, and the claim to it could no longer be brushed aside as premature or stigmatized as sedition.

In China, naturally, self-determination had a wide and ready-made field for immediate application. Apart from disabilities resulting from unequal treaties, there were areas where foreigners were exercising jurisdiction. The retention of Kiaochow by Japan would be a clear violation of the doctrine of self-determination. The limitations on Chinese customs, the numerous concession areas at ports, the maintenance of foreign troops on Chinese soil, all these seemed to militate against the self-determination of the Chinese.

Apart from these political considerations economic forces generated by the war were also helping to undermine the supremacy of the West. Japan utilized the four years of war for a planned expansion of her trade in the East. German competition had been eliminated. Britain and France, engaged in a mortal struggle when their entire resources of production had to be directed towards victory, had also left the field fairly open. India gained her first major start on the industrial road and, with the strain on British economy, Indian national capital was placed in a position of some advantage. In fact the full results of the weakening of European capitalism became evident only after the war when the pre-eminence of London was challenged by America, and British capital, though still powerful, began to be on the defensive in India. The growth of capitalist enterprise in India, and the development of industries and participation by Indian capital in spheres so far monopolistically held by Britain, like jute, resulted directly from the weakening of the economic position of Britain.

Two other results of a general character may be indicated. The first, the growth of a powerful left-wing movement in the countries of Western Europe had a direct effect on shaping events in the Eastern Empire. The Labour Party in England during the days of its growth had been closely associated with the nationalist movement in India. In fact, Ramsay MacDonald, the leader of the Socialist Party after the war, had been one of its champions from the earliest days. Similarly, Annamite nationalism had worked hand in hand with left-wing parties in France. In the period that immediately followed the war these parties had come to possess considerable influence in national affairs and, as we shall see, were instrumental in giving effect to policies which loosened the old bonds of political domination.

The second factor was, of course, the influence of the Russian Revolution which has been dealt with separately. Here it is sufficient to say that the October Revolution, as one of the results of the Great War, gave to the principles which all the Allies had accepted as their objectives a new content. Imperialism meant something totally different after Lenin's definition of it as the last phase of capitalism and his insistence that the liberation of subject peoples from colonial domination was a part of the struggle against capitalism.

Finally, the war had accelerated the pace of movements everywhere. For example, in India, the movement for independence which was confined to the intelligentsia in 1914 became a mass movement of immense proportions in 1919. Everywhere the case was similar. The *tempo* of events had acquired a momentum which few had foreseen and none had forecast in 1918. The war was a great world revolution which divided by a deep gulf the days before August 1914 and after November 1918.

One fact which stands out clear and illustrates this chasm in thought is the lack of faith in imperialist ideals in the period that followed the war. With the solitary exception of Churchill, there was not one major figure in any of the British parties who confessed to a faith in the white man's mission to rule. Successive Viceroys of India, Liberal, Conservative and non-party, professed publicly their adherence to the cause of Indian freedom. Secretaries of State from Edwin Montagu (1917-22) to Pethick Lawrence, including such stalwarts of Conservatism as Sir Samuel Hoare (Lord Templewood), claimed that they were working for the freedom of the Indian people and not for the maintenance of British rule. The French were no doubt more brave in their words, but the faith had gone out of them also.

Nowhere did this come out more clearly than in the treatment of China. Incidents which previously would have been dealt with sternly and for which territories and indemnities would have been exacted, were now only the subjects of a mild protest. Chiang Kai-shek's armies occupied the concessions at Hankow, and for months Hong Kong was subjected to an intensive trade boycott; these events would earlier have immediately led to a display of overwhelming naval strength. Britain in 1926 was prepared patiently to negotiate. Even the 'old China hands', who had watched with regret the sudden eclipse of European prestige, though they acted the Blimps in their clubs, never seriously felt that Western authority could be re-established over China by the use of gunboats. There was no conviction left of the European's superiority or sense of vision.

CHAPTER 2

INDIA

THE pomp and ceremony of a great imperial *durbar* in the historic city of Delhi to celebrate the coronation of King George V registered the high-water mark of British authority in India. Seated in the great audience hall of Shah Jehan, in surroundings reflecting the pageantry of India, King George as Emperor received the homage of the great princes and potentates. Scions of famous ancient houses acted as pages to the King and the Queen. Indian rulers felt honoured to be aides-de-camp to His Majesty. There was every evidence of public approval and no voice of protest was heard. It was, indeed, a demonstration of the might and prestige of the British Empire. And yet the proclamations announced at the *durbar* contained one act of significant surrender to popular agitation. The partition of Bengal, the masterpiece of Lord Curzon's policy, against which the people of that province had carried on an unremitting agitation, had been cancelled. Few who witnessed that solemn and imposing ceremony realized that the sun of British authority had passed the meridian on that day and that thirty-five years later the flag of Britain would be lowered on that fort.

A reminder of the changing circumstances was not long delayed. A few months later, when the Viceroy, Lord Hardinge, who had transferred the capital from Calcutta to Delhi, made a State entry into the new capital, a bomb was thrown at him by a Bengali revolutionary, Rash Behari Bose, who later found asylum in Japan and lived to be associated with the provisional 'free government of India' established by Japan during the Second World War. When the war broke out in August 1914, India was comparatively quiet. But as the war developed and its possible effects became clearer, the demand for immediate 'Home Rule', as it was then called, became insistent. Even the Conservative, Austen Chamberlain, as Secretary of State, had to agree that the time for a considerable political advance had arrived. English political thinking on India also underwent a notable change at this time. Lionel Curtis, in a remarkable political document entitled 'Letters to the Indian People on Responsible

Government', argued that parliamentary democracy with responsible government was the only line of evolution for India and therefore the next step should be the introduction of responsibility to the people in certain well-defined spheres in the provinces. An announcement by the British Government in August 1917 laid down the policy in regard to India 'as the gradual development of self-governing institutions with a view to the progressive realization of responsible government in India as an integral part of the British Empire'.

The idea of responsible government was a new departure, but it should be noted that it was only a distant objective and the immediate action proposed was only the development of self-governing institutions, and that also was to be gradual. No one in India was satisfied with the halting and illiberal announcement and the reform, known after its authors as the Montagu-Chelmsford reform, when passed by Parliament and put into operation received but little public support. Apart, however, from the controversy about the constitution there were other fields in which India made notable advances at this time. To the War Cabinet which Lloyd George established in London two Indians were nominated. India was also invited to the Imperial Conferences, the membership of which till then had been confined to the self-governing members of the Commonwealth. Her position had so far advanced internationally as to enable her to claim for herself a seat at the Peace Conference and to make her voice felt in some measure in matters affecting her direct interests.

When the war was over the general public, already dissatisfied with the measure of reforms, and the Muslims deeply resentful of the harshness of the terms proposed for the Turkish settlement, combined in a powerful upsurge of opinion which frightened the authorities in the Punjab. The Provincial Government declared martial law and took very severe measures to put down what it considered to be a rebellion. The severity of the action, especially the massacre of Jallianwalla Bagh, only further angered the Indian public and transformed the agitation to a great national movement. In England itself this wanton act of cruelty shocked the conscience of the people. It was at this time, when the nation was feeling the humiliation of Jallianwalla Bagh, that Mahatma Gandhi took the leadership of the country and started his non-co-operation movement.

Mahatma Gandhi's ideas were simple. He argued that, as the British authority in India was based on the co-operation of all classes of Indian people, a withdrawal of that co-operation must necessarily bring the Government to an end. Mr Gandhi realized that in a country of 400 million people such a programme of withdrawal of co-operation would mean first that the people should be awakened; secondly, that they should feel a moral compulsion to act; and thirdly, the movement should be rigidly disciplined and controlled and based on a principle which would be understood by all. Such a principle Gandhi claimed to have discovered in his non-violent *Satyagraha*. Muslim opinion at the time was gravely agitated by the provocative action of the British Government in dividing up the homelands of Turkey among the Western Allies, and the agitation for the restoration of the *Khalif*, which found wide support among Indian Muslims, was accepted by Mr Gandhi as a part of the nationalist programme.

The non-co-operation movement, under Mr Gandhi's leadership, passed through three stages – the first when in alliance with the *Khalifat* leaders he originated the movement and made it a mass agitation of immense power. This was between 1920-4. The second period started with the Dandi march and the Salt *Satyagraha* (1929-32). The third was the 'Quit India' movement of 1942. The Gandhian movement witnessed its final triumph in August 1947, when Britain by agreement quitted India and brought to a close the chapter of history that began with Plassey in 1757.

The period following 1919 saw also the development of constitutional and parliamentary government in India. The Montagu-Chelmsford reforms, to which we have alluded earlier, introduced parliamentary government with partial responsibility in the provinces of India. This system, known as dyarchy, placed in the hands of popular ministers, responsible to the legislature, authority over a wide range of subjects, while 'law and order' and finances continued to be in the hands of nominated British officials. Public opinion in India rejected the scheme, but it was worked through pro-British elements in many of the provinces. The dyarchical system continued in the provinces till 1936, and though owing to the opposition of the Congress and the lack of enthusiasm of the people it was not a notable political success, the period marked further retreat from the imperialist position.[1]

The most important stages in this retreat may be briefly indicated. The first was the agreement on fiscal autonomy under which the British Government in London pledged itself not to interfere with problems affecting Indian finances when both the Central Legislature of India and the Government in Delhi were in agreement. In substance this meant that British interests would not be allowed to override Indian interests in deciding the policies of the Government in Delhi. A second advance of Indian national claims and a corresponding retreat of British interests was the acceptance of the policy of discriminating protection for Indian manufactures. England herself had reluctantly given up her policy of

[1] See *Working of Dyarchy in India by Kerala putra* (K. M. Panikkar). Bombay, 1928.

free trade and adopted a system of protection for herself. She could not, therefore, object logically to the Government of India embarking on a cautious policy of tariffs for the purpose of protecting her nascent industries. Steel, sugar, cement, silk and even cotton benefited by the tariff policy, which for the first time gave India a chance to develop industrially. British vested interests, however, were powerful enough to prevent any protection being given to the shipping industry.

The establishment of a Reserve Bank for India was the first step to free the rupee from the control of the London market. The growth of Indian banking and insurance during this period was also indicative of the increasing strength of Indian capital. The boycott of foreign goods which the non-co-operation movement had used as a political weapon had helped the European industrialists to realize that the days of their unchallenged authority were numbered. Consequently there was a tendency on the part of Indian and British capital to co-operate in certain limited fields. Under the pressure of public opinion, the Government of India also embarked on a policy of nationalizing the railways. Over a period of twenty years the lines in India owned by British companies were acquired. The exclusion of British capital from so large a sphere and the management of the lines by the State were developments of considerable significance.

In the field of executive control also nationalism advanced steadily. The Indian Army, which before the Great War was officered exclusively by British officers, yielded slowly to pressure and initiated after the war a policy of granting King's Commissions to Indian cadets after a period of training at Sandhurst. The Indianization of the army was one of the demands of all the moderate parties, and a scheme of officering a certain number of regiments was put into effect as a result of parliamentary pressure. It was this group of officers, commissioned after the First Great War, who took over the command of the Indian Army at the time of India's independence. A Royal Indian Navy was created in 1924, and a beginning was made of establishing an air force, in both of which Indians were given a few commissions. Though the military forces were still predominantly British, the monopoly on which British authority in India rested was effectively breached by these measures.

In the administrative field, political pressure was able to secure that Indian appointments in superior services should reach 50 per cent of the total. The British had developed their administrative machinery on the basis of a large Indian bureaucracy guided and controlled by what were known as the superior services—the Indian Civil Service, Indian Police Service, etc. In these superior services, which were recruited by competition held in England, a number of Indians had secured admission even in the last decades of the nineteenth century. But their proportion was small. After the war, the examinations for public service were held also in India, and the increased percentage of appointments in the service effected a slow but important change in the character of government.

In the Central Cabinet, Indian representation after the war generally amounted to 50 per cent, though the key portfolios of Home and Finance were reserved for Europeans. In the provinces the proportion was even higher and sometimes even the finance ministries were entrusted to Indians. Thus in the administrative field, no less than in the political and economic fields, imperial authority had completely retreated from position to position when a new attempt was made, by the Government of India Act of 1935, to reconcile the claims of Indian nationalism with a modified imperial authority.

As already mentioned, the Reforms of 1919 failed to satisfy any section of Indian opinion, and consequently the Conservative Government of Baldwin appointed in 1928 a commission to inquire and report on the whole question. This report, while recognizing the necessity of immediate further advance, recommended only a limited self-government with provincial autonomy and a federal council for the Centre. Of course it fell far short of Indian expectations and led to further intensified agitation by all parties. In the meantime a Labour Government had come into power under Ramsay MacDonald, and a new attempt at conciliation was made by calling a series of round table conferences – 1930–3 – in which all major Indian and European interests were represented. The discussions at these conferences, in which the National Congress under Mr Gandhi participated only in one session, led to the formulation of a federal scheme of government based on self-governing provinces and princely States. Though the constitution represented in principle a substantial advance on what had been proposed in the past, the Government of India Act of 1935, as it emerged from Parliament, was an attempt to create a successor Government of India composed of feudal ruling princes and reactionary parties basing themselves on religion. Further it limited the authority of the Central Government by special safeguards for the interests of British business and capital, and by writing into the constitution clauses meant to protect and permanently uphold the rights of ruling princes and other special classes. The Congress rejected the new reforms but captured the power in the provinces in 1936, and was able to secure the nullification of the various limitations which the Act had sought to impose. It was while Congress governments were functioning in the provinces, more or less successfully, that the Second World War broke out and the constitutional experiment was given up.

It has been noticed that in the inter-war period British authority in India was in full retreat. The old idea of imperial domination had disappeared with the first war, and all the political manoeuvring of the period between 1920-9 was in the nature of delaying rearguard actions. The British authorities hoped to be able by their superior political knowledge and experience to modify and limit the independence which they knew India would ultimately acquire: they tried to do this by creating classes and interests which would support their position. The original plan was to undermine the unity of India by separating the princely States, which formed two-fifths of the area of India, and by keeping them directly under the Crown. As early as 1917, when the Montagu-Chelmsford reforms were discussed, steps were taken to constitute a Chamber of Princes, but as the question of Indian independence seemed outside practical politics no encouragement was then given to the claim of the rulers to be freed from the control of the Central Government. With the growth of the non-co-operation movement and the wide appeal of new democracy, an alliance was easily formed between the ambitious rulers of the greater States and the British reactionaries, and the theory was evolved that the suzerainty over the princes was the prerogative of the Crown and therefore the relationship of the Indian rulers was with England and not with India. This attempt to combine the dynastic ambitions of autocratic rulers with the imperial interests of Britain, however, failed through the opposition of some of the more enlightened rulers, who realized, however vaguely, that to resist national claims would be considered unpatriotic by their own subjects and that a short-sighted effort to break up the unity of India would be dangerous in the long run to themselves. The idea to create a Federal Government at the Centre by a union of provinces and the princely States originated from this, and here again the British interests sought to safeguard themselves by the creation of a centre in which the representatives of the princes together with reactionary religious groups would have a permanent majority.

The determined opposition of the nationalists and the claims of the Muslims for a separate State with complete independence rendered the Act of 1935 abortive. Realizing the failure of their efforts, the British Government, through Sir Stafford Cripps, offered complete Dominion status with certain temporary limitations during the period of the War, but the scheme failed to materialize owing to intransigeance of the Civil Services and the then Governor-General, Lord Linlithgow. Finally in 1947, India achieved her independence after the areas with a majority of Muslim population were separated to form the new State of Pakistan. The authority of the British Government ceased in India on August 15, 1947, when the King of England dropped his title of Emperor of India.

CHAPTER 3

CHINA

THE conditions following the breakdown of the Manchu Empire in China present a close parallel to those following the eclipse of Mogul authority in India. Both the Manchus and the Moguls were foreigners who established a national monarchy in the countries they conquered and for a period of two 200 years held effective authority over continental States, repelling the aggression of the foreign intruders and limiting the power and authority of the maritime nations to sea-borne trade. Both fell, as we have shown, mainly as a result of the pressure exercised from the coasts, which weakened the sources of their power, undermined their internal economy, and finally discredited them in the eyes of their own people. The immediate results in both India and in China also showed remarkable similarity. In China, as in India, a nominal authority was maintained at the centre to enable successful generals to obtain legal titles to their authority and to provide cover for aggression against others. For example, the Anfu Party in China, using the authority of Peking, finds a parallel in the Maratha General Mahdaji Scindia claiming to enforce the rights of the Grand Mogul. As in India, the viceroys of provinces in China set up as war lords, collected taxes and entered into relationship with foreign Powers. Chang Tso-lin in Manchuria was of the same type as Nizam-ul-Mulk in the Deccan and Aliverdhy Khan in Bengal; and the numerous minor bandits and generals who set up local administrations when the authority of Peking weakened were the Chinese equivalent of Amir Khan Pindara, Jaswant Rao Holkar and Dost Mohammed of Bhopal.

There was, however, one difference. While in India the rise of war lords after the breakdown of the Central Government led to the East India Company slowly conquering them one after another, or bringing them under protection and thereby establishing British authority in India, the circumstances of the period following the World War and the rivalry of the Powers prevented the same fate overtaking China. But it is necessary to emphasize that Japan's policy of territorial expansion on the mainland, by establishing subordinate regimes in Manchuria and provincial governments under its protection in the north, which we shall discuss in due course, was patterned on the British conquest of India.

The political events in China, following the downfall of the Manchus, may be stated briefly as a background. Following the abdication of the Manchus, on February 12, 1912, Sun Yat-sen, who had been elected provisional President by a hastily convened Revolutionary National Assembly at Nanking, retired in favour of Yuan Shih-kai, whom the Imperial Party had till then looked upon as its chief hope. A provisional constitution with a president, vice-president, a national advisory council and a parliament in the approved pattern of two houses was promulgated on March 10. A year later a parliament was convened, but between the revolutionaries, who constituted the majority in the house, and the president, who wielded effective power, a conflict developed which rendered administration practically impossible. Yuan Shih-kai, with no funds in the treasury and with his parliament in an obstructionist mood, chose the easy method of negotiating for a foreign loan in the hope of both overcoming his internal difficulties and securing international support for his administration. This was the opportunity that the imperialist nations were waiting for. The Great Powers – Britain, France, the United States, Germany, Russia and Japan – declared their willingness to permit a Bankers' Consortium to advance the necessary loans on condition of a clear recognition by China of their exclusive right to supply all loans. As security they demanded the hypothecation of the salt taxes which were to be administered by the maritime customs, already under foreign personnel. The United States, however, withdrew its support to this arrangement as President Wilson, then newly elected to the White House, felt that 'the conditions of the loan seem to us to touch very nearly the administrative independence of China itself'. The reorganization loan of 25 million pounds was, however, floated in the capitals of the other five Powers, and this money helped Yuan to put down a military revolt which broke out two months later. The revolt also provided Yuan with an excuse to proscribe the leading members of the revolutionary party. After this the way was clear for Yuan Shih-kai. Elections were ordered and the parliament which met chose him, by a large majority, as Head of the State. The Powers now had no further reason to withhold recognition.

It is unnecessary to go into the details of Yuan's manoeuvres, first to rid himself of parliament and later to elevate himself to the throne. The democratic feeling in the country had so grown during the four years that, though elected Emperor under the regnal title of Hung Hsien or Glorious Constitutionalism, the actual enthronement had to be postponed as a result of rebellion. Yuan himself passed away after a few months – June 1916. With his death the war lords took charge of different provinces, and for the next eleven years, till Chiang Kai-shek was able to re-establish national authority after the northern campaign, China had no effective Central Government. A nominal government existed in Peking living on the surplus revenues of the customs administration and the salt gabelle, which were under the control of foreign officials. It is not too much to say that the unity of China at this critical time was maintained by the all-China services which administered customs, salt and postal communications.

This state of affairs was brought to an end by the victorious march of the Kuomintang, an organization created by Sun Yat-sen after his withdrawal from Peking. Disappointed and deeply hurt at the support given by the Western nations to Yuan, especially their encouragement to the loan by the Bankers' Consortium, Sun retired to Tokyo and began organizing a new party. During these years his ideal was Japan, from whose statesmen he was receiving some support. Sun's view of Japan at the time was not at all unfriendly. 'Japan,' he said, 'was one of the strongest Powers in the world. Her people have given up her old prejudices, they have learnt the lessons of the West, reformed their administration, created an army and fleet, organized their finances and have done all this in the space of fifty years.'[1] This, however, was before he came under the influence of the Russian Revolution. In 1917, Sun had already set up a 'government' in the south. But failing to receive adequate support he had taken refuge within the safety of the international settlement at Shanghai. In his manifesto to the Chinese people dated July 25, 1919, Sun Yat-sen declared publicly his conviction that the Russian people will be 'the only ally and brother' of the Chinese in their struggle for freedom. Contact was soon established with Lenin, and in 1922 Adolphe Joffe came to China on behalf of the Soviet Government and met Sun in Shanghai in January 1923. A joint manifesto was issued as a result of their talks which pledged the support of the Soviets. After this agreement Sun returned to Canton, and the first effective step he took was to send Chiang Kai-shek to Moscow to study the Red Army training and military organization.

The Whampoa Military Academy was established under Chiang after his return from Moscow, and had the benefit of Russian instructors, advisers and arms. The new army that was created was meant as the instrument of national unification. To it was also attached a political propaganda organ. In 1924 the First National Congress of Kuomintang was held in Canton. Among the decisions it took was one to admit Communists to the party. Before the new army could begin its march of conquest Sun Yat-sen passed away in 1925. By 1926 the Kuomintang-

[1] Sun Yat-sen: *Memoirs of a Chinese Revolutionary*. London, p. 114.

Communist alliance had cleared all China, south of the Yangtze, of war lords and defeated Wu Pei-fu and captured Hankow and was face to face with the forces of Marshal Sun Chuang-fang, who controlled the great coastal belt. Marshal Sun, realizing the menace of the new movement to the militarists, rallied the forces of his fellow war lords, but the tide of the national movement swelled and swallowed him and his numerous army. Chiang Kai-shek stood at the gates of Shanghai, the symbol of European authority in the Pacific area.

We have anticipated events in this brief account in order to provide a background for the relationship of European nations with China during this vital period. Basically there are two facts to be remembered, the first, the absence of an effective Central Government for a little over ten years from the death of Yuan Shih-kai to the establishment of the Kuomintang Government in Nanking in 1927, and, secondly, the immense and unsuspected strength of the popular movement which, though disorganized, badly led and without any effective programme, was able to build up the reserve of strength which enabled the Kuomintang to sweep away the war lord regimes like so many toy soldiers.

Yuan Shih-kai, though at the cost of his political prestige he had succeeded in negotiating a loan of 25 million pounds, had not time to mature his political plans before the European war broke out in 1914. The preoccupations of Great Britain, France, Germany and Russia with the conflict which required the concentration of all their energies left him face to face with Japan. The Japanese statesmen naturally looked upon the war in Europe as a heaven-sent opportunity to eliminate European influence from China, and to stand forth as the paramount Power on the Asian continent. An excuse lay ready at hand. On August 7 the British Ambassador had requested Japanese co-operation in destroying German ships in Chinese waters. There was no request for a full-scale declaration of war against Germany, but Japan, taking a more generous view of her obligations under the Anglo-Japanese alliance, declared war on Germany after the issue of an ultimatum which in its phrasing recalled the German representation after the Korean War. The immediate sphere of Japanese action was China, where, without taking the least notice of Chinese rights, the Japanese, with the connivance of British authorities, landed on Chinese territory and conducted a ruthless campaign against the German concession of Kiao-chow. After the occupation of the German concession, and after having tested how far the Western Allies were in a position to interfere with Japan's policies in China, the Japanese authorities turned their attention to China itself. The Mikado's advisers were convinced that another such opportunity to solve the Chinese question 'will not occur for hundreds of years to come'. It was also pointed out that 'the present conditions in China favour the execution of such a plan'. The plan which the leaders of Nippon decided upon was presented at the first suitable opportunity.

Embodied in Twenty-one Demands (presented to President Yuan Shih-kai on January 18, 1915), this plan had been comprehensively thought out to ensure the paramountcy of Japanese interests in China for all time, to exclude other foreign interests in Chinese affairs, to reserve certain territories like Shantung and Fukien, opposite Formosa, as special spheres of Japanese influence, to place Manchuria and Eastern Inner Mongolia under the special protection of Japan, to secure control of police administration in important areas through joint administration, etc.

On May 7, Sir Edward Grey solemnly advised the Chinese Government to accept the Japanese demands. The American attitude was equally strange. As early as March 13, 1915, William Jennings Bryan, Wilson's Secretary of State, after making various formal reservations about Japan's demands on Shantung and Manchuria, agreed that 'the United States frankly recognizes that territorial contiguity creates special relations between Japan and these districts'. These assurances may be said to mark the end of European moral authority in China, for neither America nor Britain ever recovered the position they had previously held after so incautiously agreeing, in one case to the extent of even advising China to accept Japan's terms, and in the other of recognizing Japan's special relations with North China.

With her diplomatic position so strengthened, Japan felt that the time had come to force a settlement on President Yuan. On May 7, Japan gave an ultimatum to China asking for a categorical reply to the entire set of demands. The Peking Government felt it had no alternative but to agree. On May 25 President Yuan's Government signed two treaties and thirteen exchanges of notes, which at least on paper reduced China to the position of a Japanese protectorate. The American Secretary of State Bryan, feeling that he had been fooled, notified both Governments that America could not recognize any agreement that impaired the treaty rights or the territorial integrity of the Republic of China, but Japan ignored this reservation.

The treaties were ratified by the Emperor of Japan and by the Chinese President, but as the constitution of China required ratification of treaties by Parliament they were all along considered by every section of opinion in China as invalid and not binding on the Chinese Government. The history of Sino-Japanese relations from 1915 to the declaration of war between the two countries twenty-one years later is a commentary on these demands, an attempt by Japan to put into effect the paramountcy she claimed to have acquired by treaties and agreements, and an equally determined effort by China to resist all such claims by every means in her power. The ultimate and decisive failure of Japanese policy, leading to the surrender of her forces in China and the abandonment not only of her immense capital assets in China itself but her expulsion from Manchuria, was primarily due to the development of democratic forces which enabled China to fight a defensive war for eight years. The mistake that Japan made was not that she had underestimated the opposition of European nations, who she rightly felt would not fight to preserve the independence of China, but that she could not foresee that the revolution had unleashed forces of incalculable strength, and that the weakness of China as represented by Yuan and the war lords who succeeded him was no a true index of the position that was developing within the country.

Also, it may be mentioned here that Japan's policy in Asia suffered from a fundamental contradiction. Her first object was the exclusion of European authority from Asia in which she had the support and sympathy of Asian people. Side by side with this, she had also been an apt pupil of the Great Powers in their policy of expansion, and the promulgation of the Imperial Way over the peoples of Asia seemed to her to be a divine mission. A study of British methods in India gave her the inspiration of controlling the vast resources of China through methods of military power and indirect rule. Forgetting the changed conditions of the twentieth century she decided to take advantage of the international situation to put into effect a scheme by which a replica of India could be created at least in North China. The will-o'-the-wisp of imperial domination led her along the disastrous path which, after thirty years of vain and superhuman effort, lost her the position she had so patiently built up and placed her proud people under foreign occupation.

China declared war on the Central Powers, much against the wishes of Japan, who in view of her 'paramount interests, both political and economic, in China' refused to associate herself with the representation made by the Allies to China to break off relations with Germany. This attitude of Japan led to an exchange of views with the American Government resulting in the Lansing-Ishii agreement, under which the United States reaffirmed Japan's 'special relations in view of territorial propinquity' and her 'special interests in China', while Japan on her part agreed to uphold 'the unimpaired territorial sovereignty' of her neighbour. China's association with the war was, however, a success of some importance for Peking, for it gave her a voice in the peace settlement.

At the Versailles Conference, China was represented first by Wang Ching-ting (C. T. Wang) and later by Wellington Koo and Alfred Sze. Though the country was disunited, the Chinese spokesmen at the Conference represented a single point of view, the object of which was the recovery of the complete sovereignty of China. China's position was difficult because Britain, France and Italy had already agreed to the retention by Japan of the German rights in Shantung. But on this question America, whose non-territorial imperialism considered acquisition of territory as immoral, was adamant. Japanese diplomacy again gained a victory, for the Peace Conference transferred to Japan all German rights in Shantung with only oral promises on her side. On this the Chinese delegates refused to sign the Treaty of Versailles.

The Versailles decision touched off a nation-wide agitation of a kind which China had not witnessed before. The lead was taken by the students of Peking, who on May 4, 1919, staged a mass demonstration and besieged the house of a pro-Japanese Minister. For over a week the capital was in a state of turmoil involving numerous incidents with the authorities, characterized by the President of the Peking University as 'a struggle between the deluge and the beast'. Public sympathy was so obviously on the side of the students that the Government finally realized that a new power had risen in the country, and the offending Minister was publicly dismissed. A demand for the boycott of Japanese goods arose from every part of the country. In fact opposition to Japan passed from the Government to the people of the country.

It was in this atmosphere that the Washington Conference on the limitations of naval armaments in the Pacific took place. Though the Chinese had but little direct interest in the matter of naval armaments, the subject of Shantung was one of the major issues affecting the Pacific and formed the subject of a special treaty outside the Conference. Under American pressure and as a result of the persistence of the Chinese negotiators, a settlement was made under which the previous German concessions reverted to China on payment of a specified compensation. On December 17, 1922, the Japanese soldiers left Shantung and the Kiaochow-Tsinan railway line was transferred to China. This was the first diplomatic victory of China, the first retrocession of a concession and the first public retreat of Japanese aggression – achieved when China was still divided and its Central Government placed in a position of utter ineffectiveness.

Besides this specific issue, the Chinese delegation, headed by Alfred Sze, brought up before the Conference, in the form of ten general principles, the demand of China for a complete restoration of her sovereignty by the abrogation of all limitations on her jurisdiction and tariff autonomy and by the abrogation of the special privileges claimed by Powers. The Washington Conference was in fact the first international forum in which China stood forward courageously as an accuser of the imperialist nations and put the Great Powers on their defence. No one, in fact, came forward to defend these 'rights'. Even Japan, through Baron Kato, denied all desire for territorial aggrandisement, while France only ventured, an observation with apprehensions about Tongking in her mind, about the indefiniteness of China's boundaries. To this strange view Wellington Koo replied emphatically: 'The territories of the Chinese Republic were defined in its constitution' and that his delegation would not discuss this question.

The Conference also agreed on a treaty between all the nine Powers relating to principles and policies to be followed in matters concerning China. By Article I of this treaty, which was based on what was known as the Root Resolution, after Elihu Root who drafted it, the Powers concerned agreed to maintain the sovereignty, independence and territorial and administrative integrity of China; to assist China to develop and maintain an effective and stable government; to use their influence to uphold the principle of equal opportunity for the commerce and industry of all nations; to refrain from taking advantage of unsettled conditions; and to seek no special rights or privileges which would abridge the rights of the citizens of other States.

It will be noticed that these provisions were meant less to uphold the sovereignty of China than to safeguard the commercial and economic rights of foreign nations against encroachments by Japan. It was an attempt on the part of the Western nations collectively to safeguard their interests. All the same, however selfish the object, so far as China was concerned, it secured two very substantial gains. It buried the Twenty-one Demands; for Japan, in signing the Washington Treaty, had, in effect, to renounce the principles on which these demands were based. Secondly, even in respect of the claims of Western nations, it was clear that the treaty was only a defensive action, trying to protect what it was possible to protect and not a further encroachment on China's rights.

Also China had successfully raised the questions relating to her tariff autonomy, foreign post offices and extra-territorial jurisdiction. Nothing proves the changed position of Western nations as a result of the Great War more clearly than the attitude of the Powers to these demands put forward by the representatives of a State which at the time did not even have an effective central government. Wellington Koo's demand for tariff autonomy was not opposed by any Power. Though no reference was made in the treaty to China's tariff autonomy, the Powers agreed to call a conference at Shanghai to discuss the whole question. The resolution on postal agencies in China recognized the justice of the desire expressed by the Chinese Government to secure the abolition of foreign postal agencies, and the Powers concerned agreed under certain conditions to the abandonment of this privilege not later than January 1, 1923.

The Washington Conference is therefore the first important stage in the retreat of European nations, and its significance for the development of later events should not be missed. It is true that on none of the matters concerning her sovereignty did China receive immediate satisfaction; in the case of Japan, the delegates of that country even publicly maintained their position with regard to Manchuria and Eastern Inner Mongolia. But it had become amply clear that China's diplomatic position had greatly improved, and that the resistance to her demands would diminish in proportion to the authority she developed in her internal affairs. China's position was also improved by the abrogation after the Washington Conference of the Anglo-Japanese Alliance, which had enabled Japan to guard her diplomatic flank in her earlier aggression. The open distrust and opposition that the United States had shown towards Japanese policy after the war also helped to recover for China a position from which she was able to assert her rights.

After this there was but little chance of China breaking up, and the growing strength of the national movement became visible even when rival war lords were keeping up an intermittent civil war. For China the next important development was the friendship which the Soviet Union was showing towards her. Adolphe Joffe's mission to China and his agreement with Sun Yat-sen have already been described. The Western nations attached but little importance to Sun and the Kuomintang, and were inclined to consider the more prominent generals as exercising the real power of China. But the Soviets knew better. They knew that the generals would count for nothing when organized nationalism asserted itself and, therefore, while continuing technical negotiations with the authorities in Peking, the Soviets also developed political relations with the Kuomintang. Under the agreements reached by Karakhan with the Peking Foreign Office, the Russian Government gave up the concessions and renounced extra-territoriality, thus further strengthening the Chinese position in regard to these controversies with the Western Powers.

The growing strength of China was remarkably demonstrated during the agitation following the Shanghai incident of May 30, 1925, when the concession police fired on some student demonstrators. The agitation spread to all port cities, especially to Canton where British troops fired on the Chinese demonstrators. The Chinese retaliated by an effective blockade of Hong Kong and a boycott of British goods for over a year.

What was extremely significant was that in spite of this blockade of Hong Kong, boycott of British goods and intensive propaganda against Britain, there was no effective retaliation against the Chinese. Before 1914, such demonstrations would have been answered by gunboats; before the Revolution the Imperial Court would have been threatened with the most severe penalties. But in 1925, when these openly hostile activities were going on, Britain participated in the Conference in Peking to devise measures to return to China her tariff autonomy. The retreat was becoming a rout. A tariff revision commission had met in Shanghai to revise the schedule of duties in order to provide for an effective 5 per cent tariff in the interests of Chinese revenue. The Conference of 1925 was, however, for the purpose of restoring China's authority in this respect. It met in plenary session in Peking on October 26, 1925. The demand of C. T. Wang, the chief Chinese delegate, was simple: it was the removal of all tariff restrictions by January 1, 1929. This was agreed to 'in principle' by the Powers and later accepted by them as a binding decision. The decision was also taken by which the rates agreed on at Washington were immediately to be put into force.

A parallel commission on extra-territoriality also met in Peking in conformity with the decisions of the Washington Conference. The nationalists in Canton, however, considered that this was not a matter for discussion, and the Powers in trying to inquire into the operation of law courts in China were denying the sovereignty of China. The commission on extra-territoriality produced a report on the subject, recommending a series of reforms. When these were carried out, 'the several Powers would be warranted in relinquishing their respective rights of extra-territoriality.'

In the meantime a National Government in China had come into existence which was in no mood to tolerate the special position of the foreigners in China. At Nanking, Hankow and other areas in the Yangtze Valley, the nationalist troops had clashed with foreign residents. The whole attitude of the nationalists at the time showed a determination to force through these issues immediately; but after Chiang Kaishek's split with the left-wing elements and the transformation of the Revolution into a liberal nationalist regime (1927-36), a note of caution engered into its dealings. The later record of the Kuomintang should not lead us to forget its notable achievement in the first ten years of its administration, especially in the sphere of the recovery of China's authority. As these questions touch on contemporary history, we can only summarize them here without entering into any discussion.

The removal of the capital to Nanking itself affected the position of the Powers seriously. There was no 'legation quarter' at Nanking, with its own garrison, police and defence arrangements. The immense gardens, palaces and all the other paraphernalia of prestige vanished overnight by this single act. In 1928 all the Powers except Japan recognized the tariff autonomy of China, making only the usual condition of mutual non-discriminatory and most-favoured-nation treatment for their respective nations. Some of the Powers, notably Italy, Spain and Portugal, agreed in principle to the payment of taxes by their nationals. With Japan also the question of a revision of treaty arrangements was taken up. Japan at the last moment recognized the revised tariffs, but entered into a separate agreement on May 6, 1930, which safeguarded her trade interests for a period of three years by a reciprocal convention.

The more difficult question of extra-territoriality was also taken up by the Nationalist Government at the same time. On April 27, 1929, the Chinese Government addressed identical notes to the United States, Britain and France demanding that the restrictions on Chinese sovereignty 'be removed at the earliest possible date'. All the three Powers took the formal view that the recommendations of the Commission of 1926, to which the Nationalist Government was not a party, should be fulfilled in order to enable them to give up their rights. The Chinese Government not only contested this position but brought it up before the League of Nations under the clause which allowed that body to advise on treaties which have become inapplicable. Simultaneously, on December 28, 1929, the Government issued an order whereby it declared its laws should be applied to all foreign nations in the territory of China from January 1, 1930, offering at the same time to discuss with the Powers any representation they might desire to make. The reply of the Powers was that they were willing that 'January 1, 1930, should be treated as the date from which the process of the gradual abolition of extra-territoriality should be regarded as having commenced in principle'.

Also during this period the Nanking Government secured the rendition of the British concessions in Hankow, Kukiang, Chinkiang and Amoy. Wei-hai-wei was also restored. Except for the international concessions in Shanghai, Tientsin and the special regime in the legation quarter of Peking, China had practically secured the withdrawal of Western authority from the mainland. She was prevented from taking up the two major issues which still remained, the utilization of China's inland waterways by foreign vessels, including warships in the Yangtze and the international and national concessions, and the complete abolition of extra-territoriality, by the threatening situation that developed between her and Japan in the north. Japan's relationships with China do not properly come within the cope of this study, except in so far as they affect the relations of either with the West. Briefly, Japan's intervention in Manchuria in 1931 made Chiang turn for support to the Western nations, and therefore for a time he was forced to soften the attitude of hostility which the Kuomintang had followed consistently from 1924 and initiate a policy of collaboration with Europe.

In the period between 1927 and 1930, when the Nationalist Government in Nanking was negotiating its treaties with foreign governments, the unity of control which it claimed over China was more nominal than factual. Chang Tso-lin was in effective control of Manchuria till his death in 1928, and his son, the Young Marshal, had for a time carried on a pro-Japanese and anti-Russian policy. Feng Yu-hsiang, 'the Christian General', and Yen Hsi-shan, the war lord of Shansi, had refused to accept the authority of Nanking and had, with the support of minor war lords who saw their authority slipping under them, proceeded to form a government in the north. In a six months' campaign in 1930, Chiang dispersed the rebels mainly as a result of the crucial decision of Chang Hsueh-liang, 'the Young Marshal', to side with the nationalists. Not only did the Young Marshal come to the rescue of Nanking, but he seems to have realized that a policy of independence for Manchuria was no longer possible, and it was both patriotism and wisdom to place that vital area under the authority of the Central Government. Chang Hsueh-liang's accession to the Kuomintang on October 9, 1930, which was the clearest evidence of the unification of China and the acceptance of the authority of the Nanking Government over the historic territories of the past, was an event which Japan could not overlook. Her reaction was the invasion of Manchuria.

CHAPTER 4

JAPAN

In 1912, the Meiji Emperor, who had witnessed the emergence of Japan from feudal isolation to a position of unprecedented authority and strength, died in the full glory of his achievements. Japan's international position at that time was one of high prestige, and the Western Powers showed no marked suspicion or distrust of her policy. In fact they were so firmly convinced of their own impregnable position that they welcomed more than resented Japan's entry into the sphere of international diplomacy as an equal and a great Power. With condescending friendliness and appreciation, Britain had encouraged her ally in the East to build up her position originally to balance the might of Russia, and had acquiesced in the annexation of Korea and in Japan's acquisition of Russian rights in Manchuria. Though the Anglo-Russian understandings of 1907 had weakened the original purpose of the alliance, the deteriorating international situation, following the rise of German naval power, had increased rather than decreased the value of the Anglo-Japanese Alliance to Britain. Germany had established a position of considerable strength at Kiao-chow; she had also groups of islands in the Pacific and a large territory in Papua. In case of a great European war, the position in the Pacific might become menacing. For the defence of Britain's interest in the Far East in the case of a European war the Anglo-Japanese Alliance came therefore to have special significance.

When the war broke out Japan was quick to realize the opportunity it presented to her under the terms of the Alliance to stand forth as the upholder of peace and to take upon herself the leadership of affairs in the Far East. With Britain's reluctant consent she declared war on Germany, but the authorities in London were unhappy about the scope of Japanese action. Britain at this stage only desired that Japan should eliminate German naval and military power in China and not extend her operations further south on the pretext of waging war against Germany. To pacify the alarm felt by other countries, the British Foreign Office issued a statement which declared: 'It is understood that the action of Japan will not extend to the Pacific Ocean beyond the China Seas, except in so far as it may be necessary to protect Japanese shipping lines in the Pacific, nor beyond Asian waters westward of China, nor in any foreign territory except territory in German occupation on the continent of Eastern Asia.' But the Japanese did not consider this unilateral declaration as binding upon them, and a Japanese squadron appeared before the German island groups in the South Pacific, allegedly chasing Admiral Maximillian von Spee's German Far Eastern fleet.

After the Shantung campaign leading to the capture of Tsing-tao and the elimination of German influence in China, Japan, as we have already seen, concentrated on gaining a position of paramountcy in China. She soon realized that the European nations, though engaged in a mortal struggle in the West, were united in their opposition to her action, and that even her 'ally' was not favourably disposed to her, though Britain was in no position openly to oppose Japanese policy. Therefore Japan embarked on a frenzied diplomatic activity in all European capitals to secure individually from the Powers the approval of her actions in China, a kind of 'pragmatic sanction' for her ambitions. After reaching agreement with the rest of the Powers, Japan turned her attention to the United States. A special mission under Viscount Ishii was sent there, and an agreement was reached which, while reaffirming the adherence of both parties to the Open Door policy and their opposition to the acquisition of special rights or privileges which would affect the independence or territorial integrity of China, recognized 'that territorial propinquity creates special relations between countries and consequently the Government of the United States recognizes that Japan has special interests in China, particularly in that part to which her possessions are contiguous'. The contradictions in this agreement contained the seeds of the bitter hostility that developed between America and Japan in the years following the Great War. Japan understood that by this agreement America recognized her special interests in Manchuria and Inner Mongolia. The United States considered that Japan had unequivocally agreed not to claim rights or privileges which would affect the independence of China. In Japan's view her paramountcy, at least in North China, was recognized by this agreement. In the opinion of the United States, it had only recognized such interests as would not impair Chinese sovereignty or affect the Open Door principle of which she was the champion.

Satisfied that she had secured the diplomatic approval of the Powers concerned in respect of the rights she claimed under agreements entered into with Yuan Shih-kai, Japan was prepared to play a more vital role in the War. The British and the French were pressing for naval assistance in the Mediterranean against the dangerous submarine campaign which the Germans had initiated after February 1917. Since Great Britain, at the beginning of the War, had shown reluctance to agree to Japanese action outside China and had indeed given the world the impression that Japan had agreed to this limitation, it was now awkward to ask her to send forces to the Mediterranean itself. Japan, however, agreed to do so on condition that Britain and France supported her claims to the German islands south of the Equator. On this agreement a Japanese fleet under Admiral Sato, with the cruiser *Akashi* and three destroyer divisions, entered the Mediterranean – indeed, an historic event on the significance of which it may be necessary to dwell a little.

While European warships had dominated the Asian seas from the beginning of the sixteenth century, no warships from Asia had ever entered the waters of Europe. The great Turkish Navy, which under Khairuddin Barbarosa dominated the Mediterranean for a time, was in truth a Levantine and not an Asian fleet. The naval supremacy of the West in the Indian and Pacific Oceans, which began with Affonso Albuquerque in 1510, was for the first time effectively challenged in the battle of the Straits of Tsushima. The next step was the chasing of the German Pacific fleet. Now two years later, an Asian fleet had sailed into the very heart of European waters to undertake naval operations.

When the War ended Japan, as one of the Great Powers concerned in the victory, was given an equal status with America, Britain, France and Italy at the Versailles Conference. Disillusionment awaited her. President Wilson, who dominated the Conference, showed an implacable hostility to the claims of Japan. Though Britain and France were ready with the pound of flesh and gave a rather reluctant support to her claims, the American President made it clear that he considered Japan's claims to be ethically wrong and politically iniquitous. With the support of her allies Japan gained her point nominally, but as China, with American encouragement, refused to sign the treaty it was clear that the issue was not closed and that America would raise it at the earliest opportunity.

The next step was taken at Washington. The War had produced the first major shift of political influence from Europe to America. American opinion after the War had become increasingly critical of the Anglo-Japanese Alliance, as Washington had begun to foresee a conflict in the Pacific. The expansion of Japan to the island groups south of the Equator had increased the suspicion and distrust of Japanese policy that America had already begun to feel during the war years. America felt that it was the Anglo-Japanese Alliance that guarded the diplomatic flank of Japan's offensives in North China and had thwarted her attempts to limit Japan's interests. The Alliance, renewed in 1911 when the German menace loomed large, was to have expired in 1921. In England itself there was a growing feeling that since the German menace was now eliminated there was no purpose in continuing an alliance with an Asian State which limited Britain's freedom of action in the East. Also Canada, reflecting in a measure the Washington sentiment, was bitterly opposed to the renewal of the Alliance. Arthur Meighen, the Canadian Prime Minister, had been most insistent on the abrogation of the Anglo-Japanese Alliance and at the Imperial Conference, against the declared opposition of Lloyd George, Churchill and others, who feared the consequences of an antagonized Japan to British interests in the East, he was able to secure considerable support for his ideas. The declared object of the Conference was the limitation of armaments in the Pacific. With the expansion of Japan to the south, it was clear that she was bound to enlarge her navy to enable her to safeguard her distant interests. A competitive building up of naval power could in the circumstances be avoided only by international agreement.

President Harding therefore invited the nations directly concerned to a conference to discuss the Pacific problems. Japan realized that this was an attempt to isolate her, to bring up the entire question of her relations with China, especially the Shantung settlement, and to limit her activities. She therefore accepted the American invitation only after making it clear that matters which were of sole concern to particular Powers or such matters as might be regarded as accomplished facts should not be raised at the Conference. By this formula she endeavoured to safeguard her rights in Shantung which were now based on the Versailles Treaty, and her position in Manchuria which came within the category of matters which were the exclusive concern of particular Powers.

American objectives were more or less frankly stated by Secretary Hughes in the Plenary Session of the Conference. The attack on the Anglo-Japanese Alliance did not require to be pressed as Britain was only lukewarm and found in the proposal for a Four Power Pacific Treaty an excuse for not renewing the Alliance. By the Four Power Treaty Britain, the United States, France and Japan agreed to respect each other's rights and position in the Pacific area and to settle any disputes by negotiations. On the basis of this agreement the Anglo-Japanese Alliance was to be terminated. The Five Power Naval Treaty established the global ratio of 5:5:3 for Britain, America and Japan and provided that further naval fortifications should not be undertaken in the Pacific except in the Panama Canal zone, the Hawaii Islands and Alaska.

We have already dealt with the Chinese issues raised at the Conference. To China, the Washington Conference was a turning point. Though the complicated treaty structure which bound China in chains still remained, it was considerably loosened, and, apart from the Shantung settlement, the two main issues of tariff autonomy and extra-territoriality considered for so long a time as sacrosanct were ripped open and placed on the agenda for early discussions. For Japan equally it was a turning point. She realized that the European nations, including her erstwhile ally, had formed a *bloc* against her and that she was diplomatically isolated: that though the Four Power Treaty and the naval agreement temporarily safeguarded her position, American leadership in the Pacific had been firmly established, and that for the future she must be prepared to face the united opposition of the entire West.

In these difficult circumstances Japan decided on the only policy she could have followed, that is, to develop her own internal strength in a way which would enable her to safeguard her position till a new turn in the international situation brought other allies to her. She strained every effort to become a major industrial Power, to develop her air and naval forces without dependence on others, to increase her food production and to step up her trade. A planned economy, directed towards the strengthening of the nation in every aspect, was introduced and successfully carried out. But with every passing day it became clear to the leaders of Japan that without adequate resources of iron and coal, and without a guaranteed food supply, her position would remain vulnerable. These were available only in Manchuria, a great territory where she had already established herself and claimed a special position. To Manchuria, therefore, she turned, determined to make it her storehouse and arsenal.

During the period following the Revolution the vast territory lying to the north of the Great Wall in China was under the control of Marshal Chang Tso-lin, who realized from the beginning that his position of independence in Mukden rested on the support of the Japanese authorities and the Kwantung Army. As long as Chang Tso-lin was the war lord of Manchuria, direct intervention on the part of the Japanese was not necessary for the fulfilment of Nippon's strategic and economic plans. Till the rise of the Kuomintang the situation presented no serious problem. Manchuria and Inner Mongolia were in effect converted into Japanese protectorates. But with the establishment of the Central Government in Nanking and that Government's attempt to bring within its fold Chang Hsueh-liang, the son and successor of Chang Tso-lin, a new situation arose which appeared to threaten the very basis of the structure that Japan had raised in the quarter of a century following the Treaty of Portsmouth. The Chinese had from 1929 begun to construct three railway lines financed exclusively from their own resources. Two new ports, Yinkow and Hulutao, were opened in competition with Dairen to connect with the interior, thus reducing the value of the railway line which Japan controlled. Finally, when in 1930 Chang Hsueh-liang cast in his lot with Chiang Kai-shek and the Kuomintang, Japan realized that either she had meekly to abdicate her position or fight for her rights.

She decided to fight. An explosion on the tracks of the South Manchurian Railway provided the necessary occasion. On the night of September 18, 1931, the Japanese occupied Mukden. Within a few days all the strategic centres of Manchuria were occupied. China appealed to the League of Nations, and Sino-Japanese relations again became a matter of international importance. The Japanese reply was that the issue was purely a local one and could most easily be settled by direct negotiations. The diplomatic struggle in the League of Nations continued without achieving any results. The only important consequence in the first stage of the discussions was a closer participation of the United States in the deliberations of the Council, though it was not a member, thereby once again emphasizing the solidarity of Western nations against Japan.

By the end of the year Japan had occupied most of Manchuria and had begun organizing Chinese groups in her favour. On January 28, 1932, on the ground of protecting Japanese nationals in Shanghai and as a reprisal against the officially inspired boycotts, Japanese marines landed in Shanghai and attacked Chinese troops in Chapei. This naturally led to complications with the Western Powers, which felt that Japan had attacked at a point which they had so far considered as their own. In spite of the protests of the Powers, Japanese land and air forces joined in the conflict. Stimson, the American Secretary of State, demanded a formal invocation of the Nine Power Pact against Japan.

American policy in fact had taken a new turn. In regard to Manchuria, Stimson had enunciated the doctrine of non-recognition, laying down that the United States could not accept the legality of any situation *de facto*, nor did it intend to recognize 'any treaty or agreement entered into by those governments or the agents thereof infringing the treaty rights of the United States or its citizens in China, including those which related to the sovereignty, the independence or the territorial or administrative integrity of the Republic of China' . . . and that '*it does not intend to recognize any situation, treaty or agreement which* may be brought about by means contrary to the covenants and obligation of the Pact of Paris'. As soon as the incident in Shanghai began, the United States dispatched the flagship *Houston* with destroyers and an infantry regiment 'as a measure of precaution'. After the failure of the attempt to invoke the Nine Power Treaty, the American fleet was ominously concentrated at Hawaii.

Stimson's mounting hostility to Japan led him even to an attempt to mobilize public opinion through the recognized American method of public statements. In a letter to Senator Borah on February 23, 1932, the Secretary of State explained that his proposal to issue a concurrent statement, turned down by Sir John Simon, was 'a suggestion of

CHAPTER 5

ELSEWHERE IN ASIA

It was not only in India and China that European authority began to retreat after the First Great War. In Afghanistan, Nepal, Siam, Indo-China and Indonesia the situation underwent a marked change which, no doubt, was in a measure due to the altered position in India and in China. King Amanullah in Afghanistan refused to be bound by the limitations which Britain had imposed on his father's sovereignty and, taking advantage of the war weariness of the British, even opened hostilities against the British Indian frontiers. The treaty which followed the conclusion of the war recognized Afghanistan as an independent, sovereign State. The Soviet Government immediately extended recognition and Afghanistan soon entered into relations with all the major Powers and was admitted to the League of Nations.

The position of Nepal was slightly different. After the war of 1914-8 the Gurkha kingdom also claimed and obtained the recognition of her status as an internationally independent country. A Nepalese Legation was opened in London and the relations between the Indian Government and the Nepalese court were placed on an international footing. But Nepal was not anxious to go beyond this formal position for reasons peculiarly her own. Her leaders realized that diplomatic relations with other countries would inevitably raise issues connected with the status of the Nepalese King who, like the Japanese Emperor before the Meiji restoration, had been deprived of his powers and kept in the background. The historic policy of the British Government in India had been to back up the authority of the Rana family which held the hereditary prime ministership, who in their turn had given unqualified support to British rule in India. In fact, during the First Great War, when the Indian Army was fighting the battles of the Empire on the continents, it was the Gurkha Army of Nepal which to a large extent garrisoned India. The Ranas were fully aware that their authority in Nepal was dependent on British support and realized that the establishment of diplomatic relations with other countries would create for them, as it did for Japan,

Nations and Japan had come to a parting of ways. The League passed a resolution asking Japan to withdraw to the railway zone and to negotiate and settle her problems with China under the auspices of a committee of the League; it asked China to set up an autonomous Manchuria under the sovereignty of China, and further recommended that the member States should not accord recognition to Manchukuo. It was a victory for the American policy of isolating Japan. Japan for her part replied that she intended to withdraw from the League and did not consider herself bound by its decisions.

Japan had parted from Europe and was now determined to force the decision in China. Slowly and by stages she moved south, but though Japanese action found but little official opposition, as the Kuomintang was then engaged in a bitter faction fight, the national sentiment in China was steadily building up a united front against the invader. Japan, on the other hand, from her base in Jehol began to establish friendly relations with Mongol princes and to penetrate into the border areas. A Mongol autonomy movement came into existence. In Peking itself, during this period of diplomacy when Chiang Kai-shek was hesitating, a modified form of Japanese supremacy was established under what was known as the Ho-Ume-tsu agreements by which officials declared objectionable by the Japanese were to be withdrawn from Hopei Province (in which Peking is situated) and Kuomintang troops and Central Government agencies were to be evacuated from that province. North China was now treated as an autonomous area. An anti-Communist Government of East Hopei under Japanese patronage was set up. Chiang and the Nanking Government even agreed to the formation of the Hopei-Chahar political council.

Japan seemed to be treading successfully the path that Britain had cleared in India, of setting up and recognizing puppet regimes, stage by stage, in her progress. But Chinese nationalism rose up in arms. Chiang Kai-shek was forced by the Sian coup to agree to a unified front against Japan. Following this decision, and the agreement with the Communist leaders, China decided on a policy of resistance. Japan also decided to strike before national unity, established as a result of the Sian declaration, became effective. The result was the 'incident' of the Marco Polo Bridge (July 8, 1937), which opened a phase of Chinese resistance leading ultimately to war between Japan and China, which after 1941 merged into the Second World War.

Japan, as we noticed, had been diplomatically isolated after the Washington treaties. Her attitude naturally became one of hostility towards the Western 'liberal' nations. When, therefore, in 1933 Germany under Hitler again became a major Power in Europe, Japanese diplomacy recognized that the developing international situation in the West could be turned to useful account. Also Europe seemed hopelessly divided at this time. The Rome-Berlin axis had come into existence after the Ethiopian War, and between the two dictators, supported by falangist Spain, it seemed obvious that the power of the West European Powers had been effectively neutralized, leaving Japan a free hand in the East with only America's impotent anger to deal with. Germany, Italy and Spain negotiated (November 25, 1936) the anti-Comintern Pact, which gave the Far Eastern Empire an alliance of some value in dealing with the opposition of England and France. Japan thought, as it turned out mistakenly, that she had at last broken through the diplomatic blockade and was now in a position to deal with China as she liked.

This, however, was not the only reason why Japan chose to defy the world in 1937. It was clear to her that if she desired to settle affairs in a way satisfactory to herself in China, and exclude finally the possibility of a China organized against her and of a revival of Western, and in this case American, influence, it was necessary for her to act immediately. She was fully aware of the changed circumstances in China, its growing political and industrial strength and its awakened national consciousness. The Nanking regime in 1935 might have been comparatively weak and riddled with political rivalry and administrative inefficiency. But compared to the different governments that had preceded it, Chiang's administration was infinitely stronger. It was national: it had the support of an army and its authority was more widely accepted than that of any other administration after the first Revolution. If this process of strengthening and of reorganization continued unhampered for another few years, all Japan's dreams of pre-eminence in East Asia would have vanished. That Japan was not unaware of these possibilities as early as 1915 is shown by the fact that Viscount Ishii, in replying to the request of the British, French and Russian ambassadors for support of a suggestion made by their governments to President Yuan Shih-kai that China should enter the War, declared in 1915 that 'Japan could not regard with equanimity the organization of an efficient Chinese army such as would be required for her active participation in the War, nor could Japan fail to regard with uneasiness a liberation of the economic activities of a nation of 400 million people'. The dangers that Japanese statesmen had foreseen in 1915 were nearing materialization in 1931. The Kuomintang army, trained originally by Soviet advisers, was at least at that time a united fighting force. In any case, a national army had come into existence which was armed and trained in the modern way. There was also a single government away from the pressures of Peking, which had thoroughly studied the methods of modern diplomacy and was fully capable of utilizing the opportunities afforded by the League of Nations to block Japan's action. 'The liberation of the economic activities of a nation of 400 millions' which Japan dreaded was also becoming a fact. The Kuomintang Government, with the active assistance of the United States, had embarked on a policy of economic nationalism; even railway construction, so long a matter of competition between the Powers, was now being undertaken and financed directly by the Kuomintang Government. For Japan it was therefore a race against time. She must wound and disable the dragon before it recovered and reduced to naught her carefully laid plans.

At no time does Japan seem to have cherished the idea of conquering China. The pattern of her paramountcy was worked out in Manchukuo. The Hopei-Chahar Council was an extension of the same principle, and the numerous offers made to Chiang Kai-shek before large-scale hostilities broke out were also based on the idea of an indirect control of the Chinese Government and an increasing participation in economic development. It was the doctrine of the Yen *bloc* and the co-prosperity scheme.

After the Washington Conference and the success of the American policy of isolating Japan, political opinion in that country veered strongly to the view that liberal policies had failed and could not gain her national objectives for Japan. The *genro* – or elder statesmen – who had the decisive voice in political matters tried to follow a cautious policy and kept up the form of party government depending mainly on the Seiyukai, who had been in control during the war period under a statesman of great ability, Hara, who, however, was found too moderate and 'pro-Western' by the patriots, and was therefore assassinated in November, 1921. From that time to 1936 we have in Japan the strange spectacle of a parliamentary government tempered by assassinations, in which the aggressively patriotic party looked upon all political leaders as potential betrayers of the country. After an interlude of 'Government by Admirals', where party representation was only incidental, the *genro* again called to office the Seiyukai or the constitutional party dominated by capitalist interests. From 1924 a significant change came over Japanese politics, and that was the growing authority of the big industrial and commercial firms in the established parties and through them in the Government. Economic expansionism in Korea, Manchuria and North China and growing trade with South-east Asia had raised Japan's position to that of a great industrial country. The armed forces realized the importance of high finance and large-scale and heavy industry in its own scheme of things, and a tentative alliance between the two began to show itself as early as 1926. In its outward appearance, the period from 1924 to 1931 was one of bourgeois supremacy, but actually the army was taking matters in hand in Manchuria and in North China. But even in this period Parliamentary Government received a shock when Premier

Hamaguchi, whose Cabinet had participated in the London Conference and signed the treaty, was shot at by a patriot. In fact, from 1931 the service chiefs made it clear that they would not stand any nonsense. The action in Manchuria, following the Mukden incident in 1931, was taken without even the knowledge of the Cabinet; and the Premier and Foreign Minister were left to find whatever justification they could for the strong arm policy which the Kwantung Army had decided upon.

From 1931, therefore, the Cabinets were mainly composed of politicians acceptable to the armed forces, and the first of their nominees was Inukai Takushi, who had the support of the Mitsui financial interests and of the army. General Araki, the protagonist of a military democracy, who like many others was genuinely shocked at the corruption of party politics, felt that the armed forces constituted the only real democracy in Japan, and a school of thought came into being which looked upon liberalism and representative institutions as imitations from the West taking away from the glory of Nippon's traditions. This led to the outbreak of May 15, 1932, when terrorist societies composed of young officers, military cadets and students assassinated Prime Minister Inukai, hurled bombs at the residence of Count Makimo, at the Tokyo police headquarters and the offices of the Seiyukai party, all from the purely 'patriotic motives' that the Government and parties were being manipulated by vested interests and were not strong enough in resisting Western nations and eradicating subversive elements. There was a growing feeling that the Restoration of the Emperor had not fulfilled its purpose, since vested interests, corrupt politicians and parties now ruled in the name of the Emperor. It was claimed that the powers of the Emperor, who represented the nation, had been usurped by the politicians and the capitalists and that what was required now was the 'Showa' (the regnal name of the present Emperor) restoration which would rid the country of the influence of businessmen and politicians who did not think in terms of national interests. This was in no sense a reflection of the Fascist or Nazi doctrines, then fashionable in Europe, but a revival of the pure Nippon doctrine which had always been strong in Japan, and had been only in temporary eclipse during the period when the prestige of Europe stood high. With the disillusionment in respect of the West, following the Washington Treaty and the social and economic disturbances caused by the change-over to an industrialized society, and with the depression which affected the peasantry from whom the armed forces were recruited, the doctrines of pure Shinto revived again in a new form. It was essentially the same cry as 'Revere the Emperor and expel the foreigner', including, of course, the secondary foreigner who talked in terms of parliamentary government and Cabinet policies.

CHAPTER 5

ELSEWHERE IN ASIA

IT was not only in India and China that European authority began to retreat after the First Great War. In Afghanistan, Nepal, Siam, Indo-China and Indonesia the situation underwent a marked change which, no doubt, was in a measure due to the altered position in India and in China. King Amanullah in Afghanistan refused to be bound by the limitations which Britain had imposed on his father's sovereignty and, taking advantage of the war weariness of the British, even opened hostilities against the British Indian frontiers. The treaty which followed the conclusion of the war recognized Afghanistan as an independent, sovereign State. The Soviet Government immediately extended recognition and Afghanistan soon entered into relations with all the major Powers and was admitted to the League of Nations.

The position of Nepal was slightly different. After the war of 1914-8 the Gurkha kingdom also claimed and obtained the recognition of her status as an internationally independent country. A Nepalese Legation was opened in London and the relations between the Indian Government and the Nepalese court were placed on an international footing. But Nepal was not anxious to go beyond this formal position for reasons peculiarly her own. Her leaders realized that diplomatic relations with other countries would inevitably raise issues connected with the status of the Nepalese King who, like the Japanese Emperor before the Meiji restoration, had been deprived of his powers and kept in the background. The historic policy of the British Government in India had been to back up the authority of the Rana family which held the hereditary prime ministership, who in their turn had given unqualified support to British rule in India. In fact, during the First Great War, when the Indian Army was fighting the battles of the Empire on the continents, it was the Gurkha Army of Nepal which to a large extent garrisoned India. The Ranas were fully aware that their authority in Nepal was dependent on British support and realized that the establishment of diplomatic relations with other countries would create for them, as it did for Japan, the constitutional problem of the monarch's position. Nepal was therefore content to have her position recognized technically as an internationally independent State. Later, however, the Nepalese authorities took the further step of accrediting their envoy in London both to Paris and to Rome, but a reciprocal exchange of diplomatic missions with other countries was not negotiated till after the Second World War.

We have already noticed the steps that King Rama VI took in Siam to effect the recovery of Siam's unfettered sovereignty. However, it was only in the period that followed the Revolution of 1932 that Siam embarked on a policy meant to exclude Western exploitation of her national resources. Both Luang Pradit and Marshal Songgram, the two leaders of opposing camps in the public life, followed similar policies so far as this question was concerned, and during the decade of Parliamentary Government, before Japan's war with the Western nations, Siam was able to carry through a policy of economic nationalism, which in a measure was the counterpart of the recovery of her political sovereignty under Rama VI.

In Indonesia and Indo-China also, the colonial authorities realized that imperialism was in retreat. The history of the period, as in India, was one of conflicts, of large-scale national revolts, of brutal suppression by colonial governments and half-hearted attempts to find a *via media* which would reconcile nationalist aspirations with the economic and political interests of the metropolitan countries. But both the French, in spite of the intransigent utterances of her political leaders emphasizing the *mission civilisatrice* of France, and the Dutch, despite the realization that Holland's position in the world was dependent on her exploitation of the wealth of the Indies, realized that the days of their colonial domination were numbered and were only sustained by the hope that some way might be found which would enable them to prolong their hold for a little more time. Even the French and the Dutch had ceased to believe in the permanency of their authority and were fighting only rear-guard actions, when Japanese military power intervened to demonstrate alike the weakness of their colonial rule and the bankruptcy of their political systems.

The inter-war period thus witnessed the breakdown of the systems of imperial authority as a result firstly of the weakening of the capitalist system in the colonizing countries of Western Europe following the Great War and, secondly, of the strength of the nationalist forces unleashed by the circumstances of the conflict in which Asian nations were called on to take part, by the intervention of America and by the potent influence of the October Revolution. The Second World War only gave the *coup de grace* to a system which had already broken down and which could no longer function effectively.

Part VI

THE RECOVERY OF ASIA

CHAPTER I

GENERAL

SUBJECTED to the same pressure and facing similar dangers, the ancient societies of India, China and Japan, and following them the lesser States of Asia, reacted broadly along parallel lines. The renaissance of Asia has certain broad general characteristics. In the first place, it is a more or less successful attempt to reorganize society in order primarily to adjust relationships which had become obsolete, e.g., caste in India, feudalism in Japan and the stratification of life in China. The object of this reorganization was to resist external pressure. It was therefore organized from the top. Nowhere was it a movement starting from the bottom, an upsurge of social protest caused either by the sufferings or th- awakened conscience of the masses. Its strength lay essentially in the desire of each nation to conserve what was its own, and its leadership, as we shall show, was drawn from classes which, by intellectual tradition, tended to be conservative. It was not the desire for progress or for betterment that was originally at the root of Asian revival. It was the determination to resist the foreigner who was pressing his attack in all directions, political, social, economic and religious. It was the desire for national strength and not for revolutionary changes that was the main motivation of the changes in Asian communities. It is necessary to remember this when we see in the course of our narrative Brahmins preaching the abolition of untouchability, the Son of Heaven ordering reforms and the Japanese daimyos surrendering their rights without a major fight.

Secondly, it was realized from the beginning that fundamental social adjustments were not possible without a reformation of religion. Again the movement was meant to resist aggression. As the hold of religion and the extent of its external weaknesses differed greatly in the different countries of Asia, the movement for reform also assumed different aspects. In India it required a thorough re-examination of fundamental beliefs, a new interpretation of old beliefs to bring them into conformity with modern requirements, the formulation of a general philosophy in the tradition of Indian religious thought, but capable of meeting the rival philosophies of the West, and finally the creation of a genuine religious feeling and a revival of faith which could withstand the massed onslaught of Europe through its missionary organizations. In the Buddhist countries of Burma and Siam, the problem was simpler, but in China, with the ethical conceptions of the Confucian system under attack both by external forces and by internal developments and without the strength of a religious faith, this aspect of the renaissance, as we shall attempt to show, became rationalistic and liberal and therefore limited to intellectual circles. In Japan the reorganization of Shintoism and its elevation into a national cult was taken up under government auspices and formed an essential part of Japanese national revival.

The third aspect of Asia's renaissance was the attempt to assimilate the learning and thought of the West. Here, again, the approach was one of national survival and strength. Asian nations soon realized that without accepting the new learning from the West and assimilating it and using the power given by that knowledge for their benefit, there was little chance of survival, far less recovery. The overwhelming desire for Western knowledge, which was the characteristic of the intellectual life of India, China and Japan during the last three-quarters of the century, was not, as many people in Europe fondly believed, a willing acceptance of the superiority of the West over the civilization of the East, but a desire to understand the motive forces of European power and utilize it for their own benefit. Neither in literary or artistic matters nor in the field of philosophic thought was Asia to any considerable degree influenced by Europe. The literatures of India, China and Japan borrowed the forms and sometimes the formulae of European literature, but their inspiration in the main came from their own living and massive tradition, except during recent years, and that only after Europe's withdrawal had become almost an accomplished fact. In artistic creation also the development was similar. New techniques were adopted and even new forms attempted, but there was no inspiration to speak of from the West. The literary and artistic renaissance of Asia was helped by the intellectual ferment caused by the new learning, but was basically national.

A fourth and final characteristic was the emphasis on nationalism. The growth of national feeling was the direct result of the reaction against Western aggression. It should be remembered – this is a point to which we shall revert – that the sense of exclusive nationalism is not very old either in Europe or in Asia. In Asia, while Japan because of its insular position developed a certain sense of nationality – limited it should be emphasized by a strong sense of feudalism – what existed in China was a feeling of imperial greatness, comparable to that of the Roman Empire, and what kept India alive was a tradition of continuity through Hinduism. The transformation of these feelings into a sense of nationhood was an essential aspect of Asian renaissance.

Within the framework of these general characteristics the problem differed greatly in complexity. The reorganization of Indian life was much more difficult, for in India a sense of political unity which existed both in China and even to a greater extent in Japan had to be created anew. Hindu religion, with its wide ramifications touching every aspect of life, and with its caste system and its inherited customs and laws, presented a problem of immense complexity for the reformer. Also, the necessity for reform was much greater in Hinduism than in the other social structures of Asia. Political conditions under which the reforms had to be undertaken also differed radically. Japan and Siam under their national monarchies were able to direct the process and to work out the adjustments with minimum social disturbances. In India the existence of a single Government over the whole area, maintaining law and order and providing a uniform education, made it possible for the forces generated by the impact with Europe to work themselves out without interference. In China, on the other hand, the breakdown of the Central Government, the limitations imposed on the sovereignty of the Empire by the unequal treaties, and especially by extra-territoriality, the uncontrolled activities of missionaries of various Christian sects and creeds, and finally the rivalry and intrigues of the Great Powers, all anxious to establish spheres of influence and exercising power without any sense of responsibility, led to a breakdown of both the political and social structure which led to the Revolution of 1911-2. The immense significance of this difference, which left China without a strong and established social order and with its renaissance uncompleted when the new ideas of the Russian Revolution began to spread, will be dealt with later. For our present purpose, it is sufficient to note that while the movement towards reorganization was universal in Asia, and was motivated by similar factors, its results were uneven, depending largely on the political circumstances in which each country was placed and the strength of the pressure exercised on it.

CHAPTER 2

INDIA[1]

The Hindu Reformation of the nineteenth century is one of the great movements of the age which by its massiveness and far-reaching significance takes its place with the most vital developments of modern history. As it was a slow process and took place under the cover of British authority and was not always obvious to the outsider, it has so far escaped attention. A further reason why, in spite of its tremendous import, it passed unnoticed is that, by its very nature, it was an internal movement which did not touch or influence outside events. But India's independence and emergence into the modern world would hardly have been possible without the slow but radical adjustments that had taken place within the fold of Hinduism for a period of over 100 years.

In order to appreciate this movement fully it is necessary to understand what the position of Hinduism was in the beginning of the nineteenth century. 700 years of Islamic authority over the Indo-Gangetic Plains from Delhi to Calcutta had left Hinduism in a state of depression. It was the religion of a subject race, looked down on with contempt by the Muslims as idolatry. It enjoyed no prestige and for many centuries its practice had been tolerated only under considerable disadvantage in various areas. It had no central direction, no organization and hardly any leadership. When the British took over the rulership of Northern India, Hinduism for the first time in 700 years stood on a plane of equality with Islam. But a new and even more dangerous portent appeared on the stage. The missionaries, feeling that there was almost a virgin field here in a society which appeared to be on the point of dissolution, took up the work of conversion. Islam, though it proselytized by fits and starts, had no separate machinery for carrying its message to the people. The Christian missionaries were different. They used no physical force, which Islam did not hesitate to do at intervals and in limited areas. But they came armed with propaganda. In a later chapter we will narrate the

[1] This chapter is a summarized statement of a section from the author's book, *The Indian Revolution*. Bombay, 1951.

story of missionary activities. Here we shall describe only the reactions it caused within the folds of Hinduism itself. The first result of the Christian attack on Hinduism was a movement among educated Hindus in favour of a social reform of religion. The leader of this was Ram Mohan Roy (1772-1883), who may be called the father of the Hindu Reformation. Born in a Brahmin family, Ram Mohan was brought up as a strict Hindu, but educated, as all Hindus who hoped to enter public service had perforce to be at that time, in Islamic culture. He was a deep student of Arabic and Persian when he entered the East India Company's service, where also he rose to some distinction. During this period he took to the study of English, which opened to him the whole range of Western liberal thought. It was the time when the mellowed glow of the Great European Enlightenment had cast on European intellectual life an amazing serenity and sense of certainty. The light of D'Holbach, Condorçet, Diderot and the great Encyclopaedists had not died down and the dawn of the great nineteenth century thinkers, especially Bentham and the Utilitarians in England, which was destined to have so powerful an influence in the development of ideas in India, had not begun.

What Ram Mohan witnessed around him in India was a scene of utter devastation and ruin. The old order of Muslim rule had disappeared overnight, leaving behind it utter chaos in every walk of life. Hinduism in Bengal, once the centre of a devotional Vaishnava religion of great vitality, had sunk to a very low level of superstition, extravagance and immorality. A seeker after truth, Ram Mohan turned to the new religion which the missionaries were preaching. He studied Hebrew and Greek to understand Christianity better. But his scholarship was taking him at the same time to the well of European liberalism. Ram Mohan Roy was in fact the last of the Encyclopaedists. Thus he came to reject Christ, while accepting the wide humanism of European thought, its ethics and its general approach to the problems of life. His book, *The Precepts of Jesus, the Guide to Peace and Happiness*, is an interpretation of Christianity in this new light, a reply to the missionaries rather than a call to Indians.

While Ram Mohan Roy thus rejected the Christian claims, he realized that Hinduism had to be re-interpreted. That interpretation he attempted in the *Brahmo Samaj*, a new reformed sect of Hinduism, which he founded. The Samaj was not in its essence a Christian dilution of Hinduism, as has often been said, but a synthesis of the doctrines of the European Enlightenment, with the philosophical views of the *Upanishads*. As a religion Brahmo Samaj was based firmly on the Vedanta of genuine Hindu tradition, but its outlook on life was neither Christian nor Hindu, but European, and derived its inspiration from the intellectual movements of the eighteenth century.

Thus it may be said that as early as 1820 India had come into the direct current of European thought and had begun to participate in the fruits of Europe's intellectual quest. The Brahmo Samaj lived up to this ideal. Its social message was Westernization, to purge Hinduism of the customs and superstitions with which it was overlaid, to raise the status of women, to bridge the yawning gulf between popular and higher Hinduism, to fight relentlessly against caste, social taboo, polygamy and other well entrenched abuses. To the educated Hindu, who felt unsettled in mind by the attack of the missionaries, the Brahmo Samaj provided the way out.

The Brahmo tradition has become so much a part of the Indian way of life now, that one is inclined to overlook its distinctive contribution. It does not lie primarily in the fact that it enabled Hinduism to withstand the onslaught of the missionaries, but in that it introduced the modern approach to Indian problems. India started on her long adventure in building up a new civilization as a synthesis between the East and the West in the 1820s, and in that sense Ram Mohan is the forerunner of new India. It has been well stated that 'he embodies the new spirit, its freedom of inquiry, its thirst for science, its large human sympathy, its pure and sifted ethics along with its reverent but not uncritical regard for the past and prudent disinclination towards revolt'.

The spirit of reform was entering Hinduism from other sources also. In 1835 the Government of India declared that 'the great object of the British Government ought to be the promotion of European literature and science among the natives of India', and embarked on a policy of Western education, the effects of which will be considered separately. It was the devout hope of Macaulay, who was the champion of the scheme, and of many others, that the diffusion of the new learning among the higher classes would see the dissolution of Hinduism and the widespread acceptance of Christianity. The missionaries were also of the same view, and they entered the educational field with enthusiasm, providing schools and colleges in many parts of India, where education in the Christian Bible was compulsory for Hindu students. The middle classes accepted Western education with avidity and willingly studied Christian scriptures, but neither the dissolution of Hindu society so hopefully predicted nor the conversion of the intellectuals so devoutedly hoped for showed any signs of materialization. On the other hand, Hinduism assimilated the new learning, and the effects were soon visible all over India in a revival of a universalized religion based on the *Vedanta*.

It is necessary to remember that, though the Hindu religion has innumerable cults and sects, the philosophic background of all of them – including Buddhism – is the Vedanta. The doctrine of the Vedanta is contained in three authoritative texts – which are not scriptures – the

Brahma Sutras, the *Upanishads* and the *Gita*. Every orthodox sect in India derives its authority directly from these and, as has been stated in the previous chapter, the protagonists of each new religious sect have had to demonstrate how their own teachings flowed directly from these three sources. Thus it was that Sankara, the reformer of Hinduism in the eighth century, had to write his commentary on all the three. It is to the doctrines of the Vedanta, as embodied in the Upanishads, that Ram Mohan Roy turned when he also felt the need of a new religious interpretation.

The Vedantic reformation which was thus in the air found its most widely accepted exponent in Swami Vivekananda. Vivekananda was a Western-educated Bengali who came under the influence of Ramakrishna, a mystic whose personality had made a deep impression on the Bengali society of his day. Vivekananda was fired by a desire to revive Hinduism and purify its religious and social teachings. Initiated a Sanyasi, he toured the length and breadth of India spreading the gospel of Vedanta. A prolonged visit to America and a tour in England inflamed his patriotism, his desire to rejuvenate Hindu society and to give Hinduism a social purpose. His fervent declaration that he did not 'believe in a religion that does not wipe out the widow's tears or bring a piece of bread to the orphan's mouth' expresses clearly the changed temper of Hinduism. His own mission he described as follows. Answering the question: 'What do you consider to be the function of your movement as regards India?' the Swami said: 'To find the common bases of Hinduism and to awaken the national consciousness to them.' That common basis he found in the Vedanta which he interpreted in popular phraseology and preached untiringly all over India.

He not only preached this gospel, but trained up a body of missionaries, men of education, pure life and religious zeal to carry this message to the villages.

There were innumerable other Sanyasis and learned men who, though belonging to no particular sect, were preaching the same principles all over India. In fact, the revival of Vedanta in Hindu thought at the end of the nineteenth century constitutes a religious movement of national significance. It was at the end of this period that Aurobindo gave what may be called the classic exposition of the entire Vedanta doctrine in his *Essays on the Gita* and later in his *Life Divine*. By this, Vedanta may be said to have been restored to its place as the common background of all Hindu religious thought.

The unifying doctrine was the Vedanta, but the abstract conceptions of this philosophical approach could only appeal to the *elite*. Popular Hinduism continued in the old way, sectarian, devotional and based on daily rituals. But is also underwent extraordinary changes. The gnarled branches of this ancient tree either fell away by themselves or were chopped off by legislative action promoted by the reformers. Child marriage, which many Hindu communities considered as an essential part of their religion, was abolished by law through the insistence of popular agitation. The remarriage of widows was permitted. Social disabilities based on caste vanished by themselves, and the occupational basis of caste-communities was weakened. Temples were thrown open to the untouchables, and in the most orthodox province of Madras, Hindu religious endowments were placed under the control of public bodies. The movement for the regeneration of the depressed classes assumed a national character, and their participation in social and political life became a major factor in the last days of British rule. Popular Hinduism had a more vigorous life than it ever had in the immediately preceding times, but it had in the course of a hundred years changed its character and temper, though it had kept much of its form. The major difficulty of Hinduism which had made it a wild jungle growth of widely varying customs, usages and superstitions was its lack of a machinery of reform and unification. The institutions of Hinduism, which in a large measure got identified with the religion itself, were the results of certain historical factors. They were upheld by law and not by religion. Vivekananda put the point well when he wrote: 'Beginning from Buddha down to Ram Mohan Roy, everyone made the mistake of holding caste to be a religious institution. . . . But in spite of all the ravings of the priests, caste is simply a crystallized social institution, which after doing its service is now filling the atmosphere of India with stench.'

The caste organization, the joint family, the rights of inheritance and the relationships arising out of them, which in the main are the special features of Hindu society, are legal and not religious. They are man-made institutions which do not claim Divine origin or religious sanction, and are upheld by man-made laws and not by any church or priesthood. It is a truism to say that legislation of today meets the social needs of yesterday and, unavoidably, law, as a conservative force, lags one step behind social necessities. When the great codes of Hindu Law were evolved, no doubt they represented the social forces of the time, but soon they had become antiquated. The succession of authoritative commentaries would show that the urge for modifications was widely felt and, in the absence of a legislative authority, the method of a progressive interpretation in each succeeding generation was the only one available to Hindu thinkers.

The immutability of Hindu law and customs was never a principle with the authors of the great codes or their commentators. In fact, the monumental volumes of Dr Kane's *History of Dharma Sastra* would demonstrate clearly that in every age social thinkers tried to adjust Hindu institutions to the requirements of the time. If the laws are changeable it follows that the institutions which are based on such laws are equally changeable. The great weakness of Hindu society was not that the laws had remained immutable, but that the changes introduced had been spasmodic, local and dependent to a large extent on the ingenuity of individual commentators. They were not in any sense a continuous renovation of legal principles, nor a legislative approximation to changing conditions.

The reason for this lack of direction of social ideas and the failure to prevent the growth of anti-social customs was undoubtedly the loss of political power. Not only was India as a whole never under a single sovereign authority, but even the political unity of North India which existed with occasional breaks from the time of the Mauryas (320 BC) to that of Harsha (AD 637) was broken up by the political conditions of the eighth century and lost for a period of 700 years with the Muslim invasion of the twelfth century. As a result, the Hindu community continued to be governed by institutions moulded by laws which were codified over 2,000 years ago and which were out of date even when they were codified.

The Muslim State had no legislative machinery, and when for the first time India was united under the British and the entire Hindu community lived under a common administration, the authorities of the East India Company after a first effort at social reform withdrew, under the pretext of religious neutrality, from activities which they thought might cause popular upheaval. Perhaps it was a wise step, as the motive force of large-scale social reforms must come from the people themselves and legislation can only give statutory sanction to principles which have already gained wide acceptance. The reformation of the Hindu religion was therefore an essential prerequisite of social legislation.

It was only after the Great War that the legislating State came into existence in India. Under the scheme of partial self-government introduced in 1921, there was established a central legislative authority with a majority of non-official elected Indians, which was both competent to change the laws of Hindu society and to enforce obedience to such laws through the length and breadth of India. In the provinces the direction of government passed in a large measure to elected legislatures. The legislative achievements of the Central and Provincial Governments in the field of social reform have been fundamental, though they did not go anywhere as far as the public demanded. The Civil Marriage Act and the Age of Consent Act (raising the marriageable age of girls to 14) were among the more important pieces of legislation which the Central Indian Legislative Assembly enacted. The Civil Marriage Act validates marriages between men and women of different castes of Hinduism. It strikes at the very root of the orthodox Brahminical conception of caste, and annuls the laws of Manu and the other orthodox codes of Hinduism. 'The immutable law', prohibiting *Varna-Samkara* or the mixture of castes, ceased by this single piece of legislation to operate through the length and breadth of India. The Age of Consent Act was equally revolutionary. It was the custom for over two thousand years at least for large sections of people to have girls married before the age of puberty. There was not only long tradition behind the custom, but it was considered compulsory at least for Brahmins in the light of certain authoritative texts. The Indian legislature made this custom illegal, though it had so much religious authority behind it, and the performance of such marriages became a penal offence.

Thus by the end of the third decade, the Hindu reformation had made enough progress to enable the new society to direct its social forces towards general betterment.

The reformation of Hinduism has been treated in some detail, because without an appreciation of its consequences the effects of Western education on Indian society will not be fully clear. The first educational attempts of the East India Company were, it should be remembered, in the direction of reviving Sanskrit and Arabic studies. The study of English had for some time been a voluntary pursuit, and a few mission colleges, notably the college at Serampore, had helped to popularize Western knowledge. But it was only in 1835 that, under the inspiration of Macaulay, the decision was taken to promote English education in India as a Government policy. Macaulay laid down a few propositions which he considered as axiomatic. He held 'we ought to employ them (our funds) in teaching what is best worth knowing; that English is better worth knowing than Sanskrit or Arabic; that it is possible to make natives of this country thoroughly good English scholars and to this end our efforts ought to be directed'. Accepting this view, the Government of India laid down that the object of the British Government ought to be the promotion of European literature and science among the natives of India. This had long been demanded by the progressive Indian thinkers of the time, and it is necessary to emphasize a fact which has often been forgotten in recent criticism, that the demand for Western education had come primarily from Indian leaders themselves.

Following the decision of the Government, schools and colleges began springing up in provincial capitals, but a co-ordinated system on an all-India basis was put into effect only in 1854. The broad objective of this policy was enunciated in a memorable dispatch in the following words: 'It is neither our aim nor our desire to substitute the English language for the vernacular dialects of the country. . . . It is indispensable, therefore, that in any general system of education, the study of them should be assiduously attended to, and any acquaintance with improved European knowledge which is to be communicated to the great mass of people can only be conveyed to them through one or other of these languages.' Following this, the universities were started in the major capitals of Indian provinces, Calcutta, Bombay, Madras and Allahabad and a vast field was opened for missionary effort.

The Macaulayan system, under which a systematic effort was made by a powerful government to educate in a foreign language the upper classes of a vast country, has now continued for over a hundred years. India even after her independence, has not radically altered the system, for in most universities and colleges English still continues to be the medium of instruction.

The weaknesses of the system are many and can easily be summarized. It created an impassable chasm between the English educated classes and others, including those educated in the traditional way. The wastage of effort involved not only in acquiring mastery in a different language but in studying all other subjects through it was immense. A wholly disproportionate emphasis was placed on literary studies. Also the attempted transplantation on Indian soil of what was an altogether alien culture took many decades to get acclimatized, and at least in the case of the first two generations there was a noticeable tendency to create a class of men, no doubt with competent knowledge of English, but uncertain of their values, barren in their thought and unadapted to their surroundings. But when all this and more has been said and the truth of the criticism accepted, the credit balance of this unique experiment still remains substantial and impressive.

In the first place, the system of higher education in English provided India with a class imbued with social purposes foreign to Hindu thought. The continuity and persistence of those purposes achieved the socio-religious revolution on which the life of modern India is based. While British administration did little, if anything, to emancipate the spirit, to extinguish the prejudices, to eradicate the ravages of ignorant custom and pernicious superstition, to encourage and stimulate thought, the New Learning which came to India through its introduction to the English language on a nation-wide scale undoubtedly did all this. Indeed, it may be argued that the essential contradiction of the British rule in India lay in this: the constituted government upheld the validity of customs, maintained and administered laws which denied the principles of social justice, refused to legislate for changes urgently called for by society, watched with suspicion the movement of liberal ideas, while the officially sponsored and subsidized educational system was undermining everything that the Government sought to uphold. The schools and colleges taught young men the idea of liberty while the Government did everything to suppress it. In the educational system the Government created and maintained an opposition to itself on a plane where its own methods were ineffective.

The mining of the ancient fortress of Hindu custom was a major achievement, for the reason that it was uniformly spread all over India. Had the new education been through the Indian languages, the emphasis of the movement would have been different from province to province, according to the development, flexibility and character of the language used. No doubt the reformation of Hinduism would still have come about, but it would not have been on an all-India basis. There would have been no 'master plan' of change and, instead of the Hindu community being unified, it would have split into as many different units as there are languages in India, and would have repeated the pattern of Europe with its conglomeration of mutually hostile units within the same Christian community. From this development India was saved by the common medium of education which Macaulay introduced into India.

In the second place, it is a point of major significance in the evolution of India as a single nation that this uniform system of education throughout India through a single language produced a like-mindedness on which it has been possible to build. That it gave to India a common language for political thinking and action is of less importance than the creation of this like-mindedness, this community of thought, feeling and ideas which created the Indian nationality. The mind of India is united spiritually by Hindu religious thought, by the binding force of the great tradition which Sanskrit embodies and which, through the Indian languages that still reflect and convey that tradition, continues to be a living factor, and by the new community of ideas and approach which English education has spread among the dominant classes. Of these three factors, the one which unites India politically, and makes it possible for Indians to act as a single nation and build up a new society, is the last. The first two are the permanent basis of Hindu civilization. They need not and could not have by themselves created a unified nation without the cementing force of like-mindedness in politics. The unity of Hindu life and the common tradition of a Sanskrit culture are analogous to the Christian religion and Latin tradition in Western Europe, and yet by its emphasis on regional languages and the absence of a cementing factor in secular life, Europe's development was through fragmentation. Except for a hundred years of uniform education through the English language the result would have been the same in India.

Further, this education through the English language enabled India to share, not derivatively or second-hand but directly, the results of the great movement of Enlightenment in Europe. The historic and truly magnificent work of the eighteenth-century thinkers of Europe had, after a period of revolution and unsettlement, become the living thought of the nineteenth century. Through a hundred channels it was fertilizing the life of Europe at the very time that English education was spreading in India. From explosive revolutionary slogans, 'liberty, equality and fraternity' had become transformed into the respectable creed of liberalism. Even in traditional England, law was undergoing a reform which was soon to affect India also. The greatest good of the greatest number had become an acceptable formula in a country to which an exclusive Whig oligarchy had given prosperity, security and an Empire spread over the four corners of the world. To this thought India became an adopted heir, and though English administrators spoke contemptuously of natives talking the language of their masters and aping the manners and mannerisms of their betters and not understanding the inner significance of the words by which they were swearing, it is undeniable that as time went on and one generation after another grew up on these principles, the apparent contradiction of a Brahmin talking about equality and fraternity became reconciled. The Hindu middle classes had become acclimatized to European thought in a way that few people had anticipated.

India emerged by a peaceful revolution as a modern society mainly because the gradual penetration of ideas was through education spread over a fairly large and representative class. It is often alleged against the Indian system of education that it failed to filter through to the masses. On a careful examination, this criticism will be found to be unjustified. It is true that the authors of the scheme had hoped that, as a result of infiltration, Hindu society, which was then considered to be in a process of dissolution, would disappear and the population of India would be saved for Christ. This was the Grand Design which made the missionaries ardent advocates of the scheme. That hope did not materialize. In fact, far from India turning Christian, the progress of English education only led, as we saw, to a large-scale reformation of Hinduism and a more rational interpretation of its dogmas. It led to a remarkable strengthening of the hold of Hinduism on the masses and its own emergence as a leading world religion. In that sense the theory of filtering down had the very opposite effect from what Macaulay and his friends in their complacency had imagined. It is therefore no matter for surprise that the missionary educators should consider that the object on which they had spent so much money and energy had failed.

The extent to which the theory of infiltration succeeded can best be seen by the extraordinary growth of the vernaculars of India during the last half-century. Few European scholars have tried to understand the literary activity which transformed these languages into great and living vehicles of thought and artistic creation entitling most of them to places of honour in the literatures of the modern world. Languages like Hindi, spoken by over a hundred millions; Bengali, the mother tongue of seventy millions; Gujerati, Marathi, Telugu, Tamil, Kanarese and Malayalam—the least of them spoken by a population of more than fifteen millions, have all, during the last half-century, witnessed an immense amount of literary activity, the echoes of which have only very occasionally reached the West. It will hardly be denied that this activity, which is the genuine reflection of the new humanism which India has developed, is the result of the infiltration of Western ideas and thought. Indian intellectual effort has so far been judged by the work of Indian writers in English. Insignificant in number and not too original, and with very little distinctive quality to contribute, the poets, essayists and literateurs of Indo-Anglian literature, as it is called, cannot claim to represent either the modern Indian mind or be considered the examples of India's creative capacity. The genuine results of English education in India, the reaction of the Indian mind to the vital movements of European culture introduced to them through English, are to be seen in the work of Tagore, Iqbal, Buddha Deva Bose, Sarat Chandra Chatterji, Prem Chand, K. M. Munshi, Vallathol, Sankara Kurup and a host of other great writers who have enriched the literatures of modern Indian languages. Some idea of the quality of their work reached the West through the popularity achieved in Europe by the translations of Tagore's work; but, generally speaking, it has been a closed book to European scholars.

Three stages may be observed in the development of these languages. At the beginning of the nineteenth century each one of these languages could boast of a literature which contained some of the masterpieces of poetic inspiration. There were in Hindi the great works of Tulsidas, Surdas and Kesavadas; in Bengali of Vidyapati, Chandidas and Krittibas. In Tamil there was a classical literature which claimed to rival the glories of Sanskrit. In Marathi, Gujerati and the rest the position was similar. There was a poetic literature of undoubted excellence, which was greatly cherished by the people; but all the same they were vernaculars, for education was through the classics, Sanskrit or Persian. Learning and scholarship had relation only to the classical languages. It was therefore true of all these languages that they had no books which could be used as textbooks in the new educational scheme.

This period also witnessed the secularization of the vernacular literature. As mentioned before, the development of literature in these languages was almost exclusively in the realm of poetry and the themes of such poetry were predominantly religious. All the great names in the different vernacular literatures before the nineteenth century – Tulsidas, Surdas, Kabir, Mira, Vidyapati, Chandidas, Tukaram – were of those associated with devotional religion. In fact, historically, the revival of religion in the Middle Ages and the growth of vernacular literatures were two aspects of the same development. The popularization of the Rama and Krishna cults, which constituted so important a feature in the life of medieval India, was achieved through the work of vernacular poets, and as a result the literatures of what became modern Indian languages started in the nineteenth century, heavily overladen with a religious tradition. The secular tradition in these literatures was confined mainly to erotic poetry.

The secularization of literature was the work of the first part of the nineteenth century, mainly as a result of the infiltration of English ideas. For this development essential preparatory work, such as the production of authoritative dictionaries and grammars, was done in most cases by missionaries and other foreigners who had scientific training in other languages. For example, it was the German missionary Gundert who, at the beginning of the nineteenth century, wrote an authoritative dictionary of the Malayalam language. It is Bishop Caldwell's *Comparative Grammar of the Dravidian Languages* that formed the groundwork of linguistic studies in the south. The work of the Serampore missionaries in laying the foundation of the modern developments in Bengal is generally accepted.

With the foundation thus firmly laid it became possible to utilize the vernaculars in the schools. The first stage was the production of textbooks, often written under orders of the department of education, for no old-fashioned scholar was likely to come forward voluntarily to undertake this work. The period of what may be called the production of textbooks created for the first time the models for prose writing to which no serious attention had been paid in the past. Not much work which would pass as literature was produced in this period, but a standard prose style was evolved, which was greatly furthered by the growth of vernacular journalism. As everywhere else in the world, the language of journalism was artificial, but it helped the growth of new ideas, made expression flexible, and related it to the political, social and economic problems of the day.

The second stage was a period of imitation when the literary talent of the Western-educated classes came into evidence, first by the translations of English classics, and later by original works under the inspiration of Western masters. This was the period when Bankim Chandra Chatterji wrote novels in the manner of Scott, Madhusudan Dutt wrote in the style of Milton, and Dwijendralal Roy wrote historical plays following the European technique. Similar tendencies were reflected in other languages a little later, for the leadership of Bengal in this matter was widely accepted at this time.

The new generation was not satisfied with this and it found a master in Rabindranath Tagore. With the appearance of Tagore as a major influence in Indian literature, the transformation of the vernaculars into great modern languages may be said to have been completed. The new generation, of which Tagore was the representative genius and supreme prophet, struggled to give expression to the trends of India's new life. Simultaneously the movement spread in all languages. It is significant that the period also marked the growth of integral nationalism, following the partition of Bengal, the Swadeshi agitation and the appearance of the school of activists led by Tilak and Aurobindo. A great patriotic fervour becomes visible in the poetry of the period between 1903-10, the period of Jana Gana Mana, of the exaltation of Indian and patriotic motives in drama, novels and poetry.

Tagore's genius stamped this movement, not only in Bengal but everywhere in India, with the characteristics of modernism. Into the language itself he infused vitality and flexibility, provided and popularized styles and forms which broke away from old tradition, introduced an international outlook into Bengali literature and established its independent position in the world. But Tagore, though exceptional in his genius, was not a singular phenomenon. There were many notable poets and writers in other languages, who were also moved by the same patriotic fervour and the same desire to burst through the shackles of the earlier imitative period. Two are especially worthy of mention, Subramania Bharati, the Tamil poet, and Mohammed Iqbal, whose earlier work especially voiced the spirit of patriotism and revolt.

The inter-war period witnessed 'the protest of the children against the fathers'. Everywhere the search for new literary forms, experimentation with new modes of expression, the desire to get away from stereotyped emotions became apparent. Social unrest began to be reflected in literature which saw in 'realism' the ideal it was seeking. Ibsen, Dostoevski, Chekhov and others replaced the earlier enthusiasms. The Gandhian movement, which held the political stage, sent young men to the villages and re-established the primary relationship with the soil. Munshi, Prem Chand and Sarat Chandra Chatterji are perhaps the most representative novelists of this period. The novels of Bankim Chandra and of similar romantic writers became the reminiscences of school-days of many of the leaders of the generation.

CHAPTER 3

JAPAN

THE Japanese revival differed from both the Indian and the Chinese in two essential respects. In the first place, both in India and in China, the renaissance has its origin in a desire to liberalize society, as that was considered the source of democratic strength. The roots of the two movements grew out of the breakdown of these societies, which faced their leaders with a dissolution of indigenous civilizations. They had to find new ideological bases for their society or perish. In Japan, on the other hand, the motive force, as we shall attempt to show, was not liberalism but reaction. What faced the Japanese leaders was not a breakdown of their social structure but a realization that from a military point of view they were weak when compared to the Western nations. What Japan sought was not a society drawing its strength from liberalism, but a rapid assimilation of Western knowledge and techniques to make herself stronger.

Secondly, both in India and China the movements for reform were spontaneous and therefore without planned direction. They manifested themselves first as trends and intellectual questionings and, gathering force as time went on, acquired a national character by the impetus and activity of large classes, which were not moved, generally speaking, by considerations of policy, but by a desire to promote moral and social welfare as a preparation for national greatness. In Japan, on the other hand, once the relationship of national security with Western learning and forms was recognized, the renaissance was planned and operated by the Government, which never for one moment forgot the supreme necessity of maintaining national solidarity and strengthening the springs of military power.

The Japanese and Indian movements had one thing in common as against the movement in China. The essential feature of Nippon's revival was the reorganization and strengthening of the Shinto, both as a State cult and as a religion. In India also, as we have noticed, the basis of the renaissance was a reformation of Hinduism. Both countries recognized that spiritual unity was necessary for a nation if it was to maintain its individuality and build up its strength. In China, on the other hand, the missionaries succeeded only too well in creating a spiritual chaos, with the result that the Chinese New Tide – the movement for intellectual emancipation – was basically anti-religious and proceeded on the assumption that religion was a discarded superstition everywhere and had no important part to play in modern life. This suited the disillusioned Chinese intellectual whose ethical conceptions, moulded by Confucian thinking, had, as we have already seen, always tended to undervalue religious life.

In Japan, even after the policy of exclusion was enforced by Hideyoshi, there continued to exist a small group of people interested in Western knowledge. Their contacts were mainly with the Dutch, who had been permitted to establish a factory at Deshima. After Japan had been balked of her amibition to conquer the Philippines by the establishment of the Spaniards in those islands, she had watched with suspicion and interest, as we have noted earlier, the activities of European nations in the China seas. While the official attitude was one of suspicion and of fear, the group interested in Western knowledge, working through the Dutch, continued to collect information and persevere in the search for Western science. Occasionally they were able to obtain assistance from foreigners, notably from a German, Kaempfer, who was in Japan in 1690–2, and at a later period from Thunberg and Siebold.

The interest in 'Dutch' learning was intense in certain intellectual circles, though not widespread, and it is said that the annual visit of the head of the Dutch factory to Yeddo was used regularly by Japanese scholars to elicit information about scientific matters. In any case, it is clear that by the middle of the eighteenth century a group known as *Rangakusha*, or 'Dutch scholars', had come into existence, which showed a persevering curiosity in Western knowledge. As a result of the work of this group, standard European works on astronomy, mathematics, medicine and botany were translated and published or circulated among specialists.

It is significant that the interest in Japan was exclusively in scientific subjects. There was no hint in these studies of any interest in poetry, literature, philosophy or social sciences, which were making rapid strides in Europe during this period of enlightenment. While Ram Mohan Roy in India was corresponding with Condorçet, the Japanese scholars were laboriously translating textbooks on mathematics. The fact is that the Japanese were not interested in Western humanism or in the liberalization of thought, but in penetrating the secret of Western power. This is clearly brought out in the careers of men like Takashima, Sakuma Shozan, Watanabé Noboru and Takano and other leaders of the 'old men's club', which in the first half of the nineteenth century became the centre of those interested in Western knowledge. The fact that China was easily defeated by the British caused consternation in Japan and people in authority began to examine the causes of this unexpected and surprising outcome. Only the Western group had a ready reply. In a memorial which Sakuma wrote to his patron occurs the following significant passage: 'How is it that the Western countries have been able, by devotion to learning, to increase their strength to such a point that even the country of Confucius has fallen victim to their assault? *It is because foreign learning is rational and Chinese learning is not.*'

From this time, the advance of foreign learning – again in matters of direct concern to defence – was considerable. Men like Watanabé Noboru and Takano Nagahide, the former an official of some influence, a poet, painter and scholar, and the latter an author, who wrote extensively among other things on mineralogy, history and military tactics, popularized the ideas of this group, which felt that national security depended now on 'not being bettered by old maxims' and patriotism required an acceptance of the dynamics of power from the West. Their thought ranged over all important subjects of national economy, shipping, industry, forts and currency reform, recruitment to services, etc. Yokoi Shonan, one of the most influential of this group, was even a perfervid patriot, advocating frankly a world leadership for Japan, an expansionist whose ideas were to find wide popularity during the period of Japan's attempt to play a masterful role in Asia.

The alliance between the 'Western group' and the revivalists of Japan, which Yokoi Shonan represented, is of special importance. Alongside and contemporaneously with the growth of interest in Western science there had also developed a movement in favour of reactionary patriotism, associated with a revival of pure Shinto. Various sects arose which preached a 'return to antiquity' or ancient learning, which had a great influence in weakening the hold of Confucianism which had found support with the leaders of the Tokugawa Shogunate. The most notable personalities associated with this movement were Kamo no Mabuchi (1697-1769), Motoori Norinaga (1730-1801) and Hirata Atsutane (1776-1843). Mabuchi's main thesis was that the spread of Confucian ideas and the eclipse of Shinto were the real causes for 'power falling into the hands of servants and the Mikado becoming an utter nullity'.[1] It should be emphasized that the basic concepts of Shinto are the identification of Japanese national character with the Emperor, and the belief that the Emperor is descended from the Sun Goddess.

'Revere the Emperor, expel the foreigner' was the motto of the nationalist creed, which this 'pure Shinto' school had encouraged. The sup-

[1] Holtom: *Modern Japan and Shinto Nationalism*, Second Edition, 1947.

porters of the 'Western learning' had common ground with them in their attack on Confucianism, for as Sakuma had pointed out in his memorial quoted previously, Chinese learning has ceased to be rational and had therefore become dangerous. Also, some of the more forward-looking members of the Western group had already realized that a strong Central Government under the Emperor was the onlypossibility in the changed circumstances of Japan. The results of this strange alliance between Western knowledge and pure Shinto became clearly visible in the character of the Japanese renaissance which followed the Meiji Restoration.

We have already dealt in some detail with the political history of the Meiji era and the steps taken by the leaders of New Japan to assimilate Western knowledge and to transform the Empire into a modern political community. The efforts of the Meiji era statesmen were outstandingly successful in all matters which they set out to achieve. The established a Central Government, created a modern military machine, disciplined the people into a patriotic community, industrialized the country and developed its economic power, provided a national system of education, which brought into Japanese life the technical knowledge of the West, created the material set-up of a modern people, in fact transformed Japan into a great Power. It was a programme of planned Westernization, a system carefully thought out and controlled, the object of which was national strength. Only such things as were useful for this purpose or would subserve this end were accepted and others were rigidly excluded. The Meiji Emperor himself in one of his poems declared:

'Oh, how I wish to make this country inferior to none
Adopting that which is good and rejecting that which is bad.'[1]

The process by which this object was achieved has been discussed elsewhere. Here we need emphasize only the identification of community life in its widest sense with State Shinto, and the utilization of that system of ethno-centric ceremonial for the creation of national solidarity, faith in the future of Japan, and the exclusion of all thought which was contrary to the basic conceptions of the Japanese State. The Imperial Edict promulgated in the first year of Meiji declared:

'The worship of the Gods and regard for ceremonies (Shinto) are the great proprieties of the Empire and the fundamental principles of national polity and education. . . . On this occasion of the restoration (Imperial Rule) Tokio has been made the new capital and the Emperor shall reign in person. *First of all, rituals* shall be initiated and the administration of law and order shall be established. *Thus the way of religion and Government (Sai sei itchi) shall be revived.*'

The doctrine of *Sai sei itchi* or the unity of 'rites' and politic is

[1] Quoted in Yukio Osakis's *Voice of Japanese Democracy*. Yokohama, 1918, p. 108.

fundamental to the whole question of Japanese national revival, as the Imperial Rescript itself declares. The origin of this unity of the religion and the State is announced in the same edict. Even more important is the solemn proclamation issued the same day by the Emperor, which reads as below: 'We solemnly announce: The Heavenly Deities and the Great Ancestress (the daughter of the Sun God, Amaterasu Omi Kami) established the throne and made the succession secure. The line of Emperors in unbroken succession entered into possession thereof and handed it on. Religious ceremonies and Government were one and the same and the innumerable subjects were united. Government and education were clear to those above, while below them, the manners and customs of the people were beautiful. Beginning with the Middle Ages, however, there were some seasons of decay alternating with seasons of progress. Sometimes the Way was plain, sometimes darkened: and the period in which Government and education failed to flourish was long.

'*Now in the cycle of fate all things have become new.* Polity and education must be made clear to the nation and the Great Way of obedience to the Gods must be promulgated. Therefore we newly appoint *propagandists* to proclaim this to the nation. Do you, our subjects, keep this commandment in mind?'

This is the basic conception of the Japanese revival, the unity of Shinto with education and politics. In the official declaration of educational policy, issued by the Department of Education in 1937, entitled *Kokutai no Hongi* (the fundamental principles of national structure) it is laid down: 'Education in its fundamental aspects is unified with religious ceremonies and Government. That is to say, although religious ceremonies and Government and education have their own separate operations, yet in the last analysis, they are one and the same.' It should be remembered that, following the practice of modern States, Japan (under Order No. 12 of August 2, 1899) prohibited religious education in public and private schools, but the *State Shinto*, which had previously been declared not to be a religion but a training in civic responsibility, was made compulsory in all schools. Thus, while all other religious teachings were excluded – and this affected the missionaries most – Shinto was a compulsory subject to which the highest importance was attached.

The triple unification of 'rites', politics and education, which forms the basis of Japan's renaissance, though illiberal and antagonistic to freedom of thought, helped the country to come safely through the transition stage when Japan was for a time hypnotized by the achievements of Western civilization. For two decades following the Restoration, there was an extraordinary craze for Western things, an open and unbounded admiration of the West among the urban classes. Sansom describes this stage of Japanese development in the following words: 'To wear foreign style clothes and leather shoes was now correct. . . . Of course, few Japanese in 1875 or thereabouts could afford a complete foreign wardrobe, but it was usual to wear one or two articles of foreign clothing. Some interesting combinations were thus devised, such as kimono over trousers, or a broad cloth frock coat and a silk divided skirt with two swords in the sword belt. . . .

'The state of affairs is best illustrated by a song composed for children in 1878. It is called the Civilization Ball Song and was designed to impress on young minds the advantages of Western culture. They were to count the bounces of the ball by reciting the names of ten objects deemed to be most worthy of adoption, namely gas lamps, steam engines, etc.'[1]

The illiberalism and reactionary character of Japanese religious integration should not blind us to the great achievements of the Japanese renaissance in the field of science, scholarship, literature and arts generally. The new spirit of revived Japan flowed vigorously into constructive channels and in the twentieth century there was a marked revival in all spheres of intellectual activity. Meticulous scholarship and widespread research were encouraged by the universities. Japanese Buddhism showed signs of vigorous national revival. The contradictions inherent in the system stood in the way of independent political thinking, but a great deal of study, it would seem, was directed towards reconciling the forms of Western democracy, parliamentary government, adult franchise and the Cabinet system with the spirit of the Japanese system.

[1] Sansom: *The Western World and Japan*, pp. 399-400.

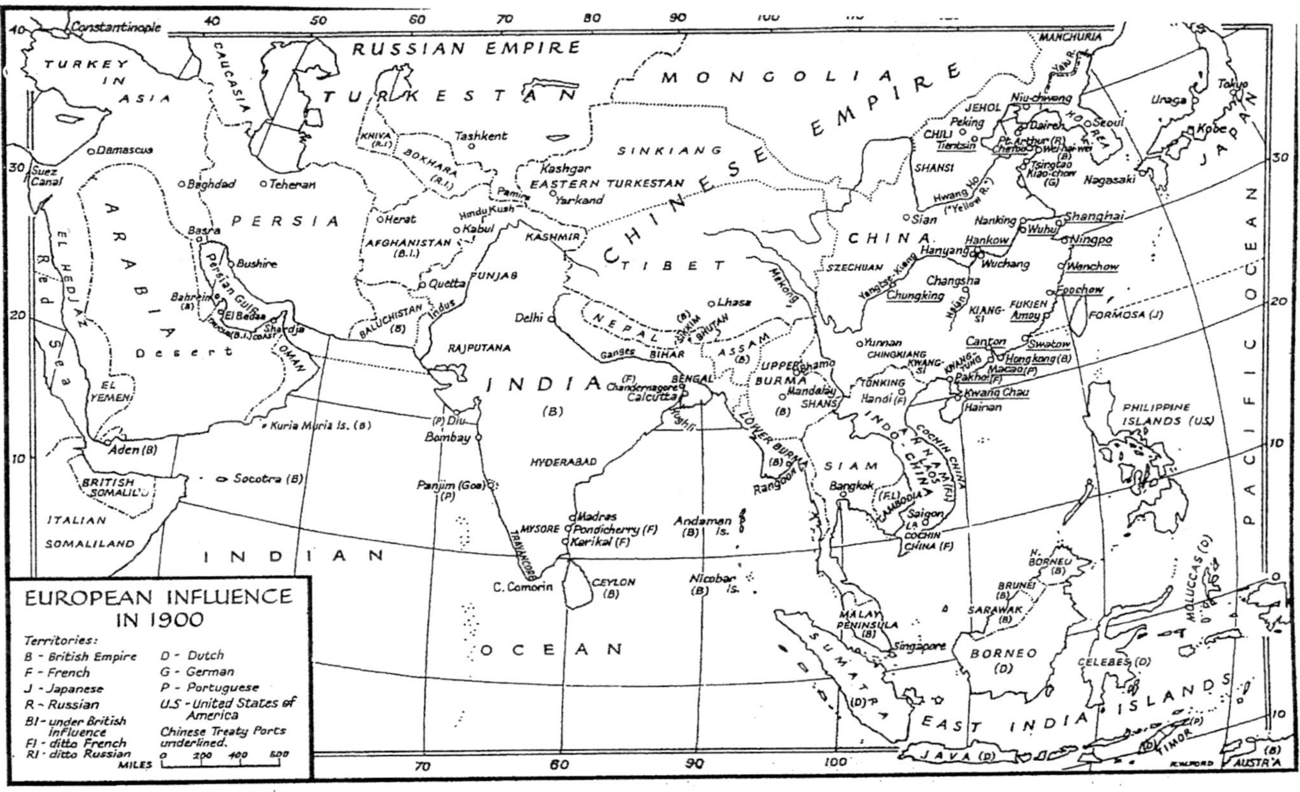

EUROPEAN INFLUENCE IN 1900
Territories:
B - British Empire
F - French
J - Japanese
R - Russian
BI - under British influence
FI - ditto French
RI - ditto Russian
D - Dutch
G - German
P - Portuguese
U.S - United States of America
Chinese Treaty Ports underlined.
MILES 0 200 400 600
RUSSIAN EMPIRE
TURKESTAN
MONGOLIA
CHINESE EMPIRE
MANCHURIA
TURKEY IN ASIA
Constantinople
CAUCASIA
Damascus
Suez Canal
Baghdad
Teheran
PERSIA
Basra
Bushire
Persian Gulf
ARABIA
Desert
EL HEDJAZ
Red Sea
EL YEMEN
Aden (B)
OMAN
Kuria Muria Is. (B)
Socotra (B)
BRITISH SOMALILD
ITALIAN SOMALILAND
KHIVA (R.I.)
BOKHARA (R.I.)
Tashkent
Herat
AFGHANISTAN (B.I.)
Kabul
Hindu Kush
Pamirs
Quetta
BALUCHISTAN (B)
Indus
PUNJAB
KASHMIR
Kashgar
EASTERN TURKESTAN
Yarkand
SINKIANG
TIBET
Lhasa
NEPAL
SIKKIM
BHUTAN
ASSAM (B)
Delhi
RAJPUTANA
INDIA (B)
Ganges
BIHAR
BENGAL
(F) Chandernagore
Calcutta
Hughli
(P) Diu
Bombay
Panjim (Goa) (P)
HYDERABAD
MYSORE
Madras
Pondicherry (F)
Karikal (F)
TRAVANCORE
C. Comorin
CEYLON (B)
Andaman (B) Is.
Nicobar (B) Is.
INDIAN OCEAN
UPPER BURMA
Bhamo
Mandalay
SHANS
(B)
LOWER BURMA
Rangoon
Mekong
SIAM
Bangkok
MALAY PENINSULA (B)
Singapore
SUMATRA (D)
JAVA (D)
EAST INDIA ISLANDS
BORNEO (D)
N. BORNEO (B)
BRUNEI (B)
SARAWAK (B)
CELEBES (D)
MOLUCCAS (D)
TIMOR (D) (P)
(B) AUSTR'A
PHILIPPINE ISLANDS (US)
PACIFIC OCEAN
TONKING
Handi (F)
ANNAM (FI)
LAOS
INDO-CHINA
CAMBODIA (F.I.)
Saigon
COCHIN CHINA
COCHIN CHINA (F)
CHINA
SZECHUAN
Yangtse-Kiang
Chungking
Yunnan
CHINGKIANG
KWANG-SI
KWANG-TUNG
Pakhoi (F)
Kwang Chau
Hainan
Canton
Hongkong (B)
Macao (P)
Swatow
KIANG-SI
FUKIEN
Amoy
Foochow
FORMOSA (J)
Wenchow
Ningpo
Shanghai
Wuhu
Nanking
Hankow
Hanyang
Wuchang
Changsha
Sian
Hwang Ho ("Yellow R.")
SHANSI
CHILI
Peking
Tientsin
JEHOL
Niu-chwang
Dairen
Pt. Arthur (R)
Chefoo
Wei-hai-wei (B)
Tsingtao
Kiao-chow (G)
Seoul
KOREA
Nagasaki
Uraga
Kobe
Tokyo
JAPAN

CHAPTER 4

CHINA

THE renaissance in China, liberal, rationalist and humanist, was late in arriving, and though its effects were notable, political circumstances prevented its natural growth; and the *New Tide* receded with almost the same rapidity as that with which it swelled. The failure of the renaissance movement, with its immense promise and early achievement, left China in a state of cultural and intellectual anarchy, opening the way for the penetration of the revolutionary ideas of Marxism.

China, even in a greater measure than India, has always shown a spirit of free criticism. The intellectual growth of China through 2,500 years has provided many notable periods when scholars and thinkers challenged accepted dogmas and gave birth to new movements. This spirit of criticism was directly inherited by Kang Yu-wei, who inspired Emperor Kuang Hsu in his tragic Hundred Days of Reform.

Kang Yu-wei, a Cantonese (born 1858), had some influence with a group of officials, mostly southerners, headed by the Grand Secretary, Weng Tung-ho, who had observed closely the lines that Japan had followed in her rise to power and had felt that what was obstructing China's progress was the refusal to learn from the West. When, on the death of Prince Kung in 1898, there was a reshuffle in Government, Weng Tung-ho recommended Kang Yu-wei to the Emperor as a person of superior gifts and outstanding ability. The Emperor was greatly impressed by the ideas of Kang, and the conviction grew on him that China would not be able to weather the storms without a serious attempt to put her internal administration in order. The first reform decree of the Emperor is a statement of this conviction and is worth quoting:

> 'We now issue this special Decree so that all our subjects, from the Imperial family downwards, may hereafter exert themselves in the cause of reform. The basis of education will continue to rest on the canons of the Sages, but at the same time there must be careful investigation of every branch of European learning appropriate to exist-

ing needs, so that there may be an end to empty fallacies and that, by zeal, efficiency may be attained. Parrot-like plagiarisms of shallow theories are to be avoided, and catchwords eschewed. What we desire to attain is the elimination of useless things and the advancement of learning which, while based on ancient principles, shall yet move in harmony with the times. The Peking University is to be made a model for the Empire, and all officials of the rank of Board Secretaries, officers of the bodyguard, expectant Magistrates, sons of high officials and Manchus of hereditary rank, are to be entitled to enter upon a college course in order that their talents may be trained to meet the needs of these critical times. No procrastination or favouritism will be tolerated, nor any disregard of these, the Throne's, admonitions.

This extraordinary attempt, which drew its inspiration from the success of Westernization in Japan, deserves some notice, though its influence was momentary. The old examination system was abolished, and subjects like political economy were introduced into the curriculum. Colleges and schools on modern lines were to be opened. A naval college was projected, railways and mining bureaus were established in Peking, and a translation department was established in charge of Liang Chi-chao. A number of sinecures were abolished. The quick succession in which the decrees were issued alarmed the conservative officials, who petitioned the Dowager Empress to take up power again. Kuang Hsu, who was aware of this intrigue, decided to strike first. He summoned Yuan Shih-kai to the palace and taking him into his confidence gave him special charge of army reform. He then entrusted him with the duty of arresting and keeping in prison the Empress Dowager. The crafty and unscrupulous Yuan went straight to Jung Lu and betrayed the Emperor's trust. The 'Old Buddha' (facing p. 160) did not hesitate a moment longer after she received the report from her favourite of the Emperor's plans. She summoned the Grand Council and secured from that body a request for her resumption of power. The reforming Emperor was promptly deposed and kept a close prisoner. Thus ended this strange interlude and the attempt of a well-meaning Emperor to reform the Empire by a programme of Westernization!

As a reformer Kang Yu-wei was in many ways a greater figure than many of the later revolutionaries, a clear thinker who realized that only by modernization of her institutions could China advance. Even more radical than Kang was Liang Chi-chao, who was associated with Kang during the hundred days of reform.

After the failure of that abortive period of hundred days, Kang escaped to Hong Kong and thence to America, and Liang Chi-chao escaped to Japan, where he founded his paper the *Hsin Min Pao* and campaigned vigorously both for new ideas and for political reform.

Liang, himself a Hunanese, had the support of some other thinkers of his province, especially Tan Ssu-tung, who refused to fly with the rest after the Empress's *coup d'état*, and met a martyr's death – the first Chinese in modern times to suffer for demanding reform.

Liang Chi-chao, from his exile, preached the gospel of the 'New People', the idea that China in the circumstances in which she found herself required a complete renovation of ideas and ideals; in fact the Chinese must emerge as 'a new people'. 'Although you change a little here and a little there, daub a bit on here and clean a bit off there, it will not help. What is required is the creation of a completely new spirit.' A scholar and writer of great ability, who shed his early monarchism and joined the republicans, Liang was a powerful influence in shaping the younger generation, and Hu Shih in his autobiography says how greatly he and his friends were influenced by the ideas and writings of Liang.

Other forces were also at work to reform Chinese society from within. Lin Tse-hsu, the famous Imperial High Commissioner in the Opium Affairs, had tried to familiarize himself with the affairs relating to foreigners. He, like the Japanese students of the West, was interested more in national security than in reform, and soon began advocating the manufacture of guns and ships in the manner of foreigners. The material that Lin collected was presented by him to Wei Yuan, a member of the Grand Secretariat, who printed and published it under the title *Hai Kuo Tu Chih*. The object of the publication was stated as follows:

'In order to handle barbarian affairs, you have to know barbarian sentiments: in order to know barbarian sentiments you have to know barbarian conditions.' Wei was a genuine reformer and he was assisted in his work by another scholar of note, Kung Tzu-chin. Their approach was that it was an age of practical knowledge and scholars should devote themselves to its acquisition. This view came to be known as the 'teachings of Kung and Wei'. Between Lin, Kung and Wei they established the Hsuan-nan Club. Of this circle a Chinese historian says: 'Of the persons who formed this club, Huang Chueh-tsu started the anti-opium campaign, Kung and Wei initiated the reform, while Lin turned out to be their leader.' These were the founders of Western learning in China.

Of a different kind was Yung Ming (graduated in Yale in 1854,) who, having had his own education in the United States, induced the Government to send a hundred scholars for study to that country. Yung Ming described his plan in the following words: 'The scheme contemplated the education of one hundred and twenty students, divided into four instalments of thirty students each, one instalment to be sent out each year. They were to have fifteen years to finish their education. Their average age was to be from twelve to fourteen. If the first and second instalments proved to be a success, the scheme was to be continued indefinitely. Chinese teachers were to be provided to keep up their knowledge of Chinese while in the United States. Over the whole enterprise two commissions were to be appointed.'

The Viceroy Tseng Kuo-fan sponsored the scheme, and the first group of thirty students left for America in 1872. The quota of 120 was completed by 1875, and, before the scheme could be fully tried out, the entire mission was recalled as a result of a new wave of reaction in 1881. It is interesting to note that many members of this first batch of 'returned students' helped China in her path of modernization.

Two other factors were at work in favour of Westernization. One was the growth of the Treaty Port Chinese, and the other, of large Chinese settlements abroad. In Hong Kong, at the treaty ports, and more especially the great cities of Shanghai and Tientsin, a large Chinese community had grown up under the protection of European Powers. In the colony of Hong Kong they lived no doubt as British subjects, but their influence in the neighbouring province of Kwangtung was considerable. In the commercial metropolis of Shanghai the comprador class had become economically and socially powerful. Though these urban communities did not count politically or socially in the time of the Dowager Empress, when influence was confined to the eunuchs and nobles of court and to the Mandarinate, nor in the country generally where the *literati* of the old school still retained prestige, yet they were a growing class and their ideas were beginning to penetrate the more intelligent and forward looking officials. The great colleges of European learning established in Shanghai and elsewhere, under the auspices of Christian missionaries, were also producing men of modern education; though they were denied political influence, because superior employment in Government service was till 1901 enjoyed by those graduating in imperial examinations, they were shaping middle class life, especially in urban areas. Also by the end of the century many young men from the cities were going to Japan and the Western countries for higher education, where they formed centres of new life, so that 'the returned students' became a factor of importance in social changes, even before the fall of the Empire

The existence of large and prosperous communities of 'overseas Chinese' in Malaya, Indonesia, the Philippines, Hawaii, the USA and elsewhere was also an important factor in the movement for Westernization The coolie traffic ('pig trade' as it was elegantly described in the 'sixties) was mainly responsible for the growth of these powerful communities, except to some extent in Malaya and Java But the children of indentured labourers showed the qualities of their race, and became economic factors of significance in the places where they settled. Though they never lost their Chinese character and were fervently patriotic, their changed surroundings and education and continuous contact with other civilizations made many of them aware of the weaknesses of Chinese society and the necessity for change in the mother country. The advocates of modernization found enthusiastic support in these overseas communities.

As long as the Empire lasted, the movement for modernization made but little progress. Even where the court made appearances of concession to foreign sentiment, as it was forced to do after the Boxer Rebellion, the Old Buddha and her advisers were able to uphold their reactionary system in internal matters. But once the Empire fell, and with it the stays and supports of the old society, the forces that were gathering during the preceding half-century began to make themselves felt. The revolution itself, as we have already noticed, proved abortive, but it had sufficient popular strength to prevent a return to the old system. The failure of Yuan Shih-kai's attempt to enthrone himself and thus restore the monarchy was of historic significance, for it showed that, though the Revolution did not have sufficient momentum or popular backing to bring about a radical social reformation in China, it definitely involved a break with the past. The imperial tradition which the great Chin Emperor Shih Huang-Ti had established, and which had lasted for over 2,000 years, was finally and irrevocably broken.

China fell at first into political and economic chaos. There were many reasons. One was the rivalry of powers exercising unseen but effective dominion over China. Another was the failure of the mandarinate and the ineffectiveness of the new classes, drawn mostly from the coast and therefore without prestige or authority among the people. Another was the break-up of the army under different war lords. It was in these circumstances that the *New Tide* or China's great movement for intellectual freedom took shape and found expression.

The centre of this new movement was the National Peking University, under its great Chancellor Tsai Yuan-pei. Its acknowledged leaders were Chen Tu-hsiu and Hu Shih. The university had been formally established in 1898 with Sun Chia-nai as Chancellor, and an English missionary, Martin, as President. The Empress, even after her *coup d'état*, had left the university untouched. Under the old regime it did not play any notable part, but with the appointment of Tsai Yuan-pei as Chancellor in January 1917 a new era may be said to have begun.

Tsai was a distinguished scholar who had been educated at Leipzig. He was a great advocate of academic freedom and one who believed that universities have the sacred duty of furthering knowledge and that their activities should not be exclusive. Tsai invited Chen Tu-hsiu, the editor of the magazine *La Jeunesse* and the accepted leader of the renaissance, to become the Dean of the College of Letters at the University. Chen

Tu-hsiu was destined to write his name in Chinese history in a number of different ways. More than even his later achievement in founding and leading the Communist Party and adding to the literature of that movement by a deviationism named after him, his five years of activity as the leader of the New Culture movement entitle him to rank high in modern Asian history. The first issue of *La Jeunesse* had appeared in September 1915, with a leading article by Chen entitled 'My Solemn Appeal to Youth'. It was a call to youth to take upon its shoulders the struggle to re-establish China's greatness. The appeal was to the patriotism of the youth of China and to its desire for free intellectual life. Its effect was indeed electric. The first issue was reprinted many times, and over two hundred thousand copies were sold. More than even the first shot fired at Wuchang, this was the real beginning of the revolution.

Even at this early period Chen Tu-hsiu had a real understanding of the situation. He analysed the problem of the ineffectiveness of China after the revolution as arising from the 'neutral attitude of the people, as if watching from the opposite side of the shore', their lack of awakening, their refusal to shed old ideas, their helpless attitude in the face of changes forced on them. He declared, therefore, that it was for the youth of the nation to come forward and the programme he set out is contained in six principles embodied in the solemn appeal: 'Independence not servility, progress not conservatism, aggressiveness not timidity, world-mindedness not narrow nationalism, practical attitude not ceremonies, scientific approach not speculation.' A year later he declared that 'the youth should be out to conquer and not be conquered; secondly, they should respect their own independent character and not be an appendix to other people; and, thirdly, they should engage in a people's movement and not in any narrow party activities'.

Chen also came out openly with his attack on the inadequacy of the old Chinese culture and thereby laid the theoretical basis of the Chinese renaissance. 'Whether in politics, scholarship, morality or literature', he declared, 'the Western method and the Chinese method are two absolutely different things and can in no way be compromised or reconciled. We need not now discuss which is better and which is worse, as that is a seaparate issue. . . . But if we decide to reform, then we must adopt the new Western method in all things and need not confuse the issue by such nonsense as "national heritage" or "special circumstances".'

How different is this language from that of the Japanese leaders, who preached the unity of 'rites', politics and education, and who sought to put modern thinking into the strait-jacket of Shinto theology. The issue between the conservative mandarins and the advocates of New Learning was squarely joined here, and Chen Tu-hsiu, with rigorous logic, carried the attack straight to the citadel of Chinese thought – Confucius himself.

To him Confucius was the enemy. In an early issue of *La Jeunesse*, I Pei-sha had published a scathing criticism of Confucius, demonstrating beyond doubt that until the time of Wu Ti of the Han Dynasty in the second century B.C., Confucianism was only a minor school of thought, and that it was the Han Emperors, realizing how useful the doctrine of five relationships was as an ideological basis for despotism, who suppressed the other sects and 'utilized Confucianism as the imperial puppet to monopolize the thought of the world and to restrict its freedom'. This attack was pressed home by Chen himself in a series of articles in the same monthly, one of which was entitled 'Confucianism in relation to Constitutional Development'. A more important attack was contained in a later article under the heading 'The Way of Confucius and Life in Modern Times'. Chen's main line of attack was that Confucianism was a total denial of human rights as it was based on the three cardinal duties: the absolute duty of loyalty to the Emperor, filial piety and the absolute submission of the wife to the husband. Stated in this form, it was clear that a modification of Confucianism to suit modern conditions was impossible and this is what the New Tide group preached. 'Down with Confucianism' was their motto.

The elevation of so radical a thinker, the leader of China's open revolt against the accepted traditions, to the position of the Dean of the Faculty of Letters in the Metropolitan University was almost like giving it official authority. Chen Tu-hsiu received powerful support for his views from the younger generation of scholars, the most notable of whom was Hu Shih. Hu Shih was a scholar of encylcopaedic knowledge, a philosopher, fully trained in the critical methods of Western thought, a scholar in the tradition of *Han Hsueh*, going to the original and not to the commentary, and above all a genuine humanist firmly believing in the value of reason in human relationship. His first contribution to the new movement was the great call for a literary revolution. The ideas were originally put forward in tentative form in 1916 by Chao Yuan-jen and Hu Shih in the *Chinese Students' Monthly*, published in America. There was an important point of difference between the two: Chao desired to give up the pictorial script and introduce an alphabet into Chinese and Hu Shih did not. To Hu Shih the more important task was to get the *literati* and the people to use the same language so that thought would not remain the monopoly of a group. He argued that what was called the Chinese literary language was a dead language, dead because it was no longer spoken by the people. 'It is like Latin in medieval Europe: in fact it is more dead (if mortality admits of a comparative degree) than Latin, because Latin is still capable of being spoken and understood, while literary Chinese is no longer auditorally intelligible even among the scholars, except when the phrases are familiar or when the listener has already some idea of what the speaker is going to say.' To meet this difficulty and provide a vehicle for thought which would reach everyone, Hu Shih boldly advocated the use of the spoken language.

Not content with the publication of his views in a students' monthly circulating in a foreign land, Hu Shih addressed a letter to Chen Tu-hsiu for publication in *La Jeunesse* suggesting a programme of literary reform, later elaborated into an article. The suggestions were modest: 'Avoid classical allusions; discard parallel construction of sentences; discard time-worn literary phrases and do not avoid popular speech. Emphasize grammatical construction; do not use sickly expressions when you are not sick; do not imitate the ancients. In short, write naturally in a language which could be understood.' But all his scholarship and the reasonableness of his arguments would perhaps have led only to a limited liberal movement if Chen Tu-hsiu had not elevated it to a revolutionary credo. Supporting Hu Shih's plea, Chen declared for 'a revolution in Chinese literature' and, as he grandiloquently declared, 'hoisted the banner of the army of Revolution in Literature'.

When *La Jeunesse* began to publish articles in the spoken language and adopted the eight points of Hu Shih, the literary revolution may be said to have been accomplished and the language emancipated from the shackles of an artificial classicism. This freedom brought forth an enormous amount of literature, translations from European languages, critical essays, original creative works, and may be said to be the starting-point of modern Chinese literature. The intellectual ferment and activity of the period is well brought out and accurately pictured in Lin Yutang's novel, *Moment in Peking*, which covers the entire period, beginning with the Boxer Rebellion and ending with the period of the Kuomintang Revolution.

It is not to be assumed that this movement for intellectual liberation and for the modernization of Chinese life and thought did not meet with vigorous opposition. Apart from ultra-Conservative Confucian scholars like Liu Shu who, in his famous letter to Tsai Yuan-pei, accused the reformers of abandoning the 'five relationships', there were others like Liang Chih-chao and Liang Sou-ming who pleaded for a better appreciation of China's national heritage and for a synthesis between the East and the West. To all these pleas the leaders of the New Tide movement, in their enthusiasm for the West, turned a deaf ear. Hu Shih, who at this period of his life had a firm faith in the all-conquering virtues of Western civilization, denounced even the doctrine of 'selective adoption' and declared that the way of salvation lay in wholesale adoption.

It is on a society which was so uncertain about its own values, and in a period of social anarchy caused by the breakdown of religion and ethics, with its intellectual classes groping towards a new life, that the explosive force of the Russian Revolution began to operate. The New Tide had achieved remarkable results, especially in its denunciation of Confucianism and in its literary revolution; but it was confined to intellectuals and had not helped to integrate society on a new basis. On the contrary, it may be said to have added to the confusion by its new ideas, no doubt as a first step towards a reintegration on a liberal and rational basis. But it never got the opportunity. When Tsai Yuan-pei and Hu Shih were advocating the acceptance of Western liberalism, the doctrines of the great anti-liberal revolution were being proclaimed in Moscow and were being enthusiastically studied by the more radical youth of all countries. It is most important in studying the problem of modernization in China to remember that the original founder of the Communist Party of China was none other than Chen Tu-hsiu, the protagonist and leader of the New Tide and editor of its organ. As early as April 1917, Chen, in an article in *La Jeunesse*, analysed the interrelation of the Russian Revolution and the awakening of the Chinese people. *La Jeunesse*, in a series of articles, identified the Bolshevik revolution with the victory of the common people, and published a special issue on Marx, edited by Li Ti-chao, another Professor of the Peking University. In July 1920, the Communist Party of China was founded with Chen as its leader. To Chen, Li and many other leaders of the renaissance, the Russian Revolution was the beginning of a more vigorous and more fundamental New Thought and New Tide.

This cleavage sounded the death-knell of the liberal renaissance of which Tsai Yuan-pei and Hu Shih were the protagonists. Their positive programme – literary revolution, revolt against Confucianism, a critical attitude in scholarship – became the common tradition of new China. By their very success they ceased to be dynamic. They ceased to have any further appeal and the more radical thinking turned away from the liberalism of the West. For another twenty years liberal thought, confined mainly to universities and academic circles, continued to exercise a certain influence on the intellectual life of China, but it gradually lost significance as a movement as it was unable to catch up with the radicalism of the people, or to put its theories into practice through institutions. The Kuomintang's movement to the right and its attempt to revive a neo-Confucianism, through controlled universities and institutions, denied the liberals whatever influence they once possessed and, from 1936 onwards, the movement for reform through enlightenment and reason may be said to have ceased finally to have any influence on the mind of China.

Why did this great movement, so promising in its beginning, so genuine in its aspirations, so convinced about its own analysis, fail after six years of intensive activity (1916–22), especially when its leaders were men of great integrity, outstanding scholarship and clear vision? The reasons seem to be simple. In the first place it came too late, at a time when the prestige of the liberal civilization of the West had been undermined by the Great War and then shattered by the Russian Revolution. Before the theories of the New Tide could be applied to social organization the rival doctrines of the Soviet Revolution, with its emphasis on nationalism in colonial and dependent countries, had overtaken China. Secondly, the social anarchy produced by seventy years of protected missionary effort made it impossible for the New Tide to organize society on a liberal basis within so short a time. Thirdly, though the doctrines of the renaissance were revolutionary in their effects, the leaders were intellectuals who were isolated from the people and could not carry their message to the masses. They had to depend on infiltration. Fourthly, there was an undoubted failure of leadership when the crisis arose. The liberals fell between two stools and proved ineffective both in dealing with official reaction under the Kuomintang minister Chen Li-fu and in stemming the intellectual tide which flowed strongly to the left. India had achieved a measure of social integration before she had to face the doctrines of the October Revolution. Japan had organized her society by identifying rites, politics and education. In China the society was an inchoate mass from which the binding force had disappeared by the failure of religion and by the continued attacks on the Confucian doctrines. The ideas of the New Tide, therefore, could only remain the creed of an intellectual class, isolated from the people.

The literature of the period following 1920 brings this out clearly. Two organizations – the Society for the Study of Literature (1920) and the Creative Society (1922) – stood for a break with the liberal tradition. The first group was headed by Lu Hsun, who, by his famous story *Ah Q*, was to become the father of modern literature in China,[1] and Shen Yenping, better known by his pen name Mao Tung. Mao Tung's trilogy, entitled *Disillusioned*, *Wavering*, and *Searching*, clearly brought out the

[1] Lu Hsun's importance in the development of modern literature requires emphasis. His first book which had influence was 'The Diary of a Madman', published in *La Jeunesse* in 1918. It was a violent attack on the greed and selfishness of human society. Its form, no less than what it contained, was so extraordinary that it startled the Chinese world. His best and most famous book, however, is the *Ah Q*, originally published as the special supplement of *Chen Pao*. Ah Q, the hero, a jobless vagabond, is an amazing character who specializes in rationalizing his weaknesses and finds arguments for comforting himself in his failures. The style in which the book is written is said to be gay and witty. The book was a merciless exposure of the weaknesses of Chinese society and has had far-reaching influence. Two volumes of his short stories *Cries* and *Hesitation* depicted village life. Lu Hsun, though never a Communist, was the chief figure in the League of Chinese Leftist writers and his work has left a permanent impress on modern Chinese literature.

struggles through which the mind of China was passing. The disillusionment with the earlier optimism arising from the failure of the Kuomintang and the liberal tradition is the basic fact which dominated the Chinese mind. The Creative Society was led by Kuo Mo-jo, historian, scholar, poet and short story writer, who at least after 1925 took up a revolutionary position in literature. Both Lu Hsun and Mao Tung became supporters of the Chinese Leftist Writers' Association, and opinion among intellectuals moved steadily to the left.

The contradictions in the Chinese renaissance movement, and the reasons for its failure, are in a measure brought out by the life of the father of China's nationalist revolution, Sun Yat-sen. Sun was born in the coastal area subject to European trade influences. Early in life he left for Hawaii, where he was brought up in an 'overseas Chinese' community and was educated in a mission school, where he was baptized as a Christian. Returning to China and working under missionary influence, he developed revolutionary activities which received their support mainly from students in Japan and America and their financial assistance from Chinese communities living in foreign countries. In the intervals of numerous attempts to stir up revolution, he lived in the safety of the foreign concessions, recruiting his adherents from the new classes who had been denied influence and power in Imperial China. At the period of the Revolution and in the years immediately following it, Sun Yat-sen's views on China approximated closely to those of the proponents of the New Tide. Like them he was against Confucianism and all it stood for: he advocated a wholesale acceptance of the West and had great confidence in the liberal traditions of European nations. In the next stage, disillusioned by the 'failure of the West', he had turned his face towards Moscow. In his manifesto to the Chinese people dated July 25, 1919, Sun declared: 'If the people of China wished to be free, like the Russian people, and be spared the lot prepared for them by the Allies at Versailles . . . let it be understood that its only ally and brother in the struggle for national freedom are the Russian workers and peasants of the Red Army'. With time this conviction only grew, for the last letter he wrote was addressed to the Central Executive of the USSR, and it said: 'You are at the head of the Union of Free Republics – the heritage left to the oppressed peoples of the world by the immortal Lenin. With the aid of that heritage the victims of imperialism will inevitably achieve emancipation. . . . Taking leave of you, dear comrades, I want to express the hope that the day will soon come when the USSR will welcome a friend and ally in a mighty, free China and that in the great struggle for the liberation of the oppressed peoples of the world both those allies will go forward to victory hand in hand.'

This transformation of Sun Yat-sen, the original champion of

Westernization, the product of a missionary school, from liberalism to open support of Leninism contains in itself the history of China's reawakening and the failure of its liberal renaissance.

CHAPTER 5

THE LESSER COUNTRIES OF ASIA

We may also deal here briefly with the movements in the lesser countries of Asia. Burma, from the time of its conquest by the British to 1937, was administered as a part of India, and the movement for national revival was greatly influenced by the developments in India. There were, however, two significant differences. The economic exploitation of Burma by Indian capitalists and businessmen and the large emigration of Indians into Burma gave to Burmese nationalism a two-fold character, anti-imperialist and anti-Indian. The Indian nationalist movement encouraged the fight against imperialism, while the British in their turn encouraged Burmese racial exclusiveness. Secondly, though with the annexation of Burma Buddhism ceased to be the State religion, its influence on the people was, on the whole, not seriously affected. While in China leaders of public opinion prided themselves on the fact that they had no religion, in Burma nationalist leaders had to profess to be devout Buddhists to gain popular support. An instance of this was the case of Dr Baw Maw, who was baptized as a Christian in his childhood; when he had become a prominent national figure, he declared that he had returned to the mother (Buddhist) church. Again public reaction to attacks on religion and clergy had been such that Thein Pe, the author of a well-known novel, *The Modern Monk*, was forced to apologize publicly for his anti-clericalism in 1945.

The Council of Buddhist Organizations, founded after the Great War (1914-19), was the first evidence of the consolidation of Buddhism under the changed circumstances of politics and of the readiness of the Burmese to base their nationalism on the unity of their religion. Thus the Burmese movement remained mainly nationalist, without any threat to the social integrity of the country or any immediate danger of social upheaval. Neither its social structure nor its religion had been seriously affected, and except among the Karens there was no large-scale missionary activity. As a result, Burma, in spite of the economic fight against Indians in the country, remained culturally within the same orbit, as the forces of education, nationalism, etc., operating in the two countries, were to a large extent similar.

Siam, under a national monarchy which from the time of King Chulalankorn showed a wise leadership, cautiously embarked on a policy of planned Westernization. The Siamese kings and their advisers knew the limitations under which they had to work, and their policy was directed towards the preservation of national independence and steady progress rather than towards the achievement of a position and importance such as Japan desired from the very beginning. King Chulalankorn realized that safety for his kingdom lay in the rivalry between France and England, and was for the time content to accept the role of a buffer State, which enabled him, through a policy of selective adoption, to modernize his State without causing undue social dislocation or disturbing the political structure of Siam. The royal family realized early the compelling necessity of adjusting itself to Western knowledge. A book about an English governess employed at the court – *Anna and the King of Siam* – gives an interesting account of the tentative beginnings of this policy under King Mankut. Soon, however, it became clear that the modernization of government required trained personnel with knowledge of Western conditions; and a State-aided policy of sending students to Europe was inaugurated. Though the students selected belonged mainly to the aristocracy, the system provided Siam with a corps of young men of generally conservative traditions who had imbibed the learning of the West and were prepared to initiate and carry out a policy of modernization. King Rama VI, who was himself educated at Christ Church, Oxford, was the leader of this movement. He established the Chulalankorn University, popularized Western literature, himself translating Shakespeare, introduced European games and generally set himself out to bring Siam in line with modern nations. Among his other achievements in the line was the organization of a youth corps known as the 'Wild Tigers', with the object of inculcating the ideals of individual responsibility and service among the youth. Civil marriage was introduced, and the king made a vigorous effort to raise the standards of civic action. Rama VI was also a journalist of considerable ability, and, writing under the pseudonym *Aswabahu* or Pegasus, he expounded aspects of national policy to his people.

In Siam, as in Burma, as a result of the strength and vitality of the Buddhist church, missionary activities had but little influence. King Rama here also led a movement for the revival of Buddhism. Under his patronage the *Tripitaka* was edited and published and attempts were made to educate and strengthen Buddhist clergy. The monarchs of Siam assumed the title of the Defender of the Buddhist Faith in imitation of the British king's title. The conservative but generally enlightened policy followed by the monarchy during the critical period between 1870 and 1920 had the effect of getting Siam through the transition without violent tumults and a disorganization of society, so that in the period following the First War she was enabled to recover her national independence in full by the gradual abolition, through negotiation, of the rights of extra-territoriality which the foreign nations possessed. The widespread system of peasant proprietorship, the vitality of the Buddhist church, and the ability with which the dynasty had handled its foreign relations, preventing the growth of bitterness against the West as in China, helped the peaceful recovery of the country.

The revolution of 1932 in Siam was directed against royal autocracy, and the system (no doubt necessary in the early days of international rivalry) of limiting the higher appointments to the rather numerous progeny of King Chulalankorn. This revolution carried forward the movement for modernization and was basically nationalist. Apart from the limitation of royal prerogatives and the introduction of a system of democratic rule, the leaders of the popular movement tended to develop a policy of economic nationalism, so that the Siamese people could free themselves from the stranglehold which foreigners had obtained on the life of the country.

In regard to both Burma and Siam, the most significant factor is the vitality of Hinayana Buddhism. In this, it contrasts with the position of Mahayana in China. Though it has been customary for European writers to underestimate the hold of Buddhism on the masses, it is undoubtedly true that the Buddhist clergy and religious organization as a whole had but little influence on national affairs in China. The Confucianism of the mandarinate prevented any social integration based on Buddhism, except in Mongolia. On the other hand, both in Siam and in Burma the Hinayana showed remarkable strength in its social organization, and was the great binding force which enabled both Siamese and Burmese societies to maintain their internal structure and resist, with outstanding success, the disruptive force alike of missionary activities and of Western ideas.

The complexity of political organization in Indo-China renders a brief statement of the position there difficult. In Cambodia and Laos, where Hinayana is strong and the form of government monarchial though under French authority, the social structure has endured, and the reform movements have been weak and not very widespread. In the Empire of Annam the Confucian principles of the court, weakened by their failure in China, as also by the more direct pressure of the French, proved a fragile defence against more aggressive ideas, while in Cochin China, under direct French administration and with the intensive activities of *Missions ét rangères* in many areas, there was a breakdown of the old system leading to the growth of many curious religious cults such as *Caodaism*. In Indo-

China the nationalism which attracted most notice was that led by the Communists. Nationalism, however, is not a new growth in Indo-China, as we have pointed out earlier. The Indo-Chinese never accepted French authority voluntarily, and their national pride and culture resisted the seductions of assimilative and associative policies of the French. But till after the First Great War there was no large-scale national movement basing itself on a scheme of internal reconstruction and reform. When that movement started, the Russian Revolution had already become a major factor in Eastern Asia, and therefore from the beginning the new nationalism of Indo-China had a Marxist bias, which later developed into Communist leadership.

In Indonesia, the Dutch had followed a policy of preserving the traditional structure of Indonesian society. Their political rule was for a long time indirect, as their interests were confined to a scientific exploitation of the resources of the country. By discouraging modern education among the Indonesians, and by evolving a system of indigenous education which kept all new ideas from schools, the Dutch were able for a very long time to prevent the growth of any national movement. They did not desire, till the end of the nineteenth century, to exercise any cultural influence. For 200 years they made no pretentions to any civilizing mission. They were concerned with the riches of Indonesia, which it is said constituted one-sixth of the national income of the Dutch.

But this enforced isolation of Indonesia from the rest of the world could not be continued indefinitely. The growth of Pan-Islamism in the Middle East and the ferment in the Muslim world were bound to affect Indonesia also. The pilgrims to Mecca and Medina brought back ideas which penetrated quickly among the masses of Indonesians. The work of the Dutch scholars on the earlier periods of Indonesian history opened a vista of past glory to young Indonesians. Also by the beginning of the century Indonesian students began freely to go to Europe, and after the First War the movement assumed significant proportions. The non-cooperation movement of Mahatma Gandhi in India, no less than the successful fight of Zaghlul and the Wafd in Egypt, created a new enthusiasm.

Originally the nationalist party, *Budi Utomo*, had begun by pressing for educational reforms, and had only a very limited political character. But from 1908, the period of the young Turk movement in Turkey and the foundation of the Muslim League in India, a new party of religious nationalism, Sarekat Islam, takes the lead. Before the movement could achieve any success, the Russian Revolution shook the Eastern world, and this had the effect of introducing an economic basis for political action in the country which had so long been dominated by religious ideas. The Islamic character of Indonesian society, apart from Holland's set policy of not disturbing social conditions through missionary activities (except in the Moluccas), had so far prevented the growth of any large-scale social reform movements in Indonesia. But the new parties, under the influence of Marxist thinking, were more convinced of the necessity of social and economic adjustments than the religious nationalists of the previous era. The significant fact may be noted that in Indonesia there is a dual inspiration for the movement which led to the recovery of independence, a strong feeling of religious unity and a growing recognition of the importance of economic and social reorganization.

BIBLIOGRAPHICAL NOTE

CHINA

Apart from the general literature listed in other chapters, the literature regarding early reform movements is contained in the following:

Yung Ming: *My Life in China and America* (1909).
La Fargue, T. E.: *China's First Hundred.*
Yung Shang-him: *The Chinese Educational Mission and its Influence.*
Hu Shih: *The Chinese Renaissance* (Commercial Press).
Hu Shih: *A Literary Revolution in China* (China in 1918 – edited by T. Z. Tyau).
Hu Shih: 'Civilizations of the East and the West', in *Whither Mankind*, edited by Charles A. Beard. New York, 1928.
Wang, Tsi C.: *The Youth Movement in China.*
Christian Education in China. Report of Burton Commission, 1922.
Chen, L. T.: *History of Chinese Political Thought during the Early Tsin Period* – adapted from the Chinese of Liang Chi-chao. London, 1934.
Hughes, E. R.: *Invasion of China by the Western World.* A. and C. Black, London, 1937.
Ah Q and the Selected Stories of Lu Hsun. Translated by Chi Chen-wang. N.Y., Columbia University Press, 1940.
Wen Han-Kiang: *Chinese Student Movement.* Kings Crown Press, N.Y., 1948.

JAPAN

The literature is again extensive. An impressive study of the whole question of the West will be found in Sansom's *The Western World and Japan.* Cresset Press, London, 1950.

On Shinto some of the more important texts are to be found in:

Balloan's *Shinto the Unconquered Enemy.* Viking Press, New York, 1945.
Modern Japan and Shinto Nationalism (Holtom). University of Chicago, 1947. [Also contains translations of important texts but is prejudiced by wartime atmosphere.]
Embre, J. F.: *The Japanese Nation.* New York, 1945.
Kato Zenchi: *A Study of Shinto, the Religion of the Japanese Nation.* Tokyo Meiyi Japan Society, 1926.
Boxer, C. R.: *Jan Campagnie in Japan*, 1600–1817. Hague, 1936.

Mclean: 'Japanese Government Documents, 1867-89'. *Transactions of the Asiatic Society of Japan*, Vol. XCII, Part I. Tokyo.
Norman, E. H.: *Japan's Emergence as a Modern State*. Institute of Pacific Relations, 1940. George Allen & Unwin.
Sansom: *Japan – A Short Cultural History*.
Satow: 'The Revival of Pure Chintao I'. *Asiatic Society of Japan*, Vol. III, Part I.
Yone Noguchi: *Japan and America*. N.Y.

Part VII

CHRISTIAN MISSIONS

CHRISTIAN MISSIONS

Christianity has existed in different parts of Persia, India and China from the earliest times. The Church in Malabar claims apostolic origin from St Thomas and in any case its existence is attested by outside authority as early as AD 182. The Nestorians were a flourishing community in Persia and we have the evidence of the Sianfu (West China) tablet that Nestorian Christianity had reached China in the seventh century. In the extensive dominions of Jinghis Khan there were many Christian communities and at the Great Khan's court there were representatives of both Oriental and Western Christianity.

The appearance of the Mongol armies in the heart of Europe had caused widespread terror and the Pope called a Council at Lyons in 1245 to discuss how the Christian world could be saved from this calamity. The Council decided to send missions for negotiating with the Mongol commanders in areas near to Europe and with the Great Khan himself.

The first missions were not religious ones. There were attempts to gather information about the Mongols, about their strength and resources. But when the Franciscan friar William of Rubruck, sent by Louis IX of France, began to discourse on Christianity to Mangu Khan (1254), he was told by the Great Khan:—

'Like the five fingers of the hand are the several ways to Paradise' – a sentiment which we shall come across often in the history of Christian efforts to proselytize the Orient.

A more important personage in the history of missionary activity in the East was John de Monte Corvino who was sent by the Pope to Kubilai Khan's court in Peking. He arrived in Peking, known at that time as Khanbaliq, shortly after the death of the Great Khan and, in spite of the opposition of the Nestorians, built a church and, learning the language, wrote the necessary literature for the Catholic ritual He claimed that the Khan honoured him beyond all other religious heads – a claim which we cannot check. His letters to Rome aroused such enthusiasm that the Pope created the archiepiscopal See of Khanbaliq

(Peking) for him. But Monte Corvino died soon after (1328) and within twenty-five years of his passing away the entire organization built up by him totally disappeared. The practice started by him of purchasing boys as slaves and then baptizing them was certainly not an edifying way of spreading the faith though it would figure in the reports to Rome as showing a promising increase in the number of believers.

The next stage of Christian activity started with the arrival of the Portuguese in Asia. The Portuguese authority in the East was based on the Bulls of Calixtus III, Nicholas V and Alexander VI, dividing the newly 'discovered' lands between Spain and Portugal and imposing on the monarchs of these countries the duty of propagating the Christian faith.

With the Portuguese christianization was a state enterprise. The king paid for the entire ecclesiastical establishment in the East. The doctrine of Padroado (jus patronatus established by the Papal Bull of 1514) vested the authority for missionary work effectively in the hands of the Portuguese crown in areas where Portugal claimed political rights. The last vestige of Padroado, the claim of approving the appointment of catholic bishops in certain parts of India, was given up by Portugal only in 1950. The Papacy took in hand the organization of the Holy Office to control missionary activities 123 years after Vasco da Gama's arrival in India.

In 1534 Goa was made a bishopric with authority extending over the entire Far East. Special instructions were issued to the Portuguese Viceroy to root out the infidels. Hindu temples in Goa were destroyed and their property distributed to religious orders (like the Franciscans) in 1540. The Inquisition was established in 1560.

In 1541, Francis Xavier, educated at Paris where he had come under the influence of Ignatius Loyola, set out for India to conquer the East for Christianity. Instead of going to the Archbishop's palace at Goa in a palanquin, he walked barefoot to a lepers' hospital and began at once washing their sores. In 1542 he established there the great college of St Paul for the training of Asian missionaries. During the next hundred years entry of missionaries into the Far East was permitted only through Goa. Thus this institution played a most notable part in Christian activity in Asia. Most of the notable European workers in the mission field in the Far East underwent a preliminary training in Goa before they were assigned to their posts. Also, Japanese, Chinese, Annamites, etc., were brought to this college for training.

Dissatisfied with such organizing work Xavier left Goa to preach to the fisherfolk along the Malabar coast. There he met with some success through his earnestness and piety. But as his consuming desire was to spread far and wide the message of Christ, Xavier soon left India for the Far East, where we shall follow his activities later.

The Jesuit missions which he established in India took up with enthusiasm the work of conversion. But progress was slow till Roberto de Nobili came to be in charge of the mission in Madura. Father de Nobili, a man of remarkable insight, after a short experience of life in Madura, reached the conclusion that Christianity would have but little success in India if it kept to its western garb and refused to understand the mind and thought of the people of the country. In 1606 he obtained the approval of the Society of Jesus to undertake a serious study of Hinduism and Madura was a centre specially suited for this purpose. Closely following the social habits of Brahmans, Nobili was able to obtain assistance from learned pandits in his search for the principles of Hindu religious thought. After years of arduous work, in the course of which he acquired a fair mastery of Sanskrit, he met in argument the learned Brahmans of Madura, in a religious discussion. This was according to the ancient well-established practice of Sastrarthavada – debates on religious topics before a learned audience. There he tried to uphold Christian doctrines in terms of Upanishadic thought. He is said to have gained the respect of even the orthodox Brahmins of the court. But the other missions could not tolerate Nobili's attempts to present Christianity in a Hindu garb. He was recalled to Rome.

Intolerance of things Indian became henceforth the characteristic feature of missionary zeal in India. Any compromise with Hindu life or religion was avoided, e.g. the eating of beef was held to be necessary as it would put the convert altogether out of the pale of Hinduism.

The same spirit of intolerance was shown by the Jesuit fathers in the Moghul court. The Emperor Akbar took great interest in religious discussions and summoned to the court scholarly Jesuit missionaries from Goa. They were received with great courtesy, but the free discussions in the Ibadat Khana (House of Worship), where the debates on religion took place, displeased the Jesuit fathers greatly. Their intolerance of other religions and their arrogant attitude towards the exponents of other faiths were unwelcome also to the Emperor. So the missionaries had to leave the capital greatly disappointed.

In 1632 the Jesuits in Bengal were said to have forcibly converted two slave girls of the Empress Mumtaz Mahal. To punish them for this rash act Shah-jehan's armed forces drove out the Portuguese from their settlement. Thousands of them were slain or taken prisoner. No further attempt was made seriously to propagate Christianity within the Mogul Empire.

After the decay of Portuguese power by 1660, active interest in mission work declined even in South India. The establishment of the Inquisition in Goa (1561) and the auto da fé (first instance in 1563) revolted the conscience of both Hindus and Muslims alike.

The Dutch and the British, who came after the Portuguese, were interested solely in trade. Moreover they were Protestants and had no sympathy with the activities of the Catholic orders. So the first phase of evangelization came to a close in India by the middle of the seventeenth century.

But we should remember some notable achievements to the credit of the Catholic missionaries during this period of Portuguese leadership. Father Estavo, an Englishman of the name of Hopkins, mastered the Indian languages and wrote an epic poem in Marathi on the life of Christ. The first printing press in India was set up by Jesuit priests in Goa. At a missionary college near Cochin, Sanskrit and Tamil were taught. It is also claimed that a Spanish lay brother, Gonsalvez, cut the first Tamil type.

The Jesuits did not limit their interest to India. Francis Xavier, it will be remembered, was attracted by further horizons. From India, in 1545, he sailed to Malacca. Here he undertook the dual work, first of reforming the Portuguese, whom he found steeped in vice, and second of preaching to the infidels. But the Malaccans, as the saint's biographer admits, 'remained indifferent to his message'.

From Malacca Xavier sailed to Amboyna where he settled down to work among the poor and lowly. He went among people stricken down by pestilence, nursed and looked after them. By his charity and piety this true soldier of God achieved a great measure of success.

While he was in Malacca, on his way back, he came across a Japanese named Anjiro, who was a fugitive from the justice of his own country. Anjiro gave him glowing accounts of the readiness of the people of Japan to receive the message of Christ. Anjiro went with Xavier to Goa, where he was entered at St Paul's for theological studies. In 1549 Xavier set sail for Japan accompanied by this disciple and reached the fief of the Satsuma Daimyo who received him with courtesy. Here he had some success as he had the gift of languages and had in a short time picked up elementary Japanese. But dissatisfied with the slow progress he was making and chafing under the opposition of the Buddhist priesthood, Xavier set out for the capital, Miyako, to try to crown his missionary efforts by converting the Emperor himself. But disappointment awaited him. He returned to Goa in 1551. The opposition of the Buddhist monks had dashed his hopes and, ignorant as he was of the Eastern religions, to him the Buddha was a demon under whose evil influence the Japanese people were living in monstrous sin. Thus his work, based as it was on ignorance and prejudice, produced negligible results. But he did not give up hopes. He wrote to Ignatius Loyola to send more workers for Japan.

While in Japan, Xavier had heard of the greatness of China. Here, he thought, was a new field for his activity. He set out for China. But waiting for a ship on a little island off the Kwantung coast the indomitable old man died (1552).

Xavier is one of the heroic figures of Christian activity in the East. He towers above all who followed him by his sympathy for the poor and the lowly, by his energy and spirit, by his utter fearlessness in the face of dangers and his supreme faith in his mission. His dogmatism and intolerance were the outcome of his blind faith; but these qualities, which roused so much animosity against him that he was inclined to see the devil everywhere, went with a true humility of spirit and a genuine sense of charity. The spirit of St Francis Xavier has been an inspiration for generations of Christian workers in the East.

Meanwhile the Portuguese establishment in Macao had become an important centre of trade. There in 1565 the Jesuits built a residence. With the arrival at this place of two Jesuit missionaries, Valighani and Ruggieri, begins the second stage in the attempts to evangelize Asia. Up to this time the attempt of the Portuguese, secular and missionary, was to carry the heathen fort by assault. The state enterprise in christianization, which the Portuguese attempted at Goa, Cochin and other fortified centres, was one of conversion by force. Even at Goa, with the Inquisition in force for a long time, the majority of the population however continued to be non-Christian. Clearly the strategy of direct assault had to be given up. Valignani and Ruggieri now attempted to evolve a new line.

The new policy was for the missionaries to conciliate the high officials and to render special service to them which would make the Christian propagandists valuable to those in authority. In order to do so, it was necessary to study the language, manners and customs of the country and conform to the life and etiquette of the circles in which they aspired to move.

In 1582 Ricci, an Italian Jesuit and an eminent mathematician, joined Valignani at Macao. Convinced as he was that influence throughout China could only radiate from Peking, he reached the Chinese capital in 1595. Unsuccessful at first he slowly won his way to favour at the court by making presents of chiming clocks and other scientific toys and by his skill in mathematics. He lived in the capital for ten years, kow-towing to the great, expounding cautiously the doctrines of his religion, and preparing the way for intensive activity at a later time.

Early in his Chinese studies Ricci had detected the conflict between Buddhism and Confucianism. Realizing that the greatest obstacle to Christianity was Buddhism, he sided with the Confucians and attacked the Buddhists. He quoted from the Confucian texts in support of the Christian doctrines and tried to show that Confucian doctrines did not conflict with Christianity.

FATHER M. RICCI

Ricci died in 1610 in full confidence that he was leaving his colleagues 'facing an open door'. Nineteen years after Ricci's death the need for reforming the Chinese calendar brought another Jesuit mathematician Adam Schall into prominence at the Imperial Court of the Mings (1629).

The work with which Schall was entrusted had more to do with astrology than with astronomy. The official calendar was to contain auspicious dates for every important event. The Jesuit mathematician did not hesitate on one occasion to interpret the sun spots as representing

ADAM SCHALL

the hostile influence of the Buddhist priests near the Ming Emperor.

A succession of Jesuit astronomers were appointed to the 'astronomical' bureau for a period of a hundred years. But there is little substance in the claims put forward by some historians that the Jesuits enjoyed immense prestige in the Ming court in Peking during this period. They could assure, however, the security of their co-workers in the districts.

But the Ming dynasty itself was in serious difficulties at this time and the reigning Emperor turned to his Jesuit 'astronomers' and asked them to manufacture cannon for him. The learned father did not hesitate to accept the task and the cannon he cast were named after Christian saints. But in spite of the artillery manufactured by the priests the Ming dynasty fell to the onslaught of the Manchus. Schall however managed to retain his post in the new regime. The Manchu monarch was naturally suspicious of the Chinese, over whom the Manchu rule had not yet become firmly established, and therefore readily continued the patronage of the foreign scholar. Schall was nominated Vice-President of the office of Imperial Sacrifice, the Superintendent of the Imperial Stud and High Honourable Bearer of the Imperial Banquet – strange posts for a Christian priest to hold!

On the accession of the minor Emperor Kang Hsi, destined to be the greatest of the Manchu monarchs, Schall was appointed one of the tutors of the youthful sovereign. But this did not save him from the hostility of the critics of Christianity at the court and for some time the learned Father had to languish in prison. He died soon after his release (1666) and his mantle fell on the Belgian Verbiest, also an able astronomer and scientist.

Though the mission was closed in Peking, Verbiest and his assistants were permitted to carry on their scientific work. The young Emperor was interested in scientific subjects and the Jesuit scholar was again appointed to the posts held by his predecessor Schall.

An edict of Kang Hsi (1671) permitted the missionaries to propagate their religion though they were warned not to teach anything contrary to the welfare of the State. This was a period of high hopes. A new rebellion had broken out and cannon had to be made again. For several years Verbiest's main activity was the making of cannon. But while the priest flourished in the sunshine of imperial smiles, the church gained little.

Before his death (1688) Verbiest had been appealing to France to enter the mission field in China. Louis XIV, in the might of his newly acquired power and the fervour of his Catholicism, was not in a mood to take into consideration the rights of Padroado by which the Portuguese claimed the sole right of evangelization in the East. He had already established in Paris (1664) the Congregation des Missions Etrangères. This remarkable institution was not an 'order' like the Jesuits but a 'congregation' – i.e. a body of priests united by a common purpose and not by common vows on discipline. Its purpose, approved by the Holy See, was that of evangelization. In 1685 six French priests left for the Far East.

Among them was Gerbillon, a brilliant linguist, who rendered valuable service to the Chinese Government during the Sino-Russian border disputes which led to the Treaty of Nertchinsk (1689). As a reward for his ability and tact an 'Edict of Toleration' was issued by the Emperor (1692) which declared that the doctrines, taught by the Europeans in charge of Astronomy and the Tribunal of Mathematics, 'are not evil' and permitted people 'to go to the churches freely to worship God'.

The Jesuits brought in medicine also as a new instrument for securing further favour. After a cure was effected in the case of the Emperor himself, the fathers were permitted to stay within the Forbidden City (the Palace enclosure) and to build a church near the palace itself (1703).

But the outwardly imposing edifice of Jesuit success, built upon dubious practices such as participation in astrology and the acceptance of office in the Board of Rites, began to crumble at the very moment of its greatest triumph. The head of the Jesuit mission as the Honourable Bearer of Dishes at the Imperial Banquet, or as the President of the Board of Rites, was not likely to find favour either in Rome or in Paris, and this was the problem that was raised at the Vatican itself, by the Dominicans.

The real issue, which was raised by them, related to the 'rites' question, i.e. how far it was possible to tolerate outward conformity with national (Chinese) practices without compromising the teachings of the Church. As formulated, it also involved such questions as to whether ancestor worship, according to Confucian practices, involved idolatry or was only respect shown to ancestors, and whether it was legitimate to establish affinities between ancient Chinese religion and Christianity in order to convey the impression that there was nothing unnational in the new creed.

In 1693 the Papacy was forced to act. The Vicar-General, sent by the Pope to China, issued a mandate condemning the practices which the Jesuits had so far favoured. The Jesuits now took a step which they hoped would settle the controversy in their favour. They appealed to the Emperor for an interpretation of the Chinese rites. The petition submitted to the Emperor was in the form of what lawyers call a leading question in order to secure from the Imperial court a clear affirmative answer. European scholars, the petition stated, were urgently begging the Jesuit Fathers in China for correct information as regards ceremonies performed in honour of Confucius, sacrifices offered to Heaven and the special rites performed for the ancestors. The Jesuits in China, according to the petition, had given as their opinion that Confucius was honoured in China as a legislator, that the rites for the ancestors were performed to commemorate the love in which they were held by their descendants, and that the sacrifices to Heaven (Tien) were addressed not to the visible Heavens above us but to the Supreme Ruler of Heaven and Earth. In the end the petitioners (the Peking Jesuits) awaited His Majesty's elucidation with respect and submission.

The Emperor's reply was that 'there was not a word that required changing', so perfect was the Jesuits' understanding of the religious conceptions of the Chinese. But the Pope naturally resented this appeal of the Jesuits to an authority outside the church in order to force his own hand. He sent a Legate to inquire into the whole question. This ecclesiastical ambassador was well received by the Emperor, but as he had to challenge the Emperor's right to decide the issue he was politely ordered to go back. On his way from Canton the Legate issued an authoritative declaration prohibiting the practices for which the Jesuits had fought so long. This declaration was represented to the Emperor as a defiance of his own views and so the Legate was arrested and handed over to the Portuguese who kept him in jail where he died (1710). The Emperor ordered that only those foreigners who accepted the rites could stay in China and that the others should depart immediately. On the other hand a Papal Bull compelled every missionary going to China to take an oath fully accepting the apostolic command regarding the rites of China.

In 1724 the preaching of the Christian religion was officially suppressed and the foreign missionaries, excepting those employed at the court, were deported to Canton.

Thus came to an end the grandiose schemes of the Jesuits in China. One point should be mentioned here on the question of conformity of Christian missionary activity with prevalent rites in a non-Christian country. The Jesuit approach to the problem of rites in China, involving as it did some of the more important aspects of Christian dogma, in search for approximation with what was fondly believed to be the original religion of China, should not be confused with the attempt of Roberto de Nobili to interpret Christianity to the Indians. Nobili no doubt advised outward conformity with Hindu practices, but on issues of dogma he was firm. He argued with Brahman scholars with all the trained ability of a Christian priest who had also mastered Hindu metaphysics, which was very different from the Ricci trick of pretending to support Confucianism against Buddhism, hoping thereby to gain favour with those in authority.

In Japan the history of Christian missions had been stormier and more heroic. After the return of Francis Xavier from Japan to India mission work continued to a limited extent mainly in the western part of the Island Empire. The feudal rulers of that part of Japan were anxious at that time to attract Portuguese vessels to their harbours mainly with the object of strengthening themselves against other feudal lords. They realised instinctively the close connection between the foreign powers across the seas and the missionaries who had come to preach the new religion.

But work in the provinces did not satisfy the ambition of the mission-

IX DEATH OF ST FRANCIS XAVIER

aries. Their eyes were set on the capital Miyako, from which Xavier had returned so disappointed. Nobunaga was then well set on his career of conquest in which he had been opposed by the powerful Buddhist monasteries. The Jesuits thus saw a chance of interesting him in their mission to the disadvantage of the Buddhist church. Nobunaga encouraged them and in 1568 he invited the Catholic missionaries to Kyoto and even gave them land on which to build a church. Under his powerful protection the missions made unexpected progress.

But unfortunately for the Jesuits Nobunaga died soon and was succeeded by the famous Hideyoshi. In the beginning he also showed favour towards the Christians, and on one occasion in his palace he is reported to have discussed with the missionaries the possibility of arranging for a large number of ships to carry his army to the mainland. The hopes of the Jesuits ran high.

But their hopes were soon dashed. In 1587, instead of the expected favours they received news of an edict condemning the missionaries and their activities and ordering their immediate departure from Japan.

Hideyoshi himself has given a convincing justification for his edict. He has stated simply that missionaries were foreigners and were preaching against the gods of Japan. Also he was fully aware of the disloyal tendencies of the nobles of the western region who, through the missionaries, were in contact with foreign Powers. In fact, the missionaries had got mixed up in political issues, and their hope had been to use the feeling against the Buddhist church in their favour, But this interference of the foreigners in the internal politics of the country recoiled on them when Hideyoshi realized the dangers involved in their activities.

The local Christian community continued to exist as a minor and obscure sect subject to intermittent persecution mainly because of its affiliations with foreigners. However in 1614 Iyeasu, the Tokugawa Shogun, made it clear that Christian teachings were no longer to be tolerated and an edict banning the religion was issued that year. A serious effort was made to root out the local Christian elements. The attitude of the Government seems to have led the Christians to intrigue with the Spaniards in the Philippines who were then talking glibly of invading Japan. A minor revolt attempted by the Japanese Christians in 1638 was put down with great severity and with this the attempted conversion of Japan came to a close.

In Japan an effort had been made to get the teachings of Christianity to the masses. While the missionaries in China had too much sense to interfere in political matters, in Japan the politics of feudal autonomy proved too tempting for the Christian Fathers and led to their undoing.

The decline of Portuguese power in Asia naturally affected Catholic missionary activity which under the *jus patronatus* was identified with the Portuguese crown. Even in the minor Portuguese possessions in India, where the church maintained an enormous organization, evangelization did not make much progress as the civil authorities had realized that undue interference with Hinduism was against their political interests.

From 1660 political activity on the coastal tracts of India was mainly in Protestant hands. By the end of the eighteenth century a spirit of evangelization permeated Protestant churches. In 1792 the English Baptists organized the first Protestant mission. The Church Missionary Society was founded in 1799 in the evangelical interests of the Anglican Church; other sects followed in their wake. All this was unwelcome to the East India Company, and the Baptist Mission under William Carey therefore settled in Serampur, a tiny Danish settlement near Calcutta. Carey was assisted by some notable men like Marshman who later laid the foundations of Protestant missions to China. A violent propaganda campaign was launched by Carey and his associates against Hinduism in Bengal which seemed to them to be in a state of dissolution. But Hindu orthodoxy reacted vigorously and Lord Minto felt obliged to prohibit such propaganda in Calcutta. Minto's letter to the Court of Directors is worth quoting: 'Pray read the miserable stuff addressed specially to the Gentoos (Hindus) in which . . . the pages are filled with hell fire, and hell fire and with still hotter fire, denounced against a whole race of men, for believing in the religion which they were taught by their fathers and mothers. . . .'

The fact that the power of the Company rested on the Sepoy army and that anything which touched the religion of the sepoys was likely to undermine their loyalty, as shown in the Vellore Mutiny, was also in the mind of Lord Minto. This predominant consideration weighed on the minds of the British in India, and the East India Company could not therefore give any direct support to Christian propaganda.

Many of the chaplains attached to the administration were, however, ardent advocates of an aggressive policy in regard to conversion and the appointment of an archbishop in India was advocated as 'it would do good among the Hindus'. The British Government was persuaded to extend the organization of its episcopacy to India, with a Metropolitan in Calcutta and numerous bishops with territorial titles, but its effect on the Hindu mind was altogether negligible.

With the abolition of the Company's monopoly in 1813, the authorities had no longer a legal right to stop the activities of Europeans who were not in the service of the Company. Alexander Duff with his Scottish Mission College was able to convert a number of young Hindus of good family. As a reaction, however, Hinduism started on its career of reform in Bengal and missionary success was halted. Only in the south in the state of Travancore did the work of conversion show any conspicuous results. Here, the Chanar community, suffering from social oppression, became the object of missionary activity and the attempt of the Maharaja to prevent social commotions led to question being raised in Parliament and the ruler being threatened with deposition. This action opened the eyes of other Indian ruling princes and there were a number of important states where no missionary activity of any kind, including schools, was permitted up to 1947.

Indirectly, however, the British Government of India gave the missionaries considerable help. Legislation protected the rights of converts to their share in Hindu joint families, and High Court decisions enabled converts to blackmail their wives to follow them into the fold of their new religion. The Government also encouraged the missionaries to work among the backward tribes.

Rather similar proselytization was taking place in China. After the exclusion decree of 1723 for nearly a century such Christian activity as existed was secret and not particularly important.

But conditions changed rapidly when the pressure of European nations forced China to open her ports first to the British (1842) and then to other nations. At the ports which were opened for trade missionaries were free to reside under the cover of extra-territoriality. The French Government, stepping into the shoes of the Portuguese, claimed to be the champions of Catholicism. The French envoy obtained an imperial decree permitting Chinese to practise Catholicism. Thus the wall was breached, and vigorous and well concerted missionary activities began under the effective political patronage of different European nations.

The French joined the second China War on the pretext – which was to become a classic excuse in China to cover political aggression – that the execution of a missionary demanded punishment. In the treaties that were concluded with the Powers in 1858, the missionaries obtained the privilege of travelling freely all over China, together with a guarantee of toleration of Christianity and protection to Chinese Christians in the profession of their faith. Thus was Christianity not only identified with Europe, but reduced to the position of a diplomatic interest of Western Powers in their aggression against China. The missionaries were clothed with extra-territoriality and given the right to appeal to their consuls and ministers in the 'religious' interests of Chinese Christians. No greater disservice, as history was to show, could have been rendered by its proclaimed champions to the cause of the Church of Christ.

It is also significant that out of the unconscionable indemnities exacted from China after the various wars, the churches received a considerable portion. The missions thus started by benefiting from the humiliations of China and by being identified in the eyes of the Chinese with aggressions against their country.

Latourette tries to justify these efforts to introduce Christianity in the wake of foreign aggression on the ground that 'it gave the converts a certain assurance of protection'. But he admits that 'it tended to make Christian communities imperia in imperio, widely scattered enclaves under the defence of aliens. . . . Many Chinese, seeing the advantage to be obtained from powerful foreign backing, feigned conversion. More than an occasional missionary promised the Chinese the support of his Government to induce them to enter the Church.'

The treaty clauses, in fact, wrote the ultimate doom of Christian activity in China. To have believed that a religion which grew up under the protection of foreign powers, especially under humiliating conditions following defeat, would be tolerated when the nation recovered its authority, showed extreme shortsightedness. The fact is that the missionaries, like other Europeans, felt convinced in the nineteenth century that their political supremacy was permanent, and they never imagined that China would regain a position when the history of the past might be brought up against them and their converts. 'The Church', as Latourette has pointed out, 'had become a partner in Western imperialism.' When that imperialism was finally destroyed, the Church could not escape the fate of its patron and ally.

Christianity in China was involved with the Taiping rebellion. At its start, this had a Christian background. But Hung Hsu-Chuan, the leader of the revolt, soon became a prophet himself, and claimed to be the younger brother of Christ, who had been given a new revelation by God. After the rebellion was crushed, the missionaries began by about 1865 to take advantage of the privileges accruing to them under the treaties and spread into the interior like a flood. They established churches and around these churches grew up small communities. Protected by foreign authority these converts looked down upon the Chinese and took up an aggressive attitude towards them. According to Tseng Kuo-fan, the greatest statesman of the Empress Dowager's time in China, 'the missionaries have created trouble everywhere. The native converts are given to oppressing those who will not embrace Christianity and the missionaries always screen the converts, while the consuls protect the missionaries.'

An enormous organization representing every sect of Christian belief was built up over the entire territory of China. For example, the China Inland Mission established in 1866 had as many as 262 stations, while the Catholic Church had partitioned the whole of China into bishoprics.

But there was not a single province or area during all this time where the common man, as well as the mandarin, did not make it clear that the missionary was an unwelcome intruder. Prince Kung said to the British Minister: 'Take away your opium and your missionaries and you will be welcome.' Not a single year passed without violent manifestations in some town or other against missionary activity. The Boxer rebellion could only be understood against this background. It was the missionary and the 'secondary devil', the convert, who were the special objects of the Boxer's fury. Indeed the Chinese Christians had to pay dearly for being 'secondary devils' suspected to be the supporters of foreign aggressors.

In Japan, the activities of the missionaries were more hedged round. Though the Emperor in the Charter Oath (1868) had asked his subjects 'to seek knowledge throughout the world', yet on the same day an official notification appeared in which it was declared that the 'evil sect of the Christians is forbidden as heretofore'. The reply to the protests of the foreign Powers was that public feeling against Christianity could only be modified slowly, and the Powers must depend on the changed situation for a full policy of religious tolerance to be made effective in Japan. In the meantime the authorities went forward vigorously with their programme of Shinto revival, identifying patriotism and loyalty to the throne with this national creed.

When the Japanese leaders were satisfied that the national position was strong enough to allow Christianity to be practised openly, they announced, as a measure of further reform, the principle of religious toleration (1873). One of the reasons for taking this step was the realization that extra-territoriality could not be abolished unless the Western world was persuaded that there was freedom for Christian activity.

By the time Christianity officially ceased to be 'an evil sect' within the Empire the Shinto religion had been strengthened and the chances of any large scale conversion to Christianity had vanished. The missionaries also realized that the recognition of the rights of Christians represented an attitude of studied neglect which was not helpful to the church. Also it is important to remember that the missionaries in Japan never secured the protection clauses which gave them practially suzerain rights in China.

The general revival of the Eastern religions by the end of the nineteenth century saw also a marked revival of Buddhism in Japan, especially of the Amida sect. From the last decade of the century, Buddhist scholarship developed in universities. This was shown in the works of scholars like Suzuki. Finally, the educational system in Japan was under national control and Christian teachings were suspected to be in conflict with the tradition of state dominance enjoined by Shintoism.

By the end of the nineteenth century Japan had emerged as a strong Power after the victory over China. The abolition of extra-territoriality which followed and the Anglo-Japanese Alliance that was negotiated gave to Japan a position of equality with other nations and with this the prospects of mission work in that country ceased to be of any great importance.

The history of Christianity in South-east Asia has also to be noticed. Early in the seventeenth century Alexandre de Rhodes, of the Society of Jesus, started his work among Japanese Christian refugeees at Faifo in Annam (1624-7). Disappointed with the meagre results of his mission he returned to Europe to interest the Holy See in this venture. Cold shouldered in Rome Father de Rhodes found warm support in France where the Mission Etrangères (founded in 1659) took up the work in earnest. Some businessmen in Rouen had established a society for the double purpose of trade and religion. It was in their ship that Bishop Lambert, selected by Father Alexandre de Rhodes for this mission, reached Tongking in the guise of a merchant (1662). The Trinh monarchs of Tongking however showed no desire to welcome missionary activity though they were willing to encourage trade with France in spite of Dutch opposition. The Dutch soon succeeded in destroying the French factory at Tongking, and the local people remained indifferent to the new religion. So there was nothing to report for nearly a century.

It was in 1765 that Pigneau de Behaine, a missionary of the Mission Etrangères, began his work in Cochin China. He was nominated Bishop of Adran in 1774. The bishop was able to render great service to the Nguen King of Hué who was then a homeless wanderer. In order to further the interests of the King in exile the bishop went to France and negotiated a treaty under which France promised to help the King regain his throne. As the promise was not carried out, Pigneau de Behaine fitted out an expedition at his own expense and restored the King to his kingdom. At the very moment of his victory the militant bishop died (1799). On account of the revolutionary struggles in France no advantage could be taken of this signal success of the French missionary. When the Bourbon restoration took place the new Emperor of Annam, Minh Mang, had become very hostile to Christian activity. In 1848 Emperor Tu Duc declared the religion of Jesus to be a 'perverse religion' and ordered ministers of this religion to be thrown into the sea.

These aggressive denunciations provided Napoleon III with an excuse for military intervention. But as T. E. Ennis writes in his 'French Policy and Development in Indo-China' (1936): 'Forty-two years after the French had taken possession of the country, missionary efforts were not imposing.' Here, as elsewhere, Christianity under the patronage of imperialism failed to attract the Asian mind.

Both in Siam and Burma the strength of Buddhism reduced the chance of large-scale conversion to Christianity. In Burma the missionaries, profiting by their experience in India, tended to concentrate their activities among backward tribes; and among the Karens they met with some success. There was thus considerable missionary sympathy for Karen separatism – a movement which at one stage was a major threat to the cause of Burmese independence.

In Indonesia, a predominantly Muslim country, Christian missionary activity was insignificant after the first efforts under the Portuguese, especially those of Francis Xavier. A main factor in the history of Indonesia in the seventeenth and eighteenth centuries was the growth and development of Islam among the pagan tribes in the interior.

We have no to trace the history in the present century. By the beginning of the twentieth century the growing sentiment of nationalism and the vigour with which Hinduism reacted left the Christian missionaries in India with but little chance of success. It is significant to note that the leaders of nationalism in India at the beginning of this century were themselves stout champions of a resurgent Hinduism. One of the main contributions of Bal Gangadhar Tilak to nationalism was his interpretation of the teachings of the Gita in terms of modern political life. Lajpat Rai was one of the leaders of the Arya Samaj, the militant puritanical sect of Hinduism which had helped to strengthen Hindu society in North India. Aurobindo Ghosh and his group of aggressive nationalists were fervent Hindus. In the south, in spite of vigorous Christian propaganda and fairly numerous conversions among the 'untouchables', the authority of orthodox Hinduism had never been seriously challenged.

Apart from the general loss of prestige which the West suffered as a result of the First Great War, the growth of nationalism, which ceased to be merely a movement of the intelligentsia, affected missionary prospects adversely. The Christian leaders in India themselves began to feel that too obvious a separation from their countrymen could not benefit them. Christianity began to show interest in Indian culture. The Heritage of India, a series of small volumes published under the auspices of the Christian National Council of India, was the first indication of this change in attitude. In fact by the beginning of the third decade of the century, the Indian Christian community had in the main shaken off the control of the Western missionaries.

Mahatma Gandhi's insistence on the removal of untouchability as an essential step in political reform took away from the missionaries what seemed to be their last profitable line of approach, for missionary activity after failing with the intellectuals, had been concentrated on the depressed classes. By way of reaction to the changed situation the churches in England instituted and encouraged movements for a national church in India. The Catholic Church, which had a better appreciation of the position, adjusted its work to the spiritual care of Christians, without emphasizing its missionary aspect.

In China, Christian hopes rose again after the fall of the Manchu

Dynasty. Sun Yat-sen, the leader of New China, was a Christian. But he soon showed that he was more interested in the greatness and welfare of China than in the promotion of Christianity. The disappointment which Sun Yat-sen felt at the attitude of the Christian Powers of the West and the influence which the October Revolution in Russia exercised on him led him away further and further from the missionaries to whom at one time he seemed to have looked for support. Moreover the rising tide of nationalism, against unequal treaties and against imperialism, was unfavourable to Christianity. The leaders of the 'New Tide' renaissance were frankly agnostic, and to them Christianity was but another manifestation of superstition, this time under a foreign garb. The Anti-Christian Federation, founded in Shanghai in 1922, asserted that Christianity was an ally of capitalism and imperialism and thus an instrument for oppressing weaker nations.

The Anti-Religious Federation organized by the Peking University students vigorously expressed its views in numerous pamphlets giving the whole story of the growth of mission work under the protection of extra-territoriality and as a handmaid of capitalist exploitation of China. That the missionaries had benefited by the weakness of China now became a serious charge against them.

Also during this period the position of the mission schools became a burning issue. The fifth annual congress of the Young China Association (1924) passed a resolution which read: 'We strongly oppose Christian education which destroys the national spirit of our people.' Next year the Peking Government promulgated regulations for the control of foreign educational institutions.

In this crisis the foreign missionaries found themselves deserted by their Chinese converts. The Chinese Christians were anxious in this period not to be considered 'secondary barbarians' or 'running dogs' of the missionaries and generally sided with the nationalist movement.

Side by side with the patronage which the Kuomintang extended to the missions during the war with Japan, when Chiang Kai-shek depended so much on American and British support, there was developing under the direction of Chen li-fu, the new Confucianism which found expression in Chiang's own book, 'China's Destiny'. China as a great field for Christian missions proved as great a mirage as India or Japan. But China suffered more from missionary activities than these other two countries. In India, Hindu society was able to resist missionary aggression, and in Japan the preventive action of the government helped to uphold the organic structure of the society. But in China the systematic undermining of social bonds through seventy-five years of missionary action under the protection of imperialist Powers led to the Revolution of 1948. Anarchical conditions in China were expected to be favourable to missionary hopes. Anarchical conditions did come about in Chinese society, but the beneficiaries were others.

We may conclude this survey with a few observations on the causes of the failure of mission activity in Asia. It cannot be denied that the attempt to convert Asia has definitely failed. In China, where conditions seemed to be particularly favourable, the collapse has been most complete.

The success of the missions need not have been so meagre but for certain factors which may be discussed now. In the first place, the missionary brought with him an attitude of moral superiority and a belief in his own exclusive righteousness. The doctrine of the monopoly of truth and revelation, as claimed by William of Rubruck to Batu Khan when he said 'he that believeth not shall be condemned by God', is alien to the Hindu and Buddhist mind. To them the claim of any sect that it alone possesses the truth and others shall be 'condemned' has always seemed unreasonable.

Secondly the association of Christian missionary work with aggressive imperialism introduced political complications. National sentiment could not fail to look upon missionary activity as inimical to the country's interests. That diplomatic pressure, extra-territoriality and sometimes support of gun-boats had been resorted to in the interests of the foreign missionaries could not be easily forgotten.

Thirdly, the sense of European superiority which the missionaries perhaps unconsciously inculcated produced also its reaction. Even during the days of unchallenged European political supremacy no Asian people accepted the cultural superiority of the West. The educational activities of the missionaries stressing the glories of European culture only led to the identification of the work of the missions with Western cultural aggression.

Fourthly, the wide variety of Christian sects, each proclaiming the errors of others, handicapped missionary work. Finally the growth of unbelief in Europe in the nineteenth century and the crisis in European civilization, following the Great War of 1914-8, and the October Revolution, broke whatever spell the different sects of Christianity had among certain classes of Asians. With the disappearance of European dominance Christianity assumed its natural position as one of the religions of Asia and the missionaries ceased to have any special or privileged position.

Part VIII

ORIENTAL INFLUENCES IN EUROPE

CHAPTER I

CULTURAL INFLUENCES

We have dealt briefly with the gradual Westernization of Asia in the nineteenth century and the gathering momentum of that movement in the first half of the twentieth century. We have shown that far from rejecting the West, the nations of Asia have been at pains to assimilate the culture of Europe in its wider aspects and to benefit by it in the reorganization of their own societies. It is now necessary to trace the influences of Asia in the life, manners, customs, and general culture of Europe during the entire period covered by our political survey. In the era of the political domination of Asia by Europe from 1860-1948, it was generally forgotten by European writers that Asia had not merely borrowed from Europe but also contributed liberally to the growth of Western civilization.

Though the intellectual contacts between Europe and Asia during the da Gama period began only in the late seventeenth century, the influence of Asia on Western European nations directly interested in the commerce of the East began to show itself fairly early. Even before the first European ships reached India and China, Indian muslin, Chinese silk and porcelain had reached Europe. With direct maritime contact this influence, on the material side, spread to many things. It was not India, but China, that had the predominant share of this influence, except in the matter of designing and printing of cotton textiles. Silks, embroideries, porcelain, lacquer, furniture, wallpaper, gardening, the roco style which dominated France and, through France, Europe for nearly half a century, evidenced a 'Chinese tide' in the first half of the eighteenth century. Porcelain, which may be said to symbolize this aspect of Chinese influence, had already been introduced into France, and in the latter half of the seventeenth century the great works at Sèvres were already producing high quality china. But with Augustus the Strong of Saxony (1670-1738) porcelain became a passion and a mania, and it gained a great vogue in Germany, France and England. Augustus, according to Reichwein, had walls, ceilings, window recesses and the like panelled with porcelain. Between 1710-12 'China' came to be manufactured at Meissen. The credit for this is attributed to Bottiger, who under the patronage of Augustus opened the factory at Meissen. Saxony became the European centre of this industry, and its riches in this respect were so great that Frederick the Great, after he had taken that kingdom in the Seven Years' War, is said to have used Meissen porcelain for payment of a part of his debts.

In England the fashion, though firmly established, did not immediately lead to the manufacture of 'China'. It took another forty years before the factory at Bow and later the new Canton factory copied Chinese designs, and it is stated that the most popular among them were the partridge and wheatsheaf patterns. The popular demand for 'China ware' was so great that a large number of factories came into existence both in England and in Germany. The Worcester factories especially became so good that only an expert eye, it was said, could detect the difference between it and the original Chinese. The Worcester patterns in Kang Hsi blue and white and *famille verte*, the Japanese Imari, and the *famille rose* of Yung Cheng and the early Chien Lung periods, attained great popularity in Europe.

Next in importance to procelain was lacquer. Early in the sixteenth century lacquer cabinets had become fashionable in the French court. By the end of the century the French seem to have gained knowledge of the process. The industry came to be established with the support of royalty, but it was only under the four Martin brothers that it achieved the artistic perfection of Chinese lacquer. The first use of lacquer in England is said to have been in 1663. Constance Simon, in her *English Furniture Designers of the Eighteenth Century*, discusses fully the history of lacquer in England, and claims that the factory in Birmingham produced better lacquer than even the French.[1]

In furniture, also, the Chinese influence was very marked. Elihu Yale, who was destined to be immortalized by the foundation of the university which bears his name, returned from his Governorship of Madras in 1699 with an immense supply of Chinese furnishings. He may be said to have set the fashion in this matter. But even before Yale, royalty had taken to Chinese and Indian tastes. Defoe, in his tour through Great Britain, noted: 'The Queen (Mary) brought in the custom or humour as I may call it of furnishing houses with China ware which increased to a strange degree afterwards, piling their China upon the tops of cabinets, scrutoires and every chimney piece to the top of the ceilings and even setting up shelves for their China ware. . . .'

[1] And why abroad our money fling
To please our fickle fair
No more from China, China bring
Here's English China ware.

Chinese cabinets and screens came into wide use with those who could afford such expensive tastes. But it was only when Thomas Chippendale, the greatest name in English furniture, drew his inspiration from Chinese designs that it began to influence national taste. Chippendale's book, *The Gentleman and Cabinet Maker's Director*, gives many Chinese designs. That they influenced the general style of Chippendale is undoubted, and one authoritative critic claims that even where his designs are not admittedly Chinese 'as in the fretwork chairs or in the frets and writing table, or in the hanging China shelves, it is discernible in small details. . . .'[1] Even the chairs entitled 'French' show in the designs on the tapestry seats, the Chinese junk, the drooping willow and the mandarin figures. By the 'fifties Chinese taste in furniture had become so widely prevalent that publications like Edwards and Darbey's *Chinese Designs of Building and Furniture* and William Chambers' *Designs of Chinese Building and Furniture* found a ready market.

Another matter of taste on which Chinese influence was decisive was wallpaper. Originally it was mostly imported. This kind of paper seems to have reached England through Dutch merchants and was part of the Dutch taste imported into England by William III. A description of the new material is found in Evelyn's Diary: 'Pictures of men and countries rarely painted on a sort of gummed calico, transparent as glass: flowers, trees, beasts, birds, etc., excellently wrought in a kind of sleeve silk, vary natural.' Patterns of wallpaper may have been brought to Europe by missionaries, but the first wallpapers manufactured in Europe in imitation of the Chinese were by Jean Pappillon in 1688. When the fashion reached its height English imitations began to appear, and one, Jackson of Battersea published a pattern book of designs in 1753. It was he who began to produce serviceable wallpaper on a commercial scale, and he was followed by the famous Chelsea and Sheringham factories, which naturalized the industry in England.

An equally permanent influence on European taste was produced by the Chinese garden. Its spiritual origins are to be traced to Addison and Pope, but it came into prominence only with the Chinese garden which Sir William Chambers laid out in the Kew Gardens in 1759, and which was widely copied in all the capitals of Europe.

It is difficult to evaluate the influence of Chinese painting on the art of Europe at this time. It is, however, undeniable that many leading landscape painters and painters in water-colours were familiar with Chinese art, and seemed to have borrowed freely from Oriental technique. Watteau, especially, shows a predilection for Chinese forms in his treatment of mountains and clouds. Watteau also introduces Chinese figures in his pictures, but they all remain curiously European. In the *La Muette*

[1] See Arthur Hayden: *Furniture Designs of Thos. Chippendale*. London, 1910.

in Paris, Watteau is said to have given free play to his Chinese fancies. Many other French painters, of whom Christophe Hult and Boucher are said to have been the most successful, followed this fashion.

Water-colour painting is said to have been borrowed from China. John Robert Cozens, whom Constable called 'the greatest genius who ever touched landscape', was the first to use the Chinese technique, which it is said 'even in detail corresponded to the Chinese method of landscape painting'.[1] Cozens' father, Alexander Cozens, in his later work is said to have been influenced by his son and, according to Laurence Binyon, his painting 'reminds one curiously of Chinese monochrome sketches'.

Rococo in architecture and the influence of Chinese ideas on the movement have been studied in detail by many experts and require no discussion here. Hudson in his admirable chapter on the subject in *Europe and China* deals with the question with expert knowledge, while Reichwein discusses the matter authoritatively and with full documentation in his treatise. The characteristics of Rococo are described thus by the former:

'Variety and multiplicity were indeed of the intention of the Rococo decorative style. Its design at its best was complex and exuberant, while yet retaining a subtle unity and balance; it delighted above all in free curves in the Chinese manner, in richly ornamented curved movements, breaking up straight lines, or in rectilinear compositions of irregular rhythm like Chinese lattice work. Its profusion differed from that of the Baroque in that it avoided all appearance of massiveness and rigidity; it favoured light springing forms. . . . It sought to modify all right-angled corners with curves and to diffuse its decoration in continuous growth without stiffness or emphasis. . . .

The movement disappeared as suddenly as it gained popularity, but its effects may still be detected in the European architectural tradition.

India's contribution to European taste in the eighteenth century or before it, was negligible except in one matter, textiles. Cotton textiles, cheap, light, washable and artistically printed, known as calicoes, malmulls, sallimpores, masuilipatam, madras, etc., and, of course, muslin, became not only fashionable in certain limited classes, but even a national habit. Neither public agitation nor even parliamentary action – e.g. the parliamentary prohibition in 1677 against cotton goods in winter months – could diminish the popularity which the lightness, the colour and pattern and, above all, their washableness gave to Indian textiles. The advocates of wool professed to be shocked by the transparency of the Indian materials: the solid worth and endurability of English woollen was recommended in a million voices, but the Indian textiles held their

[1] Reichwein, *China and Europe*, p. 125.

ground and effected a major change in the social habits of England and of Europe.

Nor were the French manufacturers less agitated about this matter. In 1701 Louvois, the Minister of Louis XIV, issued an order prohibiting the importation of muslins and *toiles blanches*. The influence of Indian textiles on the dyeing industry is freely accepted by earlier writers. One authority quoted by Reichwein (p. 48) states: 'The Indians have taught us to produce cotton stuffs, dimity and muslin and to print them in fast colours. The dyeing of Indian cloths has been imitated in Europe, though perhaps not as regards excellence and strength of colouring in such perfection as the cloths themselves.'

The social change which the habit of tea drinking introduced in England may be attributed to China and India. Originally imported from China, tea became so popular a beverage as to become a national drink. Pepys having sipped it, noted its cheering quality with appreciation. As we have seen, tea was the biggest item of British trade from China. By the end of the eighteenth century it had invaded the breakfast table of all classes, and the fashion of drinking it in the afternoon had also started. Raynal, the French philosopher and historian, was so impressed by its universal prevalence in England that he declared that it had done more for British sobriety than any laws, sermons or moral treatises. But, as in the case of Indian textiles, English economists, alarmed at the drain of gold, were eager to find arguments against tea drinking, and Arthur Young, among others, protested against the extravagance of the poor in buying it. Readers of *Romany Rye* will recall how an eccentric gentleman in a village in North England had studied Chinese characters from tea-pots, so fashionable had this habit become.

Though the British Treasury successively increased the duty on tea, the demand only continued to increase. India now entered the market. The tea plant, though native to the soil in Assam, had not been cultivated in India. In the nineteenth century India cut into the tea trade and, as tea plantations were predominantly a British interest, the popularity of tea as the breakfast and afternoon beverage of the English people was maintained without serious challenge.

A curious evidence of the Oriental fashion in England in the eighteenth century was the popularity of Asian themes on the English stage. One writer lists as many as 136 plays on Oriental subjects published or performed in England in the eighteenth century.

Contemporaneously, French theatres also were staging plays on similar themes. Voltaire's play *Orpheline de Chine*, Confucian morals in five acts, was of course a serious play based on Premares' translation of a Chinese drama, *The Orphan of Chao*. The tale had great popularity in Europe, and more than three different adaptations appeared in English.

We may conclude this aspect of Oriental influence in England with Miss Sackville-West's description of the Oriental atmosphere at Knole:

'Those were the days when the clock tower, oddly recalling a pagoda, was but newly erected; when the great rose-and-gold Chinese screen in the poet's parlour was new and brilliant in the sun; when the coromandel chests were new toys. . . . Sir Joshua's portrait of the Chinese boy squatting on the heels, a fan in his hand, and the square of his red shoes protruding from beneath his robes. It was more original to have a Chinese page than to have a black one.'[1]

[1] *Knole and the Sackvilles*, pp. 186-7.

CHAPTER 2

THE INFLUENCES ON EUROPEAN THOUGHT

FROM these exotic interests and luxurious tastes, we shall now turn to the influence that Asia had on the thought and mind of Europe. Again it was China that played a predominant rôle in the eighteenth century. The great thinkers of Europe were attracted to China and their curiosity was greatly increased by the reports received from the Jesuits at Peking. Père Le Comte's history of China had already aroused the curiosity of European scholars. The writings of the early Europeans in China were informed, objective and generally sympathetic. Translations of Chinese classics had begun freely to appear in Europe during the second half of the seventeenth century. Ignatius da Casta's translation of Ta Hsueh under the title of *Sapientia Sinica* appeared in 1662. In 1673, Prosper Intorcetta published a translation of *Chung Yung*, one of the four Chinese classics, with an appendix on the life of Confucius in Latin and in French, under the general title of the 'Polito-Moral Science of the Chinese'. A large literature grew up in the West, especially in French, which enabled European thinkers in the eighteenth century to have a fair idea of the social, ethical and political conditions of the Chinese Empire. Confucius had been discovered and popularized by the Jesuits by the end of the century, one of them describing him as 'Master and Oracle, most learned alike in moral and political philosophy'.

It should be remembered that the Jesuits had a special interest in claiming for Confucius and his teachings a near-perfection. It was their thesis in the 'Rites' controversy that the Confucian doctrines had proceeded from early revelations and that they had been received in China 'from the children of Noah'. Thus they had attempted to justify their compromises with Chinese practices. Whatever the purpose, the philosophers used the testimony of the Jesuits in the great political controversy of the eighteenth century against the privilege of the feudal classes. Here was the greatest, most populous and one of the oldest communities in the world, stable yet progressive, which had no hereditary aristocracy. Le Comte emphasized this in his letter 'on the Policy and

Government of the Chinese'. 'Nobility is never hereditary, neither is there any distinction between the qualities of people, saving what the offices which they execute make: so that, excepting the family of Confucius, the whole kingdom is divided into magistracy and communality.... When a Viceroy or Governor of a province is dead, his children as well as others have their fortunes to make, and if they inherit not their father's virtue and ingenuity, his name which they bear (be it never so famous) gives them no quality at all.' Such a discovery could not but be of the greatest help to those like Voltaire, who were engaged in a mighty struggle against the privileges of hereditary nobility. China became the example of enlightened government. As it was distant and but imperfectly known, the realities of Chinese despotism did not interfere with the theory of paternal Government. Also the great era of Kang Hsi and Chien Lung was in many ways a period which could have been held up as an example of enlightened despotism, unencumbered by the self-interest of an hereditary aristocracy. To Voltaire and those like him, it appeared that the Chinese had achieved unquestioned success in the art of government. 'They have perfected the moral science' he declared. To the religious creed of men like Voltaire, Confucianism with its reasonableness seemed to be the perfect philosophy for the civilized man.

The fashion in this matter was set by Leibnitz. In 1689, the philosopher made the acquaintance of Father Grimaldi, who had returned from China after a period of missionary work at Peking. He had already familiarized himself with Chinese thought through available translations, and in his preface to *Novissima Sinica* he gives full expression to his admiration of what he understood to be Chinese politics – morality. 'The condition of affairs among ourselves seems to me to be such that, in view of the inordinate lengths to which the corruption of morals have advanced, I almost think it necessary that Chinese missionaries should be sent to us to teach us the aim and practice of natural theology as we send missionaries to instruct them in revealed theology.' Leibnitz was continuously working for the interchange of civilization between Europe and China.

By the time of Voltaire sufficient material was available for people to come to their own independent conclusions. The pro-Chinese school was led by Voltaire who, in his *Essai sur les Moeurs* (1760), declared that the philosophers had discovered in China a new moral and physical world. To him Confucius, as presented by the Jesuit apostles of the most Holy Sage, seemed to be the perfection of a philosopher, prophet and statesman. In the works of Confucius, Voltaire 'found the purest morality' which appeals only to virtue, 'preaches no miracles' and is not couched 'in ridiculous allegory' – all, it will be noticed, shafts directed against Christian theology. He held up the Chinese as worthy of imitation, and asked 'what should European Princes do when they hear of such examples? Admire and blush and, above all, imitate.'

Diderot, Helvetius and other *philosophes* of the Encyclopaedia seem to have been equally impressed by the civilization and culture of China. In fact, they put the best interpretation they could on the material supplied by the enthusiastic Jesuits and drew liberally on it to drive home their arguments against a society based on the twin pillars of a propertied nobility and a church, both enjoying vast privileges and, at least in the case of the latter, using its immense authority against freedom of thinking. China was the convenient armoury provided by the enemy himself from which they drew their most destructive weapons.

After all, those who reported on the question were Catholic missionaries, and the enthusiasm for Chinese philosophy had penetrated the 'holy of holies' of Western academies, the theological faculty of the University of Paris. Nothing could have suited Voltaire and his friends better than to turn against the Church the admiration so loudly expressed by the Jesuits for the non-Christian society of China. And it became to the philosophers of the Enlightenment an argument and an example, a society based on morals and not on the Church, a government which did not depend on a privileged class, a gradation of values in which scholarship ranked high, a system which seemed to entrust authority to those who were learned and therefore presumed to be wise, a political structure which did not exalt the military – in fact everything which to the liberal thinkers of Europe seemed wanting in Europe.

It is not to be assumed that this enthusiastic Sinophilism did not meet with violent opposition. At the very start of the Chinese movement in Europe, Fenelon had come out openly against it in a book entitled the *Dialogues Among the Dead*. Here Socrates faces Confucius, and has not much difficulty in exposing (to the author's satisfaction) the foolishness of the claims of the Chinese to a superior civilization. This view found an even more celebrated champion in later times in Rousseau, who could see nothing valuble in the Chinese point of view as it was advocated by Voltaire and his school. 'If neither the ability of its Ministers nor the alleged wisdom of it laws . . . has been able to protect this realm against subjection by ignorant and rude barbarians, of what service have been all its wise men?' he asked. He saw no beauty in the Chinese garden.

The influence of China on the physiocrats was perhaps more logical and certainly more abiding. Quesnay, the founder and the original thinker of the school, drew his inspiration mainly from Chinese sources. His *Tableaux Economiques* is said to have been an ingenious translation into mathematics of a Chinese doctrine attributed to Fo Hi. Again Quesnay's object was to attack the immunity from taxation which the territorial nobles claimed. Here the Chinese model came in most useful, for in China no one was exempt from imperial taxes and, as in all Asian countries, payment to the State was calculated in terms of production from land. His Chinese inspiration is not denied but rather it is affirmed with pride by his disciples. The elder Mirabeau – the self-proclaimed Friend of Man – declared in the funeral oration of his master: 'The whole teaching of Confucius is aimed at restoring to human nature that first radiance, that first beauty which it had received from heaven, and which had become obscured by ignorance and passion'. He therefore exhorted his countrymen to obey the Lord of Heaven . . . 'never to make passion the measure of action but rather to subject it to reason. It would be impossible to add anything to this splendid diadem of religious morality; but the most essential part still remained to be done – to bind it upon the brows of the earth and this was the work of our master'. Quesnay is claimed to be the heir and successor to Confucius. The influence of the physiocrats in economic thought and in educational theory has been profound and the influence of China had in this case more effect than the admiration which Leibnitz, Voltaire and others expressed for the moral philosophy of Confucius and his school.

With the eruption of the French Revolution the influence of both the *philosophes* and the physiocrats vanished, and with it also the admiration of China, which was so notable an intellectual fashion in the eighteenth century. Nineteenth-century Europe, in the pride of its power and the feeling of superiority which went along with it, had but little use for China or India. But new forces were at work. The close of the eighteenth century had opened the till then closed book of Sanskrit to European scholars. In that sense the translation of the *Bhagavad Gita* by Charles Welkins, with an introduction by Warren Hastings (1785), and the translation of *Sakuntala* (1789) by Sir William Jones are landmarks in the relations between Asia and the West. During the years that followed, Sanskrit study was taken up seriously and the knowledge of the *Upanishads*, through translations, had a profound effect on the philosophy of Schopenhauer and Nietzsche. Also, the philological researches to which the study of Sanskrit gave birth opened up vast fields of knowledge which had great psychological results. The discovery that Sanskrit, Persian, Greek and Latin had a common origin, and that the Aryan race had a common tradition, dominated much of the social thinking in the nineteenth century. That the theory in the hands of the latter-day advocates of racism led to wild extravagance does not detract from its importance.[1]

Though its influence at the time was limited – almost negligible – the

[1] For a summary statement of Indian influences in the nineteenth and twentieth centuries see Radhakrishnan: *Eastern Religions and Western Thought*. Oxford, 2nd edition, 1940, pp.247-51.

translation of the sacred books of the East, especially the *Bhagavad Gita*, the *Upanishads* and the scriptures of Buddhism – later supplemented by the work of the Pali Text Society – prepared the ground for the great influence that Vedanta and Eastern thought generally came to exercise on the minds of a section of European intelligentsia at a later period. But even in the latter half of the nineteenth century, the influence of Indian Vedantic thought was clearly marked in the writings of such outstanding thinkers as Emerson and Thoreau. Edwin Arnold's translation of the *Gita, The Lord's Song* and his *Light of Asia*, both of which even after half a century continue to be popular favourites, also marked the growing influence of Indian religious thought. In the first half of the twentieth century, beginning perhaps with the publication of Tagore's *Gitanjali*, Hindu religious thought attained an independent position of importance in European religious circles. It was a slow process, not a question of fashion, or a temporary reaction against some established doctrines, but the gradual and almost imperceptible penetration of ideas.

The work of the great 'popularizers' should also not be forgotten. Max Müller in regard to India, Giles and a host of others in regard to China, Lafcadio Hearn in matters Japanese were great influences in their day; and that tradition, though it has tended to become more and more specialized, plays an important role in the cultural life of Europe even today. In fact, T. S. Eliot has claimed that Chinese poetry had in a measure passed into the literary tradition of Europe through the translations of Waley and others, while in regard to Indian literature, if its poetry cannot be said to have made any deep impression, the number of volumes which are published every year about Indian thought bear witness to the unfailing interest in the perennial philosophy of India.

Better understanding of the Asian mind – Indian and Chinese – had one further consequence which needs emphasis. It had been almost a dogma of European thought that everything of value arose in the regions that touched the Aegean Sea. Religion, philosophy, art and even science, it was claimed, originated in this area. In fact, for all civilization a Greek origin was postulated. A persistence in this belief was responsible in the early years of Oriental research for the futile attempts made to date events in Asia, especially Indian history, to periods where they could be conveniently adjusted to developments in Greece. That belief in a monopoly of wisdom for the Greeks had to be reluctantly abandoned, as a result of increased knowledge of Asian civilizations. The liberalization of the Furopean mind consequent upon the recognition of the fact that all nations have contributed towards the growth of human civilization, is a gain of considerable significance.

It is not to be understood that the influence of Asia on Europe, even in the field of thought, has always been beneficial or progressive. In the matter of political and legal theory, it generated a movement of reaction which had considerable influence in England. From Wellington to Curzon, the tradition of conservatism found a steady stream of recruits from among those whose political experiences were coloured by their association with the government of colonial or dependent empires. The theorist of this reaction, who exercised a very considerable influence, was Sir Henry Maine, whose experience of India is clearly reflected in his great work on ancient law. Others, like James Stephen-FitzStephen and Alfred Lyall, who provided the new Toryism with an intellectual background, were also men of Asian political experience. Nor could the influence of an ever-increasing number of people with commercial, missionary and administrative experience in Asia, all united in a disbelief in the equality of man and in democracy, fail to change the quality and temper of the metropolitan countries themselves.

A final result of the unequal impact between Asia and Europe was the growth of the feeling of colour superiority. Many observers have noted that in the eighteenth century there was very little of this feeling of colour among the Europeans either in India or in China. In fact in the eighteenth century the feeling towards the Chinese was generally one of respect, while in India there had not developed that feeling of racial arrogance which was to be the marked characteristic of the Europeans in the latter half of the nineteenth and the first three decades of the twentieth century.[1] The reasons for the growth of this feeling may have been many; but that it was largely due to the political domination which Europeans came to exercise, and looked upon as their right by the middle of the nineteenth century, would seem to be obvious. The very fact that such a feeling was not very widespread in countries which remained independent, like Japan and even Siam, should conclusively prove its political origin.

[1] An English observer coming out from England said of 'the commercial men in India that many had lived so long among the Asians as to have imbibed their worst feelings and to have forgotten the sentiments of civilization and religion: they were as cruel as covenanters without their faith and as relentless as inquisitors without their fanaticism'. Quoted from *The British in Asia* by Guy Wint, p. 127.

CONCLUSION

The period of maritime authority over Asia, beginning with Vasco da Gama's arrival and ending with the departure of the Western fleets from their bases on the Asian continent, covers an epoch of the highest significance to human development. The changes it directly brought about and the forces it generated in the countries of Asia in contact with Europe for a period of 450 years, and subjected to Western domination for over a century, have effected a transformation which touches practically every aspect of life in these countries.

Though it is impossible to anticipate what Asia will make of these influences in the future, and how the different Asian countries will transmute the experiences, ideas and institutions in the crucible of their racial characteristics, history and social tradition, there is no gainsaying the fact that the massiveness of the changes that have already taken place, the upsurges which have radically transformed their ancient societies, and the ideas that have modified their outlook, involve a qualitative break with the past which justly entitles the changes to be described as revolutionary. The period of European control of the States of Asia is a dividing line in their history, for both by resistance and by adaptation they have had to call forth new vitality and consciously adapt themselves to new ideas by which alone they were able gradually to recover their independence and strength.

As we have noticed, the European expansion towards the East began as a crusade. It was the beginning of one of the great Crusades, the Eighth Crusade we might call it. The leadership of this movement was inherited from Henry the Navigator, not only by Manoel the Fortunate and Joao III, but by Affonso Albuquerque and other leaders of Portuguese expansion who looked upon themselves as genuine crusaders. Every blow struck at the Moor was, in their view, a victory for Christendom. The attack on the spice trade, as Albuquerque clearly explained to his soldiers at Malacca, was an attack on the financial prosperity of the Muslim nations, an aspect of economic warfare the significance of which both the Muslim Powers and Portugal fully realized. This crusading attitude had certain significant results. With the non-Muslim peoples and rulers of Asia, the relations of the Portuguese were not, generally speaking, unfriendly.

The crusading and anti-Muslim aspect of European expansion in Asia ceased to be a major factor by the beginning of the seventeenth century, owing to two important reasons. In the first place, the Protestant movement had broken up the unity of Christendom, and the religious fanaticism which was previously directed against Islam was now turned to civil war in Europe. The Wars of Religion, which devastated Europe for over a century and ended only with the Treaty of Westphalia, tended to obliterate the memory of the Muslim menace, which ceased from then to be a 'primary motive' in European history. The second was the Battle of Lepanto where Don Juan of Austria, for Christian Europe, destroyed the naval power of the Turks. After that victory the menace of Islam became less and less, though the Ottoman power was still formidable and capable on occasions of carrying the war to the gates of Vienna. But the Western European nations were no longer afraid of the Turk.

The crusading spirit was replaced, so far as the Catholic countries were concerned, by a spirit of evangelization. The upsurge in the Catholic religion, of which the most characteristic expression was the Society of Jesus, saw in the East great prospects of evangelization. The Portuguese monarchy was deeply influenced by this, and we have from this time a new urge which sent Jesuit fathers to the courts of the Grand Mogul, the Chinese Emperor and the Shogun. This urge weakened a little with the arrival of the Dutch and the English in Asian waters, for till the beginning of the nineteenth century Protestant churches did not feel the call of converting the heathen and entering seriously into the mission field. But in the nineteenth century, and up to the First European War, evangelization again becomes a major urge in European relations with Asia. It may indeed be said that the most serious, persistent and planned effort of European nations in the nineteenth century was their missionary activities in India and China, where a large-scale attempt was made to effect a mental and spiritual conquest as supplementing the political authority already enjoyed by Europe. Though the results were disappointing in the extreme from the missionary point of view, this assault on the spiritual foundations of Asian countries has had far-reaching consequences in the religious and social reorganization of the peoples. We have already in a previous chapter attempted to assess the reactions of this movement in the recovery of Asia. All that need be said here is that in surveying the influences of Europe on Asian countries, it is necessary to keep in mind the unbroken religious urge of European expansion, and take into consideration the immense non-official and voluntary effort that it represented. Indeed, it might be appropriately said that while political aggrandisement was the work of governments and groups, and commerce the interest of organized capital, mission work was the effort of the people of the West to bring home to the masses of Asia their view of the values of life.

Religion, however, was only one aspect of European expansion. Even with the Portuguese, who in the beginning equated the establishment of a monopoly in spice trade with religion, trade soon overshadowed the religious aspect of their work. With the arrival of the Protestant Powers trade became for a time the only consideration. There was little contact outside commercial relations. If by an Act of God the relations of Europe with Asia had ceased all of a sudden in 1748, little would have been left to show for two and a-half centuries of furious activity. Even in India there would have only been a few ruined forts on unfrequented coasts, some churches erected also in coastal areas by the Portuguese, a small community of half-castes, regretting the days when they were people of prestige – hardly anything more. In the trading period, 1610–1758, Europe influenced Asia but little.

In the period of conquest (1750–1857), however, the situation began to change. Asian leaders began to feel that the strangers had become a menace and had to be taken seriously. It is not surprising that the first serious interest that the Asian leaders began to show was in cannon-making, army organization and military equipment. But apart from this justifiable curiosity in respect of military matters shown by a few people in power, there were others who were interested in the intellectual and spiritual strength of the European nations. Ram Mohan Roy and his school in India and the Rangakusha school in Japan are examples of this changing attitude towards Europe. Citizen Tipoo as a member of the Jacobin Club of Seringapatam, Ram Mohan Roy in correspondence with the leaders of the Enlightenment in Europe, and public meetings in Calcutta to congratulate the liberal revolutionaries in Spain were symptoms of an intellectual awakening and a sense of world-community which was dawning on Asia.

The most significant single factor which changed the intellectual relationship of Europe and Asia was the French Revolution. Few people today realize the immense influence of the French Revolution outside Europe. Negroes in Haiti, Tipoo in Mysore, Dutch radicals in Indonesia, all felt the ripples of this movement. The reforms of Dandaels in Java were a direct result of it. Wellesley's aggressive policy leading to the conquest and annexation of large areas of India was one of its indirect consequences, for it was the fear of the revolutionary French that provided the main motive of his policy of conquest. But it is not in this sense that the doctrines of the French Revolution – 'liberty, equality and fraternity' – came to have a pervading influence on Asia. As a revolution the developments in France had but little immediate influence on the Asian people. In the period that followed the Napoleonic experiment, the doctrines of the Revolution had become the common inheritance of European liberalism. Modified and made respectable by the reformers in the period immediately following the Napoleonic era, they became the mental background of European statesmen. Education could no longer be neglected in the possessions of European nations. Codes of modern law had to be provided; and even the Dutch had to pay lip service to the interests of the Indonesians when they recovered the lost colony of Java. Slowly a liberal tradition penetrated the policies of European nations.

Not only did the French revolutionary doctrines become in due course an influence on European thought in relation to the East, but they provided the Asian peoples with their first political ideology. Indian writings of the first period of nationalism hark back to the principles of this school. Ram Mohan Roy and his followers, petitioning for the abolition of *Suttee*, for education in English, for greater freedom for women, though they quote from Hindu scriptures in justification of their reforms, are really thinking in terms of Rousseau, watered down to meet Indian conditions. European inspiration of the Asian reform movements of the first half of the nineteenth century cannot be denied.

The nineteenth century witnessed the apogee of capitalism in Europe. That this was in a large measure due to Europe's exploitation of Asian resources is now accepted by historians. As Hobson, the historian of Imperialism, observes: 'The exploitation of other portions of the world, through military plunder, unequal trade and forced labour, has been the one great indispensable condition in the growth of European capitalism.' It is the riches of Asian trade (and American) flowing to Europe that enabled the great industrial revolution to take place in England. But with the establishment of capitalism as the dominant economic structure of the colonizing nations, an immense and far-reaching change took place in the relations of the West with Asia. In the eighteenth century, conquest was for the purpose of trade. In the area you conquered, you excluded other nations, bought at the cheapest price, organized production by forced labour to suit your requirements, and transferred the profits to the mother country. In the nineteenth century conquest was not for trade but for investment. Tea plantations and railway construction became major interests in Britain's connection with India. Vast sums were invested in India for building railways. 'Of the loans for Indian Railways,' says an English writer, 'about one-third went to pay the home charges in London, something under one-third was spent on wages and administrative expenses, largely paid to English engineers, and something over one-third on British rails and engines and in paying British ships to bring them to India.'[1]

The third phase of European relations with Asia, which begins with the middle of the nineteenth century, is the period of imperialism in the true sense of the word. The transformation is completed earliest in

[1] Quoted in Carrington: *British Overseas*, p. 479.

India, which provides the pattern for the rest, for the Dutch in Indonesia, for the French in Indo-China, for all the nations in respect of China. The imperialist relationship, involving large-scale capital investment, had the result of importing into Asia advanced technical skills and scientific knowledge. Railway construction, which was the main field of capital investment, required the importation of engineers. Rivers had to be spanned, tunnels had to be built, and the lines, once constructed, had to be maintained. Imported technical skill, except at the highest levels, became too costly, and as a result engineering colleges and schools became unavoidable. The spread of technical knowledge in the East, of which this is merely an example, was a necessary result of capital investment. It was not possible to keep Asian nationals out of this knowledge, for returns on capital depended on finding technical skill locally. In regard to industry also, a similar movement became noticeable. European industries established in Calcutta, Bombay and Shanghai had to depend, at least in their lower levels, on locally trained personnel. With the advancement of knowledge among local populations it became impossible to prevent Asian capital from encroaching on European industrial monopolies. In India, cotton mills began to spring up in Bombay and Ahmedabad. In Shanghai, which had become practically a European city, Chinese industrialists found no difficulty in setting up factories in imitation of European models. Railway construction in China, which was a subject of furious international competition, when it was first taken up, soon became an activity of the Chinese Government. Thus, in its primary aspect, imperialism as an export of capital carried into Asia the seeds of its own destruction.

In its second aspect, that is territorial expansion for providing areas for exploitation, European imperialism in the nineteenth century, under the humanitarian impulses of the liberal movement, embarked on a policy of education, welfare schemes and even political training. Direct administration of vast populations naturally created new interests. The administrative authorities had no direct connection with or interest in trade, the officers being, at least according to English tradition, recruited from the middle classes with public school training. So in India, and to some extent in Indonesia, a contradiction developed within the structure of imperialism in which the administrative authorities were inclined to emphasize the welfare aspect of their work, while the commercial interests still considered the territories as areas for exploitation. The conflict between the two views came out into the open in India in the controversy on the Ilbert Bill and in the successive movements to resist political reforms, of which the inspiration and the leadership lay always with big business. Nor was it less apparent in places where the power exercised indirectly as in China. The bitter controversies between the

Shanghai and treaty port merchants' opinion on the one hand and the Foreign Office on the other in dealing with China, which we have discussed earlier, is another instance of this contradiction. In fact political authority, combined with the humanitarian ideals of the era of peace, brought a sense of responsibility towards 'the backward peoples'. No danger to the supremacy of Europe was suspected as being inherent in this development, for even at the end of the nineteenth century the Europeans – even the most progressive among them – were convinced that their superiority was divinely ordained and was safe at least for centuries to come. The idea that the Chinese, weak, immobilized and without industrial potential, could stand up and fight the European within a measurable time, or that Indians could compete with the British in trade or industry, or that the hundreds of Indonesian islands could be united in opposition to the Dutch, would have sounded ludicrous to a European in the Augustan age of imperialism. Therefore the humanitarian ideal of educating the Asian people and of encouraging them to develop at least those skills which were necessary for the more effective discharge of the white man's mission, was pursued without any sense of fear.

Also, the complexities of direct administration of vast areas like India and Indonesia made it necessary to develop a large body of indigenous administrative personnel. In the period of trade there was no such necessity. In the period of imperialism this was unavoidable.

The apparatus of modern States, run largely by local talent, had to be built up, providing the Asian peoples both with administrative training and with knowledge and understanding of the mechanism of modern government. This is particularly important, for one of the main differences between the earlier periods of history and the political systems that developed in the nineteenth and twentieth centuries lay in the vast administrative systems which touched every aspect of life which the State organizations of the nineteenth and twentieth centuries represented. In the eighteenth century, neither in Europe nor in Asia was there a government which was also an administration in the present-day sense. In the latter half of the nineteenth century European countries, having had to deal with more and more complex problems of industry, commerce, social and economic welfare, organized the vast mechanism of modern administration, which neither Frederick the Great nor Napoleon could have conceived, and which earlier political thought would have resisted bitterly as encroachments on liberty.

The Asian State-systems, though essentially bureaucratic and therefore 'administrative' and not political, were, however, limited to land administration and defence. The administrative system which the Crown developed in India and which every colonial administration felt compelled to develop in its territory, not only provided the first conception of the modern State to the Asian mind, but equipped it with the mechanism necessary to realize it in time. Even in regard to China, this is a development which has not received sufficient attention. The organization of the imperial customs department under Western leadership, and the growth of posts and telegraphs, provided China with the pattern of new administration.

The third aspect of territorial expansion – of the era of imperialism – was the popular sentiment of responsibility for 'moral wellbeing' which found its most characteristic expression in the missionary work. The conscience of the people, especially of the Protestant countries, was aroused by the fact that in the areas directly governed by them or under their influence hundreds of millions lived and died without the chance of salvation. We have already seen the zeal and blind devotion of men like William Hudson Taylor, the founder of the China Inland Mission. He was only the most notable example among thousands of serious-minded, pious men who devoted themselves to the cause of evangelization and spent their lives in the different countries of Asia. Though the results of their religious activities were negligible and often led only to reactions which they least expected, their interest in the life and wellbeing of the common people, and their efforts to break down the barrier of race, had the benefit of bringing the West nearer to Asia. Also, their educational and medical work in the interior of India, China and Burma had far-reaching consequences.

It is necessary to emphasize that the contact between the peoples of the East with Europeans began really only in the era of imperialism. In the 300 and odd years that preceded it (from 1498 to 1858) this contact was limited, even in India, to narrow circles, and had not penetrated even into the ruling classes. With direct administration, development of educational systems, exploitation instead of trade, the contact gradually extended to different levels. Slowly Asian youths began to find their way to European seats of learning. We have seen how Japan began with a planned system of sending selected young men to understand the secrets of Europe. China's 'first hundred' promoted by the Great Viceroy Tsang Kuo-fan was an abortive attempt in the same line. The first impulse which took young Indians across the seas was not to probe the mysteries of European life, but the more material consideration of a chance to compete in the Civil Service examinations. But soon this movement assumed immense proportions, and a large proportion of the students who went to Europe were dedicated to the study of such subjects as engineering, medicine, forestry, geology and chemistry apart, of course, from law and social sciences. A similar movement took large numbers of Indo-Chinese students to Paris and Indonesians to Leyden. The prestige of German technical advances attracted a growing number to the universities of the Reich.

The essential point for our purpose is that in every one of the countries of Asia, the leadership in the movement which ultimately displaced European supremacy belonged to those who had been trained by the West under the aegis of imperialism. Not only Mahatma Gandhi and Jawaharlal Nehru, but the founders of the Indian National Congress and the successive generations of Congress leaders were trained in the West. In Japan, it was the group of explorers sent to the West by the Shogunate that led the movement for the reorganization of the State. In China, though the deposition of the Manchus was not the work of Western-educated people, the building up of the revolutionary movement that followed was led by men of Western training. In Indonesia, Indo-China, Burma and Ceylon it is the men and women educated in the West – the 'Wogs' (Westernized Oriental gentlemen) as the European contemptuously called them – that provided the leadership.

It will thus be seen that in the relationship between the East and the West, the vital period which witnessed the realization of European ambitions and generated at the same time the movements which led to its destruction was the period of Imperialism. The period that followed, that of Europe in Retreat (1918–42), is dominated by two factors, the October Revolution and the rise of Asian nationalism. It is beyond the scope of this treatise to deal with the former. To the growth of nationalism, especially as a reaction to the dominance of the West, we may now turn.

Nationalism is indubitably the most significant development in Asian countries during the last hundred years of European contact. It is often stated by European writers that Asian peoples had no sense of nationalism or even of nationality till they came into contact with European peoples. This criticism ignores the fact that in Europe itself the doctrine of nationalism developed mainly as a result of resistance to Napoleonic aggrandisement. No doubt England and France had deep-seated patriotic feeling, but in the multi-national Empire of the Habsburgs, which included Lombardy as well as portions of Poland, patriotism had to be equated with dynastic loyalty. It is, therefore, not unreasonable to emphasize that the development of nationalism in Asia, as an over-riding loyalty to a State embodying a continuous tradition and supposed to represent a single people, was a parallel growth to the same movement in Europe and arose out of similar circumstances, that is, resistance to foreign rule. The prophets of nationalism who influenced Asia were Mazzini and the Irish patriost struggling to achieve the national independence of their respective countries.

In China, Japan and to a lesser extent in India, the sense of patriotism was strong and deeply imbedded in people. Even though the reigning dynasty was foreign, the love of the Chinese people for their country was such that their resistance to external aggression never weakened. In Japan, patriotism had always been a dominant national characteristic and, as we have noticed from the first contact with Europe, Japan's thinkers began seriously to concern themselves with the problems of safeguarding their independence. Even in India, Arthur Wellesley (later Duke of Wellington) was struck by the patriotism and national spirit of the Marathas, the only national monarchy at the time, and when foreign rule spread over Hindustan, national and patriotic sentiment was strong enough to organize an armed rebellion which destroyed the East India Company and shook the foundations of British authority. The nationalism which developed as a result of European contacts was different from this. It was the acceptance of the doctrine of a national personality, of an identification of all the people within the territory with the individuality of the State, of a belief in a kind of mystic brotherhood of the people that constituted the nation. Indian nationalism, for example, emphasized the *Indian-ness* of their people, of their common bond of history, civilization and culture, mystically united to the land of Hindustan. Similarly in Japan, the doctrines of 'pure Shinto' were extended to cover a unity of the Japanese people, their unique and continuous history, their special mission in the world. Even in China the Han race became the basis of the new nationalism.

This cult of the nation required in many cases a new historical background, for without a common history a nation cannot exist. In many Asian countries, especially India, such a history with a national purpose seemed hardly to exist. India had an undoubted geographical, cultural, social and even religious unity in the sense that all through its history ran the main thread of Hindu religious development. But political history was practically unknown except as myths and legends. From the identification of Sandrocottus as Chandragupta Maurya to the excavations of Mohenjodaro and Harappa, from the deciphering of the inscriptions of Asoka to the comprehensive survey of epigraphic records all over India, the material for the writing of Indian history was provided by the work of European scholars. Even more striking is the case of Indonesia, where a few European scholars, mostly Dutch, reconstructed from inscriptions the history of the great empires of Java and Sumatra which provided Indonesian nationalism with a solid historical basis. In this sense it cannot be denied that European scholars and thinkers, by their labours in the interests of knowledge, enabled India, Ceylon and Indonesia to think in terms of historic continuity.

Nationalism is also a pride in cultural achievement – a sense of being common successors to a proud cultural heritage. No one had to tell the

Indians, Chinese and Japanese about the richness of their inherited culture and, in fact, it was their conviction that they were superior to others. To this we shall revert later. But it is well to recognize here that the rationalization of this belief at the present time is due to the recovery and interpretation of the culture of India and China by Western scholars. The paintings of the Tunghuan caves were not known to anyone until discovered by the Hungarian scholar Sir Aurel Stein. Similar is the case with the caves of Ajanta and Bagh in India. When the Asian peoples recovered from the 'first intoxication of the West', as Yone Noguchi called it, they were able to fall back and find sustenance for their intellectual self-respect in a culture which had attracted some of the superior minds of the West. In fact, while resistance to political domination of Europe provided the motive force of the new nationalism, its justification and strength lay in a growing appreciation of its own culture to which European scholarship had also materially contributed.

If nationalism developed directly by resistance and indirectly by the recovery of historical sense and pride in cultural achievement as a result of Western contact, the sense of Asianism is exclusively the counterpart of the solidarity of European feeling. Before the end of the nineteenth century there was no such feeling as Asianism. But in the beginning of this century we find the great Japanese artist Okakura Kakuzo opening a book with the startling declaration 'Asia is one'. Undoubtedly there is much that is common in the tradition of non-Islamic Asia, in religious approach, social organization, art, and so on. From Japan to India the civilizations of Asian countries are united by certain common features which cannot be explained solely by the influence of Buddhism. Ancestor-reverence and family relationships, both of which are outside the sphere of Buddhism, are common features of the social organization of the non-Islamic East. While there is no doubt, as many Western observers[1] point out, that there are fundamental differences between the Hindu and Chinese attitudes towards life, especially the attitude of the Chinese *literati* whose practical Confucian outlook impressed the Western observers, it is equally true that there is a community of thought and feeling between the common peoples of India and China, which it is not possible to overlook.

It should also be remembered that the European nations in emphasizing their solidarity, their *European-ness* in dealing with Asian countries, inevitably gave rise to a common feeling of Asian-ness. Even in India, where nationals of other European countries enjoyed no political rights, the division was between Europeans and Indians and not between Englishmen and Indians. The exclusive clubs in India were not for

[1] See the writings on China by Lowes Dickinson and Bertrand Russell especially.

Englishmen, but for *Europeans*. Special schools and educational facilities that existed were also for Europeans. In China, where all European countries enjoyed political privileges, the European communities went to great lengths to present a united front. Even when the Franco-German War was being fought in Europe, the pressure of the doctrine of European solidarity against Asians compelled the German Minister to line up behind his French colleagues in the affair of Tientsin. Similar was the attitude of the Powers to Japan during the period of negotiations for treaty revision. Japanese efforts to sign bilateral treaties were frustrated on numerous occasions by the desire of the Western countries to stand together. From 1880 to 1914 – during the period of imperialism – the Europeans were united against Asia, and this attitude, in its turn, gave birth to a sense of Asianism which even the aggressive actions of Japan and its proclaimed policy 'of standing in with the West' did not seriously undermine.

There is a view generally held by many European writers that the changes brought about in Asia by the contact with Europe are superficial and will, with the disappearance of European political authority, cease to count as time goes on. They point out that the vast masses in India, China, Indonesia and even Japan have remained unaffected by the changes in their countries, and that the penetration of Western ideas has been confined to limited classes: that the great Oriental religions have held firm under assault, that the life in the East in spite of the appearance of great change moves in the familiar old grooves. The view is therefore advanced that with the elimination of European political authority Asia will revert to type and the Western influence will be gradually swept away by the indigenous ways of life.

This point of view would seem to be based on a superficial reading of history. Though the Hindus, the Chinese and the Japanese liked to believe that their own cultures were superior they could not deny either the superiority of Western knowledge or the greater strength – though not the stability – of the European social and economic organization. They were convinced, after a short period of intoxication, that their own religious and moral systems were superior but they had ample proofs to satisfy them that Europe was intellectually centuries ahead of them. European learning, therefore, earned the respect of all Asians during a whole century and, what is more, European social and economic organization provided a norm which, in part, they accepted enthusiastically and, in part, was forced upon them by world conditions. This had never happened before, at least in the history of India and China. Five hundred years of Muslim authority in North India had not forced the Hindus to change their social ideas in regard to caste and untouchability – in fact, it had strengthened them. Hundreds of years of foreign rule had not forced the Chinese to question the validity of Confucian teachings or doubt the canonical value of the *Book of Filial Piety*. To-day, however, as a result of the contact with the West, untouchability has been abolished and caste no longer is king in India. Confucius has ceased to be the Most Holy One in China where the slogans of the youth movement execrate him. There is no doubt, therefore, that the changes that have been brought about in Asian life by the contact with Europe are radical and far-reaching, and will not disappear as many observers are inclined to think with the rise of a new Asian sentiment.

It would be useful at this point to examine the major features where Western influences are likely to be permanent, and the extent of these influences on Asian societies in general.

The first and perhaps the most abiding influence is in the sphere of law. In all Asian countries the legal systems have been fundamentally changed and reorganized according to the post-revolutionary conceptions of nineteenth-century Europe. The first country in which this change was introduced was India where, under the influence of Thomas Babington Macaulay, new legal principles were systematically introduced and applied. I may quote here what I have written elsewhere in this connection: 'The legal system under which India has lived for a hundred years and within whose steel frame her social, political and economic development has taken place, is the work of Macaulay... The establishment of the great principle of equality of all before law in a country where under the Hindu doctrines a Brahmin could not be punished on the evidence of a Sudra, and even punishments varied according to caste, and where, according to Muslim law, testimony could not be accepted against a Muslim was itself a legal revolution of the first importance. Few, indeed, who compare Macaulay's code with its great predecessors, whether those of Manu, Justinian or Napoleon, will cavil at the claim that the Indian penal code was a great improvement on the previous systems.'[1]

The imposing and truly magnificent legal structure, under which the 483 million people of India, Pakistan and Burma have lived during the last 100 years, has changed the basis of society in a manner which few people realize. Though the personal laws of different communities may be different, the penal law is the same for all. This has been supplemented by a vast corpus of legislation, which has profoundly affected every kind of social relationship. The position of women in India, for example, has undergone changes which Hindu thought even fifty years ago would have considered revolutionary. Even the personal law of the Hindus, in respect of their succession, inheritance, marriage, joint family and the set of what may be called their special social organization, has been

[1] *A Survey of Indian History*, p. 257.

greatly modified by the legal systems now in force in India. There can be no going back on this – in any case to the old Hindu ideas. The transformation brought about by the new legal doctrines of the West is a permanent one and is likely to outlast the more spectacular changes in many other fields.

The transformation of legal systems is not confined to areas which were directly administered by colonial Powers like Indonesia, Indo-China and Burma. Japan voluntarily brought into force a modern system of law which has been in operation now for over half a century. It was on the strength of the liberal and modern character of its legal system and judicial administration that Japan was able to obtain the early abrogation of extraterritoriality in her Empire. In China, though the elaborate civil and criminal codes introduced by the Kuomintang have now been discarded, the tendency has not been to go back to the legal systems of the pre-revolutionary era but to introduce something which is considered even more progressive. At least in the realm of family relationships the new laws are more advanced than in any Western country.

Economic structure may break down, leading to widespread misery; political organizations may disappear under the impact of new revolutionary forces. In these spheres Asian societies may conceivably be thrown back after a period. But it is difficult to imagine how the basic ideas of the new legal systems could be changed so easily, unless civilization itself is extinguished in these areas. For such a pessimism there is no valid reason in countries like India, China and Japan where elaborate legal systems survived unimpaired even periods of dreadful confusion and anarchy. We may therefore assume that the great changes brought about in social relationships by the introduction and acceptance of new legal systems under the influence of Europe will be an abiding factor in the civilization of Asia.

It is not possible to speak with the same certainty about the political and social structures brought about as a result of the conflict with Europe. The forms of Government, the nature of political rights, democracy in its widest sense, local and municipal administrations – these may all disappear, change their character or survive only in attenuated and unrecognizable forms in certain areas. And yet at the present time they constitute the most spectacular change in Asia. No country in the East is now governed under a system of 'Oriental Despotism'. Even Japan, where the divinely descended Emperor reigns in an unbroken line of succession, is now clothed will all the paraphernalia of a democratic constitution. In fact, the norm of Government in the East has become a republic. While in Europe there are still six sovereigns and a Grand Duchess, in non-Islamic Asia there are only three monarchies (Japan, Siam and Nepal), while all the nations which acquired their independence or threw off foreign domination have been proclaimed republics. India, Burma, Indonesia and China, seats of ancient empires and kingdoms, are all now republican governments. It may be a temporary phase, for no political system can be considered permanent. But it is fairly certain that even if democratic institutions in Asia, as in some Latin American Republics, get metamorphosed into something quite different from their original shape and form, or do not develop in the spirit of genuine vigour, the principles of 'Oriental despotism' will not come back. 'Oriental despotism' has at all times reflected certain ideas and principles accepted generally by the people. Those ideas and principles no longer find any acceptance. Once the thread is broken the *mystique* of the doctrine also ceases.

So, while the new democratic institution in Asia may not last beyond a few generations or may become transformed quite early into replicas of Liberian democracy, it would yet be true to say that the principles of government that Asia has accepted from the West constitute a major and qualitative change whose influence will penetrate far into the future. The new social structure has to be reflected in new political institutions. Further, the commercial economy resulting in the participation in world trade; industrialization, bringing along with it both the power of accumulated wealth and of organized labour; the growth of organized city life, different from that of the great capital towns of the past; all these, and numerous other factors, render a reversion to the old political structures, based as they were on a rural economy and on land tax, altogether out of the question. No doubt the political structure of the Asian countries, though they may now copy the institutions of the West, may in time evolve their own patterns which may not too closely follow the traditions of Europe. But any return to a purely Asian tradition is ruled out by the growth of social, economic and political forces which no country in Asia had to deal with in the past.

The growth of great cities, themselves centres of political and economic dynamism, is a result of European contacts, the immense significance of which has not been fully appreciated. There was a great, urban life and culture previous to the arrival of Europeans in India, China and Japan. The very word *nagarika*, a town-dweller, means a man of sophisticated culture and refined tastes, and has been used in that sense from at least the third century BC. Great towns like Benares, Pravag, Broach and Surat, unconnected with courts and kings, have flourished in India through historical times. But in general they represented neither political nor municipal life. The *nagarika* did not convey the meaning of citizen. The towns and cities in India, when they were not great capitals, were merely great centres of population, sometimes important from the point of view of trade, often from the point of view of religious sanctity. They did not involve any civic tradition. The same was the case in China.

The new cities, which grew up as a result of European contacts, Bombay, Calcutta and Madras, Shanghai, Tientsin, Singapore, Colombo, Jakarta, etc., represent a new principle: the organization of the city as an independent unit. In Madras, Calcutta and Bombay we have the full paraphernalia of European city life, with sheriffs, mayors, corporations and aldermen. From this point of view, the organization of the Municipal Committee of Shanghai by the British merchants, and its phenomenal growth during a period of seventy years, may represent a greater and more far-reaching change than the control exercised by the foreigners on the imperial court.

It is the city that has created the wealthy middle classes in India, China and other Asian countries. The emergence of the middle classes both as leaders in political and economic life and as reservoirs of essential scientific skills, has been in the main the outcome of the new life in the cities. The possibility of the great cities surviving as centres of civilization, even if regression sets in elsewhere inside the countries of Asia much in the same way as in medieval Europe, cannot be overlooked, and if that happens the credit for the survival of the new life in the great cities will certainly belong to Europe.

Another point, one which arises directly out of Europe's long domination over Asia, is the integration of vast territories into great nation States of a kind unknown in the previous history of Asia. India, for instance, all through her long history, had never been welded together into a single State as she is now. Her territorial unity was in the past emphasized by the unity of Hinduism, by the similarity of Sanskrit culture and by a political impulse which led every leading Empire in India to undertake the task of conquering and bringing under one dominion the territory extending from the Himalayas to Cape Comorin. This relentless urge moved every dynasty of importance in the past; but it was never realized.

Even under the British, vast areas, amounting to nearly two-fifths of the territory of India, were under the rule of semi-independent princes. For the first time in history, India has been integrated into a single State living under the same constitution and subject to the same laws. Unquestionably this was the result of a hundred years of British administration which imposed a unity on the peoples of India, both by the machinery of Government which it created and by the forces of resistance to which it gave rise. Even more striking is the case of Indonesia. In the past these islands had never been united into a single political organization. Nor was it ever the dream of the great Empires of Java and Sumatra to weld the whole archipelago into one State. The

Sailendra monarchs of Srivijaya, in the greatness of their maritime strength, never dreamed of claiming suzerainty even over the whole of Java, let alone Borneo, Moluccas and the innumerable islands of the Sundas. When the Europeans arrived in the islands there was no feeling of Indonesian unity. The present unity of the islands is therefore the result of the 450 years of contact with Europe, and the political and economic ties created by the Dutch.

Even in regard to China, the resistance to Europe has brought about an integration of territory the importance of which cannot be overlooked. From the earliest times to the time of the Kuomintang Revolution, the great provinces of China, though governed under the direct orders of the Emperor, were not subjected to uniform policies. As we have seen, even in matters relating to war, the whole Empire was never engaged. During the Opium War of 1839–42, only the Kwantung Government was involved, and the court in Peking did not even know how the matter was progressing. The war with Japan in 1895 was more the responsibility of the Viceroy of Chihli than of the Imperial Government. The Empire was in fact a loose confederation of viceroyalties, kept together by the sense of unity of the Chinese peoples, the system of central appointments and the authority of the Emperor. Faced with the difficulty of dealing with European Powers, the Peking Government slowly transformed itself into a central administration with a Foreign Office, created only under the pressure of the Powers, a national army and a few central departments like customs administration. It was only after the Kuomintang Revolution (1925–7) that the first effective steps were taken to convert China into a nation State with a proper central administration, a regular national army and defined national policies with regard to important matters. And yet, the Kuomintang was not wholly successful, as old-time war lords like Yen Hsi-shan in Shansi and the Muslim 'Ma' war-lords in Kansu and others refused to give more than nominal allegiance to the Central Government. But the forces of integration were at work, and the unification of China, completed by the People's Republic, was but the consummation of the tendencies already in operation.

So far we have discussed the changes in the social and political institutions which arose directly from Asia's contact with Europe. A vaster and perhaps more significant change is in the realm of ideas, which it is not possible to discuss in this treatise. What the introduction of modern sciences, history and wider knowledge of the world has done to the mind of Asia is a supremely fascinating subject of inquiry. What the outcome of that fermentation will be no one is yet in a position to foresee or forecast. Obviously, it has affected every aspect of life, religion, arts, language, processes of thinking and speculative philosophies which had long held sway over the minds of men. If the Eastern religions and philosophies have not been displaced, and in fact are stronger today, it does not mean that they have not undergone profound changes. As against other religions and other philosophies they have more than held their own; but they have also had to undergo subtle transformations to resolve the conflicts which modern science, more than rival religions, forced on them. Thus the new interpretations of Buddhism and Hinduism reflect in a large measure the influence of modern ideas, mostly arising from contact with Europe.

Philosophy and religious thinking, however much they may influence the people in general, are the special interests of the intellectuals. But not so the language, and it is here that the influence of Europe has been most noticeable. From the great literatures of China, India and Japan to the minor languages spoken only by a few million people, everywhere the influence of the West overshadows past traditions. The Literary Revolution in China (1918–21) will perhaps be considered in future a more significant event than the many revolutions that country has undergone in this century. Today in China the forms of writing which are followed show little or no influence of the classics, and are modelled upon the literature of the West. The Chinese novel today does not follow the *Dream of the Red Chamber*, or the story of the three kingdoms, but is created in the mould of Tolstoy, Turgenev, Romain Rolland, Thomas Mann and Maxim Gorky. The short story, which is the most popular medium, has no classical models in Chinese literature. Its origin is almost wholly Western, and the work of Lu Hsun, Mao Tun and Kuo Mo-jo is more related to the genius of de Maupassant, Chekhov and the modern progressives than to any writers of ancient Chinese. During the past twenty years in China all creative writing has been dominated by Europe.

The instance of India is even more significant. In the great languages of India there was at first no revolutionary break with the past. In fact, till about 1914, though the Western forms of writing had taken deep root in the languages, and novels, short stories and dramas were popular and had gained a hold on the public mind, it was the classical tradition that was still dominant. In poetry especially, India, with its 3,000 years of literary inheritance, clung to the forms and manner of Sanskrit classicism, modified to a great extent by the literary renaissance of the Middle Ages. Even in Tagore, a true product of Victorian culture, the dominance of Sanskrit traditions was clearly visible. He used every known Western form: drama, short story, lyrical poetry, essay; but the voice that spoke was of one nurtured on the epics of Vyasa and Valmiki, the poetry of Kalidasa and Jayadeva and the songs of Vidyapathi, Kabir and Mira. During the last thirty years, however, the literatures of the great Indian languages have undergone a revolutionary change. They are no longer concerned with the refinements of classical style. They borrow freely from all the literatures of the West, the drama from Ibsen, Shaw, Pirandello and Chekhov, the short story and the novel from their French and Russian masters, and poetry from the latest schools in Europe. No longer have they any concern with the lotus and the moon, the swans, the *chatakas* and other time-worn symbolisms of the past.

The new art forms, especially in prose, owe little or nothing to the earlier Indian traditions. It may in fact be said that the thought of Europe is at last being acclimatized in India by the popular literature of the last quarter of a century. The social and political content of the new writing is essentially cosmopolitan, influenced widely by the breakdown of the old society in Europe and by the dynamism of Marxist thought in the widest sense. Also it is not only through literature in its creative aspect that this message is being spread. Weeklies, magazines, newspapers, cinema films and radio constitute the ever-widening popularity of the new literature. 'There is no writer under forty today,' says Mulk Raj Anand, 'who will deny that at one time or another he did subscribe to the dominating influence of the Progressive Writers' Association, which was formed in 1935. And the movement which this body generated has unleashed a tremendous amount of poetry and prose in which the conditions of our existence are constantly related to the extreme limit of possibilities.' In fact, it is the New Life – not Europe – that finds its voice echoed in a thousand mouths.

This, few will deny, widens every day the gulf between the past and the present in Asia. It is the change in the language that is in many ways the most far-reaching transformation in Asia, for it is not merely the reflection of the changed mind but is in itself the instrument of continuing changes, for the new languages of Asia represent a new semantics, a new world of ideas and thought which is reaching a larger and larger circle every day. It is significant to note that an immense development of broadcasting was one of the first things that every new State in Asia took in hand after it achieved its independence and, significantly, too, India, China and Indonesia have embarked on a policy of developing their national literatures in order to make them capable of popularizing modern ideals.

It should, however, be emphasized that the increasing acceptance of new ideas, though generated by contact with the West and of late greatly influenced by the October Revolution and the prestige of Communist thought, does not involve a break in the continuity of the great Asian civilizations. The Chinese, Indian and other civilizations, though modified by new ideas and enriched by new experience, continue even in an increasing degree to emphasize their special characteristics. In South and South-east Asia and in Japan this, to a large extent, is the result of the strength of the reorganized religion. The failure of the Christian attack on Hinduism, Buddhism and, of course, Islam, left them stronger and more vigorous as a result of the adjustments they were called upon to effect. In China, where the missionary activity achieved the limited success of breaking down religious traditions, the attachment to national civilization is still profound and is strengthened by racial and psychological characteristics which cannot be easily changed. Thus, though the influence of Europe and the penetration of new ideas have introduced vast changes in Asia, and may lead to even greater changes, Asian civilizations will continue to develop their marked individuality and remain spiritually and intellectually separate from Christian Europe.

One strange aspect of Asian political conception which it took a long time to change was the conviction, in India and China especially, that the world outside did not matter. The average Hindu did not know of the existence of countries and peoples outside India. Europe became real to him only in the nineteenth century after the British had established dominion over India. Two wars had to be fought before the Chinese could think of European nations as anything more than barbarian tribes occupying the outer regions of civilization. Imperial Commissioner Lin, addressing Queen Victoria in 1842, speaks in all seriousness and honesty of her being 'the chieftainess of the tribe'. The world, to the Chinese, even in the nineteenth century, revolved round the Central Kingdom, which was seriously described as the Celestial Empire. The States on the outer periphery of China accepted this claim, and the Chinese people were convinced that even if important countries existed in distant areas, they could in no way be compared in power, greatness and civilization with their own.

It was only during the second half of the nineteenth century that the Asian peoples awoke to the fact that Asia was only a part – and by no means the most important then – of a greater world of which previously they had no knowledge. Gradually the picture became clear to them, first to the Japanese and slowly to the others. The growth of Asia's importance in the twentieth century as a result of the demand for tropical materials, and the emergence of Japan as a great Power and the gradual transformation of China, first as a playground of European rivalries and later as a danger spot, led naturally to a greater realization of Asia's role. After the First Great War, when the leadership of the West passed to America, which unlike European States is also a Pacific Power, Asia was brought more directly into the whirlpool of world politics.

The new Asian States, therefore, can no longer revert to a policy of isolation or pretend ignorance of the existence of other countries. China,

India and Indonesia – apart, of course, from Japan – have therefore no mean roles to fill in the politics of the present-day world. That arises directly from the transformation caused by Europe's former Empires over the East.

The effects of Asian contacts on Europe, though considerably less, cannot be considered insignificant. The growth of capitalism in the seventeenth, eighteenth and nineteenth centuries, in itself a profound and revolutionary change, is intimately connected with the expansion of European trade and business into Asia. The political development of the leading Western European nations during this period was also related to their exploitation of their Asian possessions and the wealth they derived from the trade with and government of their Eastern dependencies. Their material life, as reflected in clothing, food, beverages, etc., also bears permanent marks of their Eastern contacts. We have already dealt briefly with the penetration of cultural, artistic and philosophical influences, though their effects cannot still be estimated. Unlike the Rococo movement of the eighteenth century, the spiritual and cultural reactions of the nineteenth and twentieth centuries are deeper and have not yet fully come to the surface. The influence of Chinese literature and of Indian philosophical thought, to mention only two trends which have become important in recent years, cannot be evaluated for many years to come. Yet it is true, as T. S. Eliot has stated, that most modern poets in Europe have in some measure been influenced by the literature of China. Equally the number of translations of the *Bhagavad Gita* and the *Upanishads*, which have been appearing every year, meant not for Orientalists and scholars but for the educated public, and the revival of interest in the religious experience of India, are sufficient to prove that a penetration of European thought by Oriental influences is now taking place which future historians may consider to be of some significance.

Also, archaeology has seriously affected the faith which was so firmly held in the past that everything of value developed on the shares of the Mediterreanean. The past of the Great Asian peoples has gradually come to be considered as part of the general heritage of civilized man, and this may in time lead to a breakdown of the narrow Europeanism, which considered everything outside the experience of the West as of secondary importance. These subjects are merely alluded to here to indicate that the influence of the contacts between Asia and Europe is not wholly one-sided and that now, since the political domination of Asia is a thing of the past, the results of the interpenetration of culture may be even more fruitful.

INDEX